CARL E. WILLGOOSE

Boston University

third edition

THE CURRICULUM

IN

PHYSICAL

EDUCATION

PRENTICE-HALL, INC., Englewood Cliffs, New Jersey 07632

LIBRARY OF Congress Cataloging in Publication Data

WILLGOOSE, CARL E
  The Curriculum in physical education.

  Includes bibliographies and index.
  1. Physical education and training—Curricula.
I. Title.
GV361.W48 1979   375.6137   78-12428
ISBN 0-13-196303-1

© 1979 by Prentice-Hall, Inc.
Englewood Cliffs, New Jersey 07632

Printed in the United States of America

10 9 8 7 6 5 4 3 2 1

Editorial/production supervision
and interior design by Charlotte Leonard
Cover design by Richard LoMonaco
Manufacturing buyer: Harry Baisley

PRENTICE-HALL INTERNATIONAL, INC., *London*
PRENTICE-HALL OF AUSTRALIA PTY. LIMITED, *Sydney*
PRENTICE-HALL OF CANADA, LTD., *Toronto*
PRENTICE-HALL OF INDIA PRIVATE LIMITED, *New Delhi*
PRENTICE-HALL OF JAPAN, INC., *Tokyo*
PRENTICE-HALL OF SOUTHEAST ASIA PTE. LTD., *Singapore*
WHITEHALL BOOKS LIMITED, *Wellington, New Zealand*

Contents

Preface

to

the First Edition

Sometime early in the second century Marcus Aurelius wrote in his *Meditations*, ". . . observe always that everything is the result of change, and get used to thinking that there is nothing nature loves so well as to change existing forms and to make new ones like them."

If this ancient philosopher had been a twentieth-century curriculum builder he could hardly have expressed his function more clearly, for here is embodied the essential truth underlying program development in physical education. Indeed, the needs of the learner and society itself keep changing from year to year. These changes may appear so slight that they go unnoticed, yet they require a modification of the existing program.

The purpose of this book is to help awaken the reader to the need for redirection in physical education, and to assist him in the process of developing a curriculum for both boys and girls at all grade levels. The principles of curriculum development are brought to bear on the aims and objectives of physical education in the hope that school programs will be carefully developed and become more effective as conscientious instructors and coaches strive to provide the finest teaching possible.

The text is divided into three parts. *Part One: Foundations of Education* takes a look at Western civilization today and discusses societal changes and human needs. *Part Two: Curriculum Considerations* is devoted to the nature of the curriculum, its planning, and its ultimate organization. *Part Three: Implementing the Curriculum* is a practical consideration of what is to be taught, how much, and in what sequence for all grades, for both boys and girls. Emphasis is on a broad and varied program—a progressive and complete approach to class instruction, developmental and remedial programs, the mentally retarded, and intramural and interscholastic sports. Inquiry, invention, and innovation in physical education programs are examined along the way. Throughout the chapters the emphasis is not so much on curriculum items themselves as on their effective use with children of all ages. It is in this connection that factors such as teaching stations, flexible scheduling, team teaching, and dedicated teachers have a significant influence on program.

Physical education is a unique part of the curriculum. It is more than a game, a dance, a stunt. Ultimately it offers a way of life, and teaching it challenges the best efforts of every instructor. In most schools it can be made considerably better through serious attention to purpose, pilot studies, and creative planning. Much of this may be accomplished locally when professional spirit is high and teachers actively seek the best means of developing effective programs. As Ernest Bentley has said, "We seldom assault truth, but we do violence to it by default." Physical education teachers, therefore, are more than instructors in an activity; they are dreamers and truth seekers.

CARL E. WILLGOOSE

Preface

to

the Second Edition

In the last several years there has been a substantial amount of change and innovation in educational programs. In hundreds of school systems an admirable effort has resulted in the whole process of schooling being more pertinent to the needs of society and more vital in the lives of young people. In physical education this has been demonstrated through wider school–community programming of sports, dance, and recreational activities for people of all ages; more time assigned to curriculum development activity; a sincere bolstering of girls' and women's programs; a movement toward extensive multiple-use facilities; alternative programs to meet individual strengths and weaknesses, and increased experimentation with flexible scheduling, performance objectives, mini-courses, independent study, student contracts, differentiated staffing, and evaluation practices which can be effectively interwoven with teaching routines.

Such an expression of concern for youth is predicted on the growing awareness of the cardinal role of physical exercise and meaningful skills in the maintenance of both physical and mental health, longevity, and the prudent use of increased leisure time. Moreover, by coupling these items with the "joy of living" component it becomes very plain that the role of physical activity is an extensive one that needs to be more clearly understood. It is for this reason that professionals in physical education have been searching for a more descriptive name for the field—a name that will embrace all of the objectives and consequences of human movement. Yet it appears that calling the field movement arts, human movement, kinesiology, or sports education somehow limits rather than broadens the comprehension we now have of physical education. In any case, the search will continue for a way to help everyone to better understand the field. The prime purpose of this book is to move in this direction through improved curriculum development practices that should result in more justifiable and stronger programs—programs upon which boys and girls thrive, and in later years support with their monies because they have so thoroughly enjoyed the experiences inherent therein.

CARL E. WILLGOOSE

Preface

to

the Third Edition

When the renowned physiologist, Bruno Balke, was asked why he believed so strongly in physical education, he replied that it is essential to the living of a full life that one be acquainted with the broad variety of movement patterns that contribute to the development of intricate subcortical and cortical functions and help measurably to prepare people for mental and psychological encounters. R. Tait McKenzie would have agreed. As a physician and pioneer in physical education McKenzie considered the "joy of effort" the crowning reward of human movement—a response not at all unlike that of a Martha Graham dancer, that the "joy of activity" is the *sine qua non* in men and women.

Discovering a number of self-fulfilling movement activities for each individual is a worthy educational goal, one that clearly calls for imaginative and fascinating programs designed to provide students with *choices* at an early age. Through a preplanned exploration of many movements, it is possible to work activity choices into life styles and patterns of living in such a way as to advance well-being and contribute to a rich and full existence in the years ahead.

Although this edition gives appropriate space to the issues, trends, and needs in physical education, its primary thrust is directed toward curriculum improvement. Therefore, attention is focused on a number of school and community settings, alternative programs, research and change, student competencies, program content and organization, the needs of the special student, and the intricate relationship between program objectives and evaluation procedures. In this approach to the curriculum, one's ear should be cocked to catch the faint voice of Prometheus calling for a more rewarding life, triggering the release of human energies in search of something better through the medium of physical education.

CARL E. WILLGOOSE

xii

part one

FOUNDATIONS

OF

EDUCATION

Examining
the Expanding Society

chapter one

> Why build the city glorious if man unbuilded goes? In vain we build the
> world unless the builder also grows.
>
> EDWIN MARKHAM

Mindfully observant of human needs and purposely directing his words
to the very core of societal issues, the educator-poet Markham focused on the
social and economic abuses of a hundred years ago. In his widely known poem,
"The Man with the Hoe," he made life, limb, and the spirit of the individual
important.

Participants in the steady advance of Western civilization have been
more than slightly preoccupied with the multitude of technological and
industrial forces contributing to their welfare. For the most part, this has been
an upgrading process both in terms of material goods, new skills, and lifestyles
that include intellectualization, creativity, and self-fulfilling leisure. On the
other hand, the age of big business, big government, and industrial clout has
given birth to a civilization that is so concerned with the production of goods
for power, affluence, and comfort, that what happens to the individual as
illnesses and disorders result, is played down. Thus, beautiful plastic articles
are made at the expense of the worker who may develop vinyl-chloride
poisoning and liver damage; and very often the production line job is so
routine, repetitive, and dehumanizing that good pay and economic security
are not sufficient to offset general fatigue, "worker blues," and psychosomatic
illnesses. People still talk about the diseases of civilization as some kind of a
necessary evil that is inadvertently linked to "progress." There are symptoms,
such as overweight and obesity, coronary heart attacks, hypertension,
chronic fatigue, gastric ulcers, low-back pain, degenerative arthritis, poor
mental health and general unhappiness, and a number of hypokinetic conditions resulting from sedentary living.

3

The Developing Awareness

In *Man's Search for Himself*, Rollo May said that "one of the few blessings of living in an age of anxiety is that we are forced to become aware of ourselves."

In recent years developing society has demonstrated an encouraging degree of anxiety over the consequences of technological advances in a continuing space age that manages to raise questions relative to human welfare and survival. The non-polluting and energy-giving qualities of nuclear power is weighed against injuries due to the improper handling of radio-active wastes; positive genetic advances from DNA recombinant research is measured against the possible creation of new and damaging life forms; polluting toxicants are controlled by environmental impact studies and United States Environmental Protection Agency regulations; and communities of people are studied in efforts to reduce industrial pollution, substandard housing, sewage and garbage discrepancies, street violence, crime, joblessness, and neighborhood lethargy and indifference that breed inactivity, resignation, and despair. Rollo May is right when he talks about awareness, for, precisely, by anxiously looking at ourselves in the total scheme of things, the pattern of life as influenced by physical education does take on meaning.

The true worth of physical education, or of any education, is in how the education affects values, judgments, and commitments. In terms of physical well-being, people who understand themselves have fewer accidental injuries and diseases and recover sooner from illness than those who do not. They have what Abraham Maslow long ago characterized as an "appreciation of the body," which leads, by extension, to the personality. They are the healthy, self-actualizing people.[1] They know what to do and are moved to a state of action. They are not indifferent to the consequences of their behaviors. There is a sensitivity to the delicateness and dearness of life. There is a profound awareness of the potentialities of a fully awakened human being. They perceive a clear relationship between the well-being of the citizen and the healthy development of the society itself.

Achieving such a level of comprehension and feeling is far from reality for large masses of people. For many, life has become aimless, without significance, less inventive, and simply comfortable with things as they are. Achieving a fullness of expression through an attentive mind and body remains only a potentiality at best.

The Romans, like us, were affluent. They also had a standard of living unparalleled in the history of the world. They too enjoyed the "good life" and had free time to think, plan, and be creative if they chose to do so. Unfortu-

---

[1]Abraham Maslow, *Toward a Psychology of Being* (New York: D. Van Nostrand Co., Inc., 1962), p. 196.

4

nately, they didn't choose to think beyond the materialistic, matter-of-fact conditions of the moment. They became a dying race, and the great civilization came to an end precisely because its people were very comfortable in their way of life. They resisted change. They became soft in mind, spirit, and flesh and became viewers of the passing scene rather than participants in its evolution. Failing to realize what was going on, they chose to be at ease and smug at a time when the world demanded not smugness but sensitivity, not satisfaction but struggle, not weakness but strength.

Civilization will indeed be destroyed by the cumulative effect of the forces around it if the individual citizen remains rigid. Always before him or her is the task of formulating a new culture, with new beliefs, goals, sanctions, patterns, and group responsibilities. As an active agent in change, the educator must provide for democracy by promoting vigorous personal activity and a capacity for criticism, comparison and correction of deficiencies.

A Nation of Participants

During the first half of the century philosophers of physical education, such as Jesse Feiring Williams, Jay B. Nash, Frederick Rand Rogers, and Charles H. McCloy, stressed the need to educate youth as *participants* in the passing scene, not merely as spectators viewing the activity and accomplishments of others from afar. This type of education was one way, perhaps the most important way, to a highly productive and rewarding life. This concept is not new—the Greeks had it—and it applies significantly to the broad realm of human movement.

Following World War II, the one-time officer of the Austro-Hungarian army turned dance choreographer—Rudolph Laban—urged his followers to study and focus attention on the value of human movement in the everyday lives of the citizenry. Ten years later Dwight Eisenhower, moved by research findings indicating a lack of concern for the physical capacity of both youth and adults, established the President's Council on Youth Fitness.[2] A short period later John F. Kennedy found himself presiding over a somewhat sedentary population and made his now famous remark that "we do not want a nation of spectators, but a nation of participants in the vigorous life."

In observing the developing society it becomes clear that the prevention of disease and poor health in general is ultimately an individual responsibility with major overtones of cooperative group action. The key word today is prevention. The key process is in collective action with a nation of eager participants.

By 1973, after a year of nationwide hearings and study, the President's

[2]This was subsequently changed to the President's Council on Physical Fitness and Sports in order to embrace a wider dimension of human activity.

Committee on Health Education cautioned that it was imperative to *educate* for health and well-being, for it was no longer possible to stem the tide of human illness, despair, and misery by improved medical and surgical techniques, more hospitals and social workers, more clinical psychologists, more sophisticated health care centers, and more "repairmen." The message called for prevention. There must be an education of the public relative to how to live in order to stay free from the variety of infirmities of mankind. Thus, the physical wherewithal *to do,* to move efficiently and understandably, is an indispensible *quality* which at long last seems to warrant top priority—"an idea whose hour has come" (Carlyle).

In 1974 the Bureau of Health Education was established at the Center for Disease Control in Atlanta (Public Law 93-641) to be a focal point for illness-prevention activities by the federal government. By 1977 preventive medicine and health education efforts were beginning to be noticed in the society at large. The bureau described its educational function in terms of the following concrete actions:[3]

1. informing people about health, illness, disability, and ways in which they can improve and protect their own health, including the more efficient use of the health care delivery system
2. motivating people to want to change to more healthful practices
3. helping people to learn the necessary skills to adopt and maintain healthful practices and life styles
4. fostering teaching and communication skills in all those engaged in teaching consumers about health
5. advocating changes in the environment that facilitate healthful conditions and healthful behavior
6. adding to knowledge through research and evaluation concerning the most effective ways of achieving the above objectives

Note that in numbers two and three above, attention is directed to healthful skills, practices, and life styles. The implications relative to the role of physical activity and human movement programs in advancing health status and preventing illness are clear. What is not always clear, and needs to be emphasized, is the fact that programs of *prevention* and programs of *treatment* in a community do not have to compete with each other. They can be integrated. Moreover, health-care dollars do not have to be spent on curative medicinal care to the near exclusion of preventive care.[4] School health education funds should be spread widely enough to include the upgrading of physical education programs from kindergarten through college.

[3]"Health Education and Public Law 93-641," *Focal Points*, Atlanta: Ga.: Bureau of Health Education, Department of Health, Education, and Welfare, July 1977, pp. 2–4.

[4]Morton S. Hilbert, "Prevention," *American Journal of Public Health*, 67 (April 1977), 353–56.

The Automated Age

Scientific discoveries are transforming the life of the individual on a scale increasingly hard to comprehend. Industry, growing more automated, is producing unheard-of amounts of material goods for all. Accompanying such plus items as nuclear energy, improved communication-instrumentation, and medical technology are system analyzers and sophisticated computers that have replaced a number of human beings on the production line. Moreover, as these changes occur, the individual's self concept and ability to master natural forces will also change. Technology will permit more creativity, particularly if advantage is taken of the choices available, which in time will allow greater freedom to be human.

Although we should not worry that science and technology will create a "sick" and impersonal society in which people are robbed of their freedom and humanity, it is nevertheless true that the possibility exists if an educational effort to control them is not made. The task of the school and community involving 100 million school children is to prepare people for the world of the automated machine and an increasingly production-line way of life. The question raised by J. B. Nash a decade ago is still germane. If only about 15 percent of the workers of the nation are in the so-called learned professions, what type of education should be advocated for the other 85 percent?[5] How rich can we make the lives of the masses if the boredom of routinized automation is to be made bearable? How can we give people something to struggle for—to master, to conquer—so that they can achieve self-respect and dignity?

This is no small problem. By the tens of thousands people dread going to work. Some need three drinks at lunch to help them make it to quitting time that evening. This feeling has been called the "blue-collar blues," the "blahs," and other names indicating the boredom, aimlessness, and mental fatigue that come from America's superefficient way of dehumanizing what people do for a living. Thus, an increasing number of workers who hold steady jobs find little meaning in their work and come to work late, stay out "sick," get drunk or drugged, and even engage in acts of product sabotage.

The Meaning of Overpopulation

Throughout the world the population explosion has focused on what it means to have an increasing number of people per square mile. In this connection, the growth of the American city threatens the welfare of its inhabitants. The increasing number of families that have left the farm and

[5]"Leisure, Curse or Blessing?" in *Recreation: Pertinent Readings* (Dubuque, Iowa: W.C. Brown Co., 1965), p. 2.

7

migrated to metropolitan areas and away from smaller towns has created staggering health, housing, and transportation problems that will persist for years to come.

In 1610 there were 210 settlers in this country; in 1960, there were 180 million people. By 1972, there were close to 210 million people. Of these almost 75 percent lived in or near big cities. There will be considerably more people by the year 2000 despite the measurable drop in the nation's fertility rate—a record low of two births per woman in 1976. If this rate remains constant there will be over 250 million people by the year 2000.

Northern and western Europe and the United States have been moving toward a low population growth rate for several years. The lowest, very close to 0.0, is in East Germany. Generally, population growth is lowest in the most industrialized, urbanized, and educated nations. Thus, the high population density in countries like Japan, Netherlands, Belgium, England and Wales, and West Germany does not threaten the collective welfare of the citizenry as it does in parts of Asia, Africa, and South America where illiteracy, overbreeding, and overcrowding continue to exist.

Overpopulation must not be defined solely in terms of population density. To be meaningful, overpopulation must be viewed in terms of "optimum population size"—an expression attributed to Paul and Anne Ehrlich as they related optimum population to the "quality of life" or the "pursuit of happiness."[6] Such expressions are obviously somewhat abstract and subjective until they are related, for example, to human nutrition, natural resource depletion, and thermodynamic limits. The question of what size population the earth can support in comfort is an old one and a constant one. Information pertaining to nonrenewable resources has to be balanced against programs of energy conservation and population control.

A few years ago an international group of outstanding scientists, sociologists, industrial managers, and educators met in Rome and combined their thinking and research on world population problems and their numerous ramifications. This Club of Rome focused on environmental polution, the rate of depletion of natural resources, the ability to increase food supplies, the rate of industrialization, and the growth of population.[7] Their computerized findings from statistical data predicted that the continued depletion of resources and the ignoring of ecological items would lead eventually to widespread disease, famine, and strife. The prevention and hope factor, said the group, lies in arriving at "a steady-state society on a worldwide basis in which collective action prevails." Without collective action the civilization would collapse in less than a century. This prediction scared a few people and caused

[6]Paul R. and Anne H. Ehrlich, *Population, Resources, Environment: Issues in Human Ecology* (San Francisco: W.H. Freeman and Company, 1972), pp. 199–200.

[7]Donella H. Meadows and others, *The Limits of Growth: The Club of Rome's Project on the Predicament of Mankind* (New York: Signet, 1972).

a number of scientists to indicate serious flaws in the study. So a second Club of Rome study was undertaken with new dynamic models set up by regions of the world. Its report was that if the world social and economic order were seen as totally interrelated, population growth could proceed at a gradual pace indefinitely.[8] In short, "collective action" would ensure a steady growth, for example, in nutrients and energy resources. This "collective action" amounts pretty much to an immediate world cultural revolution in which the industrialized nations work more with the less fortunate nations and revolutionize some of their values and beliefs.

A further ramification of overpopulation in the big cities deals with the affluent population and how well it likes its environment. How well do the dwellers in Boston, Chicago, and San Diego tolerate their overcrowding? By 1985 well over half the United States population will be located on the east and west coasts and in the region of the Great Lakes. Thousands thrive in the crowded areas as others regularly escape to desert, shore, or relatively uncrowded mountain areas every weekend. The Ehrlichs suggest that an urban area is overpopulated if many people feel that they have too little space and no means of escape.

Quite significant from an educational viewpoint will be the difficulty of crowding more and more people into a small space, causing problems of transportation, crime, air, noise, and water pollution, drug addiction, and numerous other issues having to do with physical and mental well-being. Consequently, the needs of urbanites and the people in the skyrocketing suburbs will have to be carefully reviewed.

The educational implications are numerous. The role of the physical education and recreation specialists is extremely relevant in bringing youth and adults together to find ways to enjoy their forced proximity to one another. This is necessary if violence is to be reduced in the cities. The greater the crowding, the greater the violence rates. As privacy is threatened humans squabble and fight, frequently against unseen forces. They suffer the stress of apprehension and anxiety, of fear and anger, and either resign themselves or rebel. Rollo May points out that aggression and violence are basic to the human power of the individual.[9] Moreover, they can be creative, permitting the individual to affirm or assert himself or herself. People who know where they are going, or are at least quite determined, assert themselves in a number of ways all the time. However, when the need to assert oneself is blocked, the stage is set for aggressive behavior. And when there is no outlet, violence follows. It is not surprising, therefore, that explosive or physical activity through games, dances, and sports helps provide a wholesome outlet for aggressive feelings. James F. Conant, President Emeritus of

8Mihajlo Mesarovic and Eduard Pestel, *Mankind at the Turning Point: The Second Report to the Club of Rome* (New York: E.P. Dutton & Co., Inc., 1974), ch. 1.
9*Love and Will* (New York: W.W. Norton & Co., 1969).

Harvard University, recognized this fact and pointed out in *Slums and Sub-urbs* that if he were to name the one educational program that potentially could do most to reduce just one city problem—that of school dropouts—he would select physical education. Indeed, good programs of interscholastic and intramural sports are available to command the attention of young people. However, most school systems are in need of major improvements within this area.

As the need for recreation and physical education space increases, the city alone will be unable to meet the requirements, and the adjoining sub-urban areas will become involved. For too long the middle classes have departed to the suburbs and left the central cities increasingly dominated by slum dwellers who require city services (police, fire, welfare, health, educa-tion) but who can contribute little in taxes. The problems of the city are no longer merely urban; they are suburban and regional. Before long it will become absolutely necessary to combine urban and suburban school bound-aries. Already, educational parks have been established to provide a quality education for all pupils in a large region; they cut across geographic, economic, and social boundaries to draw pupils to better physical education facilities and programs and better education in general.

The Health of the Citizenry

Death rates have declined in the United States, but life expectancy is greater in a number of other countries. England, Canada, Netherlands, France, and Sweden have greater life expectancy. Swedish females live about two years longer than United States females (77.4 years), while life expectancy of Swedish males is about four years greater than that of United States males (72.0 years).

Longevity seems to relate more to how one lives than to one's geo-graphical location or to other variables. Individual health practices are signifi-cant. Both the California Human Population Laboratory (California Depart-ment of Health, Alameda County) and the Longevity Research Institute of Santa Barbara, California support this view. Mortality rates drop off as posi-tive health practices increase. The Human Population Laboratory studied seven personal health practices—sleep, eating breakfast, diet in general, weight status, physical activity, alcoholic beverage consumption, and smok-ing. The results showed a direct and statistically significant association with age-adjusted mortality rates. Mortality rates declined with the number of health practices observed. For men, 8.8 times as many died among those with three or fewer of the seven favorable practices as compared with those who practiced all seven; for women the figure was smaller but still high, 3.6 times as many.

Except for the mortality from influenza and pneumonia, which remained unchanged, death rates for each of the major causes of death were lower in 1976 than in 1975. Accidents are still the principal cause of death, and the major cardiovascular diseases lead as the cause of death at age 35 and over. In females, cancer follows accidents as the principal cause of death.

Despite the increase in longevity, the great reduction in human disease, and the gradual movement from superstition and ignorance to a somewhat scientific viewpoint regarding health, it is still not possible to say with certainty that good health today has become general. Indeed, the more complex civilization becomes, the more one must depend on modern knowledge and techniques from the health sciences in order to survive.

Hippocrates taught that each disease of mind and spirit arises from a natural cause. Even one's values have much to do with health-building and health-destroying activities. Unfortunately, large numbers of people suffer from "value illness"; that is, they know what they are supposed to do to keep well, but they fail to do so. They know about the recovery power of proper relaxation, but they do not rest. They understand how tobacco smoking can cause death from lung cancer, but they do not give up cigarettes. They know how alcohol affects driving ability, but they drive after drinking. They appreciate the role of regular exercise in weight control, yet they do little to alter their sedentary way of living.

In a real sense, modern society is characterized by the spectacle of humans fighting for perfection while knowing little about where they are headed. Their efforts all too often fail to produce the peace of mind they seek. In an environment where speed, status, comfort, and economic success are high marks of achievement, it is not uncommon to find men and women who cannot adjust to the increasing pressures. Some become overfed and underactive. Others literally "burn themselves out" with insecurity, fear, anxiety, worry, jealousy, anger, and hatred. Resulting tensions refuse to stay bottled up. They make their presence known in headaches, indigestion, gastrointestinal upsets, restlessness, sleeplessness, irritability, and fatigue.

It is a mass age, an age of routines performed by human cogs in an industrial and political setting. It is an age of scientists, dynamic labor leaders, business tycoons, and public relations experts. It is an epoch of psychological stress leading to ulcers, coronary heart disease, low back pain, mental disorders, and the tension syndrome. With it all, there are battalions of "experts," pill-takers and tub-thumpers to leach us of our many ills—both real and fanciful.

Despite the health education, physical education, and medical science efforts to make changes in our way of life, the staggering statistics underscore the fact that the task ahead is great indeed.

Specifically:

1. Heart disease causes over a million deaths per year. Coronary arterial disease continues to spread as does hypertension, with 15 to 20 percent of the adult population affected.

2. Approximately 50 percent of all hospital beds in the United States are occupied by mental patients. A Senate committee has estimated that 10 percent of public school children are emotionally disturbed and in need of psychiatric guidance.

3. Human drive and high aspiration for personal achievement frequently set the stage for a number of psychosomatic disorders. Working at top speed with great intensity tends to elevate uric acid levels. One theory that uric acid acts as a stimulant to the brain carries with it the corollary that uric acid, a nitrogenous waste product of the body's metabolism, also helps cause the painful inflammation of the joints (gout). Great and prolonged human drive, especially under somewhat stressful conditions, frequently leads to the tension syndrome and disrupts normal physical and mental functions.[10] At the other extreme is evidence that boredom and monotony rank high as underlying factors contributing to poor mental health.

4. Over 500,000 new cases of cancer are discovered each year. If proper treatment were started in time, the high death rate could be reduced one-third. There were approximately 380,000 deaths in 1977.

5. Accidents are the greatest threat to life and limb in childhood. Some 55,000 people die each year in automobile accidents; 1,900,000 are disabled, and 1,600,000 are injured but not disabled. Another 9000 people die each year from drowning despite widespread programs of swimming and water safety instruction. The government and the automobile industry have become concerned over a "design for safety," something more than seat belts. 45 million people are injured a year in some kind of accident, and another 98,000 are killed. Deaths related to drowning, pedestrians, bicycles, industry, and the home are numerous enough to warrant a spirited educational effort both in and out of schools.

6. Approximately three out of five men in their fifties are overweight. Half the women beyond the age of forty are more than 10 percent above their desirable weight. Even half the men in their thirties are at least 10 percent above their optimum weight. Separate studies of adolescent obese boys and girls clearly indicate a large number of such children. Moreover, these children have been carefully observed to be significantly less active than nonobese children. Other studies show that in many communities girls lead a very soft existence. Not only are they overfed, they don't exert energy to do *anything* often enough. They are passive and altogether too dependent on their parents. In fact, there is almost a symbiotic relationship to the mother. Also, obese adolescent girls seem to be much more knowledgeable about weight problems than they are about solutions. Canning and Mayer compared 225 obese female adolescents and 213 controls and discovered an obsession on the part of the obese with their weight, to such an extent that areas of personality, looks, and emotional overtones became involved in the issue.[11] Interestingly, the girls were aware of the role of exercise but lacked

---

[10]See especially Hans Selye, *The Stress of Life* (New York: McGraw-Hill, 1953). See also a discussion of metabolic stress and human performance by G.W. Brooks and Ernest Mueller in *The Journal of the American Medical Association*. (February 7, 1966).

[11]Helen Canning and Jean Mayer, "Obesity: Analysis of Attitudes and Knowledges of Weight Control in Girls," *Research Quarterly*, 39 (December 1968), 894–99.

the first-hand knowledge to get started. People need to know, says Jean Mayer, that exercise and diet are not alternatives but rather complements.

7.   The physical fitness of both youth and adults has been improving steadily since 1958, but it is clear that for many individuals the personal level of physical capacity for leading an active life is far below what it might be. The President's Council on Physical Fitness and Sports has demonstrated what can be done to improve physical fitness when adults as well as children are exposed to better-quality physical education programs carefully designed to meet individual weaknesses. However, large numbers of people are bothered by hypokinetic disease and inadequacies associated with a sedentary type of living which requires very little physical energy to prevail. Women suffer needlessly from menstrual discomfort, backaches, and general fatigue due in part to inadequate muscle tone.

8.   Millions of people have poor teeth. Generally, cavities are found to be developing faster than teeth are being filled. By the time a child reaches school, that child has one to three carious teeth. At age 12 or 13, he or she has five permanent teeth attacked by caries. From here on, the decay rate rises sharply. However, in those communities where the water is flouridated, the decay rate for the younger population is decidedly reduced.

9.   More than 500,000 teenagers yearly acquire a venereal disease. According to the United States Public Health Service, there has been a nationwide increase of more than 500 percent in venereal disease since 1958, and it is now considered pandemic. Large numbers of middle-class citizens see VD as a problem largely of the poor, yet it is increasing in the suburbs among the sons and daughters of business and professional people. Including unreported cases, VD afflicts over 3,500,000 Americans annually, over half of whom are under 25 years of age. Programs of sex education are still far from adequate.

10.   Alcoholism and drug addiction are on the rise and are primarily symptoms of poor mental health. One in every 18 drinkers will become an alcoholic. Untreated alcoholism shortens life 12 years and contributes to many types of fatalities—with over half the nation's traffic deaths involving drunken drivers. According to one researcher, young people start with alcohol and graduate to the use of drugs by age 18. Faced with 750,000 heroin deaths, many private and public institutions are seeking preventive measures as well as controls. According to the National Institute of Mental Health, marijuana use has increased and involves as much as 90 percent of some groups of high school students. The nonmedical use of such drugs as amphetamines and barbiturates is contributing to a rising death toll on the highways, juvenile delinquency, violent and bizarre crimes, suicides, and other anti-social behavior. In short, drug-taking has become a recreational pastime—a real challenge to the very meaning of the word recreation. There is a disquietude among the youth in many sections of the new society that combines desperation with aggressiveness.

11.   Suicides take nearly 25,000 lives a year. This figure should probably be much greater, partly because many suicides are unreported on account of the moral and religious stigma attached to suicides. Also, it is highly probable that a certain percentage of all categories of violent death are in reality suicides. Adolescent suicides are increasing because of the inability to face defeat and to find a meaningful existence. The number of suicides *attempted* is ten times the number that result in death.

12. Approximately 90 percent of the urban population lives in localities that have air
     pollution hazards—radiation, smoke, smog, fumes, and chemicals. The au-
     tomobile is a top-ranking culprit, producing a large number of the contaminants
     found in the air. High concentration of air pollution can cause acute illness and
     death. Of even greater importance are the health effects of the ordinary levels of
     air pollution to which most people in the country are exposed day and night, for
     years on end. Long-term exposure to air pollution has been associated with many
     chronic respiratory diseases, such as asthma, bronchitis, emphysema, and lung
     cancer. Enough is known today to control the source of the problem. Fortunate-
     ly, the public is awakening to the complexity of the ecological process.[12]

13. Superstitions exist throughout the land. They are part of the daily existence of the
     bright scholar as well as the dull and ignorant. They are difficult to combat
     because they are concealed beneath the veneer of education. Superstitions,
     when combined with misconceptions, prove to be a tremendous obstacle to a
     healthy citizenry. They make it easier for people by the thousands to become
     faddists of some kind, or worse still, followers of quacks.

Problems of the Aged

People are living longer; the population is growing older. It is not at all
unrealistic to base the education of children now in school on the probability
that a high percentage will live past ninety and many beyond one hundred
years.

Coronary heart diseases, arthritis, and chronic fatigue are significant
health problems for the aging population. With thousands of people retiring at
ages sixty and sixty-five, there are other problems too. Studies by the Life
Extension Institute show that the three primary factors that determine happiness in retirement are health, money, and the number of interests people had
developed during their earlier life. This last factor is particularly meaningful
when one considers the nature of a lifetime education in preparation for two or
three decades of retirement. Studies indicate that the happiest oldsters are
those who stay in their home communities and keep busy by carrying on
regular physical, mental, and creative activities. Moreover, weight control,
daily walking close to an hour a day, and adequate sleep each night appear to
be most beneficial. The secret of rewarding life in retirement is to be interested in what is taking place. Boredom alone can be reason enough for
fatigue.

Dr. Theodore G. Klumpf told the White House Conference on Aging
that the average person in the United States today is in an appalling condition chiefly because of mechanized living and that the "usual activity" of the
elderly person nowadays is finding "the shortest distance between two

[12]See especially Carl E. Willgoose, *Environmental Health* (Philadelphia: W.B. Saunders Co., 1979).

chairs." Moreover, said Dr. Klumpf, many people really believe that "a stiff, flabby, creaking, groaning, knocking, weak, tired, breathless body is normal for age sixty." The fault here is the culture; for old age is life's end product, the outcome of the values and structures life has been given by society.[13]

Most people don't wear out; they rust out. In this respect, the playground-movement champion, Joseph Lee was quite right when he said that "we don't cease to play because we grow old; we grow old because we cease to play." Thus, the way to *keep* lively is to *be* lively; the way to stay active is to move. Energy begets energy, and the only way to develop the capacity to expend more and more energy (dynamic fitness) is to keep increasingly active. Strength, endurance, balance, flexibility, and agility can be attained in no other way. However, only recently have older people in senior centers, convalescent, and retirement homes been exposed to the fitness message. The Department of Health, Education, and Welfare's Administration on Aging and the President's Council on Physical Fitness and Sports have promoted programs and implementation procedures for older citizens. They have stressed walking, jogging, and free exercise according to three progressive levels of intensity set forth as red, white, and blue sequences. Note the total body involvement reflected in the sample of order of exercises in Figure 1-1.[14] The program is more effective when daily activity-exercise schedules are kept by the participants and when alternative and supplemental activities, such as gardening, swimming, rowing, cross-country skiing, chopping wood, bicycling, and dancing, are engaged in on a regular basis.

The National Association for Human Development in cooperation with the President's Council on Physical Fitness and Sports, under a grant from the Administration on Aging (HEW), has been conducting a national program to develop model exercise and fitness activities for people over sixty years of age. It is becoming quite successful in reaching many people.

Open Space and Well-Being

There is today an urgent need to promote a healthful environment, free from pollutants and various intoxicants, and to preserve a fair share of the land for recreation and physical education purposes. Wadsworth wrote, "Let nature be your teacher," and Henry David Thoreau praised the wilderness as he criticized society and technological progress. In seeking communication with woodchuck and snowstorm, he derived something from the simple life.

[13]See Simone De Beauvoir, *The Coming of Age* (New York: G.P. Putnam's Sons, 1973) and "Old Age: End Product of a Faulty System," *Saturday Review*, April 8, 1972.
[14]President's Council on Physical Fitness and Sports, *The Fitness Challenge in the Later Years*, Washington, D.C.: HEW Administration on Aging, 1976, p. 9.

RED Program Sequence	WHITE Program Sequence	BLUE Program Sequence
	Exercises * to be performed in the following order.	
Walk 2 minutes	Walk 3 minutes	Alternate Walk (50 steps) Jog (50) 3 minutes
Bend and Stretch	Bend and Stretch	Bend and Stretch
Rotate Head	Rotate Head	Rotate Head
Body Bender	Body Bender	Body Bender
Wall Press	Wall Press	Wall Press
Arm Circles	Arm Circles	Arm Circles
Wing Stretcher	Half-Knee Bend	Half-Knee Bend
Walk 2-5 minutes	Wing Stretcher	Wing Stretcher
Lying Leg Bend	Wall Push-Away	Alternate Walk (50 steps) Jog (50) 3 minutes
Angel Stretch	Walk 5 minutes	Leg Raise and Bend
Walk-a-Straight-Line	Lying Leg Bend	Angel Stretch
Half-Knee Bend	Angel Stretch	Walk-the-Beam (2-inch by 4-inch beam)
Wall Push-Away	Walk-the-Beam (2-inch by 6-inch beam)	Hop
Side Leg Raise	Knee Push Up	Knee Push Up
Head and Shoulder Curl	Side Leg Raise	Side Leg Raise
Alternate Walk (50 steps) Jog (10) 1-3 minutes	Head and Shoulder Curl (arms crossed on chest)	Head and Shoulder Curl (hands clasped behind neck)
Walk 1-3 minutes	Diver's Stance	Stork Stand
	Alternate Walk (50 steps) Jog (25) 3-6 minutes	Alternate Walk (50 steps) Jog (50) 5 minutes, gradually increasing to walk 100 steps — jog 100
	Walk 1-3 minutes	Walk 3 minutes

*Illustrations of each exercise and figures for number of repetitions or length of time to perform it, appear on pages 10-18 (Footnote 14). Where two figures are given, start at the lower figure; gradually increase the repetitions or duration over a period of days or weeks until you can perform the higher number.

FIGURE 1-1.

Over the decades American and Canadian voices have cried out about the vanishing woodlands and the rape of nature by bulldozers. Fortunately, the environmental movement has come of age, and industrialists and others are willing, as well as required, to stop further damage to the living space. Large numbers of people are rallying behind groups such as the Sierra Club, the National Audubon Society, the Wilderness Society, the Conservation Law Foundation, and the United States Environmental Protection Agency.

Collective action to upgrade the environment has been slow because (1) complex ecosystems are difficult to study; (2) demonstrating ecologic change is somewhat rudimentary; and (3) the medieval view of humans as "superior" creatures in the natural environment prevails. Also, individualism and hedonism have been growing steadily since World War I. This noncollective approach to life and living has not helped community conservation and environmental improvements. The era of the "here now" philosophy, the "instant gratification," "instant success," "buy now-pay later," and "eat, drink, sleep, and be merry for tomorrow we may die" has not been conducive to the sacrifice of personal comforts for the good of the overall environment. Moreover, the concept of stewardship rather than an "ordained" ownership of the land has been difficult to overcome. Early settlers conquered the land, and it was their land despite the pronouncement of Thomas Jefferson that "while the landowner holds title to the land, actually it belongs to all the people because civilization itself rests upon the soil." However, the wisdom and words of Woody Guthrie are still modifying the attitudes of people everywhere, as his son Arlo continues to sing, "This land is your land, this land is my land . . . this land was made for you and me."

Local and state conservation commissions are beginning to be more active everywhere, for they believe that rural life has something to offer in addition to what can be provided by the urbanized countryside. In man's effort to "get away from it all" to the environment of nature, he is refreshed and may gain perspective and a reverence for life. In any case, more and more land is being purchased with the state and community cooperating in the planning and financial arrangements. Moreover, under legislation passed in 1965, the federal government pays a large share of the cost of purchasing open areas to be used for conservation, parks, and recreation. The demand for recreation workers will continue to increase as people understand the need for open space in their own communities rather than in open space 50 or 100 miles away.

Recreational Trends

During the past several decades the amount of recreational involvement in the United States and Canada has been considerable. In fact, the satisfaction of leisure needs and interests has become a key economic factor in national well-being as participants crowd into stadiums, theaters, museums, and music halls, and as they invest in hobbies and culture activities. The increasing free time in an affluent society has generated an interest in recreation so vast and comprehensive that the era has already been nicknamed "The Golden Age of Sport." The findings of the Rockefeller Report, limited to outdoor recreation alone, indicated in 1962 that Americans were turning to outdoor recreation in such numbers that the future would bring a tidal wave.[15] It is now being experienced.

The rise in sports and sports-related activities has been nothing less than phenomenal since the end of World War II. Sports have become a way of life for whole families, with something readily available for grandparents and preschool grandchildren. Private and public horseshoe and shuffleboard courts were unavailable two decades ago but are commonplace today and are used throughout the year by retired men and women all over the country. Skiing, which started in the United States with a single rope tow in Vermont in 1934, has grown from a shoestring operation providing fun for a few "outdoor nuts" to a multimillion-dollar business, with an increasing number of ski lifts added yearly as new ski areas are developed and old ones improved.

Figures prepared by the Athletic Institute support the fact that most people in the United States are today taking part in sports, previously the activity of the wealthy. Millions of waterskiers and owners of expensive power boats enjoy the lakes and rivers. The number of golfers is approaching the 12 million mark. Along with the usual team sports, there are other activities, such as archery, bowling, table tennis, roller skating, handball, skin diving, and scuba diving, and camping of all kinds. Add the fantastic increase in bicycling for all ages and the construction of home and community swimming pools, and it becomes clear that sports activity is popular and rewarding.

For example, tennis with 29 million participants is a real growth industry and entrepreneurs find it hard to keep up with the demand. Tennis courts are being added at a rate of thousands a year, with a mushrooming of indoor courts. Like many sports today, tennis has shifted from the domain of the affluent to the level of the common man playing on the municipal playground court. It has become democratized, professionalized, inexpensive, year-round, all-weather, all-hour—and, probably, the nation's fastest-growing sport.

Do-it-yourself recreation is continuing to boom. Arts and crafts, chess, and backpacking into the semiwilderness show phenomenal growth. In the latter case more than six million Americans in 1973 strapped 30-pound packs

[15]Outdoor Recreation Resources Review Commission, *Outdoor Recreation for America, a Report to the President and to the Congress,* Washington, D.C.: United States Government Printing Office, 1962, p. 25.

on their backs and headed off for adventure—this number of Americans has quadrupled in the last decade. Many are seeking to escape the pressures and constraints of urban life. Many have the desire for a strong dose of the Protestant Ethic—the work and "character-building" effort in the face of great body fatigue and the tormenting adversities of the weather.

Along with the boom in attendance at major athletic events, in individual sports participation, and in family recreation, there is also an increasing amount of community-school recreation. In countless communities the schools are open day and night, weekends, and all summer for citizens of all ages, with programs encompassing a wide variety of physical, intellectual, and creative activities. One of the largest total community-school programs in the nation occurs in Flint, Michigan, a city of more than 200,000 people, where over 12,000 visitors a year come just to observe what is going on. So great is the size of the undertaking that approximately 70 agencies and businesses in Flint offer their assistance each year.

The Flint program is thorough and extensive. It is indicative of what will occur in more and more large city areas as populations swell and people in close proximity to each other try to meet the need for physical activity. Moreover, the increasing number of recreation programs will reflect the leadership of communitites like Flint by placing competition second to participation.

In reviewing the United States Census Bureau figures on municipal leisure services in large cities it becomes apparent that expenditures for recreation have risen steadily since about 1909, the greatest rise occurring between 1936 and the present. Along with the increase in the number of municipal parks, playgrounds, and recreational programs in general, there has been a steady increase in amusement parks and theme parks, such as Disneyland, which reflect the culture and extended life cycle of the times. Linked to this growth is a renewed family orientation where doing things together as a family is the objective. Theme parks keep a whole family involved for a whole day. Municipal leisure service groups are beginning to do the same thing. As Margaret Mead and others have pointed out, it was once wrong to play so hard that it affected one's work; now it is wrong to work so hard that it may affect family life.

Although the disease "spectatoritis" has long been on the American scene, there is little evidence that it is disappearing as more people engage in physical activities. In fact, as the population increases and people congregate in or about the large and crowded metropolitan areas, there is an ever-deepening danger that opportunities for full personal participation will be inadequate unless long-term planning for recreational needs is carried out by leaders in the big cities. This concern is of particular significance in the planning of physical facilities, both in and out of the city, sufficient to meet the needs of people for individual and group sports, hiking, camping, and other physical activities. Will Durant recognized this when he spoke clearly on this point:

> The wisest of our citizens will not be those who merely enjoy the spectacle; but will be those who climb up out of the pit and onto the stage, and lose themselves in action.

In this spirit, numerous ways are pursued to get into the action without being a player. Sport has its active viewers, listeners, and readers. It has its teachers, coaches, and managers. Among its arbitrators are referees, score-keepers, and judges. Among the entrepreneurs are owners, promoters, and manufacturers. And one shouldn't forget trainers and photographers.

Since recreation has the potential of immediately involving the personal and social values of a participant, there is a significant task ahead for teachers of physical education. Ultimately, the quality of the recreational endeavor relates to the preparation of the participants in the numerous individual and group skills—games, sports, dances, and other movement-related activities. Coupled with this is the need to learn "how" to play and how to employ recreational pursuits in a manner that will offset the anguish of mental and physical labor—an anguish always associated with human virtue.

In examining the culture to see just where leisure fits in, Fred Martin describes leisure as a continuing search for meaning. The "search" is especially germane to physical education. Says Martin:

> It was at the 21st Olympics that a slight but splendidly controlled fourteen-year-old Romanian gymnast captivated the world by achieving perfection in her sport, her art. Nadia Comaneci personified an ideal that many are urged to strive for but few are thoroughly convinced can be reached. In one week we were treated to a series of gymnastic exhibitions by this young woman that call to mind George Leonard's elegant portrayal of sport and excellence in *The Ultimate Athlete* and Richard Bach's urging in *Jonathan Livingston Seagull* that "There's a reason to life! We can lift ourselves out of ignorance, we can find ourselves as creatures of excellence, intelligence and skill," and that "there is such a thing as perfection . . . and that our purpose for living is to find that perfection and show it forth."
>
> That our culture is intensely caught up in a continuing search for meaning, purpose, identity, and related notions is evident from the struggles that such quests have provoked within religion, education, philosophy, politics, and other areas of human activity. What men, women, and children once derived from the church, work, and the family seems to have been dispersed and appears to be much sought for in what we now call *leisure*. The all important sense of well-being and its harmonic overtones—satisfaction, gratification, achievement, joy, etc.—are increasingly expected as outcomes of the leisure experience. The

study and discussion of the leisure phenomenon and its relation to culture is considered important for many reasons. But it is through its relationship to our search for meaning that such efforts become increasingly significant.[16]

Leisure, Education and Freedom

As indicated, the recreational movement is focusing on the true meaning of leisure. Thus, the full meaning of the word "leisure" needs to be understood. In the past, to different people it has meant different things ranging from the philosophic to the ethical. Eventually, according to Margaret Mead, it became linked with recreation and revitalization, rewards for duty done.

The word "leisure" comes from the Latin word *licere*, meaning "to be permitted freedom or opportunity to do something." In the medieval university, the first degree an individual earned was the "licentiate," also derived from *licere*. Education, leisure, and freedom have thus a common root. In fact, education and leisure are so closely related that leisure may be considered a nonwork activity wherein one has the freedom to continue learning—a kind of continuous schooling.

In its finest sense, leisure provides an opportunity for the individual to become refreshed, rejuvenated, and recreated. Leisure time activity without significance is not enough to satisfy; neither is insignificant work. Fullness results when recreation and work go together. "The struggle for existence," writes Nash, "has not been man's greatest enemy. Very often, it has been a stimulant to his lagging, puttering spirit. In the process of evolution, an unorganized nervous system became a brain and, later, when man was 'kicked into activity by a hostile environment' he found he could build an airplane, paint a picture, construct a bridge, write a novel, cure a disease, and create a civilization."[17]

Today men and women are free, without any moral stigma, to use their time exactly as they choose. And they have indeed been doing just that for a number of years. Perhaps the ultimate question one must ask is whether twentieth-century Americans are wise enough to plan the use of their non-work time so that their civilization will flower instead of decline. The society is linked to the aspirations of each individual member. How he or she fills leisure time, says Bertrand Russell, is "the last product of civilization." Arnold

[16]Fred W. Martin, "Leisure, Culture, and the Continuing Search for Meaning," *Journal of Physical Education and Recreation*, 47 (October 1976), 2.

[17]Jay B. Nash, *Recreation: Pertinent Readings*, p. 4. See also Lin Yutang, *The Importance of Living* (New York: John Day Co., 1937), p. 150, where it is stated that culture is essentially a product of leisure and that the man who is "wisely idle" is the most cultured man. The wisest man, says Yutang ". . . is he who loafs most gracefully."

Toynbee and other historians remind one that no society has ever survived with a great amount of free time. The need for an education for leisure, therefore, must be given close study as the new age ripens and evolves. If this kind of education is efficient it may reap for the individual not only intellectual and physical satisfaction, but creative, artistic, and spiritual satisfactions sufficient to contribute to an ultimate inner growth. The former president of Yale University, A. Whitney Griswold, has said,

> Now we stand on the threshold of an age that will bring to all of us more leisure than all the aristocracies of history, all of the patrons of art, all of the captains of industry and kings of enterprise ever had at their disposal. . . . What do we do with the great opportunity? In the answers that we give to this question, the fate of our American civilization will unfold.[18]

The balance between work and play or freedom and control is always a precarious one. Too much of one limits the influence of the other. When Dubos discussed *equilibrium* as a fundamental concept in ecology he also applied it to the civilization itself.

If physical education, or any other kind of education, is to contribute to the concept of equilibrium—a balance in living—and reach the untapped resources of human beings, it will have to bridge the gap between the work-stress world of the individual and the somewhat utopian state of meaningful recreational activity. In so doing, it will fortify the individual for both the world of work and the world of play.

In this transient world the establishment of roots is difficult because of the constant change in people's relationship to things, places, and people. So much is temporary; and the unpredictability of future changes is threatening. There is evidence of increasing withdrawal—not only in the youth subculture, unable or unwilling to cope with the stress-filled environment, but a partial withdrawal by thousands of ordinary adults who reduce themselves to states of semiconsciousness with alcohol or television. However, more and more people are escaping the overstimulating man-made environment into a pristine natural environment through camping, backpacking, mountain-climbing, and hiking. The life goals of these people, and how they can be achieved, have been carefully studied and related to the overall values of living.

Sport as an Art Form

Certainly if mass recreation is to continue to be a blessing and to enrich life, opportunities for active engagement must be as available as occasions for sitting and viewing the sporting event as an art form.

[18]Quoted in Richard Kraus, *Recreation and the Schools* (New York: Ronald Press, 1964) p. 12.

A significant reason for the wide acceptance of sports today by participants and receivers alike is the intrinsic feelings developed for the display of high-quality skills—artistic accomplishments that frequently rival the finest performances at theater and music hall.

In the American past, sports served several functions, the least of which was artistic because art was generally equated with the stage, gallery, and studio. It comes as no surprise, therefore, that when music is added to the performance of figure skating, gymnastics, and synchronized swimming, these activities come alive through association, gain color, and take on a kind of form that elicits a genuine emotional response from the spectator. Superficially, the music makes the difference, but really the activities can stand by themselves.

In recent years the qualities of the aesthetic—the cultivation of excellence—has gone beyond the art-by-association activities to individual and team sports. Thus, the balance, rhythm, and direction of the performance on the trampoline and diving board depicts the beauty of the human in specialized movements. The stick-handling in ice hockey and the lacrosse catch-and-pass are equally as beautiful. Kovich expresses this viewpoint very well when she says:

> The spectator cannot divorce man from his movements. Sport is a truly human form of art, for it is not just the product of man's abilities which is on display; it is man. Research in electromyography has shown that observers mimic in a minute way the movement patterns of the performer, thus including a form of restrained participation. As the performer feels the art he is creating, so can a perceptive spectator feel the same quality, although not to the same extent. Whether intended or not, there is silent communication between the performer and the spectator. Empathy with the elements of force, space, and time in the world of the performer and his movement can account, in part at least, for the spectator interpeting the movement as meaningful and beautiful.[19]

Sports participation as an art form, directly or indirectly, will continue to grow throughout the world because of its cultural significance. This was noted long ago by Cozens and Stumpf when they stated that "sports and physical recreation activities belong with the arts of humanity. Such activities have formed a basic part of all cultures, including all racial groups and all historical ages, because they are as fundamental a form of human expression as music, poetry and painting."[20]

[19]Maureen Kovich, "Sports as an Art Form," *Journal of Health, Physical Education and Recreation*, 42 (October 1971), 42. See also John Loy and Gerald Kenyon, *Sport, Culture and Society* (New York: Macmillan, 1969), Part 3.

[20]Fredrick W. Cozens and Frances S. Stumpf, *Sports in American Life* (Chicago: University of Chicago Press, 1953), p. 1. See also the filmstrip *Art and Sport*—a joint effort between the American Association of Health, Physical Education, and Recreation and the National Art Education Association. (Comes with script from AAHPER.)

Dance in America

As a primary form of artistic and social expression dance has no equal. From the days of primitive man or woman to the present it has met the fundamental human need to express oneself. Since the medium of expression is through the movements of the total body it has been natural to link dance in general with physical education as well as the arts.

Through a body-movement orientation, dance becomes a topic that overlaps the broad fields of aesthetics, education, religion, and medicine. It fulfills the aspirations to worship, to engage in courtship, to express tribal or national loyalties, to express both artistic and creative urges, to assist in the therapeutic process, and to provide a means for social or recreational group activity.[21]

Dance in its many forms is flourishing in Western society today. The creative and concert forms (ballet, modern, modern jazz, ethnic) are appearing in numerous small communitites that heretofore had no dance programs at all. There is a renewed interest in social dancing, including rock-and-roll, ballroom, folk, square, and round dancing. Dance clubs and community dance programs sponsored by recreational centers are on the increase. A recent, continuing-series program on television that met with tremendous success was the *Dance In America* show. Each of the hour-long programs was an independent entity aired by Public Broadcasting Service (PBS) stations. What stimulated thousands of listeners was the nature of the dance documentary in which directors, choreographers, and dancers discussed repertory, backgrounds, artistic goals, and the training of bodies.

What has occurred to make dance a vital part of the educational and cultural scene is an awakening by the general population to the significance of dance in their lives. The awakening has brought classical ballet, avant-garde modern dance, and earlier Martha Graham-variety black dance jazz, hoofing, gymnastics, and other dance forms into the local communitites.

Although less than a quarter century old, regional ballet is increasing, and several amateur companies have climbed the step up to a professional level. The observer of dance in the American scene will see and feel much that ultimately relates to his or her recreational and educational interests. Walter Terry champions the dance movement when he describes Eugene Loring's *Billy The Kid*, with its great Aaron Copland score, opening and closing with an unending processional of American pioneers moving ever forward to new frontiers: "Individuals falter, some return to a remembered security, but the

---

[21]See elaboration by Richard G. Kraus, *Recreation Today: Program Planning and Leadership*, 2nd ed. (Santa Monica, California: Goodyear Publishing Co., Inc., 1977), p. 449.

march goes on, the quests continue, the adventure never ends. To me, this is what our American dance, on TV or live, is all about."[22]

The Exercise Movement

It no longer causes undue attention and "smart" remarks by onlookers to appear in and about the community in gymnastic attire, tennis shorts, or the nonconforming uniform of the jogger. Laughing children and barking dogs have given way to a sense of wonderment, and even envy, as men and women alike work to trim the waistline, bolster the heart muscle, and simply enjoy the fruits of regular exercise—formally or otherwise.[23] The eight million joggers, of course, are only a part of the exercise scene.

FIGURE 1-2. Maintaining adult fitness on a day-night jogging track. (Courtesy Institute for Aerobics Research, Dallas, Texas)

A few years ago the Opinion Research Corporation conducted a national adult physical fitness survey consisting of detailed personal interviews with

[22]Water Terry, "On TV: America's Dances and Dancers," *Saturday Review*, June 25, 1977, p. 46.

[23]It wasn't many years ago that some people took delight in quoting the late President Hutchins of the University of Chicago who liked to say, "Whenever I feel like exercising I lie down until the feeling goes away," or Shakespeare, "It is better to rust to death than to be scoured to death from perpetual motion."

almost four thousand men and women, twenty-two years old or over, living in private households within the United States.[24] The question of exercise was raised. As can be seen in Table 1-1, for all activities except weight training by both sexes and walking by men, the greatest participation in physical fitness activities was found for men and women in New Suburb-One Family situations. The least exercise was recorded by women in city apartments. Walking is the most prevalent activity.

Table 1-1. Present Adult Participation in Exercise for Housing Types by Percentages

EXERCISE FORMS	A	B	C	D	E	F	G
			Men				
Walking	46	39	37	40	44	30	44
Bicycling	13	11	18	21	17	14	12
Swimming	14	17	18	26	16	10	18
Calisthenics	13	9	14	24	11	7	15
Jogging	8	3	8	14	8	8	9
Weight Training	7	3	7	5	5	4	7
			Women				
Walking	35	39	43	55	41	32	49
Bicycling	2	17	18	31	23	17	15
Calisthenics	9	14	15	23	18	9	21
Swimming	9	11	10	18	13	8	15
Jogging	2	1	3	6	3	3	5
Weight Training	0	1	1	0	1	0	0

Code: A City Apartment D New Suburb-One Family
  B City-Multiple Family E Old Suburb-One Family
  C City-One Family F Rural-One Family
  G Suburb and Rural-Multiple Family
Courtesy: The President's Council on Physical Fitness and Sports

Some of the more significant findings having a bearing on society's acceptance of movement activities are as follows:

1. More than 55 percent of adults engage in exercises covered by the survey. Next to walking, bicycling, calisthenics, and swimming are most popular. Jogging and weight training follow in order.
2. Frequency and length of participation are greater for those with some college education and increase with income.
3. Men and women with consistent weights are the most active.
4. Most individuals give good health as their main reason for exercising. Men gave enjoyment, pleasure, and relaxation as the reason for exercising, while women tended to stress weight control.

[24]President's Council on Physical Fitness and Sports, "National Adult Physical Fitness Survey," *Physical Fitness Research Digest,* Washington, D.C.: U.S. Govt. Printing Office, April 1974.

5. White men and women were better informed than nonwhites. There was less awareness by both men and women in city apartments.
6. About 95 percent of men and women had taken physical education during their school years, with high school the dominant education level. Some 90 percent felt that it was good for them.
7. Sports in which the greatest number of adults participated were baseball, basketball, football, track, and field for men, and basketball, softball, and volleyball for women. Those with the greatest sports participation were younger, had more education, had higher incomes, were in the professional and managerial classes, were Caucasian, and had an adult weight comparable to their weight at age twenty-one.

This survey certainly pointed to the need for better elementary and junior high school programs of physical education, to a continuing need for an education in the lifetime or carry-over sports, and to weaknesses in adult physical fitness practices. A major need is to make easily accessible paths for bicycling, jogging, and walking; greater opportunity for swimming, and a stronger effort to disseminate information to the public on the value of exercise in the total effectiveness of the individual. The supportive research is available, and organizations, such as the President's Council on Physical Fitness and Sports, exist to be helpful even on the local level.

Today, a number of excellent community programs are taking place in the country. A superb example is in the city of Brookings, South Dakota, where an elaborate jogging-exercise course has existed since 1973. The course combines jogging trails and exercise stations, and provides users of all ages with a pleasant and beneficial recreation experience. The one and one-half mile trail with twenty stations is located next to existing golf course facilities in order to provide users with necessary drinking water, rest rooms, and parking space. Its attractiveness and challenge is conducive to wide community use. The course layout and station details are fully diagramed and explained in an attractive booklet, which was prepared in 1977 after four years of course evaluation.[25]

It has been said that there is an unprecedented obsession with physical fitness due to an overdose of television-sports or the fear of coronary occlusion or the reduction of sexual ability. There probably is some evidence, but the more reasonable argument in support of expanding exercise programs suggests a swing away from the materialism—comfort values of *homo sedentarius* toward what has been called "new feeling states."

It feels good when capillaries throb and muscles perform. When 88 million adults over eighteen years of age participate in physical activity,

[25]Contact Paul E. Nordstrom at South Dakota State University, Brookings, S.D., for a copy of *The Brookings Jogging-Exercise Course*, 32 pages.

they do so not simply because of quixotic resolve, Spartan determination, or evangelistic tenacity, or even because of a desire to keep up with the Joneses. Rather, they realize that they need not be exhibitionists or superathletes to possess healthy bodies. George Leonard, author of *The Ultimate Athlete,* expressed it well when he said, "We are discovering that every human being has a God-given right to move efficiently, gracefully, and joyfully."

To Travel Hopefully

In a Promethean sense there is a better world out there—a world that can provide a richer existence for most civilized people if they are properly inspired and guided. Human aspirations rise with the help of the educator, but the helping task is of considerable magnitude in an environment of complex communitites.

Society is filled with people determined to reach their goals—often at any cost. Pressure begins to mount in the early years as the mania for speed and social status begins to build up. There is little time to relax and considerable time to worry about not succeeding and "losing face." This isn't a new phenomenon. Crile wrote about it when he said ". . . the whole history of man is only the terror of standing second." In a close-knit society, this terror is real, and it is probably responsible for more stress and tension than most people realize. Ambition is desirable; so is striving and reaching toward acceptable goals. Unfortunately, large numbers of individuals strive and climb—all over the other fellow—only to reach their goals having missed something along the way. They miss the joy of traveling.

If we learn anything at all about the present condition of adult mankind, it should be that the problems, diseases, and inadequacies of the moment did not suddenly appear; rather, they emerged gradually, having been established during the early elementary school years. That is to say, backaches, ulcers, gastrointestinal pains, hypertension, obesity, chronic fatigue, coronary thromboses, and the neurotic and psychotic behavior related to such feelings as anxiety, apprehension, worry, fear, hatred, and jealousy are all tied directly to a pattern of living. A sense of values formed early in life, coupled with the proper skills and knowledge, set the stage for good health in more ways than one. The part played by physical education in that period can be most fruitful.

To learn *to travel hopefully* is a fine goal to embrace. People seldom reach their goals; it is the process of striving that counts. The relationship of this idea to the maturation of Western civilization has commanded the attention of Nash and other physical educators for half a century. It is Nash who expresses the Stevenson philosophy that man must forget that he is indefatigable and take time to rest because there is a possibility that "we shall never reach the goal; it is even more than probable that there is no such place, and if we live for centuries and were endowed with the powers of a god, we should find ourselves not much nearer what we wanted at the end. . . . Little do you know your own blessedness; for to travel hopefully is a better thing than to arrive."[26]

The challenge to physical education, as a vital part of the total education effort in the years ahead, is of considerable consequence. Never have we achieved the widespread and general understanding of the true nature and potentialities of physical education necessary for its full development and function. Some progress is being made as human movement is studied in its fullness; and with the determination to start right away to seek excellence in programs, the next several decades might well usher in a "golden era" of physical education heretofore unknown in Western civilization.

QUESTIONS FOR DISCUSSION

1. Is change inevitable? Is it always necessary? Is there danger that too many changes coming too fast will tend to cause mankind to overlook certain long-standing truths that have made civilization what it is?

2. The way our society evolves has many implications for the physical educator. One of these has to do with a meaningful philosophy of leisure. Do you believe that leisure is necessary only as a respite from work, or is it valuable in itself as an end to which work is directed?

3. Does education have some responsibility for consciously changing culture patterns? Or do educators simply exist to keep alive the existing truths?

4. John Lear writes about "social accounting" (see Selected References), which is based on the premise that changes in perceptions, interpretations, and reactions, as well as changes in social situations themselves, can be identified by special "social indicators." One of these indicators is the way time itself is spent. From your experience and reading, comment on how people react when questioned about *how they use their time*. Are there keen explanations or emotional reactions?

5. One of the liabilities of modern education, according to Norman Cousins, is that it has contributed to a compartmentalization of knowledge and that what is needed today is an understanding of the interrelationships within the entire province of knowledge. Do you agree or disagree with this view? How do you see it relating to physical education?

[26]*Philosophy of Recreation and Leisure* (St. Louis: C.V. Mosby, Co., 1953), p. 218.

SUGGESTED ACTIVITIES

1. Defend the statement by Blanche Drury (McGlynn reference, p. 112) that physical education should muster all its forces to study all manifestations of movement, from early childhood to geriatrics, in an ever changing environment.

2. Physical education is becoming stronger, especially when good programs are presented. However, school members frequently have reservations about supporting programs. Arrange to talk with one or two school board members relative to the way they feel about the contributions of physical education, particularly when money is in short supply and time is needed to innovate other school programs. Share your findings with classmates.

3. Compare the views of Herbert Spencer with those of Jay B. Nash relative to the significance of work and leisure in the life of our society.

4. Ask several eighty-year-old men and women
   a. how many hours a day they worked in making a living
   b. what new products or inventions impressed them the most during their teen years
   c. who their heroes were as they grew up
   d. what games they played in youth
   e. how, generally, they used leisure time during their youth

5. Examine the history of physical education. What part did it play in the education of youth for leisure
   a. at the time of Homer
   b. during the Dark Ages
   c. during the American Colonial period
   d. during the pre-World War II period

6. In his utopian book, *The Shape of Things to Come*, H.G. Wells assumed that scientific thinking, modern engineering, and public education, by their intrinsic worth, would prepare a kind of future that an educated middle-class citizen could approve. Later, when he wrote *Mind at the End of Its Tether*, he had become disillusioned as he noted that Nazi Germany scored higher on scientific rationalism, engineering, and public education than did any other European nation. Take a moment to examine this observation. Are there implications here of any particular signficance? Do educational goals and programs need very careful definition as they relate to a civilization? Write out some specific implications for educators and others who build a society "close to the heart's desire."

7. Examine the several effects of sports on the culture. Give particular attention to sports as an art form. Readings by Cozens and Stumpf, Loy and Kenyon, Bryant J. Cratty, Celeste Ulrich, and Ernst Jokl will be

especially helpful (see Selected References). In carrying out this activity, it may be helpful to list some of your findings so that they can be employed in class discussion to illustrate differences of opinion.

SELECTED REFERENCES

ALLEN, DWIGHT W., and J.C. HECHT, *Controversies In Education.* Philadelphia: W.B. Saunders, 1974.

ARNOLD, NELLIE, "Leisure: Revolutionary Creator of a Planetary Society," *Journal of Physical Education and Recreation,* 47 (October 1976), 32–34.

BATES, BARRY T., "Scientific Basis of Human Movement," *Journal of Physical Education and Recreation,* 48, (October 1977), 68–73.

BOSSERMAN, PHILLIP, and NELSON BUTLER, "The Leisure Revolution: It's About Time," *Journal of Physical Education and Recreation,* 47 (October 1976), 27–31.

BUCHER, CHARLES A., "National Adult Physical Fitness Survey," *Journal of Physical Education and Recreation,* 45 (January 1974), 23–26.

———, "Change and Challenge," *Journal of Physical Education and Recreation,* 46 (December 1975), 55–56.

BUTLER, GEORGE, *Introduction to Community Recreation.* New York: McGraw-Hill, 1976, pp. 225–30.

CONANT, JAMES F., *Slums and Suburbs.* New York: McGraw-Hill, 1961.

CRATTY, BRYANT J., *Social Dimensions of Physical Activity.* Englewood Cliffs, N.J.: Prentice-Hall, Inc., 1967.

CROSS, GERTRUDE, "The New Leisure Class," *Parks and Recreation,* (June 1977), p. 33.

DUBOS, RENE, *Man Adapting.* New Haven: Yale University Press, 1965.

EHRLICH, PAUL K., ANNE H. EHRLICH and JOHN P. HOLDREN, *Human Ecology: Problems and Solutions.* San Francisco: W.H. Freeman and Company, 1973.

FELSHIN, JAN, *More Than Movement: An Introduction to Physical Education.* Philadelphia: Lea and Febiger, 1972.

FREEMAN, W.H., *Physical Education in a Changing Society,* Part III. Boston: Houghton Mifflin Company, 1977.

HART, MARIE M., ed., *Sport in the Sociocultural Process* (2nd ed.). Dubuque, Iowa: W.C. Brown, 1976.

HAWKINS, DONALD E., and DENNIS A. VINTON, *The Environmental Classroom.* Englewood Cliffs, N.J.: Prentice-Hall, Inc., 1973.

HIGGINSON, JOHN, "A Hazardous Society?" *American Journal of Public Health,* 66 (April 1976), 359–64.

JOKL, ERNST, *Medical Sociology and Cultural Anthropology of Sport and Physical Education.* Springfield, Ill.: Charles C. Thomas, Pub., 1964.

KAPLAN, MAX, and PHILLIP BOSSERMAN, eds., *Technology, Human Values and Leisure.* Nashville, Tenn.: Abingdon Press, 1971.

KENNEDY, JOHN F., "The Soft American," *Sports Illustrated,* (December 26, 1960), pp. 15–17.

KRAUS, RICHARD G., *Recreation Today* (2nd ed.). Santa Monica, California: Goodyear Publishing Co., Inc., 1977.

LEONARD, GEORGE, *The Ultimate Athlete.* New York: Viking Press, 1975.

LEAR, JOHN, "Where Is Society Going? The Search for Landmarks," *Saturday Review,* April 15, 1972.

LINEBERRY, WILLIAM E., ed., *Priorities For Survival.* New York: H.W. Wilson Co., 1973.

LOCKHART, AILEANE S., and HOWARD S. SLUSHER, eds., *Contemporary Readings in Physical Education* (3rd ed.). Dubuque, Iowa: W.C. Brown, 1975.

LOY, JOHN W., and GERALD S. KENYON, *Sport, Culture and Society.* New York: Macmillan, 1969.

LUCAS, CHRISTOPHER J., *Our Western Educational Heritage.* New York: Macmillan, 1972.

MARTIN, ALEXANDER REID, "Leisure and Our Inner Resources," *Parks and Recreation,* (March 1975), p. 1.

McGLYNN, GEORGE H., *Issues in Physical Education and Sports.* Palo Alto, California: National Press Books, 1975.

McKINNEY, WAYNE C., and PHYLLIS M. FORD, "What is the Profession Doing about Education for Leisure? *Journal of Health, Physical Education and Recreation,* 43 (May 1972), 49–51.

MILIO, NANCY, *The Care of Health in Communities.* New York: Macmillan, 1975.

MORTON, ROGERS C.B., "Leisure and the Environment," *Journal of Health, Physical Education and Recreation,* 44 (January 1973), 36–37.

NASH, JAY B., *Philosophy of Recreation and Leisure,* Dubuque, Iowa: W. C. Brown Co., 1965.

RICH, JOHN M., *Challenge and Response: Education in American Culture.* New York: John Wiley and Sons, 1974.

SCHWEITZER, ALBERT, *The Philosophy of Civilization.* New York: Macmillan, 1949.

SILBER, JOHN R., "The Pollution of Time," *Bostonia,* 45 (September 1971), 9–15.

TOYNBEE, ARNOLD, *Greek Civilization and Character.* New York: New American Library, 1961.

ULRICH, CELESTE, *The Social Matrix of Physical Education,* Chapter 2. Englewood Cliffs, N.J.: Prentice-Hall, Inc., 1968.

VANDER ZWAAG, HAROLD J., *Toward a Philosophy of Sport*. Reading, Mass.: Addison-Wesley, 1972.

VEBLEN, THORSTEIN, *The Theory of the Leisure Class*. New York: Mentor Books, 1899.

WILLGOOSE, CARL E., "Value Illness," *Journal of Health, Physical Education and Recreation*, 36 (March 1965), 19–21.

———, "Recreation: An Attitude of Mind," *Education*, (September 1960), pp. 42–44.

Educational

Paths to Virtue

chapter two

This thesis grows out of the concept of human nature as rooted in meaning and of human life as directed toward the fulfillment of meaning. The various patterns of knowledge are varieties of meaning, and the learning of these patterns is the clue to the effective realization of essential humanness through the curriculum of general education.

PHILIP H. PHENIX
PREFACE TO *REALMS OF MEANING*

A few years ago the American Academy of Physical Education adopted the theme "Realms of Meaning" for philosophic discourse. The topic was selected because Philip Phenix had expounded admirably on the process of integrating different segments of knowledge in order to give a deeper meaning to existence.

All too often an education offers only isolated bits of information with little effort having been made to relate the parts to each other. Needed is an integrative effort in which the physiological and physical aspects of living are viewed with respect to the social, psychological, and aesthetic dimensions. Advancing this concept can bring about what Rosenfeld calls a "new consciousness," in which the individual demonstrates an essential awareness and understanding of the physical self as the yeoman of the brain and mind.[1] The concept is not new, but it requires updating from time to time. Whitehead said as much in his day: "There is only one subject matter of education, and that is life in all of its manifestations."

By concentrating on meanings in education, Phenix has brought general education down to a practical level on which learnings must be seen by the individual as having such substance that they have a bearing on life at the

---

[1]Albert Rosenfeld, *Mind and Supermind* (New York: Holt, Rinehart, Winston, 1977).

moment. One can understand that he considers the humanities a scholarly discipline, and human movement an essential experience.

> The sense of movement is inherent in every human activity. . . . All perceptions . . . are accompanied by motor reactions. No other instrument is as elaborate, sensitive, and responsive as the human body. This is why the arts of movement are so important for the expression of human meaning.[2]

While treating the same topic, Victor Frankl reminds his followers that the word "meaning" comes from the Greek word "logos" which not only is translated as "meaning" but also as "spirit."[3] There was a spirit in ancient Greece with its cultural emphasis on physical education that has no comparable counterpart. It is not only that physical education was more prominent in Greek life than in any other culture before or since, but even more significantly, as Siedentop has indicated, competitive athletics was the central focus of the culture and a primary criterion by which civilization was distinguished from barbarism.[4] Moreover, a large part of Greek life centered in the palaestra and the gymnasium, and the Greek youth received sports skills instruction from shortly after dawn to midday. This experience formed the core of his education. It was an education to fulfill all human needs. The values from competition were intrinsic, not extrinsic and material. The goal was embodied in the concept of *arete*—excellence in performance and noble behavior. This was what Homer described as he wrote about the lives, personalities, and deeds of the early heroes who sought a conduct of just and righteous living.

Now one asks if the day has passed when we can have the benefit of such singleness of purpose. Have the remnants of the Greek ethic been so diluted that they provide no real influence for the society or the educational systems? Albert Schweitzer would say no, and go on to show how civilizations come about—not by ignoring the past, but by "thinking out ideals which aim at the progress of the whole, and then so fitting them to realities of life that they assume the shape in which they can influence most effectively the circumstances of the time."[5]

Life Styles and Human Totality

Cardiologist John L. Boyer moves directly to encounter the question of needs by asking that the *life style* of America be examined. What is there about the life style? What does the physician see in hundreds of people who go

[2]Philip J. Phenix, *Realms of Meaning* (New York: McGraw-Hill, 1964), pp. 165–66.

[3]Victor Frankl, *Man's Search For Meaning* (New York: Washington Square Press, 1970), p. 82.

[4]Daryl Siedentop, "Differences between Greek and Hebrew Views of Man," *Canadian Journal of History of Sport and Physical Education*, 2 (December 1971), 30–49.

[5]Albert Schweitzer, *The Philosophy of Civilization* (New York: Macmillan, 1949), p. 9.

through his office in a year? Says Boyer, "You see people . . . striving frantically for things; a great sense of urgency, striving to obtain things, to get things, and they talk about things . . . and they struggle against time, always struggling to make a deadline . . . ambitious, competitive, impatient, aggressive, and enslaved by time and number." They are unaware of their own bodies and how much they can tolerate. Their education has not made them fully conscious of themselves.

The pursuit of life is not merely a massing of mental and physical quantities, but qualitative, too. And this, says Oberteuffer, is the crucial issue for physical education in today's schools. He asks,

> What meaning does it have? What experience does it offer in the direction of that meaning? Does it make a contribution to man in its entirety? . . . To survive, the physical education programs of the day must recognize the totality of man and be constantly mindful that man lives in a social setting, not in isolation.[6]

William Glasser refers to poor-quality life style as a condition that occurs when people lack the vitality and strength to find the happiness enjoyed by others. Missing is the perception and dynamism to overcome difficulties associated with fulfillment, pleasure, recognition, and a sense of personal value. In his Positive Addiction theory, in which people have a positive life style, Glasser states that runners are in a most favorable category.

> I only have to think of putting on my running shoes and the kinesthetic pleasure of floating along, the pleasure of movement starts to come, I get a feeling of euphoria, almost real happiness . . . when I am happy I am running well, when running well I am happy. It is the platonic idea of knowing thyself. Running is getting to know thyself. Running is getting to know yourself to an extreme degree.[7]

No doubt, this is the "peak experience" that Maslow describes as producing profound changes in an individual. He finds numerous activities that trigger peak experiences. In speaking of music and movement his comment contributes much to the significance of a life style.

> . . . it fuses over into dancing or rhythm . . . for me they melted together . . . I don't know whether you want to call that music, dancing, rhythm, athletics or something else. The love for the body, and a reverence of the body—these are perfectly good paths to peak experiences.[8]

[6]Delbert Oberteuffer in the foreword to *Background Reading for Physical Education*, by Ann Paterson and Edmond C. Hallberg (New York: Holt, Rinehart and Winston, 1965).

[7]William Glasser, *Positive Addiction* (New York: Harper and Row, 1976).

[8]A. H. Maslow, "Theory of Human Motivation," *Psychological Review*, 50 (1953), 376.

George Leonard states that it may seem strange that physical education should rank high in the reform movement and the building of new life styles. How could we have misplaced this kind of education in the first place—"something that is so obvious, so persistent, so *close;* the human body"?[9]

Educational Objectives

The aim of education cannot be defined until the aim of life has first been determined. The goal of human life, says Maxwell Garnett, is that human societies should aim at making progress and advance steadily toward the fulfillment of some far-reaching purpose.[10] Seneca would have agreed, and he called attention to the fact that the greatest part of progress is the *desire* to progress. Desire is a key word.

Objectives mean something when there is personal striving to make progress in a definite direction. To make progress, humans need what John Dewey referred to as a "means of execution." That is, something has to happen if an aim or objective is to be realized. The word "education" bears this out, for it comes from the Latin word *educere,* meaning "to lead forth" or "draw out." It therefore suggests "drawing out" something latent or potential in a person. It suggests a change in some particular direction. *Education, therefore, may be defined as a process of changing behavior to aim toward certain preconceived goals.*

The essential purposes of education have not varied to any great degree in a century. What Herbert Spencer wrote in the nineteenth century on the question of "What Knowledge Is of Most Worth?" does not depart significantly from modern ideas.[11] For Spencer, education was concerned with (1) life and health; (2) earning a living; (3) family rearing; (4) citizenship; and (5) leisure. This list does not differ very much from that of the *Cardinal Principles of Secondary Education* of 1918.[12] The goals listed are health, command of fundamental processes, worthy home membership, vocation, citizenship, worthy use of leisure time, and ethical character. As far as health and physical education are concerned, both sets of purposes stress health as the primary aim and point to the need for education for leisure.

It is quite apparent that some of the first writers on education—such as

[9]George Leonard, "The Rediscovery of the Body," *New York,* December 27, 1976, pp. 34–39.

[10]J. C. Maxwell Garnett, *Education and World Citizenship* (London: Cambridge University Press, 1921), p. 315.

[11]Herbert Spencer, *Education: Intellectual, Moral and Physical* (New York: Appleton-Century-Crofts, 1860).

[12]Commission of the Reorganization of Secondary Education, *Cardinal Principles of Secondary Education,* Washington, D.C.:, Bureau of Education, 1918, Bulletin 35.

Socrates, Comenius, Locke, Rousseau—were just as enthusiastic about healthful living and its relationship to other educational objectives as were more recent educators such as Horace Mann, James, Dewey, and Piaget. Moreover, the goals they envisioned did not differ essentially from the 1946 and 1961 purposes of the Education Policies Commission—self-realization, human relationship, economic efficiency, and civic responsibility.[13] Up to this time any differences in stated objectives had been mostly a matter of emphasis.

Not until the 1966 report of the American Association of School Administrators appeared was an entirely new look at the times and the needs of man taken. This admirable publication, *Imperatives in Education,* sets forth in concise fashion the essentials that should be at the forefront as "curriculums are modifed, instructional methods revised, and organizational patterns reshaped to meet the educational needs of this country in one of its most dynamic periods."[14] More specifically, the report identifies the following nine imperatives in education:

1. to make urban life rewarding and satisfying
2. to prepare people for the world of work
3. to discover and nurture creative talent
4. to strengthen the moral fabric of society
5. to deal constructively with psychological tensions
6. to keep democracy working
7. to make intelligent use of natural resources
8. to make the best use of leisure time
9. to work with other peoples of the world for human betterment

Not only do these imperatives reflect the changing times, they hold considerable significance for teachers of physical education. Moreover, there are also implications for health education programs and recreational activities. In short, these nine points, according to which the educational program must be revised and reshaped, are particularly meaningful in the long-range planning activities of both the small-town instructor and the large-city director of health, physical education, and recreation.

[13]Educational Policies Commission, *Policies for Education in American Democracy,* Washington, D.C.: National Educational Association, 1946. See also *The Central Purpose of American Education,* Washington. D.C.: National Education Association, 1961. In the latter report (p. 15) it states: "The central purpose of education is to develop rational powers of the individual or capacities to think and reason. Basic to this development is physical health since disease defects and disability may interfere with learning."

[14]American Association of School Administrators, *Imperatives in Education,* Washington, D.C.: American Association of School Administrators. 1966.

Physical Education Objectives

Physical education is concerned with the art and science of human movement. However, its ultimate objective is to employ movement in order to contribute to the physical, mental, and social goals of education. For this reason, physical education might properly be defined as education through physical means, primarily through large-muscle activity.

The major objective of physical education is the development and maintenance of (1) physical fitness and motor skills; (2) social efficiency; (3) culture; (4) recreational competency; and (5) intellectual competency.

Teachers of physical education must be willing to scrutinize and carefully reappraise existing physical education goals and the emphasis that is given to these goals from time to time. Perhaps the matter of emphasis needs more attention. Certainly, as one reviews the history of physical education, it becomes clear that some objectives have been slighted in the past while others were overemphasized. There have been periods of great attention to posture and mental health, character development through sports participation, and body awareness through movement exploration; and periods in which the development of physical fitness almost replaces the name of physical education.

There is no easy way to bring about needed improvements in the curriculum. However, *all* goals can be given proper consideration. If they are, the major objectives of physical education will be kept in balance.

From time to time some professionals have asked whether physical education should have a hierarchy of objectives. Such a hierarchy could bring extra attention to certain objectives that appear to be of major importance in a particular year or decade. However, it could also be unfortunate, as it might make some objectives more important than others. Harrison Clarke is one of a number of people who oppose a hierarchy of objectives, but he concedes that certain boys and girls who are below standard in physical fitness components should be identified and provided with programs designed to meet their individual needs. This position is taken because of the recognition that the improvement and maintenance of physical fitness are unique to physical education. No other subject-matter field in education makes this type of contribution to youth.

Physical Education—What's in a Name?

What is wrong with the expression "physical education"? Why are some professionals in the field anxious to change to a new name? What designation might replace "physical education"?

Historically in this country, "physical culture" was the terminology employed to designate the field. Because of the association of "physical" with

FIGURE 2-1. The joy of movement—for spectators and participants alike. (Courtesy, American Alliance for Health, Physical Education and Recreation)

"culture" it had broad implications and great promise, but it was downgraded in the eyes of the public because of a popular newsstand magazine of the same name that concentrated on the "body beautiful." About the same period, and owing somewhat to the influence of military preparedness programs, the term "physical training" was used. The emphasis was on fitness and training in certain physical skills. Because the word "training" began to be appraised by educators in general as a kind of indoctrination and a much too narrow word, it was dropped and subject-matter areas such as physical training, vocational training, and manual (industrial arts) training were upgraded to "education."

The designation "physical education" rose in popularity during the twenties and thirties because it clearly linked physical activity to the ultimate purposes of education. It was described as an "education *through* the physical" and gained strong support from such leaders as Thomas Wood, Luther Gulick, Clark Hetherington, Jesse Feiring Williams, Jay B. Nash, Karl W. Bookwalter, and Frederick Rand Rogers. Hetherington's definition of physical education and his objectives have been widely accepted, and have had a significant effect on current educational efforts in the nation's schools and teacher-preparation institutions.

In the past several decades there has been increasing dissatisfaction expressed concerning the appropriateness of the name "physical education."

Rosalind Cassidy, Professor Emeritus at UCLA, voiced her disapproval as far back as 1927, stating that the designation was semantically unsound and focused on a mind-body dichotomy. In 1954 the late Charles H. McCloy acknowledged that it was not a very good term, but he could not come up with a substitute name. He confessed that he did not like "sports education" or simply "sport" because it had overtones of gambling and horse-racing that would not be acceptable to a large number of people.

More recently criticism has been made that the term "physical education" does not adequately characterize the development and conservation of the body mechanism as the producer of purposeful movement patterns and skills—does not convey the idea that it is concerned with perceptual-cognitive content, and does not really tell or stand for the whole story of what is involved in human movement. There are, of course, large numbers of professionals in this field who oppose any change of name at all. People like Josephine Rathbone, Arthur Esslinger, Harrison Clarke, Donald Matthews, Lloyd Messersmith, Charles Bucher, and others would disagree with Cassidy and say that "physical education" has not encouraged a mind-body dichotomy at all, but has done much to bring the societal influences, psychological parameters, and biokinesiological aspects of the human being closer together—perhaps more than any other subject-matter area in the curriculum. Moreover, why not retain a term that has finally become understood?[15]

To the average person the term "physical" suggests or implies movement. Messersmith questions whether the substitution of another term would solve the problem and give the public a better understanding and appreciation of the field. Such action could detract from rather than enhance status and understanding in the eyes of the general public to whom the problem of semantics is not so acute. This is a valid point, for there is always the need to clearly and precisely convey the business we should be about in our field of endeavor. In short, perhaps the nature of the term employed is less important than the quality of the work produced by the members of the profession.

The name-change discussion, however, will not rest and be nicely settled by the foregoing remarks. Any enduring effort to explore accurate terminology is sound and reasonable and will continue to provoke a number of viewpoints. In terms of the nation as a whole, there are several educational institutions in which name changes have already been made, and there has been considerable discussion in state and local workshops and teacher-preparation institutions as well as in the general sessions of the American

---

[15]For a full discussion of the pros and cons relative to the designation "physical education" see *The Academy Papers* (Quality of Life through Human Movement), The American Academy of Physical Education, 1972. Copies may be obtained from Dudley Ashton, Business Manager, 2070 Eastern Parkway, Louisville, Ky. 40204.

Academy of Physical Education. Some of the suggested designations for the field are as follows:

1. Human movement. Physical education might well be called human movement, since human movement is symbolic of human existence. Peter Karpovich tells the story of an ancient philosopher who believed so strongly that motion is the essential characteristic of life that he coined the phrase: "Moto ergo sum" or "I move, therefore I exist." He may have been a somewhat odd, if dedicated, man, because when he became hoarse and could not talk, he would raise his hand and move his index finger as a symbol of existence.[16]

This concept of movement is more than mental, physical, social, and perceptual. In its broadest educational sense, human movement is all-encompassing, and its advocates suggest that potentially it is the most significant experience in the learning program when fully described. This may appear to be a somewhat exaggerated statement bordering on chest-thumping by euphoric physical educators. This is hardly the case, however, because a careful examination of all movement—both directed and nondirected, motivated and nonmotivated—clearly relates to the involvement of the total person. Moreover, this is not just a rebirth of the classical concept of the whole person, but is something that can be attested to by almost any modern practitioner of medicine, clinical psychology, and religious counseling.

Naming the field "human movement" is based on historical and contemporary evidence that movement is fundamental to human functioning, is related to culture and society, may be an aesthetic experience, has meaning and significance, and has persistent and dynamic forms.[17] Furthermore, there are three underlying concepts: (1) humans move to survive; (2) they move to discover and understand their environment; and (3) they move to control and adjust to their environment. The proponents of "human movement" base their case on the present-day need to be more descriptive of what is involved in the motor function of the human. Moreover, they do not limit their description to movement exploration activities, but include all developmental and adapted physical activity, dance, and athletics.

2. Movement education. Perhaps the most popular substitute designation for physical education is "movement education." The rationale for its acceptance is very much the same as that for human movement. Cassidy sees movement experiences as a means of achieving self-identity, self-value, self-esteem, self-reliance, and self-actualization in the development of the

[16]Peter V. Karpovich, "Moto Ergo Sum," in Charles A. Bucher and Myra Goldman, eds., *Dimensions of Physical Education* (New York: C.V. Mosby Co., 1969), p. 157.
[17]See Robert Singer and others, *Physical Education: An Interdisciplinary Approach* (New York: Macmillan, 1972), pp. 4–6.

responsible, socially aware, creative person. This might be likened to the social efficiency or character-development objective so often stressed in the past by Hetherington and, in the present, by Maslow, Erikson, Harrison Clarke, and Charles Bucher. In any case, the name "movement education" is preferred by a number of people because it focuses on the word "movement" in a way that appears to be broader in scope than does the word "physical." Fait sees "movement education" as "an explorative activity . . . form of problem solving within the field of physical education."[18] Lorena Porter sees "movement education" as that part of the physical education curriculum concerned with body management—controlling the body in movement patterns because one understands the way the body can move in relation to the many forces exerted upon it.[19] Schurr describes it as the "vital core of the whole school program of physical education," carried out in an "experiential manner" and laying a foundation for the further application of knowledges . . . to the learning of work-skills and the various game, sport, exercise, and dance activities which are the basis of the active leisure-time pursuits of youth and adulthood."[20] Kirchner also subscribes to the view that "movement education" has a specific connotation and is a part of the broad field of physical education. It is a means by which the student *understands* all movement in order that the simple-to-complex physical education skills may be developed.[21]

3. Kinesiology. The proponents of "kinesiology" point out that their topic is already known and respected as the science of human movement and is a logical substitute for the name "physical education." Moreover, there is increasing agreement that the understanding of movement behavior hinges on the study of the human as a moving being. Thus, the term "kinesiology"—made up of "ology," the study of, and "kinesis," movement—is quite descriptive and parallels such designations for the fields of psychology, sociology, physiology, and so forth. MacKenzie makes a strong case for this word to serve as a term for the subject matter.[22] From the root word *Kinesi* he coins the new word, *Kinesics*. The thesis is that the study of human movement—kinesiology—involves moving, feeling, and thinking about movement, and is an integral part of liberal education.

[18]Hollis Fait, *Physical Education for the Elementary School Child: Experiences in Movement*, 2nd ed. (Philadelphia: W.B. Saunders Co., 1976), p. 110.

[19]Lorena Porter, *Movement Education for Children*, Washington, D.C.: American Association of Elementary-Kindergarten-Nursery Educators, 1969, p. 5.

[20]Evelyn L. Schurr, *Movement Experiences for Children*, 2nd ed. (Englewood Cliffs, N.J.: Prentice-Hall, Inc., 1975), p. 226.

[21]Glen Kirchner and others, *Introduction to Movement Education* (Dubuque: William C. Brown Co. Pub., 1970), p. 16.

[22]Marlin M. MacKenzie, *Toward a New Curriculum in Physical Education* (New York: McGraw-Hill, 1969), pp. 9–10.

4. Anthropokinesiology.   Actually the term "anthropo-kinesi-ology" (man, movement, the study of) is a more accurate designation of what physical education focuses upon. It is a variation MacKenzie supports. But the word is too long.

5. Developmental motor performance.   In the AAHPER (American Association for Health, Physical Education, and Recreation) publication *Tones of Theory* (1972), much was made of the human movement phenomena as a total response of the individual. Implicit in this response is a wide variety of motor performances and related performances having to do with expressions of ideas, sentiments, attitudes, and so forth. To capture this viewpoint, Laura Huelster and others would substitute "developmental motor performance" for physical education.

6. Movement arts and sciences.   If physical education is being defined as the art and science of human movement, then, says N. P. Neilson, why not call the field "movement arts"? The name would be generalization and serve as one umbrella over all activities classified into subgroups. Dudley Ashton champions this view, but would relate more to the ancient Greek ideal and designate the area "movement arts and sciences."

7. Physical education and sports.   A number of individuals, sensing the value of a sports education, do not feel that physical education tells the whole story. Although sports have always been a part of physical education, sports now require some additional visibility. Recently the President's Council on Physical Fitness added "and Sports" to its name in order to call attention to the place of sports in the lives of people. Earl Ziegler concurs; so does Robert Yoho when he points to the definite acceptance of women in competitive sports and the need for women to identify with the sports terminology. Says Yoho, to employ the term "movement arts" would be pure folly.

8. Sports education.   Suggested by Seward Staley several decades ago, this term was never accepted—chiefly because it appeared to be a limiting designation. When it is a means to an end that fosters physical development, humanistic attitudes, art forms, and cultural contributions, it is a valuable term. Tom Sheehan sees "sport" and "sport education" as the central focus of attention.[23] Edward Shea of Southern Illinois University feels the same way and sees a greater possibility for the academic synthesis of all physical activities within the broad contextual environment of sport. Interestingly, Professor Liselott Diem of Germany reports that "sport" rather than "physical education," is becoming a descriptive term there. In Germany it is sometimes referred to as "sport sciences."

9. Other terms.   Because muscular effort prevails in the realm of physical activity, the term *ergonomics* has been suggested as a substitute

[23]Thomas J. Sheehan, "Sport: The Focal Point of Physical Education," *Quest*, 10 (1968), 59–67.

designation for physical education. Another suggestion is the term *human conservation*. Still another is *human physical sciences*. Leonard Larson feels that this designation would nicely cover all the professional activities, such as health education, recreation, adapted physical education, sports medicine, preventive medicine, and so forth.

It should be clear by now that the concern to enlighten general educators and the public alike to the full meaning of physical education is serious business. Whether to change the name or to do a better job of describing the nature and potential of the field will be an unresolved question for years to come. Kleinman doesn't think that the name "physical education" is understood as meaningful and significant on the highest level of existence because it is too often seen only in terms of sports and games.[24]

There is not what Siedentop calls a "discernible consensus view" on what to call the field because of how the concept of human movement is interpreted.[25] Is movement a unitary concept or a part of a larger package of concepts? Certainly it is expressive, interactive, communicative, and essential for survival. And because motor reactions accompany all other perceptions (perception sorts sensory input and determines motor output), speaking in terms of a unitary concept—viewing the body, its efforts and relationships as a whole—becomes easy.[26] Says Phenix:

> The fundamental concept of the arts of movement is the organic unity of the person. . . . If learning is to be organic . . . this union of thought, feeling, sense, and act is the particular aim of the arts of movement . . . nowhere else is the coordination of all components of the living person so directly fostered.[27]

Germane to the discussion are the recent writings of Cheffers and Evaul and the earlier writings of Ruth Abernathy and Maryann Waltz in which human movement is looked upon as the *discipline* that incorporates a body of knowledge, and physical education is the *profession* that applies that knowledge.[28] In subscribing to this distinction one recognizes that human move-

[24]Seymour Kleinman, "The Significance of Human Movement: A Phenomenological Approach," in Bucher and Goldman, eds., *Dimensions of Physical Education*, pp. 150–53.

[25]Daryl Siedentop, *Physical Education: Introductory Analysis*, 2nd ed. (Dubuque: William C. Brown Co., Pub., 1976), p. 142.

[26]For a review of Laban's considerations useful in describing movement see Lawrence Locke, "Movement Education—A Description and Critique," in Roscoe Brown and Bryant Cratty, eds. *New Perspectives of Man in Action* (New York: Prentice-Hall, Inc., 1969) p. 208.

[27]Phenix, *Realms*, p. 310.

[28]John Cheffers and Tom Evaul, *Introduction to Physical Education: Concepts of Human Movement* (Englewood Cliffs, N.J.: Prentice-Hall, Inc., 1978), p. 38. Ruth Abernathy and Maryann Waltz, "Toward a Discipline: First Steps First," *Quest*, 2 (April, 1964), 1–2.

ment and physical education are not synonymous. Physical education is quite specific, as it modifies the person in terms of broad educational goals. It is, therefore, an applied field which employs movement experiences as a means of reaching the aims of education.

Much of the dilemma as to what to call the field, what designation carries the greatest meaning, involves a failure to recognize what Warren Fraleigh calls a *multitheoretical viewpoint,* in which several kinds of concepts contribute to the broad context of physical education.[29] Celeste Ulrich supports this view and sees physical education drawing from many areas of theory and the many concepts of movement through fitness activities, dance, sports, and others, contributing to the multitheoretical base.[30]

Perhaps the most satisfactory way to bring this discussion of what to name the field to a close is to make a plea for a more descriptive interpretation of just what physical education is and what it hopes to accomplish. It does indeed have meaning, for wherever one looks there is consistent evidence of the unique manifestations of movement phenomena serving a variety of purposes. Perhaps the admirable words of Lois Ellfeldt are appropriate: ". . . instead of movement as a baseline we might, in one grand Alice-in-Wonderland gesture, turn the whole thing upside down and think of physical education as a great golden funnel down which splashes an ever-increasing variety of movement experiences."

Physical Fitness and Physical Activity

Defined briefly, physical fitness is the capacity for activity. It is a positive quality and is closely related to diet, exercise, rest, and emotional outlook. It is often referred to as organic vigor or vitality—the physical element of behavior that permits the person to be active. It is demonstrated through physical performance. Although related to health in general, it is more specific when carefully evaluated. For example, several persons may be thoroughly checked by the school physician and found to be free from disease and defects, and yet they will vary in the degree to which they can perform physically. Some will tire in walking a short distance; others may run the same distance without being winded. The greater the physical fitness, the greater the physical endurance and precision of movement. The greater the physical fitness, the longer a person will be able to keep going; he or she will be able to perform more efficiently and at greater speeds and to recuperate faster from fatigue.

Harrison Clarke, research consultant to the President's Council on

[29]Warren Fraleigh, "Resolved That Physical Education Is Multi-Theoretical Rather Than Uni-Theoretical," *The Academy Papers,* No. 7 (1973), p. 10.

[30]Celeste Ulrich, "A Multi-Theoretical Crusade," *The Academy Papers,* No. 7 (1973), p. 19.

*sine qua non = an absolutely
indispensible or essential thing*

Physical Fitness and Sports, points out that undergirding physical fitness is an organic soundness consisting of three components: (1) muscular strength; (2) muscular endurance; and (3) circulatory-respiratory endurance. The effectiveness of all body movements, whether large- or small-muscle in nature, depends upon the status of these three components.

The Unique Role of Physical Activity

Conrad wrote, "Man is born; he struggles; he dies"—a pretty short life history. The key word here is "struggles." Life is a struggle. The capacity to perform is the *sine qua non* in the individual. With it, one is able to strive to achieve a certain happiness. This is accomplished "not by acquiescing with what is but by struggling for something else, not by accepting but by doing, not by receiving but by giving, not by rest but by activity."[31]

It is through the manifestations of the muscular system—through activity—that our species makes itself known as a human animal. Says Tyler, "The muscles are the organs of the will." Through them, humans speak, execute, and express themselves in a thousand ways. The very quality of

FIGURE 2-2. An education through the physical is accomplished in a variety of ways. (Courtesy, Nissen Corporation)

[31]Shailer U. Lawton and Frederick R. Rogers, *Educational Paths to Virtue*, I (Newton, Mass.: Pleides Co., 1937), 47.

the musculature, therefore, relates to all human activity. Poor health and lowered physical capacity reduce one's *ability* to perform mental tasks. Learning itself depends on muscle action. John Dewey wrote of this when he referred to "learn by doing" and the virtue of reinforcing a learning situation by physical activity. Comenius noted, "Intellectual progress is conditioned at every step by bodily vigor. To obtain the best results, physical exercise must accompany and condition mental training." Gesell, Jersild, and the Swiss psychologist Piaget found that a child's earliest learning is motor in nature and forms the foundation for subsequent learning.

Individuals approach their potential mental capacity only when they are capable of putting thoughts into actions. There is really nothing strange about this, because the end of a train of thought is action. William James made this clear when he spoke of the whole neural mechanism as essentially a machine for converting stimuli into reactions. And Maxwell Garnett amplified the James position by pointing out that uninterrupted and undissipated thoughts are conclusive thoughts, which leave the brain and "give rise to some form of bodily activity. And this is the normal ending of every train of thought."[32]

As one continues to investigate the role of activity in education, it becomes increasingly clear that the quality of muscle fiber has as much to do with learning as the nature of the intellect. In fact, the intellect cannot be divorced from the flesh. The human organism is a totality, and learning is accomplished as a totality.

Because thinking and acting cannot be separated, the role of activity in the education of youth is most signficant. What kind of activity shall there be? Many experiences in which thought and action are combined are needed. Dance is an example of a physical education activity in which the individual can both think and act. Movement exploration is another.

Moreover, the activated muscle sense (kinesthetic sense) may be the most important human sense. It is possible to operate without eyes and ears but not a kinesthetic sense. It is this muscle sense, created through muscle action, that stimulates the mind. In fact, the mind can become a blank when the "organs of the mind" are relaxed. Thus, by relaxing eye, tongue, and mouth muscles, we make thoughts disappear and the mind is quiet. In this connection we should remember that muscles are 40 percent sensory organs and only 60 percent motor.

The only way the mind obtains leverage upon matter, and can "materialize" mental events, is through movements that are made possible by *quality* muscle tissue—tissue physically fit to meet the demands of the vigorous life.[33]

[32]J. C. Maxwell Garnett, *Education and World Citizenship* (London: Cambridge University Press, 1921) p. 273.

[33]Review the superb account of mind-body relationships described by Ernst Jokl in *Medical Sociology and Cultural Anthropology of Sport and Physical Education* (Springfield, Ill.: Charles C. Thomas, 1964).

In view of this, it is not surprising to find numerous references in the literature of human development to physical condition and learning potential. The correlation between intellectual or academic achievement and physical capacity is low, but positive. Terman recognized this years ago when he said that good things tend to go together. More recently, Charles A. Bucher brought together the findings of a large number of research studies conducted independently over a number of years. He was able to confirm the relationship between motor skills and academic achievement, as well as the relationship between physical fitness and grade-point average.[34]

Perhaps one of the most convincing discussions relating physical condition to intellectual productivity is to be found in the literature pertaining to the educationally subnormal boys and girls. An increasing body of evidence indicates that systematic and progressive physical conditioning yields marked mental as well as physical improvement and improvement in social adjustment. Says Paul Benoit, ". . . there is a new feature in the expectation that the appropriate planning of physical activity for the retarded can affect personal capacity for thought and action. If we raise the degree of well-being, alertness, and interest in reality and action, the individual's attention span will expand, with the result that he will have the benefit of more awareness, more associative perception, more thought . . . physical education is now regarded as an essential tool, indeed as a primary tool, in inducing optimal mental development."[35]

Perceptual-Motor Development

The nature of perceiving has been studied for many years and has been closely linked to the motor process. In fact, the quality of a movement performance by anyone is dependent on accuracy of perception, as well as the ability to interpret a number of perceptions into a series of coordinated motor acts. In the case of children, a good feeling for the body—a good image of the body—contributes to the development of many perceptual skills needed in classroom activities. In this respect physical education is unique in providing experiences designed to initiate and maintain locomotor abilities, physical fitness, body image, balance, flexibility, agility, laterality and directionality, and manipulative abilities.

Perceptual theorists, for example, Hunt, Piaget, Bruner, Wilkin, and Gagne, call attention to the necessity of sensory-motor integration in the hierarchy of human development. The holistic view of human functioning

---

[34]Health, Physical Education, and Academic Achievement," *NEA Journal*, 54 (May 1965), 17.

[35]J. Paul Benoit, "Extending the Mind through the Body," *Journal of Health, Physical Education, and Recreation*, 37 (April 1966), 28–29. See also the excellent article by Julian V. Stein in the same issue (p. 25), entitled "The Potential of Physical Activity for the Mentally Retarded Child." See also Muriel R. Sloan's report, "Physical Education: Multiperspectivity," in *The Academy Papers*, No. 8 (September 1974), 16–26.

clearly associates the self or ego with the body. Von Bertalanffy said a number of years ago, "Take this proprioceptive experience away and no consciousness of myself is left."[36]

    With the increasing emphasis on upgrading educational programs and opportunities for the wide variety of handicapped children, considerable attention is being given to those individuals with perceptual-motor weaknesses. The outcome is that there is a wealth of research evidence supporting the relationship between one's physical ability and acceptance of self.[37]

Physical Activity and Well-Being

    If for no other reason, a physical education is essential to personal well-being because of its physiological consequences. The tremendous amount of research to back up this statement may be quickly summarized as follows:

    1. Physical activity relates to weight control. Desirable weight is basically a matter of correct balance between energy intake and energy expenditure. Men tend to put on excess fat at an earlier age than women. But, past the age of forty, a higher percentage of women than men are more than 20 percent over their "best" weight.

    Although there are a number of causes of human obesity, considerable evidence indicates that physical inactivity and food intake in excess of needs are the major etiological factors. When the physical activity of obese men and women is compared with that of the nonobese (matched for age, occupation, and socioeconomic background), there is a clear indication that obese people are far less active. In several studies of adolescent boys and girls, Bullen and Mayer have been able to demonstrate that the obese adolescents are significantly less active than the nonobese.[38] In fact, even when they are actively taking part in a sport or game, they are expending less energy than their nonobese playmates. Another benefit associated with exercise in weight control is that weight lost through exercise is more lasting than loss through dieting. Moreover, exercise may produce changes in body proportions and composition that are desirable and at the same time not change weight appreciably.[39]

    Although a lean person in good condition may eat more following

[36]Ludwig Von Bertalanffy, "The Mind-Body Problem: A New View," *Psychosomatic Medicine,* 26 (January, 1964), 29–45.

[37]See comments by Robert J. Sonstroem in "Attitude Testing Examining Certain Psychological Correlates Of Physical Activity," *Research Quarterly,* 45 (May 1974), 93–103.

[38]Beverly Bullen and Jean Mayer, "Adolescent Obesity," *American Journal of Clinical Nutrition,* 14 (1964), 211.

[39]Ernst Jokl, *Nutrition, Exercise and Body Composition* (Springfield, Ill.: Charles C. Thomas, 1964).

exercise, the increased activity will burn up the extra calories consumed. The overweight person does not respond in the same way to exercise. Because he has large stores of fat, moderate exercise does not stimulate his appetite; only when he exercises in greater amount will his appetite increase. Caloric expenditure in daily activities and exercise varies considerably in terms of the activity. Table 2-1 indicates the number of calories a 150-pound person burns up in an hour.[40]

Working with the health teacher and others in the school, the physical educator can do much to reduce not only the weight of the adolescent but also the frequently passive, withdrawn, lonely, and isolated feelings of the individual. A special weight-watchers physical education class has worked in a number of situations. The concern for body image and its relationship to self-concept is a significant area which can be improved to some degree by giving increased attention to motor performance. Obesity is consistently encountered as a cause of physical unfitness among boys and girls, men and women, but the results of controlled exercise programs on body composition through simple walking, jogging, and running are measurable.[41]

TABLE 2-1

Rest and Light Activity	50–200	Badminton	350
Lying down or sleeping	80	Horseback riding (trotting)	350
Sitting	100	Square dancing	350
Driving an automobile	120	Volleyball	350
Standing	140	Roller skating	350
Domestic work	180		
		Vigorous Activity	over 350
Moderate Activity	200–350	Table tennis	360
Bicycling (5½ mph)	210	Ditch digging (hand shovel)	400
Walking (2½ mph)	210	Ice skating (10 mph)	400
Gardening	220	Wood chopping or sawing	400
Canoeing (2½ mph)	230	Tennis	420
Golf	250	Water skiing	480
Lawn mowing (power mower)	250	Hill climbing (100 ft. per hr.)	490
Bowling	270	Skiing (10 mph)	600
Lawn mowing (hand mower)	270	Squash and handball	600
Fencing	300	Cycling (13 mph)	660
Rowboating (2½ mph)	300	Scull rowing (race)	840
Swimming (¼ mph)	300	Running (10 mph)	900
Walking (3¾ mph)	300		

[40]Adapted from the report *Exercise and Weight Control*, available without charge from the American Medical Association, Department of Health Education, 535 N. Dearborn St., Chicago, Illinois 60610.
[41]Dorothy L. Moody and others, "The Effect of a Jogging Program on the Body Composition of Normal and Obese High School Girls," *Medicine and Science in Sports*, 4 (Winter 1972), 210–13.

To stress the fact that the role of exercise in weight control has been minimized, Mayer calls attention to a large body of research showing that physical inactivity is the single most important factor for the increasing number of overweight people in modern Western societies. Contributing to the obesity is a breakdown in the energy-balancing mechanism in the hypothalmus at the rear base of the brain, which occurs when too little exercise is taken. Intensive physical activity, such as progressive weight training, in only six to ten weeks time will reduce skinfold and absolute and relative fat, increase muscle girth, and contribute significantly to lean body weight.

In the Tecumseh, Michigan, Community Health Study—a large ongoing epidemiological investigation of an entire community—active individuals, as expected, were consistently leaner but became fatter with advancing age and less activity. Perhaps the most important finding, however, was the relationship between the lack of activity and fatness as it contributed to high serum cholesterol levels and poor heart-rate response to moderate exercise. When the fatness was eliminated there was essentially no relationship between this estimate of work capacity and serum cholesterol. [42]

2. **Physical activity needs for women and girls are the same as for men and boys.** This point is frequently overlooked when a program of physical education for girls is being organized. Lack of physical activity in a girl's childhood is related to chronic low back pain, a common complaint of new mothers. A five-year study of women patients with debilitating backache revealed that a large number of women patients had had backache problems for years that were aggravated by household jobs, lifting, sexual relations, and childbirth. [43] These young women were not obese. However, muscle tone was poor and posture and stance ungainly, and they had poorly developed abdominal muscles and facial tissue, a protruberant abdomen when standing and lordosis. Significantly, there was a common history of inactivity from early childhood—no physical education, no bicycling, little dancing, and no walking or bowling. Hans Kraus has written at length on the relationship of exercise to low back pain; and Raab and Kraus have stressed the need for movement in the prevention of disease. [44] Also, the beneficial relationship of good abdominal tone and regular exercise in reducing menstrual pain has

[42]Henry J. Montoye and others, "Fitness, Fatness, and Serum Cholesterol: An Epidemiological Study of an Entire Community", *Research Quarterly*, 47 (October 1976), 400–408.

[43]Evalyn S. Gendel, "Pregnancy Fitness and Sports," *Journal of the American Medical Association* (September 4, 1967), 751–54. See also "Fitness and Fatigue in the Female," *Journal of Health, Physical Education and Recreation*, 42 (October 1971), 53–54.

[44]Hans Kraus and Wilhelm Raab, *Hypokinetic Disease* (Springfield, Ill.: Charles C. Thomas, 1961).

been well established for nearly a quarter century by Golub and other scientists.[45]

A full physical education curriculum for girls and women is medically sound. On more than one occasion, Clayton Thomas, Medical Director of Tampax, Incorporated, and a member of the AAU National Sports Medicine Committee, has said that there is no evidence whatever that vigorous physical education and athletics are harmful to women. There are no stresses that can in any way harm reproductive organs or interfere with the menstrual cycle.

It is long past the time to encourage participation in carry-over individual and group activities and team sports instead of merely sandwiching them in. Fortunately, the female image is changing. The old arguments about the loss of femininity when a girl demonstrates her athletic ability are fast disappearing. In late 1972 women received official support when both the Eastern Collegiate Athletic Conference (ECAC) and the Massachusetts Secondary School Principals Association, which oversees schoolboy sports, made rule changes permitting women to play on men's teams in noncontact sports if there were not a comparable women's team on the campus. This action afforded a real boost to women's programs and encouraged schools to offer a wider range of women's sports.

Presently, many girls and women still lead a rather sedentary existence, containing not enough activity to tax the cardiovascular system. Complaints of fatigue upon exposure to mild physical activity are common; however, conditioning for life "work loads" is becoming more common, and girls enjoy it. When one high school girl was questioned about physical education, she said, "I like it because it makes me look and feel better. It helps me use up extra energy . . . and develops a nice body."

3. Muscle tension can be relieved by moderate exercise. In a survey of psychiatrists and their recommended treatments, 98 percent of the practicing psychiatrists agreed that moderate exercise will relieve tension, and 93 percent were prescribing moderate exercise in this order: walking, swimming, golf, and bowling. Exercise, when combined with psychotherapy, lowers blood pressure and relaxes muscle groups. Biofeedback research indicates that the ordinary person can be taught to control neuromuscular tensions. Even the teacher in the classroom can teach children to relax. In fact, in the decade ahead, the teaching of the means to relaxation may become one of the most important items in the physical education curriculum. In describing individuals of all ages, deVries illustrated the close relationships between reducing neuromuscular tension and regularly prescribed physical activity. The process also reduced anxiety.[46]

[45]Leib J. Golub, "Problems of Dysmenorrhea," *Philadelphia Medicine*, July 1, 1955, p. 87.
[46]Herbert A. deVries, "Physical Education: Does Physical Activity Promote Relaxation?" *Journal of Physical Education and Recreation*, 46 (September 1975), 53.

4. Lack of physical activity relates to coronary heart disease. A large number of Americans of all ages are underactive. Dietary habits and inactivity contribute to a rise in serum cholesterol and arteriosclerosis. Historically the evidence is impressive. The basic work of Morris with mail clerks and mail carriers confirmed the fact that coronary heart disease is about twice as common among less physically active people, and that walking is significantly more beneficial than sitting or standing.[47] Morris and Crawford studied autopsy hearts and discovered that 21 percent of the men whose jobs required light physical activity had small multiple heart scars, while only 4.9 percent of men whose jobs required heavy physical activity had scars.[48] A study of blood brothers in Boston and Ireland showed that those who remained in Ireland were more physically active and had lower serum cholesterol levels and less heart disease than their brothers in Boston.[49] A number of studies showed that coronary attacks come two to three times as often and are more severe in people who lead relatively inactive lives.

Over 3600 San Francisco longshoremen, studied over a 23-year period for factors that predisposed to fatal coronary heart disease and stroke, showed conclusively that the more sedentary jobs were associated with higher death rates.[50] These findings were interpreted to signify that physical activity influences myocardial function more than the atherosclerotic process. Moreover, the more strenuous the job, the lower the risk of heart attacks.[51] Rose and co-workers earlier reported similar findings, but discovered that with an increase in occupational physical activity there tends to be some reduction in the atherosclerotic condition.[52] Also, Rose concluded a year later that as little as 20 minutes of walking each day might help to protect a person from coronary heart disease. Cooper set forth a comparable view after studying heart attacks in thirty-five to forty-four year old men in Austria, where the attack rate is only 36 per 100,000 men as compared with the United States,

[47] Harold Kahn, "The Relationship of Reported Coronary Heart Diseases to Physical Activity of Work," *American Journal of Public Health*, 53 (July 1953), 1058–67.

[48] J. N. Morris and M. D. Crawford, "Coronary Heart Disease and Physical Activity of Work," *British Medical Journal*, 2 (1958), 1485.

[49] Fred J. Stare, "Nutritional Challenges for Physicians," *Journal of the American Medical Association* (December 2, 1961).

[50] Ralph S. Paffenberger, Jr, and others, "Characteristics of Longshoremen Related to Fatal Coronary Heart Disease and Stroke," *American Journal of Public Health*, 61 (July 1971), 1362–68.

[51] Ralph S. Paffenberger, Jr., and others, "New Study Backs Physical Work to Aid Heart," *American Journal of Epidemiology* (March 1977), p. 125.

[52] G. Rose, "Physical Activity and Coronary Heart Disease," *Proceedings of Royal Society of Medicine*, 62 (1969), 1183.

where the rate is 91 per 100,000 men.[53] Cooper reasoned that the wide difference was related to the daily physical activity and possibly effective secondary school physical education programs that carry over into adult life.

Interestingly, there have been no documented deaths from coronary heart disease or cerebral arteriosclerosis among marathon finishers of any age. Therefore, the American Medical Joggers Association has postulated that marathon runners have immunity to coronary heart disease as long as they maintain their fitness.[54] The degree of protection against coronary heart disease diminishes among runners who jog and train at distances under six miles. These findings are in keeping with British studies in which heavy recreational physical activity contributes to fewer electrocardiographic abnormalities and incidences of hypertension.[55] Also, a number of Veterans Administration studies have demonstrated the combined role of diet and exercise in reducing angina, hypertension, cerebral and cardiac restrictions, gout, and high cholesterol and triglyceride conditions. In one dramatic study of vascular disease cases, one half of a group of hospital patients was advised to walk daily (control group), and one half was asked to do the same along with a carefully controlled diet (experimental group). Later, when being evaluated on a treadmill walking test, the control group improved 302 percent, while the experimental group improved 5,820 percent, nearly 18 times more than the control group.[56] One wonders if the late cardiologist Paul Dudley White was not right when he cried aloud for bicycle paths to combat the push-button devices which have in recent years replaced muscle activity. Seneca's remark nineteen centuries ago that "Man does not die, he kills himself" is more true today than when the words were spoken.

One of the most extensive reports documenting the role of past and present physical activity in the prevention of coronary heart disease was researched by Fox, Naughton, and Haskell of George Washington Univer-

[53]Kenneth Cooper, "Heart Attacks, Men Ages 35–44," *Journal of the American Medical Association* (February 8, 1971).

[54]Thomas J. Bassler, "Marathon Running and Immunity to Heart Disease," *The Physican and Sports Medicine* (April 1975), 281.

[55]L. Epstein and others, "Vigorous Exercise in Leisure-Time, Coronary Risk Factors, and Resting Electrocardiograms in Middle-Aged Male Civil Servants," *British Heart Journal* (April 1976), p. 403.

[56]Nathan Pritikin and others, "Diet and Exercise as a Total Therapeutic Regimen for the Rehabilitation of Patients with Severe Peripheral Vascular Disease," Paper presented to the American Congress of Rehabilitation Medicine, Atlanta, Georgia, November 19, 1975.

sity.[57] (Dr. Fox is medical consultant to the President's Council on Physical Fitness and Sports.) The following information is adopted from their work:

TABLE 2-2

Physical activity may:

Increase	*Decrease*
Coronary collateral vascularization	Serum lipid levels
Vessel size	Triglycerides
Myocardial efficiency	Cholesterol
Efficiency of peripheral blood	Glucose intolerance
distribution and return	Obesity-adiposity
Electron transport capacity	Platelet stickiness
Fibrinolytic capability	Arterial blood pressure
Red blood-cell mass and blood volume	Heart rate
Thyroid function	Vulnerability to dysrhythmias
Growth hormone production	Neurohormonal over-reaction
Tolerance to stress	"Strain" associated with
Prudent living habits	psychic "stress"
"Joie de vivre"	

The long-term Framingham Heart Study, now associated with Boston University, graphically supports the significant role of physical activity in the lives of the men studied. Physical activity lowers tryglycerides, but its greatest benefit is to improve collateral heart circulation, so that should a heart attack occur, there will be capillary routes available to help carry the blood supply in the heart muscle.

The intricate relationship between underactivity, overweight, and cardiovascular disease suggests that physical education skills have more to do with living a full and balanced life than was previously suspected.

5. Physical activity improves functional efficiency at any age. This is because human biological design has not changed; humans are still meant to be active, not sedentary creatures. During World War II, Howard A. Rusk, M.D., pioneer in rehabilitation of servicemen, found that hospital readmissions were reduced as much as 25 percent because the men were being sent back to duty in much better physical condition. Special exercise helped reduce the convalescent period for most diseases 30 to 40 percent. And for older people, Theodore Klumpf, M.D., has demonstrated that fatigue is the greatest obstacle to a happy, useful life, and that the best prescription for fatigue in older citizens is physical activity. Paul Dudley White said the same

---

[57]S. M. Fox, J. P. Naughton, and W. L. Haskell, "Physical Activity and the Prevention of Coronary Heart Disease," *Annals of Clinical Research,* 3 (1971), 404–32.

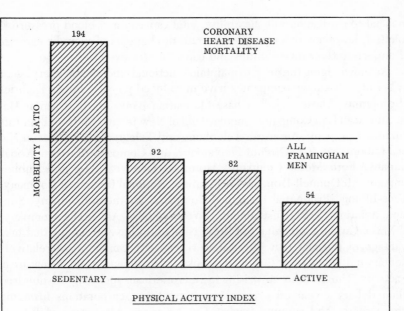

CORONARY
HEART DISEASE
MORTALITY

194

MORBIDITY RATIO

92

82

ALL
FRAMINGHAM
MEN

54

SEDENTARY ——————————————— ACTIVE

PHYSICAL ACTIVITY INDEX

1. In the Framingham study the "least active" men had more than three times the risk of "most active" males.

2. High level physical activity confers protection against severe manifestations of coronary heart disease by:

   A. Stimulating the development of collateral circulations when the coronary blood flow is impaired.

   B. Helping to prevent overweight with attendant benefits of lower serum lipid levels, lower blood pressure, and reduced cardiac work load.

FIGURE 2-3. Coronary Heart Disease and Physical Activity. (Framingham Heart Study Report, U.S. Public Health Service Pub., No. 1515)

thing: ". . . exercise sufficient to cause muscular fatigue is the best antidote I know for nervous strain and insomnia. It can helpfully replace most of the tranquilizers and sedatives of today."[58]

Referring to muscle use, Kottke makes it clear that too much rest in any body system reduces efficiency. Significantly, as one grows older and limits the amount of muscular activity, it is the sensory-motor system that is put off balance and that causes a marked reduction in sensory perception and intellectual functions.[59] However, short-term physical training by older men is

[58]Paul D. White, "Health and Sickness in Middle Age," *Journal of Health, Physical Education and Recreation*, 31 (October 1960), 21.
[59]Frederic J. Kottke, "The Effects of Limitation of Activity Upon the Human Body," *Journal of the American Medical Association*, 196 (June 6, 1966), 825–30.

beneficial to cardiac output, flexibility, vital capacity and blood pressure.[60]
Too often, however, older people overrate the benefits of sporadic exercise
and underrate their own abilities and capacities for exercise.

Acknowledging the need to maintain functional efficiency at every age, a
number of well-known companies have introduced physical fitness facilities
and programs. These include Chase-Manhattan Bank, Marriott Motor Ho-
tels, American Can Company, Standard Oil of New Jersey, Metropolitan Life
Insurance Company, American Telephone and Telegraph, Brookhaven National Laboratory, E.I. DuPont DeNemours and Company, Eastman Kodak
Company, Ford Motor Company, Motorola, Goodyear Tire and Rubber
Company, McDonnell Douglas Corporation, National Insurance Company,
Owens-Illinois, Prudential Insurance Company, Raytheon Company, Sun-
strand Aviation, Texas Instruments, Westinghouse Air Brake Company,
and Xerox Corporation. Many of these companies have programs that take
advantage of the fact that physical work capacity can improve relatively
sedentary individuals in as little as six weeks' time, depending on the nature of
the activity. Thus, it is not surprising to find Americans spending two hundred
million dollars a year on exercise equipment and corporations installing
exercise rooms and running tracks. The American Association of Fitness
Directors in Business and Industry reports that 82 percent of their representative companies employed full-time fitness program directors in 1977.

6. Physical activity aids in the adaptation to stress   (worry, anxiety,
apprehension, fear, hate, jealousy, anger) by improving the sensitivity of the
adrenal glands so that they provide more steroids to counteract stress. In
general, exercise improves the functioning of the total glandular system. The
sexual response, for example, is stronger among active people than among
sedentary ones. Kinsey noted this, and others have done the same with an
extensive list of research references. It was further confirmed by Masters and
Johnson.[61] Hans Selye also related the ability to handle the stress of living to
regular exercise and other positive health habits.[62] There is also evidence that
emotional stability is enhanced through physical activity.

Fifteen years of tracing the medical histories of 3500 men convinced
cardiologists Friedman and Rosenman that the majority of the heart victims
fail to adapt to the socioeconomic stresses brought on by excessive ambition,
overwhelming aggressiveness, high-level competitiveness, impatience, and

[60]Victor Buccola and William J. Stone, "Effects of Jogging and Cycling Programs on
Physiological and Personality Variables in Aged Men," *Research Quarterly*, 46 (May
1975), 134–39.

[61]William H. Masters and Virginia E. Johnson, *Human Sexual Response* (Boston:
Little, Brown and Co., 1966), p. 266.

[62]Hans Selye, *The Stress of Life* (New York: McGraw-Hill, 1953).

slavishness to the clock.[63] These men are classified as Behavior Pattern Type A personalities. Missing in their lives is a basic understanding of recreational needs and appropriate skills. Moreover, they have higher blood cholesterol levels, a significant degree of underlying atherosclerosis, more rapid blood clotting, and a much higher prevalence of coronary heart disease than their counterparts. Simply stated, the Behavior Pattern Type A personality lives with a high-risk factor involving the intricate relationship between the central nervous system and associated environmental stresses. Enjoyable physical activity can be almost stress-free. When stress occurs, epinephrine and norepinephrine are produced by the adrenal medulla and sympathetic ganglia of the central nervous system. If one exercises, the epinephrine is used up during the excitation. Were it not used up and continued to build up, there would be a risk of developing necrosis on cardiac tissue which precipitates cardiac failure. Both Hans Kraus and Hans Selye have found this to be true following postmortem examinations of coronary heart-attack victims. It is advantageous, therefore, to seek activity when one is "up-tight" and thereby assimilate hormones that might otherwise damage the heart.

7. Longevity relates to physical activity. One reason why several studies have failed to show that physical activity increases the longevity of man is because control of such factors as diet, stress, occupation, genetic factors, and other items was not sufficient. However, the extensive research by Hammond shows rather definitely a difference in longevity between individuals who take part in heavy exercise and those who do not exercise.[64] Table 2-3 is especially significant in showing the benefit of exercise as one grows older.

The work of deVries at the University of Southern California indicates that functional ability and "physiological age" can be extended for older people through controlled programs of walking, jogging, swimming, and relaxing. As fitness improves, self-esteem rises, and as inner sense of worth occurs there follows a stronger will to live.[65] Since this in turn reduces the mortality rates for a number of cardiovascular diseases, it becomes an obvious contributor to longevity.

[63]R. H. Rosenman and others, "Coronary Heart Disease in the Western Collaborative Group Study: A Follow-Up Experience of Two Years," *Journal of the American Medical Association*, 195 (January 1966), 86. See also Edwin Kiester, Jr., "Your Personality Can Be a Matter of Life or Death," *Today's Health*, 51 (February 1973), 16–19.

[64]E. G. Hammond, "Some Preliminary Findings on Physical Complaints from a Prospective Study of 1,064,004 Men and Women," *American Journal of Public Health*, 54 (1964), 11–29.

[65]Michael P. Briley, "How To Cope With Stress," *Modern Maturity*, August/September, 1977, p. 8.

TABLE 2-3   Deaths per 100 Men by Degrees of Exercise (N = 461, 440)

Age	No Exercise	Slight	Moderate	Heavy
45–49	1.06	0.56	0.38	0.23
50–54	2.08	0.80	0.55	0.33
55–59	3.60	1.58	0.85	0.59
60–64	4.90	2.32	1.19	0.92
65–69	10.33	3.85	1.74	1.38
70–74	11.02	4.92	2.60	1.56
75–79	16.05	6.55	3.46	1.96
80–84	16.43	8.49	3.96	4.49
85–plus	22.13	12.08	5.67	2.78

Social Efficiency

Simply stated, social efficiency is the ability to get along with others and exhibit desirable standards of conduct. It is a kind of social well-being akin to mental and emotional health. School physical education contributes measurably to development of social efficiency by providing learning situations in which pupils can express themselves through initiative, perseverance, courage, cooperation, followership, leadership, self-restraint, and loyalty to the group. A limited physical capacity sometimes handicaps an individual in pursuing social goals.

More than any other subject in the curriculum, physical education is organized to deal specifically with the elements of proper social behavior. Through appropriate games and dances, pupils assume their responsibilities when working with each other. Cooperation is born out of a feeling for others or group consciousness. From this awareness of others develops—somewhat experimentally at first—a degree of participation through followership and leadership. Significantly, it is the freedom within the rules of the play situation that gives birth to sportsmanship. This concept alone may be one of the most important concepts in education. In fact, Johan Huizinga, the historian, holds that history reveals a pattern that has the characteristics of play, in that freedom and independence of collective action establish themselves only on the firm basis of rules. Without rules, freedom is meaningless, and without freedom, there is no long-term survival.[66] This is the area in which the sports movement has much to offer. It encourages a degree of freedom with proper restraint and in keeping with the rules of the game. Moreover, the power of the word "sportsmanship" is universal. It is probably the clearest and most popular expression of morals in vogue today.

[66]Reported in Jokl, *Medical Sociology and Cultural Anthropology of Sport and Physical Education* (Springfield, Ill.: Charles C. Thomas, Publishers, 1964), p. 136.

Sociology of Play and Sports

I care not who makes the laws or even writes the songs if the code of sportsmanship is sound, for it is that which controls conduct and governs the relationship between men.

—MARCUS TULLIUS CICERO

Sport and play have deep roots in the culture and in the humanities simply because they provide life enrichment and fulfillment opportunities. This is brought out in commendable fashion by Cozens and Stumpf as they demonstrate the role of sports in the progress of civilization, with special emphasis on the relationship between sports and national vitality. They depict the games as the "touchstone for understanding how people live, work, and think."[67] People learn how to live with others through the sport experience.

FIGURE 2-4. Sport as an art form. An example of balance in action as the shoulder charge is demonstrated—the only legal body contact permitted in soccer. (Courtesy, Hubert Vogelsinger)

[67]Frederick C. Cozens and Florence S. Stumpf, *Sports in American Life* (Chicago: University of Chicago Press, 1953).

Sports, therefore, are an education in themselves. Because they relate directly to play, they become a means of escape from the stresses and strains of work and routine.

A strong case for a sociology of sport in the tradition of the social sciences has been made by several sociologists and historians; and Loy and Kenyon have done an especially fine job of bringing this all together.[68] They define sports sociology as the "study of sport in society as it affects human development, forms of expression, value systems, and the interrelationships of sport with other elements of the culture." In the light of this definition, how can sports education be anything other than of prime concern to the educator? Aside from the health and social experience, Loy and Kenyon view the sports experience in terms of the independent dimensions of pursuit of vertigo, aesthetic experience, catharsis, and ascetic experience. The vertigo event, at some risk to the participant, is provided through the thrill of speed, acceleration, sudden change of direction, or exposure to dangerous situations. The aesthetic experience is captured through the several senses. Catharsis is achieved through the release of tension built up by frustration. The ascetic experience is seen as the punishment one endures in a competitive situation, and in extended training periods, as the gratification received from achievement is delayed.

This is the underlying way in which the sports experience contributes to personal growth. Moreover, research tends to bear this out. A number of studies show a positive relationship between personality traits and social adjustment and high levels of skill and play involving sporting activities. Cooper found this true with athletes who had greater social adjustment, ascendency, and higher emotional stability than nonathletes.[69] This was also thoroughly demonstrated over an eleven-year period in the Medford, Oregon Boys' Growth Study in which personality and psychological characteristics were related to maturity, fitness, and general motor ability.[70] Positive relationships were shown, as measured by psychological inventories, peer status indicators, teacher evaluations, and a self-concept instrument. Findings showed that the individuals high in general motor ability tended to be more sociable, dependable, tolerant, competitive, and popular with their peers. Boys low in general motor ability were inclined to have feelings of insecurity,

[68]John W. Loy, Jr. and Gerald S. Kenyon, *Sport, Culture and Society* (New York: Macmillan, 1969). See also John W. Loy, Jr., "A Case of the Sociology of Sport," *Journal of Health, Physical Education and Recreation*, 43 (June 1972), 50–52.

[69]Lowell Cooper, "Athletics, Activity and Personality: A Review of the Literature," *Research Quarterly*, 40 (March 1969), 17–20.

[70]H. Harrison Clarke, ed., "The Totality of Man," *Physical Fitness Research Digest*, Washington, D.C.: President's Council on Physical Fitness and Sports, January 1972, pp. 1–14.

difficulty in social relationships, emotional instability, and negative self-concept.

Interestingly enough, it is the opportunity to display one's general motor ability (so highly correlated with game skills) in a group sport situation that fosters efficient social actions. One simply *has* to make an adjustment in order to function in a social interest group; for the group by definition, says Bryant Cratty, "is a collection of people mutually interacting to solve a common problem. Influencing group performance are such variables as the size of the group, its leadership, the nature of the task, . . . the influence of affiliation needs versus achievement needs on the part of the members, and the cohesiveness of the group."[71] In short, this is the way the participant finds himself as he struggles for higher levels of performance. The spirit of the Athenians is reborn each time the player comes to grips with himself in the struggle for perfection. Thus, the athlete does not retreat from life, but immerses in it completely, and experiences a joy of mind, body, and spirit. This Delphic spirit, possessed by the adventurous who climbed Delphi mountain, demands that the athlete does the best he or she can. This is the way the "peak experience" in sports is attained—an experience "in which the individual has an ecstatic, nonvoluntary, transient experience of being totally integrated . . . functioning fully, and in complete control of the situation."[72]

The social efficiency objective takes on even greater magnitude when the inner purposes of play are considered. Cowell and France sum up the several values of play in education. They ask: Why is the play of children important? Their answer includes the following points:

1. because it is a wholesome safety valve of prehuman origin for aggressions and other drives
2. because it allows the organism to test not only its ordinary powers, but its originalities, before responsibilities are too critical
3. because it bears some relation to the business of life, being in some measure "the young form of work"
4. because it provides wholesome compensations for frustrations and failure experienced in other areas
5. because it provides opportunities for creativity
6. because it satisfies psychic hunger for activity, achievement, belonging, and recognition and similar needs
7. because it affords the normal mechanism for release of imagination and a legitimate means for needed occasional escape from reality

[71]Bryant J. Cratty, *Social Dimensions of Physical Activity* (Englewood Cliffs, N.J.: Prentice-Hall, Inc., 1967), pp. 40–41.
[72]Brian W. Fahey and Dorothy J. Allen, *Being Human in Sport* (Philadelphia: Lea & Febiger, 1977).

8. because it provides opportunities for experiencing thrills and successes, as well as proper dosages of risks and failures making for character-building
9. because it develops an individual's resources for effective adjustment to solitude
10. because it develops a give and take, a subordination of the self and a loyalty to the team, that are of great social value
11. because it has moral significance, providing for improvement of values concerning fair play, cooperation, and other social virtues
12. because it encourages attention and therefore personality integration, since interest is inherent in the activity itself without extraneous or interest-distorting motivations.[73]

Culture

I look forward to an America which will not be afraid of grace and beauty . . . which will reward achievement in the arts as we reward achievement in business or statecraft . . . which will steadily raise the standards of artistic accomplishment . . . which will steadily enlarge cultural opportunities for all of our citizens.

JOHN F. KENNEDY

The least considered objective of physical education, perhaps because it is least understood, is the development of the cultured person. Culture is not something ethereal that cannot be grasped. It is practical. It involves a deep appreciation for life's activities, and is associated with the rich and full life. Teachers of physical education who develop appreciation for rhythm and music through specific sport skills and dances and who employ form and color in creative activities are helping to develop the cultured person. Moreover, every teacher of physical education who successfully teaches a pupil a *useful motor skill* is contributing to the cultural objective. The very meaning of culture substantiates this.

In general, the mark of a cultured person is refinement in mental and moral powers as a result of particular training and enlightenment. The cultured person feels a concern for a number of things. Careful cultivation, the product of learning that enriches and fills with appreciation, and appreciative attitude toward all the arts show a person to be cultured.

Art, in its many forms, enriches human experiences, both as participant and as a spectator. Sports and games are capable of doing the same thing. Max Reinhardt said that the immortality of the theater is derived from the eternal longing of the human mind to be transformed. Jokl recognizes that this statement applies equally to sports because sports, a medium of communica-

[73]Charles C. Cowell and Wellman L. France, *Philosophy and Principles of Physical Education* (Englewood Cliffs, N.J.: Prentice-Hall, Inc., 1963), p. 113.

tion, have unlimited range and appeal to human emotions.[74] René Maheu, the French philosopher and former UNESCO head, sees sport as a variety of culture. Maheu developed the viewpoint that spectator sports are the true theater of our day when he said:

> Think of the tens of thousands who fall silent as the athlete prepares to jump and shout with relief as he soars upward. . . . This participation by the spectator as well as the performer, this close link generating a current of sympathy, under- standing, and support from the nameless crowd of watchers or listeners to the individual taking the stage and expending himself . . . takes us back to the theater of Greece. That is why sport . . . is able to release and, in the Aristote- lian sense, to "purge" the emotions of the spectator, just as effectively as any work of art in general and of the theater in particular.[75]

There is one more reason why the physically educated person is a cultured person. This has to do with the development of the kinesthetic sense or consciousness within the body structure for specific skilled movements.[76] This appreciation developed through the kinesthetic sense is an artistic ex- perience and is comparable to other appreciations one has for the fine arts, literature, and music.

Accomplishing a difficult skill and the gradual learning of a new skill involve the same nervous pathways and end in a neural pattern no less important to artistic appreciation than stimuli received through other senses and smaller muscle groups. A man or woman listening to a symphony, for example, upon hearing the music, may unconsciously close the eyes and relax the body in the fullest appreciation. The art lover may be completely "lost in space" as he views his favorite works in the gallery. Likewise, the golfer may hit the ball so perfectly or serve the tennis ball so accurately that he or she experiences a feeling of supreme satisfaction. The reactions of music and art lovers and the skilled sports person are the outward manifestations of the cultured person. All three persons have a fine artistic sense, two through small muscle sensorimotor responses and the third predominantly through large muscle sensorimotor response.

It is the *feeling* that counts in a discussion of culture. A Boston music critic wrote that music expresses the inexpressible and that words were inadequate to describe music. It was a penetrating thought by a man who must

[74]Ernst Jokl, *Medical Sociology and Cultural Anthropology of Sport and Physical Education*, p. 37.
[75]René Maheu, "Sport and Culture," *Journal of Health, Physical Education and Recreation*, 39 (October 1963), 18–21.
[76]For a full elaboration of this proposition see article by Carl E. Willgoose, "Culture and the Kinesthetic Sense," *Journal of Health, Physical Education and Recreation*, 18 (March 1947), 149–50.

FIGURE 2-5. A cultural entity—the delight of liftoff. (Courtesy, Dorothy R. Stanley)

continue to try to describe the indescribable. The same can be said in attempting to describe the feeling that one gets from viewing highly skilled movements. Just as it is easier to describe the crowd than the music at a symphony performance, it is likewise easier to describe the spectators at a football game or tennis match than the rousing impact of the physical activity itself. Yet it is the feeling that both participants and spectators depart with that has cultural overtones.

There is another concern for the cultural objective that relates to cultural pluralism and the need for a multicultural physical education, particularly in American and Canadian society. Ethnic games and dances make a contribution. In fact, dance as a part of the broad human movement area has much to offer education. As a creative performing art it is concerned with technique, composition, improvisation, aesthetic principles, communication, and the formation of symbols. Therefore, its participants gain deep appreciations for movement, to their advantage culturally. Dance will always have a place in physical education and, in fact, thrive when the physical education administration subscribes to the creative development and personal expression of movement.

Recreational Competency

Aleksandr Kuprin, the Russian novelist, says that man is born for great joy. To find life worth living he must either have joy in his life or have some hope of joy. It is the joy that refreshes him and recreates him. The whole

66

organism is involved. Recreation, therefore, is more than a game "just for fun." It is an act of restoration of the individual to his normal self by a renewal of the physical, mental, and spiritual state. Moreover, it is more than a simple motor act; it involves the higher centers of the brain where the desire for divergence and refreshment is felt. Recreation, therefore, is an attitude of mind. It is as much akin to mental health as it is to physical well-being.[77]

The recreation function is far greater in importance than it may appear to be. In a world of increasing tensions, physical and psychological, there must be an antidote. Although glands attempt to adjust to the constant demand of stress by pouring out excess hormones to keep the body in balance, this cannot go on without appropriate relief. As Canadian physiologist Hans Selye points out, the glands succeed for a while, but in the end the defense mechanism itself breaks down—arteries harden, blood pressure rises, heart disease develops, arthritis strikes. Happiness itself is related to freedom from stress. An individual must have hope, faith, and self-respect—if not in work, then in recreation.

With the coming of the machine culture the need to recreate more and work less is almost a fact. What should the twentieth-century individual have in the way of an education sufficient to provide him with recreational competence? How much of this competence is the concern of the physical education instructor?

Recreational skills, a large number of which are physical, need to be mastered early so that the individual can participate in and learn to enjoy the various activities well enough to want to carry them on through a lifetime. The paramount need, therefore, is for developing a *quality performance* of skills. Skills poorly taught, poorly learned, and weakly participated in can hardly be expected to carry over into adult life. The truly fruitful experience is one that leaves the participant in a state of mental and physical exhilaration sufficient to promote peaceful relaxation and appreciation. Moreover, quality experience will contribute to both health and cultural objectives—a product of the rational use of leisure.

Intellectual Competency

It is not the purpose of physical education to become an academic discipline by introducing intellectual experiences into the curriculum. However, it is very much the responsibility of the physical education instructor to consider ways and means of *insuring* a continued participation in physical activities through an adequate knowledge and understanding of the values inherent in the activities. Generally, this cannot be done in the average

[77]See especially, "Recreation: An Attitude of Mind," by Carl E. Willgoose, in *Adult Leadership*, 8 (June 1959), 37.

physical education class without some preplanning that will involve lecture materials, special films, group and independent study, and the measurement of understanding.

Persons defend things they thoroughly understand. Moreover, they tend to act in keeping with their convictions. One must understand why physical skills are beneficial and why exercise is necessary, and appreciate the unique role of recreational activity in providing for the rich and full life. Also, there is considerable evidence that people of all ages do not know how to behave at games. They are ignorant of game rules and game procedure and frequently unfamiliar with game strategy. Furthermore, many spectators lack the background to appreciate fully the activity and the sports as part of the culture of Western civilization.

Some years ago Supreme Court Justice Byron R. White expressed the idea that intellectual power and physical vigor were natural allies; together they counted for much more than either one alone and even more than the sum of the individual parts.[78] Perhaps this is another way of saying that if students understand not only the "what" and "how" but the all-important "why" of physical education they will lend enlightened support to its programs in the years to come.

Human Values

Joseph Wood Krutch wrote, "The most stupendous of man's inventions was not the wheel, or the wedge, or the lever, but the values by which he has lived."[79] The true worth of a civilization, therefore, is found in its values, beliefs, judgments, and commitments.

Values are not always articulately expressed, but they are evident in the attitudes of people toward almost everything they come in contact with. They come to the forefront in politics, religion, and education, when inner feelings are challenged. Moreover, they are subject to change—slowly. Every generation tests the values it has inherited against new and fresh circumstances. Values inherent in physical education, therefore, must be appraised in terms of the changing times.

Involved in this value question, of course, are the ultimate questions individuals in a society have to ask about themselves. How sensitive to life are we? Just how precious is life anyway? What are the potentialities of a fully able

---

[78]Byron R. White, "Athletics: . . . 'Unquenchably the Same'," in Bucher and Goldman, eds., *Dimensions of Physical Education*, p. 29.

[79]Joseph Wood Krutch, *The Measure of Man* (New York: Bobbs-Merrill, 1954), p. 172.

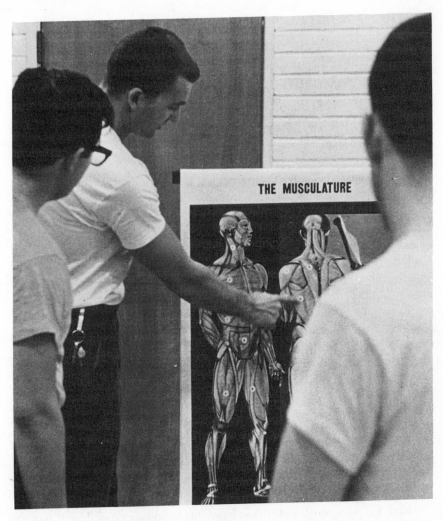

THE MUSCULATURE

FIGURE 2-6. Lasting values are developed when something more than skills are taught. (Courtesy, American Alliance for Health, Physical Education and Recreation)

human being? What connection do we see between the fully able citizen and the development of the society itself?

One wonders just how much indifference to life exists. What is the connection between insensitivity and indifference to living the full life and value illnesses? Why do seemingly educated people fail to act according to what they know or believe? Where is their normal vitality? Somewhere here is the message of humanity—of human growth and perfectibility.

QUESTIONS FOR DISCUSSION

1. In their book, *The New Professionals,* Gross and Osterman make it very clear that "virtually every one of the major professions is deeply troubled," and most are in the process of renewal, reconstruction, reform and, occasionally, revolution.[80] If this is so, where do you see the profession of education? Is it meeting individual and societal needs? Are physical education professionals (which include teacher-preparation personnel) tied to the past so much that they find it hard to become part of the renewal process?

2. As civilization becomes more complex, is there a tendency for education to become somewhat divorced from life? Is this true of physical education as contrasted with other subject-matter areas?

3. Marvin H. Eyler, in a superb study of the origins of contemporary sports (*Research Quarterly,* December 1971), indicates that there was a substantial increase in the number of sports introduced during the nineteenth century. This seems to parallel the increase in leisure time brought about by the Industrial Revolution. Comment on what effect this information might have on sports participation in the next decade.

4. The intensity of play, says Johan Huisinga, finds no explanation in biological analysis. This is because play is a psychological entity—concerned with emotions, mirth, and fun. If this is correct, then play must satisfy important psychological needs. Would you agree? What about play that is no longer fun? Is it still play, or is it work?

5. Freeman and others have asked if physical education is the best name for the field. How would you express yourself on this subject?[81]

SUGGESTED ACTIVITIES

1. Examine the programs of several school systems to see what concern they have for perceptual-motor development, handicapped children, quality skills promotion, and multicultural physical education.

2. Formulate a list of contributions of physical education to physiological, psychological, and sociological development. Be prepared to share this with others so that one enlarged list of contributions can be put together. The literature is rich in useful evidence (see Selected References at the end of this chapter).

[80]Ronald Gross and Paul Osterman, eds., *The New Professionals* (New York: Simon and Schuster, 1973).

[81]William H. Freeman, *Physical Education in a Changing Society* (Boston: Houghton Mifflin Co., 1977), pp. 11–18.

3. Develop a short position paper relative to the adequacy or inadequacy of the designation "physical education." Be certain to consider existing definitions, purposes, and the viewpoint held by general educators and the public at large.

4. "Play is an attitude," said Luther Gulick, the founder of the Camp Fire Girls. This was the basis of his philosophy. Make a collection of a number of definitions of play as expressed by philosophers, recreationists, educators, psychiatrists, and others. How do these definitions relate to play as an attitude? How do they relate to play as a means of education? As a means of therapy?

5. It has been said that the average person rarely speaks of the values that lie at the heart of his or her way of life. Ask four different people what they believe are the two or three most important values of life from their particular standpoint. Suggested people to talk with are: (a) a social studies teacher; (b) a physician; (c) a clergyman; and (d) a businessman.

6. Sports sociology is relatively new, but with the anticipated growth of sports in the future, it may become firmly established. Review some of the writings that provide avenues for further inquiry—both in the physical education area and in the social sciences. Set down on paper the several directions in which you think sports sociology can go. See especially the writings of such individuals as Sutton-Smith, Singer, Riesman, Loy, Ziegler, Sage, Gerber, Sheehan, Kenyon, and Vander Zwaag (see Selected References at end of the chapter).

7. Human needs are not always realized by educational goals unless the planners of these goals are very much aware of both the aspirations and problems of mankind. Formulate a list of obstacles that stand in the way of achieving educational goals. Consider negative items, not only within the culture, but at the local school and community level.

8. Survey a number of teachers of physical education in several different school systems in order to determine the half-dozen or more primary reasons why physical education objectives are not being realized.

SELECTED REFERENCES

ABERNATHY, RUTH, and MARYANN WALTZ, "Toward a Discipline: First Steps First," *Quest,* 2 (April 1964).

ALLEN, DOROTHY J., and BRIAN W. FAHEY, *Being Human in Sport.* Philadelphia: Lea & Febiger, 1977.

BARROW, HAROLD M., *Man and His Movement: Principles of His Physical Education* (2nd ed.), Philadelphia: Lea & Febiger, 1977.

BELLOC, NEDRA, "Relationship of Health Practices and Mortality," *Preventive Medicine,* 2 (January 1973), 67.

BOOKWALTER, KARL W., and HAROLD J. VANDER ZWAAG, *Foundations and Principles of Physical Education.* Philadelphia: W.B. Saunders Co., 1969.

BRILEY, MICHAEL P., "How to Cope with Others," *Modern Maturity,* (August/September 1977), 8.

BUCHER, CHARLES A., *Foundations of Physical Education* (7th ed.), St. Louis: C. V. Mosby Co., 1973.

BURTON, DIANNE E., "Shaping the Future," *Journal of Physical Education and Recreation,* 47 (March 1976), 20–24.

BURTON, ELSIE C., *The New Physical Education for Elementary School Children.* Boston: Houghton-Mifflin Co., 1977.

CHEFFERS, JOHN, and TOM EVAUL, *Introduction to Physical Education: Concepts of Human Movement.* Englewood Cliffs, N.J.: Prentice-Hall, Inc., 1978.

CLARKE, H. HARRISON, *Physical and Motor Tests in the Medford Boys' Growth Study.* Englewood Cliffs, N.J.: Prentice-Hall, Inc., 1971.

CORBIN, H., *Education for Leisure,* Englewood Cliffs, N.J.: Prentice-Hall, Inc., 1973.

DRURY, BLANCHE J., "The Movement Medium," *Issues in Physical Education and Sports,* ed. George H. Mc Glynn. Palo Alto, California: National Press Books, 1974, p. 89.

EDGERTON, V. R., "Exercise and Growth Development of Muscle Tissue," in *Physical Activity: Human Growth and Development,* ed. G. L. Rarick, New York: Acad. Press, 1973, pp. 1–31.

EDINGTON, D. W., and V. R. EDGERTON, *The Biology of Physical Activity.* Boston: Houghton-Mifflin Co., 1976.

ELLIS, M., *Why People Play.* Englewood Cliffs, N.J.: Prentice-Hall, Inc., 1973.

FELSHIN, JANET, *Perspectives and Principles for Physical Education.* New York: John Wiley & Sons, 1967.

FIELDING, LAWRENCE W., DONALD H. STEEL, and MARVIN H. EYLER, "Spencer's Philosophy of Play—An Overview," *Canadian Journal of History of Sport and Physical Education,* 3 (December 1972), 1–15.

FRANKEL, LAWRENCE J., and BETTY B. RICHARD, *Be Alive as Long as You Live.* Charleston, W. Va.: Preventacare Publications, 1977.

FRANKL, VIKTOR E., *Man's Search for Meaning.* New York: Washington Square Press, 1970.

FROST, REUBEN B., *Physical Education Foundations-Practices-Principles.* Boston: Addison-Wesley Publ. Co., 1975.

GALLAHUE, DAVID L., PETER H. WERNER, and GEORGE C. LUEDKE, *A Conceptual Approach to Moving and Learning.* New York: John Wiley & Sons, Inc., 1975.

GERBER, ELLEN W., *Sport and the Body: A Philosophical Symposium.* Philadelphia: Lea & Febiger, 1972.

GLASSER, WILLIAM, *Positive Addiction*. New York: Harper & Row, 1976.

HARPER, WILLIAM A., and others, *The Philosophic Process in Physical Education*. Philadelphia: Lea & Febiger, 1977.

HEILBRONER, ROBERT L., *An Inquiry into the Human Prospect*. New York: W.W. Norton & Co., 1975.

HIGGINS, JOSEPH R., *Human Movement: An Integrated Approach*. St. Louis: C.V. Mosby Co., 1977.

HUNT, MAURICE P., *Foundations of Education*. New York: Holt, Rinehart and Winston, 1975, Part III.

INGRAM, ANNE, "Art and Sport," *Journal of Health, Physical Education and Recreation*, 44 (February 1973), 24–27.

JOHNSON, WARREN R., *Science and Medicine of Exercise and Sports*. New York: Harper and Row, 1964.

JOKL, ERNST, *International Research in Sport and Physical Education*. Springfield, Ill.: Charles C. Thomas, Pub., 1964.

"Keeping Fit: America Tries to Shape Up," *Newsweek*, May 23, 1977, p. 78.

KROLL, WALTER P., *Perspectives in Physical Education*. New York: Academic Press, 1973.

LABAN, RUDOLF, *The Mastery of Movement* (2nd ed.), pp. 1–20, 86–101. London: MacDonald and Evans, 1960.

LEIFER, WALTER, ed., *Man and Sport*. Munich: Max Huber, 1972.

LEONARD, GEORGE, "The Rediscovery of the Body," *New York*, 10 (December 27, 1976), 34–38.

LEY, KATHERINE, "Teaching Understandings in Physical Education," *Journal of Health, Physical Education and Recreation*, 42 (January 1971), 20–22.

LOCKE, LAWRENCE F., "Movement Education: A Description and Critique," in *New Perspectives of Man in Action*, eds. R.C. Brown and B.J. Cratty. Englewood Cliffs, N.J.: Prentice-Hall, Inc., 1969, pp. 200–226.

LOY, JR., JOHN W., "A Case for the Sociology of Sport," *Journal of Health, Physical Education and Recreation*, 43 (June 1972), 50–52.

METHENY, ELEANOR, *Movement and Meaning*. New York: McGraw-Hill, 1968.

METZGER, PAUL A., *Elementary School Physical Education: Readings*. Dubuque, Iowa: W. C. Brown Co., 1972.

MILLER, DONNA MAE, and KATHRYN R. E. RUSSELL, *Sport: A Contemporary View*. Philadelphia: Lea & Febiger, 1971.

MONTAGUE, MARY ELLA, "Dance is Affective and Therefore Effective Education," *Journal of Health, Physical Education and Recreation*, 43 (March 1972), 87–88.

NEAL, PATSY, *Sport and Identity*. Philadelphia: Dorrance and Co., 1972.

OXENDINE, JOSEPH B., "Social Development: The Forgotten Objective?" *Journal of Health, Physical Education and Recreation*, 37 (May 1966), 23–25.

PETERSON, CAROL ANN, and SCOTT LEE GUNN, "Leisure Counseling: An Aspect of Leisure Education," *Journal of Physical Education and Recreation*, 48 (April 1977), 25–29.

PIAGET, JEAN, *Play, Dreams and Imitation in Childhood*. London: William Heinemann, Ltd., 1951.

RAAB, WILHELM, and HANS KRAUS, *Hypokinetic Disease*. Springfield, Ill.: Charles C. Thomas, Pub., 1961.

ROSENFELD, ALBERT, *Mind and Supermind*. New York: Holt, Rinehart & Winston, 1977.

SAGE, GEORGE H., *Sport and American Society*. Reading , Mass.: Addison-Wesley, 1973.

SEIDEL, BEVERLY L., and MATTHEW C. RESICK, *Physical Education: An Overview*. Reading, Mass.: Addison-Wesley, 1972.

SHEEHAN, THOMAS J., "Sport: The Focal Point of Physical Education," *Quest*, 10 (1968), 59–67.

SHEPHARD, ROY J., *Endurance Fitness* (2nd ed.), University of Toronto Press, 1977.

SIEDENTOP, DARYL, *Physical Education: Introductory Analysis* (2nd ed.), Dubuque, Iowa: W. C. Brown Co., 1976.

SINGER, ROBERT N., *Physical Education: Foundations*, Chap. 1. New York: Holt, Rinehart & Winston, 1976.

———, DAVID R. LAMB, JOHN W. LOY, JR., ROBERT M. MALINA, and SEYMOUR KLEINMAN, *Physical Education: An Interdisciplinary Approach*. New York: Macmillan, 1972.

SPARKMAN, ROBERT R., *Exercise in the Office*. Carbondale, Ill.: Southern Illinois University Press, 1977.

———, "Easy Isometrics," *Family Health/Today's Health*, May 1977, p. 48.

STEINHAUS, ARTHUR H., "Your Muscles See More Than Your Eyes," *Journal of Health, Physical Education and Recreation*, 37 (September 1966), 38–40.

WELSH, RAYMOND, *Physical Education: A View Toward the Future*. St. Louis: C. V. Mosby Co., 1977.

WICKSTROM, RALPH L., *Fundamental Motor Patterns*. Philadelphia: Lea & Febiger, 1977.

WILLGOOSE, CARL E., "Culture and the Kinesthetic Sense," *Journal of Health, Physical Education and Recreation*, 18 (March 1947), 149–50.

———, "Physical Fitness: Our Primary Objective," *Journal of Health, Physical Education and Recreation*, 30 (November 1959), 32–33.

———, "Value Illness," *Journal of Health, Physical Education and Recreation*, 36 (March 1965), 19–21.

ZIEGLER, EARLE F., and MARCIA J. SPAETH, *Adminstrative Theory and Practice in Physical Education and Athletics*. Englewood Cliffs, N.J.: Prentice-Hall, Inc., 1975.

part two

CURRICULUM

CONSIDERATIONS

The Student

and

the Curriculum

chapter three

Students have their own unique reactions to the educational process. They range from the Georgie Smiths who feel "trapped like rats" to those who genuinely enjoy school. The feelings may change because of differences in teachers and the passing of time—a model student in elementary school dropping out in high school, a difficult student being "reached" by a gifted teacher. Their perceptions of what is going on about them are not always correct or even rational. Yet these perceptions are a major factor in determining how well they can function in school.

Educators like to speak of learning as, ideally, a partnership between teacher and student. Too often the reality is teacher versus student. Listen to the conversations in the teachers' lounge about the "little bastards"—or to the kids walking home talking about "old grouches" and "Gestapo gym teachers." Each group can provide evidence for its own views; kids who actively torment teachers and teachers who actively torment kids.[1]

DWIGHT W. ALLEN

Beneath the surface, frequently camouflaged behind their protestations and frustrations, are the real concerns about where youth is headed. To understand young people fully, one must realize that they live in an intense present—a "here now" environment. Much of what seems important lies either in the immediate life situation or in the rather near future. To be effective, therefore, physical education must get close to the students' personal value system of the moment. Youth must experience events, says Joseph Conrad in *Lord Jim*, that ". . . reveal the inner worth of man; the edge of his temper, the fibre of his stuff; the quality of his resistance; the secret truth of his pretenses not only to himself but to others."

[1]Dwight W. Allen and Jeffrey C. Hecht, *Controversies in Education*, (Philadelphia: W. B. Saunders Co., 1974), p. 441.

The Youth of Today

Boys and girls appear desperate, arrogant, and disruptive, and they seem to be running away from the world in which they live because the forces of education are too weak to hold them down, fire their imagination, arouse their intellectual being, and challenge their muscles.

Fortunately, most elementary and secondary school students are quite normal in terms of what they will tolerate of school subjects and programming. As Charles Silberman pointed out in his Carnegie Corporation study, children will sit by the hour in school and never ask "why." But many have an impatient idealism that can be satisfied only by exposure to meaningful programs. While some students become upset and turn to alcohol and objectionable behavior, most rise above temptations.

Young people will identify with the kind of programs that permit them to explore and feel the forces around them. From an early age they are ready to identify with persons, situations, and the skills of cognition, sociability, and physical movement. Erik Erikson said as much in *Dimensions of a New Identity* when he encouraged the educator to discover a means for the identification outlet.[2] This will boost self-concept, or self-image, for how the young person feels will determine how he or she will act. If a girl feels clumsy or inept, she will not move with grace. A boy who feels stupid will present a noncomprehending face to his world.

The Physical Education Potential

Physical education was made for youth. It is the one subject in the curriculum that appeals frequently to large numbers of children—chiefly because of the chance to run, jump, dance, and express themselves through movement. There is also an opportunity, as George Leonard has written, "to read their own bodies" as well as read books,[3] and to test and know themselves. Moreover, if physical education is properly presented as a group activity and a humane activity that will bring people of many persuasions together, youth will "buy" it and drop some of their hostility to the system. Jerome Bruner relates to this view by pointing out that in the schools today there is very little organized cooperative activity in which students can really interact with each other. Most joint enterprises are extracurricular—social, political, or artistic—and do not really challenge the fiber of individuals. Properly conceived, there is more opportunity to get at these group interactions through games and sports than has heretofore been communicated. True, intramurals and interscholastic sports have existed for some time.

[2]Erik Erikson, *Dimensions of a New Identity* (New York: W. W. Norton & Co., 1974), p. 124.

[3]George B. Leonard, *Education and Ecstasy* (New York: Delacorte Press, 1969).

Unfortunately, in hundreds of schools today they fail to involve seriously more than a small part of the student population.

From Philosophy to Objectives

Sir Ronald Gould told his Canadian and American teachers that they would be less than professional if they wanted someone else to think for them and tell them what to do. Fundamentally, it is the responsibility of every teacher-to-be and teacher-in-fact to think deeply of the ultimate purposes and existing practices in education. Philosophizing is an earmark of the professional person.

Among physical educators, from the supervisor of the department to the instructor in the gymnasium, the act of rationalizing the program—of thinking and struggling with diverse viewpoints—is as germane to program development as are space and facilities. In fact, to rely solely on others to think out and prepare lists of desired pupil competences and curriculum content is to miss experiencing some of the richly challenging activities that endear the profession to the teacher. Moreover, teachers, like other builders of a civilization, need goals to establish and strive for. Through the process of resolving their doubts and convictions they can achieve the personal fulfillment that is the ultimate hope of free people everywhere. Ideally, therefore, supervisors and curriculum coordinators are only helpers in the process of program change. They lead you, as Gibran expresses it, to the "threshold of your own mind."[4] What happens beyond that point is up to the teacher.

There is hardly a time in the life of the teacher when he or she fails to experience some feeling of helplessness after looking over a nicely prepared list of educational aims. Indeed, utopia seems a long way off. Traveling toward it—let alone reaching it—is an ambitious undertaking. Yet it is necessary to state lofty aims and purposes in clear terms.

Focus on Specific Objectives

In discussing objectives, it is customary to proceed from the major aims or remote goals to the near-at-hand goals, frequently referred to as specific objectives. In curriculum building, the immediate or specific objectives are related to learning experiences. The problems of setting forth such objectives are essentially problems of determining desirable ends for learning. Briefly, the specific objectives are important for the following reasons:

1. The objectives are statements of educational *intent* expressed so specifically as to establish criteria for selecting and organizing what is to be taught. In this respect, a

[4]See the section on teaching in *The Prophet,* by Kahlil Gibran (New York: Alfred A. Knopf, 1923), p. 64. Here Gibran elucidates on the behavior of the skillful teacher and leader, saying, "If he is indeed wise he does not bid you enter the house of his wisdom, but rather leads you to the threshold of your own mind."

good educational objective defines both the behavior desired in the learner and areas of human experience through which this behavior is to be developed.

2. Specific objectives encourage teachers to move from the more general to the particular activities that foster skills and understanding.
3. Objectives may be made so specific that both teacher and student know exactly what they are trying to accomplish in a unit of work or in a daily lesson. For example, the student with a clear picture of what he is trying to accomplish in gymnastics will learn the skills sooner.
4. Specific objectives, when reduced to immediate goals, focus on three types of human behavior: cognitive, psychomotor, and affective. This taxonomy provides a useful tool both for determining what must go into the curriculum and for evaluating the results of teaching.[5] The most specific education program, therefore, will identify the concepts (cognitive realm), skills (psychomotor realm), and values or attitudes (affective realm) that will be used as guides in the selection of specific learning.

The literature in the physical education field contains listings of specific objectives that would be suitable for giving direction to teachers and students alike. Frequently, these lists serve to indicate the function of physical education and therefore have some merit for school use. One such listing of functions, admirably stated in terms of teaching goals, was developed by Cowell and France. It reads very well and is more specific than a list of aims. It does not attempt to spell out particular learning objectives for any one activity. The functions it describes are as follows:

1. To develop not only muscles and other organs, but to stimulate growth and development of the individual as a personality with respect to appropriate social and psychological outcomes as well.
2. To develop a wide range of physical attributes, such as muscular strength, good body mechanics, flexibility, agility and ability to resist fatigue.
3. To provide situations demanding judgments in time and space and gradually in more complicated game situations: to establish situations favorable to creative intelligence.
4. To encourage activities involving grace and rhythm and improved reaction time as well as a wide range of individual and team game skills conducive to participation and its resultant benefits.
5. To contribute to the realization of the democratic ideals in the daily life of pupils in the gymnasium and on the playing field.

[5]For a review of this taxonomy see the material of John I. Goodlad in *Planning and Organizing for Teaching*, NEA Project on Instruction (Washington, D.C.: National Education Association, 1963). See also David R. Krathwohl, Benjamin S. Bloom, and Bertram B. Masia, *Taxonomy of Educational Objectives, Handbook II: Affective Domain* (New York: David McKay Co., 1964). See also Benjamin S. Bloom, J. Thomas Hastings, and George F. Madaus, *Handbook on Formative and Summative Evaluation of Student Learning* (New York: McGraw-Hill, 1971).

6. To foster healthy social growth by providing friendly and sociable contacts by means of games, sports, camping, and related activities.
7. To encourage close cooperation with the general health and guidance services within the school for well-coordinated programs to achieve optimum health, both mental and physical, for each child.
8. To coordinate activities of the school-centered recreation program with that of the community.[6]

The closer one moves toward considering pupils and their learning experiences, the less general and more precise the objectives become. At this level of refinement, the objectives must relate to factors such as age, sex, and the characteristics of growth and development. The following objectives, listed at random in Table 3-1, are examples of immediate and *exact* requirements:

TABLE 3-1

Example	Grade Level
Takes turns and shares playground equipment	K–2
Catches a rubber volleyball thrown from a distance of 12 feet	1–2
Bats a pitched ball thrown from a distance of 35 feet to over home plate, 2 out of 5 (girls) 3 out of 5 (boys)	5–6
Develops a wholesome boy-girl relationship in coeducational activities	5–8
Executes a giant swing on the high horizontal bar	9–12
Evaluates own progress in the development of physical fitness	6–8
Walks, runs, skips, slides, and gallops in rhythm to music	1–3
Broad jumps, one foot take-off, at a distance equal to his own height	2–4
Dances to the waltz, polka, schottische, and mazurka and understands the music appropriate for each	6–7
Plays in groups happily and takes directions given by the teacher or a student leader	1–3

These examples might be referred to as pupil competencies or proficiencies, or achievement goals.

Behavioral Objectives in Physical Education

In recent years considerable attention has been given to *behavioral* objectives. The preceding examples would nicely fit the behavioral objective category because they focus attention on specific behavior—knowledge, attitudes, and skills. Taking the lead from the *Taxonomy of Educational Objectives* (see footnote 5), the proponents of this approach to educational goals set

[6]Charles C. Cowell and Wellman L. France, *Philosophy and Principles of Physical Education* (Englewood Cliffs, N.J.: Prentice-Hall, Inc., 1963), p. 30.

FIGURE 3-1. Faces reflect involvement in the affective domain. (Courtesy, American Alliance for Health, Physical Education and Recreation)

up behaviors in terms of cognitive, affective, and action domains. Anything that can be observed directly or indirectly can be fashioned into a behavioral objective. This includes *all* behaviors—emotional responses, attitudes, motor skills, reading, liking an activity or person, becoming frustrated or pleased, staying with a task, and so on. The desired student behavior is set forth in terms of action words. Examples of key words that can be used to describe a behavior are in Table 3-2. The chief advantage of establishing student behavioral objectives is that from the beginning, the attention of the instructor is specifically directed toward the *action domain*. When this occurs the teaching routine in the gymnasium or on the playing field is effectively coupled with the evaluation. Fortunately, this is far easier to do in physical education than it is in other subject-matter areas. The execution of an individual or game skill, a dance routine, or a sport technique is more readily observable than some of the projected behavior resulting from a course in English literature or social studies.

In the Omaha, Nebraska, public schools behavioral objectives are written to be read by the students and employed to advance student-centered learning.[7] The gymnasium is behavior-centered and is thought of as a learn-

[7]Robert D. Schrader, "Individualized Approach to Learning," *Journal of Health, Physical Education and Recreation*, 42 (September 1971), 33–35.

TABLE 3-2

Cognitive Domain		Affective Domain	Action Domain
(*Actions related to knowledge and understanding about physical education*)		(*Feelings about physical education*)	(*Skills in physical education*)
describes	evaluates	aware	demonstrates
investigates	relates	sensitive	runs
analyzes	distinguishes	sympathetic	walks
portrays	selects	pleased	swings
explains	discriminates	conscious	hits
interprets	chooses	elated	catches
develops	determines	values	passes
differentiates	applies	appreciates	throws
		prizes	jumps
		feels	dances
		excited	plays
		joyful	leaps
		inspired	

ing laboratory with listening stations, viewing stations, reading stations, discussion stations, practice areas, and evaluation stations. The program is task-oriented with the teacher acting as a facilitator. When students have completed one task based upon the learning objective, they move to another. Their objectives tell them (1) under what conditions they will learn, (2) what they are to learn, and (3) how they will behave when they have learned.

Examples

Given a tumbling mat and after a brief warm-up period, you will be able to perform the headstand for a period of three seconds demonstrating the form illustrated.

In the swimming pool you will be able to swim elementary backstroke in a leisurely fashion demonstrating the form shown in the loop film.

One of the most complete descriptions of physical education objectives was developed by Leonard Larson and set forth as qualitative standards.[8] These are standards, not norms. They identify what is desirable and what is possible for an individual to achieve over a period of years. There are five categories of objectives:

Objective One: Normal Expectancies of Individual Health
Objective Two: Normal Expectancies of Neuromuscular Development

[8]Leonard A. Larson, *Curriculum Foundations and Standards for Physical Education* (Englewood Cliffs, N.J.: Prentice-Hall, Inc., 1970), pp. 475–528

FIGURE 3-2. Behavioral objective for the high balance beam is to demonstrate coordination and confidence. (Reprinted from *Instructor,* copyright© October 1972)

Objective Three: Knowledge, Understanding, and Appreciation of the Human Organism in Activity
Objective Four: The Individual as a Social Being
Objective Five: The Individual as a Self- and Group-Adjusting Organism

Each set of objectives is carefully spelled out in detail and in progression. Moreover, most of the objectives are written in terms of observable behaviors. Although the Larson standards are not set up as typical behavior objectives, a careful study of them will reveal that they do serve the same purpose because each requirement leads to the *application* of knowledge and understanding.

The Student and Goal-Setting

As a crucial step in the learning process, the participation by students in goal-setting has had the support of educators for several years. Research has shown consistently higher levels of achievement by pupils who have set performance goals than by those who have not.[9] Achievement-oriented performances in the motor domain apparently arouse within subjects a concern for the standard of excellence whereby success/failure is produced, an element of challenge exists, and the subject is willing to accept responsibility for the performance outcome.[10] Where the objective requires a greater risk by the student and is more competitive, there appears to be a higher personal motivation to meet the objective.[11] However, there remains a need to explore the effects of goal-setting through established behavioral objectives for a wide range of motor skills, particularly for skills that are generally a part of the whole curriculum.

After studying the effect of goal-setting on the learning of a gross motor task, Mary Barnett discovered that the task's being student-centered and objectified was not reason enough for higher final performance scores.[12] Hollingsworth had found essentially the same thing a year earlier.[13] According to Barnett, a possible explanation is that goal-setting sessions did not occur soon enough. This observation ties in with Ostrow's interpretations on the need to understand the behavioral objective and accept responsibility for the performance outcome. It also relates to Hunt's concern that when a behavioral objective or other student goal is set up, there is a tendency for it to be just one more teacher-prescribed item.[14] In addition to their authoritarian cast, the objectives frequently appear to the student as somewhat totalitarian in that all students are supposed to learn the same motor skills, concepts, facts, and so forth. If behavioral objectives, or any variety of student goals, are to be effective, they must be seen as a function of personal and cultural needs. At this point many programs oriented toward behavioral objectives fall apart. Students cannot relate to them properly if they are conceived and presented as just more tasks to perform. The humanistic dimension is necessary. In fact,

[9]E.A. Locke, "The Relationship of Intentions to Level of Performance," *Journal of Applied Psychology,* 50 (1966), 60–66. See also E.A. Locke and others, "Motivational Effects of Knowledge of Results: A Goal-Setting Phenomenon," *Psychological Bulletin,* 70 (1968), 475–85.

[10]Andrew C. Ostrow, "Goal-Setting Behavior and Need Achievement in Relation to Competitive Motor Activity," *Research Quarterly,* 47 (May 1976), 174–84. See also M.G. Wade and R. Martins, *Psychology of Motor Behavior and Sport.* (Urbana: Human Kinetic Publishers, 1974).

[11]G.C. Roberts, "Effect of Achievement Motivation and Social Environment in Risk Taking," *Research Quarterly,* 45 (March 1974), 42–55.

[12]Mary L. Barnett, "Effects of Two Methods of Goal Setting on Learning a Gross Motor Task," *Research Quarterly,* 48 (March 1977), 19–23.

[13]Barbara Hollingsworth, "Effect of Performance Goals and Anxiety on Learning a Gross Motor Task," *Research Quarterly,* 46 (May 1975), 160–69.

[14]Maurice P. Hunt, *Foundations of Education: Social and Cultural Perspectives* (New York: Holt, Rinehart and Winston, 1975), p. 466.

the perceptual psychologist Arthur W. Combs agrees and will not support the use of behavioral objectives unless they are used as a part of the teaching process.[15] Instead of simply posting it, a motor-skill objective should be discussed, demonstrated, and worked in class, then tested with an evalua- tion feedback process of which the student is a part.

1. allows one to learn about the activity,
2. " " " practice the activity,
Competency-Based Programs *3. " " " be tested.*
4. " " appraised & discussed in terms of performance

A competency is a solid ability or proficiency. In the human-movement *Life* domain, a competency might appear in written form as a behavioral objective. *Style* The assumption behind competency-based instruction (CBI) is that general motor skills, sport skills, knowledges, and social behavior can be identified in all parts of the physical-education program. Competencies are defined and stated in advance of instruction, and there is a progression in competencies that the learner must follow. As proficiency is demonstrated, the learner moves ahead to the more difficult activities. The student sees clearly that the responsibility for the learning lies with him or her.

Those educationists who dislike competency or performance-based edu- cation feel that it controls behavior much too closely. James Day calls it "skill training" that neatly packages items to be learned—an arrangement in keep- ing with the behavioral work of Pavlov, Watson, Thorndike, and B.F. Skinner as they shaped, conditioned, and modified behavior through a rigid structure that tended to limit the freedom of the student to explore.[16] Although this reasoning may apply to a number of subject matter areas, it does not seem to apply so strongly to physical education. In fact, Dowell sees the com- petency/performance organization for learning as a readiness arrange- ment that allows students to learn about an activity, to practice the activity, to be tested, and to have the performance appraised and discussed in terms of individual life styles.[17] Moreover, a pretest may be taken to see if the cognitive and skill levels are high enough for the student to be excused from learning the activity.

In several schools about the country, individualized learning-program manuals have been prepared so that the student can thoroughly study the concepts and competencies surrounding a particular physical activity. In the

[15]Arthur W. Combs, *Educational Accountability: Beyond Behavioral Objectives,* (Washington, D.C.: Association for Supervision and Curriculum Development, De- cember 1972).

[16]James F. Day, "Let's Hear It for Performance-Based Education: A Resounding No," in L. Golubchisk and B. Persky, *Innovation in Education* (Dubuque: Kendall/Hunt Pub. Co., 1975), p. 191.

[17]Linus J. Dowell, *Strategies for Teaching Physical Education* (Englewood Cliffs: Prentice-Hall, Inc., 1975), p. 100.

Quincy, Massachusetts, public schools the physical-education curriculum is a student-centered learning system (SCLS) that represents a deliberate effort to implement a system of education that is learner-responsive. It has been in use since 1971 and has been revised several times. Student motivation appears to be high because the student works with the teacher to build a program of studies consistent with personal goals and aspirations. Motor skills are evaluated when a unit of work is introduced. Appropriate learning activities and the wide use of media are regular occurrences. Self-learning is encouraged through several approaches. The specificity of competencies is set forth in keeping with pertinent concepts. Illustrated in Figure 3-3 is an organization in which adjacent numbers refer to detailed instructions appearing elsewhere in school materials. Example A is the development of perceptual abilities suitable for the lower grades. Example B is suitable for early secondary school use.

At the University of Rhode Island individual learning programs were established primarily to attract students and motivate them toward improving their physical education skills and toward a thorough understanding of the particular activities. Figure 3-4 illustrates part of an Activity Learning Packet for intermediate swimming. Note that it provides answers for questions related to the development of concepts and competencies in the area. It could be adapted to almost any school with a swimming program, media outlets, and a performance-minded teaching staff.

The Nature of Curriculum

Although the word "curriculum" has already been used several times in this chapter, little attempt has been made to examine its meaning until now. This is because any detailed discussion of curriculum is ideally preceded by a study of educational philosophy and purposes.

The word curriculum is derived from the Latin word *currere*, which means "to run." It was associated with the running of races and with race courses; one might say with tongue in cheek that it had a physical education orientation.

The more common definitions of a curriculum describe it as "a work schedule" or "any particular body of courses." The derived word, as well as the definitions, seems to suggest an orderly plan and progression. One does not arrive at a schedule or course without having engaged in some kind of planning and organizing.

In the American public school, the word curriculum is an all-inclusive term referring to the total program in the schools. All of the academic programs and the extra-class activities, such as band, glee club, student council, yearbook, and intramural and interscholastic athletics are included

Example A

C.C. 01. Development – Man is master of himself: man acquires, develops and understands motoric skill patterns through movement.

G.O. 001 The learner develops perceptual abilities through exposure for stimuli which impinge upon the higher brain centers for interpretation.

IO 01 Develop concepts of laterality.

P.O. 0010 The student will perform movements involving both sides of the body.

0020 The student will perform movements utilizing one side of the body.

02 Develop concepts of balance.

0030 The student will maintain body balance from a static position.

0040 The student will perform activities from a moving position.

03 Develop concepts of body image.

0050 The student will identify body parts.

0060 The student will move within a prescribed area.

04 Develop concepts of spatial awareness.

0070 The student will move in various directions with controlled body movements.

0080 The student will move in various ways while avoiding objects.

05 Develop concepts of visual acuity.

0090 The student will differentiate through movement shapes, forms and sizes.

IO 06 Develop the skills associated with visual tracking.

P.O. 0100 The student will follow objects with coordinated eye movements.

07 Develop the skills associated with visual memory.

0110 The student will demonstrate through movement an ability to recall previously observed patterns.

08 Develop concepts related to auditory acuity.

0120 The student will demonstrate through movement an ability to differentiate between sounds.

FIGURE 3-3A.

09   Develop concepts associated with auditory tracking.

    0130 The student will demonstrate through movement an ability to distinguish the direction of sound.

10   Develop the skills associated with auditory memory.

    0140 The student will demonstrate through movement an ability to reproduce sounds that have previously been heard.

11   Develop the skills associated with tactile discrimination.

    0150 The student will demonstrate through movement an ability to distinguish among the textures of objects.

12   Develop the skills associated with eye-hand coordination.

    0160 The student will catch an object at a height above the waist.

    0170 The student will catch objects at waist height.

    0180 The student will catch objects below waist height.

    0190 The student will throw an object into/against a specified goal.

P.O.   0200 The student will catch an object projected from another object.

    0210 The student will catch an object projected from his own hands.

    0220 The student will catch an object projected from another person.

    0230 The student will perform overhand throwing.

    0240 The student will perform underhand throwing.

    0250 The student will perform sidearm throwing.

    0260 The student will strike/hit an object.

13   Develop the skills associated with eye-foot coordination.

    0270 The student will kick an object from the side of the foot.

    0280 The student will kick an object from the front of the foot.

    0290 The student will kick an object from the back of the foot.

    0300 The student will kick an object into/against a specified goal.

    0310 The student will block an object.

FIGURE 3-3A. *Continued.*

Example B

C.C. 02   Adaptation: Man moves in space; while moving in space, man acquires and utilizes the elements of space, time, force , and flow while adapting basic motor skill patterns to competitive, creative, and expressive environments in physical education. This provides opportunities for self–actualization within the physical, mental, and social environments of individual and group activities.

    G.O. 004   Adapt basic motoric skill patterns associated with aquatics to life saving.

        P.O. 0010   The student will identify when it is safe to swim.

            0020   The student will identify where it is safe to swim.

            0030   The student will identify hazards relative to the aquatic environment.

            0040   The student will identify safety practices relative to the aquatic environment.

            0050   The student will identify safety and rescue equipment.

            0060   The student will perform reaching rescues.

            0070   The student will perform wading rescues and assists.

            0080   The student will perform free floating supports.

            0090   The student will perform throwing assists.

            0100   The student will perform surfboard rescues.

            0110   The student will perform rescues by an untrained swimmer.

            0120   The student will demonstrate the use of the rescue tube.

            0130   The student will identify the conditions affecting rescue.

            0140   The student will perform takeoffs from various places.

            0150   The student will identify the principles of the approach strokes.

            0160   The student will perform approach strokes.

        P.O. 0170   The student will identify the principles of making contact with a victim.

            0180   The student will perform the various approaches.

            0190   The student will identify the principles of the various carries.

            0200   The student will perform the various carries.

            0210   The student will remove the victim from water.

            0220   The student will identify the principles of the various releases.

            0230   The student will perform the various releases.

FIGURE 3-3B.

0240 The student will identify the principles of the various escapes.

0250 The student will perform the various escapes.

0260 The student will identify the principles of the various defenses.

0270 The student will perform the various defenses.

0280 The student will perform searching for a submerged victim.

0290 The student will perform the rescue of a submerged victim.

0300 The student will describe the job of a lifeguard.

0310 The student will describe small-craft safety techniques.

0320 The student will perform small-craft safety techniques.

0330 The student will identify the principles of ice safety.

0340 The student will identify the principles of ice rescues.

0350 The student will describe survival swimming in a civilian emergency situation.

0360 The student will perform skills necessary to survival swimming in civilian emergency situations.

0370 The student will identify respiratory emergencies.

0380 The student will perform artificial respiration.

0390 The student will perform cardiopulmonary resuscitation.

0400 The student will identify the general directions for giving first aid.

0410 The student will perform emergency first aid for bleeding.

0420 The student will perform emergency first aid for shock.

0430 The student will perform emergency first aid for spinal injuries.

0440 The student will perform emergency first aid for burns.

0450 The student will perform emergency first aid for heat-related injuries.

0460 The student will perform emergency first aid for sudden illnesses.

FIGURE 3-3B. *Continued.*

Intermediate Swimming
(University of Rhode Island)

What can the student expect to get out of this activity?

        This learning packet has been designed for you to improve your swimming skills in order for you to become safely active in the wonderful world of Aquatics. If you are interested in "water fun" such as: sailing, boating, canoeing, water skiing, skin and scuba diving, you will need to become a proficient swimmer before you can safely learn to participate in these and other pleasurable activities. When you have accomplished the skills in this packet and have turned the last page, you will have opened the door to an environment that covers 3/4's of our earth.

What is the purpose of this packet?

1. To develop a safe swimmer with intermediate skills.
2. To refine the swimming strokes: crawl, back crawl, breast stroke, side stroke, inverted breast stroke, elementary backstroke, and survival swimming.
3. To learn the preliminaries of springboard diving.
4. To develop your knowledge and skills in the areas of personal safety and help others in distress.

How does the student use this packet?

        This packet is merely a guide. If you use it well you will avoid many problems. Read the table of contents. Any questions you have regarding swimming should already be listed there. After reading the entire table of contents decide which question is most important to you and turn to the section of the Packet which contains the answer to that question. Then refer to your second most important question and its answer. Implement the answers when action is called for or implied. In this manner progress through the entire set of questions, answers, and outside reading and performance experiences.

        There is no need for undue haste in completing the progressive goals in this packet. Concentrate on good form and stroke perfection. Progress at your own rate.

What knowledge areas and standards must be attained to get credit in this activity?

1. Discuss the reasons for the health and safety rules which apply to swimming pools.
2. Discuss the basic aquatic principles (outside reading)
    a. the principles of buoyancy
    b. force as applied to movement in water
    c. resistence as applied to movement in water
    d. laws of motion
    e. laws of levers
3. Discuss the mechanism of drowning and the importance of treatment after a near drowning.
4. Discuss the principles of rescues.
5. Discuss the principles of disrobing.
6. Discuss the physiological contribution of swimming to fitness.
7. Discuss water maintenance of safe health conditions for swimmers.
8. Discuss the principles of diving safely into the water.
9. Discuss aquatic breathing.

What skills and proficiency must be attained to get credit in this activity?

1. Survival float for 5 minutes, demonstrating your ability to survive with the arms only and the legs only.
2. Tread water for 1 minute, using only legs for last 30 seconds.
3. Survival travel stroke one length of the pool.
4. Swim mechanically correct one length of each of the following strokes: elementary back, breast, inverted breast, side, overarm side, crawl, trudgeon, trudgeon crawl, back crawl, and butterfly.
5. Execute a surface dive in 10' water and swim underwater for 20 feet using a double glide stroke.
6. Demonstrate direct and indirect forms of resuscitation.
7. Execute on-shore rescues: reaching assistance, extension assistance, throwing assistance, and wading rescue with an extension.

FIGURE 3-4.

92

8. While fully dressed, inflate a shirt you are wearing, remove pants, and inflate.
9. Execute an open turn for each of the strokes.
10. Execute the following dives and preliminary dives:
    running front dive from one meter board; preliminary back dive.
11. Swim 18 lengths of the pool in 12 minutes.

What primary and supplimentary sources of information are recommended to attain the knowledge required to pass the written examination?

1. Swimming Loop film cartridges available for viewing in our pool office - check out films from men's issue (5081)
2. 16 mm film - viewing to be announced at lab sessions
    a. Drownproofing
3. Books - on closed reserve for 101 K and 105 P classes
    at URI Library.
    a. Aquatics Handbook, Gabrielsen, Spears, Gabrielsen
    b. Swimming and Water Safety, Amer. Red Cross
    c. Swimming, Midtlying (Saunders Activity Series)
    d. Teaching Swimming, Ferinder
    e. Swimming and Diving, Ormbruster, Allen, Billingsly
    f. The Science of Swimming, Counselman
    g. Lifesaving and Water Safety, Amer. Red Cross
    h. Swimming, Gambril

What activities and drills will help the student learn the skills?

1. Participate in laboratory activities.
2. Have students of advanced level classes help you.
3. Attend meetings at the beginning of swimming classes.
4. Learning is by participation — practice the strokes observed in the texts, loop films, and 16 mm films.

Where can the student find information on how to perform the needed skills and description of additional activities and drills to help learn the skills?

1. View loop films on swimming strokes.
2. Any of the swimming texts in the Library.
3. Go to intramural and competitive swim meets at URI.

Where can the student go to practice this activity?

1. URI pools at recreation hours — posted in aquatics area.
2. URI pools during your regularly scheduled swim class.
3. YMCA or other commercial pools.
4. Anywhere you can find a pool of water.

Where can the student go to study this activity?

1. The best place is in the URI Library (closed reserve)
2. Observe swimming team practices — when balcony is open
3. Observe the beginning swimming classes.
4. Observe and participate in swimming labs.

Where can the student get the equipment to practice this activity?

1. Bathing suits, towels, and caps are secured at the towel room in the locker rooms.

Who administers the written test for this activity?

The Learning Laboratory Supervisors anytime the Laboratory is open. Note the open hour lab schedule on the bulletin board in the locker rooms. The knowledge test is composed of multiple choice questions.

When and how often can the student take the written test for this activity?

You can take the written test anytime the swimming laboratory is open. See the open hour schedule on the bulletin board in the locker rooms. You may take the test as many times as necessary to pass. Seventy percent correct is required to pass.

FIGURE 3-4. *Continued*

Who administers the skill test for this activity?

Miss Seleen or Mr. O'Leary during posted laboratory hours. If for some reason we cannot get together at this time, we will agree to another meeting.

When and how often can the student take the skill test for this activity?

Tests will be given during the swimming laboratories and at the assigned time of test dates. Talk to us about any problems on attending the open laboratories. Tests may be taken as many times as needed. Seventy percent correct is required to pass.

Who does the student see about problems?

Mr. O'Leary (5909) or Miss Seleen (2975). If you are unable to see us during posted times, we will schedule an appointment with you.

FIGURE 3-4. *Continued.*

and considered important. Therefore, the term "co-curricular" activity has replaced the older term "extracurricular" activity to describe activities other than studies.

The curriculum is a body of experiences that lies between objectives and teaching methods. It commands a central position (see Figure 3-5). It is a full program of things to do that will realize the original aims and objectives. But it is not foolproof, for its success with boys and girls will always depend on sound teaching methods, effective teaching materials, and proper evaluation techniques. In short, the human factor—the teacher—has much to do with the achievement of curriculum objectives. It is quite possible, therefore, to think out and develop a fine course of study, only to find that it only partially does the job for which it was intended because some teachers failed to grasp its significance or were indifferent to its content. An elementary school curriculum guide, for example, may give a detailed breakdown of pupil activities associated with the learning of soccer skills. However, the teacher may resort to his or her own way of teaching the skills, which may not involve the same experiences set forth in the physical education guide. If, when they are evaluated, it is evident that the pupils are not doing very well, the fault may be

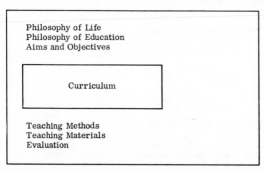

FIGURE 3-5. The central position of curriculum.

that of the teacher who ignored the guide and acted independently. Obviously, there is room for some flexibility when following a course of study. However, the teacher who tries to work within the framework of a well designed course of study and periodically checks pupil progress will generally contribute as planned to the achievement of prearranged objectives.

Curriculum Models

The separate subjects curriculum.   Since 1951, there has been in this country an influential and unprecedented curriculum reform movement. It has reached into thousands of classrooms, gymnasiums, shop classes and laboratories all across the land.

The movement focuses on the academic subject rather than on the whole curriculum. This *separate subjects curriculum* is often called by other names, such as the subject-matter curriculum, the scientific subjects curriculum, and the discipline-centered curriculum. Students study each subject that the school has to offer for a certain amount of time each day. The emphasis is almost exclusively on the subject as a separate entity in the curriculum: not on science, but on chemistry, physics, and biology; not on social studies, but on history, economics, and geography. Little attempt is made to relate one school subject to another. For example, physical education is taught without reference to health or safe living. With this approach, there is a tendency for students to learn isolated facts and skills without seeing them as a part of life in general.

The separate subjects approach creates few immediately visible problems for the secondary school physical education program, in which teachers have been prepared in a major field and in supporting disciplines. It does, however, create problems for the elementary school.

In all but a very few states, elementary teachers are prepared as generalists rather than as subject-matter specialists. All too often, they have a weak physical education background. Also, they must choose what to teach, because there is a limit to the number of separate subjects that can be taught within the time available. Therefore, some schools have left out physical education altogether, or limited it in time allotment and content. There is considerable evidence, however, that many elementary school people are questioning the assumption that the aim of schooling is accomplished by concentration in the separate subjects.

Total curriculum.   The *total* curriculum emerges from the awareness that students need a balance between their many competencies and their kinds of understanding in order to survive in a world of varied influences. In a limited sense, this is something like the *broad-fields curriculum* in which subject-matter areas are grouped together. This type of curriculum may group such items as spelling, writing, reading, grammar, oral communication, and literature under the broad topic of "language arts." Health, safety, and physical education may be grouped together for they possess many features in common. Health may also be taught under the broad heading of science. The total curriculum helps students see relationships between several subjects learned in one general area.

There are advantages in this kind of curriculum. Subjects struggling for proper recognition in the program (art, music, health, physical education, industrial arts, and so forth) have a chance to be identified collectively as an essential part of the total school program. Also, as the number of subject-matter areas is reduced, the number of teaching periods is also reduced, and it is possible to lengthen the time of each period so that the instructor can work without interruption in order to more fully develop the student's skill and appreciation.

Experience indicates that both health instruction and physical education are more successful when taught as separate subjects. However, this does not mean that they could not be effective as a part of the total curriculum model if it were properly organized. The integration and correlation of subject matter is not a new idea.

There is a continuing dilemma whenever one attempts to compare the virtues of the subject-matter curriculum with those of the total curriculum. The knowledge explosion suggests the need for breadth, but the power to deal forcefully with any aspect of the knowledge explosion demands depth.

Humanistic curriculum.   Humanism is defined by Webster as "a way of life centered upon human interests or values." When we are concerned with the curriculum, it seems an idealistic approach to the conduct of schooling. It may have more to do with method than with program, for it is grounded in the principle of respect for individual personality. Goodlad supports it because it focuses on what kind of persons students should be—rather than strictly upon what they know about processes, items, and things.[18]

The humanistic or "existential" curriculum plays down the mastery of subject matter and emphasizes programs based on needs. From time to time there have been other curriculum patterns employing a similar approach. These include some varieties of the *activity curriculum* and the *emerging curriculum*, both of which call for a good amount of creativity on the part of the teacher.

At present, the humanistic curriculum is difficult to implement. Goodlad prefers a nongraded system designed so that each child will advance at his or her own best rate. This structuring will be difficult. If planning successfully for developing skills and knowledge is hard, consider how much harder it may

[18]John I. Goodlad, "The Educational Program to 1980 and Beyond," *Designing Education for the Future*, No. 2, ed. E.L. Marphet and C.I. Ryan (New York: Citation Press, 1967).

be to plan for "human interests and values." In any case, the humanistic curriculum serves to illustrate the extremely close relationship between a curriculum plan as such and the warm, personal methods and techniques of a teacher. This is to say that the *art of teaching* can never be divorced from the program of studies.

Caldwell indicates that the emergence of a physical education in accord with the directions of humanistic design would be characterized by a thrust toward Maslow's "self-actualization"; and movement exploration activities seem to be a means of achieving this end.[19] Moreover, to achieve this goal, says Caldwell, it will mean "the elimination of the jock, the throw-out-the-baller, the military martinet, the professional who died on the vine nine years ago, the incompetent and uncaring who masquerade as teachers while fostering student passivity, obedience, conformity, and dependence."

Siedentop believes that humanistic efforts in physical education will eventually be demonstrated by teachers selected more for their therapeutic and social qualities than for their knowledge.[20]

> The development of skill in sport and dance will remain an objective, but less and less attention will be paid to it as physical educators shift their focus to the affective aspects of activity. Less time will be spent in actually practicing the skills and more time will be spent in introspection, discussion, and other group-oriented techniques associated with humanistic educational methodology.

Felshin supports the Siedentop modification on the mastery of skills but does not rule out the attention required to obtain quality motor skills. In short, the affective domain is not to be overlooked. Moreover, she sees the humanistic emphasis contributing to a shift from "programs based on the competitive models for human striving and behavior to bases in a humane focus in which meaning and relevance and capacity and ability are the primary values."[21]

It is apparent today that the rights of the student determine in part the nature of the curriculum in all areas of education. Therefore, curriculum planning in physical education must consider the student's right to choose, the right to safety, the right to be informed, and the right to be heard. Clearly,

[19]Stratton F. Caldwell, "Toward a Humanistic Physical Education," *Journal of Health, Physical Education and Recreation,* 43 (May 1972), 31–32.

[20]Daryl L. Siedentop, "The Humanistic Education Movement: Some Questions," in George H. McGlynn, *Issues in Physical Education and Sports* (Palo Alto: National Press Books, 1974), p. 13.

[21]Jan Felshin, "Cultural Considerations for Physical Education," in George H. McGlynn, *Issues in Physical Education and Sports* (Palo Alto: National Press Books, 1974), p. 153.

humanism applies as much to sports and exercise as to other scholastic subjects and programs.[22]

The mini-course curriculum.   When it appears desirable to concentrate on a particular skill, knowledge, competency, or contemporary problem, the short and intensive course approach is warranted. Such courses are purposely made attractive and especially relevant to the lives of pupils. Glatthorn feels that they should deal with some critical issues or problems that students face. They should focus on the practical aspects and be essentially a discrete course where sequence and reference to other parts of the program are of little consequence.[23]

In physical education, chiefly in the secondary school, mini-courses are offered in such areas as sport safety, officiating, drownproofing, relaxation techniques, weight training, and selected sports skill development.

The alternative curriculum.   In recent years, alternative settings with new courses have appeared in numerous school systems. There, the teachers' role is critical, for the students in alternative programs require humanistic teachers to provide much needed stability and familiarity.

Program differentiation is not new. Good teachers have always sought alternative paths to meet the particular shortcomings of certain youth. The differentness of the programs and atmosphere, as well as the element of student choice, makes school attractive to students in need of individual and small-group attention. The alternative curriculum in physical education, or in any other subject matter, can be a limited one within a school, or it can be comprehensive and involve a total school population.

The Physical Education Curriculum

In his many commendable writings pertaining to physical education, Jay B. Nash always stressed the need to take a close look at what is happening to individual boys and girls. Are they developing their bodies, skills, and interests according to plan, or are they simply lost souls in the American school system? Are they swelling with enthusiasm for life, for movement, and for expression as a result of physical education and related subjects, or are they simply jumping about, working up perspiration, and taking a shower two or three times a week in the name of physical education?

Well over a decade ago Bucher spoke out for the development of a new physical education.

[22]Melvin L. Thornton and others, "Humanistic Needs in Sports, Exercise and Recreation," *Journal of Physical Education and Recreation*, 47, (February 1976), 8–9.

[23]Allan A. Glatthorn, *Alternatives in Education* (New York: Dodd, Mead and Company, 1975), p. 104.

Education has a *new* math, a *new* English, and a *new* physics. We should also have a *new* physical education. The first step in achieving this goal might be a major curriculum study to identify, through scientific means, the basic concepts of physical education and then assign responsibilities for each grade and education level—K through College—for fulfilling and teaching these concepts. The final blueprint would be a sequential and progressive developmental pattern for teaching skills, knowledges, appreciations, and other aspects of our professional programs. The *new* physical education would give direction to all physical educators as to *what skills are to be taught* and *when; what knowledges are* to be imparted and *when; what fitness standards* are to be achieved and *when;* and *what social outcomes* are to be expected and *when.* The progression to be followed, the sequential development to be adhered to, and the desirable standards to be met would be clearly delineated. The sum total of all experiences would result in graduation from our schools and colleges *physically educated* students.[24]

In the year 1969 John Nixon addressed himself to the same topic of curriculum reform and called for a "macro-cosmic approach to physical education" from which would emerge a continuous performance curriculum from kindergarten through college. Shortly thereafter, the Physical Education Division of the American Association of Health, Physical Education and Recreation commissioned three committees to develop guidelines for a total program. These were published in 1971 and served the needs of many teachers at the local public school and college level when educational administrators needed to know just where physical education was headed.[25] These publications were not in the category of models, or comprehensive plans or patterns.

By 1973 the Academy of Physical Education was giving full discussion to the question of national models from which to develop local programs. A case was made for the creation of a flexible model of some real substance—a program pattern that could be used as a guide almost anywhere. Such a display of a model program would go beyond the material found in state and local curriculum guides and be suitable for national distribution.

Although there is a long way to go, there is some evidence that a fair amount of progress is already being made toward an improved physical education. Throughout the country, numerous curriculum conferences have been held at local and state levels for the express purpose of preparing a soundly based and attractive course of study. Communities that never had

[24]Charles A. Bucher, "A Ten-Point Program for the Future of Physical Education," *Journal of Health, Physical Education and Recreation,* 38 (January 1967), 26–28.

[25]Publications were: (1) "Essentials of a Quality Elementary School Physical Education Program," (2) "Guidelines for Secondary School Physical Education," and (3) "Guide to Excellence for Physical Education in Colleges and Universities," *Journal of Health, Physical Education and Recreation,* 42 (April 1971), 41–53.

even the simplest skeleton outline of a program have recently worked out their program particulars on paper and have plans for a revision in a year or two. Many of these same communities have upgraded their teaching methods, enlarged their indoor and outdoor playing spaces, added new supplies and equipment, and improved their programs by the addition of frequently overlooked items, such as a better choice of lead-up games, circuit training routines, skill progressions, movement exploration, mini-courses, challenge activities, and coeducational teaching.

The quickening tempo of school programing in physical education is encouraging. If ever there was a time to think in terms of a full and effective curriculum for "all the people's children," it is now. Status and trend studies indicate that there is a real desire in America today to promote physical education from the "minor" category to a prominent place in the total school operation. Specifically

1. The number of health and physical education teachers in elementary and secondary schools has increased at a rate which is greater than the increase in school enrollments and is due to new teaching positions having been established.

2. Approximately 65 percent of United States boys and girls now have physical education three to five periods a week. The movement toward daily periods has increased at all grade levels, but is especially noticeable at the senior high school level.

3. Attention to physical fitness on a personal basis has increased to the point that a number of schools promote physical fitness clubs in which regular jogging and bicycle riding is carefully programed.

4. Requirements have increased in several states at the secondary and elementary levels in the last ten years.

5. Accreditation standards as well as laws and regulations have been improved in forty states in the last fifteen years.

6. Students vitally interested in programs are requesting a voice in curriculum design. In many cases it is they who are saving programs that have changed from being required to being elective.

7. Movement education, movement exploration, guided discovery, and problem solving have been introduced to an increasing number of elementary school programs.

8. Program innovations have been widespread, and include open laboratory provisions for individualized physical education through viewing and listening stations, reading stations, discussion stations, and practice stations.

9. Elective programs are popular at the high school level because they provide an opportunity to perfect skills in activities personally selected by upper-level students.

10. Working under the supervision of the director of physical education are "Community Sports Specialists" who teach lifetime sports to junior and senior high school physical education classes off campus.

11. Adult physical education programs in the schools are on the increase throughout the nation as both men and women demonstrate their need for adult fitness,

weight control, and instruction in a favorite physical activity or sport. An increasing number of business and governmental organizations are providing similar opportunities.

12. Statewide and regional conferences, workshops, and clinics are being held in almost all states every year in an effort to continue to upgrade the competency of teachers and supervisors of physical education.

Although there are many better programs today than there used to be, there is a strong tendency simply to repeat each year what went on the year before. Needed are long-range longitudinal studies of physical education and physical recreation "behaviors" demonstrated by adequate samples of adults who have graduated from school systems in several parts of the country that have provided: (1) physical education on a daily required basis, such as in California; (2) on a voluntary participation basis, and (3) no physical education except interscholastic athletics. If such studies followed large samples of men and women for intervals of 5–10–15 years, it could be ascertained once and for all whether physical education experiences really make a difference in adult life.

The Teaching Dimension

The worth of a curriculum of study depends in the end on teacher effectiveness. Although it is not the purpose of this text to delve in depth into how teachers carry out their function, it is most unrealistic not to comment at all.

Carefully developed program content and quality teaching practices in physical education present a tightly interwoven situation. It is one in which physical activity is pointed in the direction of motor development and the advancement of social skills and self-concept, but this situation is dependent upon the variety and duration of many class-time behaviors. Psychologist Carl Rogers made it clear that students will learn only what they want to learn and that teachers are first and foremost provocateurs who set the stage for student learnings. Thus, as Anderson says, "The essential character of physical education is not to be found in curriculum guides, textbooks accounts, or other idealized program descriptions, but in the day-to-day realities of physical education classes."[26] Interestingly, the "day-to-day realities" associated with the learning behavior of individual students suggest a much wider study of the relationship of class-time activity to teaching success. Laubach worked out a way of monitoring the behavior of individual students, which Anderson

[26]William G. Anderson, "Videotape Data Bank," *Journal of Physical Education and Recreation,* 46 (September 1975), 31–35.

employed to evaluate class-time behavior. In his videotape study (see Table 3-3), he found students engaged in a number of behaviors, a large amount of which was simply awaiting further instructions:[27]

TABLE 3-3

Student behavior	Mean percent of time
awaiting (inactive)	18.8%
playing game	18.7
receiving information	15.8
relocating	11.4
practicing motor skills	11.0
performing exercises	7.8
assisting others	2.9
exploring movement alternatives	2.5
diverging	2.0
getting equipment	1.6
performing expressive movements	1.0
giving information	.4
off monitor (not visible)	5.2

The most striking revelation associated with this study is the contrast between physical education teachers and classroom teachers in terms of the patterns of communication employed. Classroom teachers show repetitive cycles of talking, with students listening, whereas in physical education the teacher-talking is followed by *student movement*—a happening that makes the gymnasium and playing field a distinctive educational setting in which the opportunity is present to act immediately on what has been taught.

When students not only participate in physical activity but also truly share in decision making, they exhibit a higher self-concept than that of those students who do not participate.[28] Employing the Cheffers Adaptation of the Flanders Interaction Analysis System (CAFIAS) to identify the various teaching patterns, the Schilling Body Coordination Test to measure the development of motor skills, and the Martinek-Zaichkowsky Self-Concept Scale to measure student self-concept, it was possible to show that a teacher-directed approach contributes significantly to the development of motor skills, and a student-sharing approach has a definite positive effect on the development of self-concept.[29] In short, the *how* of teaching is every bit as important in terms of achieving predetermined objectives as are the development and distribution of the program of study.

[27]Ibid, p. 33.

[28]Thomas J. Martinek, "The Effects of Horizontal and Vertical Models of Teaching on the Development of Specific Motor Skills and Self-Concept In Elementary Children" (Unpublished Doctoral Dissertation, Boston University, 1976).

[29]Thomas J. Martinek, Leonard D. Zaichkowsky, and John T. Cheffers, "Decision-Making in Elementary Age Children: Effects on Motor Skills and Self-Concept," *Research Quarterly.* 48 (May 1977, 349–57.

QUESTIONS FOR DISCUSSION

1. The variety of sports items purchased by youth shows that peer-group interests and practices measurably influence the teaching process. In planning a series of lessons on a particular sport skill, how might you take advantage of peer-group influences?

2. William VanTil, writing in *Curriculum: Quest for Relevance*, expresses the viewpoint that tomorrow's educated citizen will need more liberal education in the Greek sense of the word than ever before. He feels that mankind will soon have the leisure to cultivate grace and beauty, and states therefore, that physical education should regain the place it had in the Greek curriculum. How do you feel about this viewpoint?

3. Why is a study of aims and objectives frequently referred to as a "dry" topic?

4. How well structured should a newly prepared curriculum be if it is to be flexible and subject to change?

5. Writing from Indiana, David A. Field sees a real need for improved accountability procedures in physical education (see Selected References). He believes that this can be accomplished by spelling out in precise terms exactly what behavior objectives are expected of the student. What are your comments? Where are the problems here?

SUGGESTED ACTIVITIES

1. Students progress in physical education when teaching behavior is both humanistic and skillful. Student-teacher interactions can now be assessed scientifically. Look up the Cheffers Adaptation of the Flanders Interaction Analysis System (CAFIAS) and see how well it applies to the teaching of physical education. (See Selected References under Cheffers and Zaichkowsky.)

2. Obtain a copy of a curriculum guide that has recently been developed by a local school department of physical education. Study its purposes (usually outlined in the beginning) to see whether they qualify as remote aims or near-at-hand objectives. How adequate do they appear to be?

3. Arrange to talk with a number of men and women students from a high school that is considered to have a reasonably good program of physical education. Find out what the students like and dislike about the program. Have any of them ever been asked to provide student input to faculty program-planning sessions? What do they think of the idea, and what might they have to offer?

4. Examine several state and local curriculum guides of recent origin to see how they present their long-range goals and near-at-hand objectives. Are

concepts more popular than behavioral objectives as a means of objectifying the program? Are there statements in the guide that attempt to alert the teacher to the means of tying objectives to evaluation practices?
5. Review some of the basic works in the area of motivation and interests of today's students. General psychology and psychology of learning texts should be helpful. Is there a practical application of the research, or does the research appear to be essentially theory?

SELECTED REFERENCES

ANNARINO, ANTHONY A. "Physical Education Objectives: Traditional vs. Developmental," *Journal of Physical Education and Recreation,* 48 (October, 1977), 22–23.

BLOOM, BENJAMIN S., J. THOMAS HASTINGS, and GEORGE F. MADAUS, *Handbook of Formative and Summative Evaluation of Student Learning.* New York: McGraw-Hill, 1971.

BURNS, RICHARD W., *New Approaches to Behavioral Objectives.* Dubuque: William C. Brown Co., Pub., 1972.

BURTON, ELSIE C., *The New Physical Education,* chap. 2. Boston: Houghton Mifflin Company, 1977.

CHEFFERS, JOHN T., and others, *Interaction Analysis: An Application to Nonverbal Activity.* Minneapolis: Association For Productive Teaching, 1974.

CUMMINGS, L. L., and others, "Performance and Knowledge of Results as Determinants of Goal-Setting," *Journal of Applied Psychology,* 55 (October 1971), 528–38.

Education Policies Commision, *The Central Purpose of American Education,* Washington, D.C.: National Education Association, 1961.

FIELD, DAVID A., "Accountability for the Physical Educator," *Journal of Health, Physical Education and Recreation,* 44 (February 1973), 37–38.

GALLAHUE, DAVID L., PETER H. WERNER, and GEORGE C. LUEDKE, *A Conceptual Approach to Moving and Learning.* New York: John Wiley and Sons, Inc., 1975.

GIRDANO, D.A., and D.D. GIRDANO, "Performance-Based Evaluation," *Health Education,* 8 (March/April), 13.

GLATTHORN, ALLAN A., *Alternatives in Education.* New York: Dodd, Mead and Company, 1975.

HASS, GLEN, *Curriculum Planning: A New Approach* (2nd ed.), section 3. Boston: Allyn and Bacon, Inc., 1977.

HELLISON, DONALD R., *Humanistic Physical Education.* Englewood Cliffs, N.J.: Prentice-Hall, Inc., 1973.

HUNT, MAURICE P., *Foundations of Education: Social and Cultural Perspectives*, part 3. New York: Holt, Rinehart and Winston, 1975.

KRATHWOHL, DAVID R., "Stating Objectives Appropriately for Program," *Journal of Teacher Education*, 26 (March 1965), 70–74.

LARSON, LEONARD, *Foundations of Physical Activity*, New York: Macmillan, 1976.

LOCKE, E.A. and others, "Motivational Effects of Knowledge of Results: A Goal-Setting Phenomenon," *Psychological Bulletin*, 70 (1968), 474–85.

MATSON, FLOYD W., "Humanistic Theory: The Third Revolution in Psychology," *The Humanist*, 31 (March-April 1971), 6–11.

MILLER, JOHN P., *Humanizing the Classroom*. New York: Praeger Publishers, 1976.

RARICK, G.L., ed., *Physical Activity: Human Growth and Development*. New York: Academic Press, 1973.

SHAPIRO, DIANE C., "Knowledge of Results and Motor Learning in Preschool Children," *Research Quarterly*, 48 (March 1977), 154–58.

SINGER, ROBERT A., *Motor Learning and Human Performance*. New York: Macmillan, 1976.

SMITH, BRUCE C., "The Dynamic Tension of the Human Potential Movement," *Health Education*, 8 (May-June 1977), 32–33.

VANTIL, WILLIAM, ed., *Curriculum: Quest for Relevance*. Boston: Houghton Mifflin Co., 1971.

ZAICHKOWSKY, LINDA B., LEONARD D. ZAICHKOWSKY, and THOMAS J. MARTINEK, "Self-Concept and Attitudinal Differences in Elementary School Children after Participation in a Physical Activity Program," in J. Salmela, ed., *Mouvement*, October 1975.

Planning

the Physical Education

Curriculum

chapter four

It is most important that those who are constructing our school curriculum shall maintain an overview of the total situation. . . .

HAROLD RUGG

Although it is used to identify a field of study, the term "curriculum" is more appropriately used to illustrate a *plan* for education. Such a plan is founded on theory and research and past professional practice, and is designed for the purpose of achieving predetermined objectives. It is important, therefore, to follow the Rugg admonition ". . . maintain an overview of the total situation;" otherwise, a limited approach to planning may occur. This requires a rather orderly process of gathering, sorting, selecting, balancing, and synthesizing relevant information from a number of sources in order to design appropriate goal-reaching experiences.

The finest curriculum is always subject to change. Publius Syrus said in 42 B.C. that "it is a bad plan that admits of no modification." Admirable accomplishments in education almost always occur as the result of careful planning. In the long run things left to chance seldom succeed. In the affairs of men, said Lao Tzu, there is a system. A *reasonable* plan for each community should be the near-at-hand objective. Begin gradually, run pilot programs, solicit comments, evaluate results, and then with this background of experience the physical education effort can safely be extended.

Curriculum Development

The roots of the curriculum field go back to the days of Johann Friedrich Herbert (1776–1841), a German educator whose ideas were widely accepted in America. Herbert taught that learning required an orderly attention to the

106

selection and organization of subject matter. Moreover, he applied his views to physical education as well as to the other educational fields, and he was one of the early philosophers to recognize the essential nature of a properly conceived and structured program of physical activity.

Through the years, school systems became "curriculum-conscious" as they developed and revised subject matter plans.[1] By 1966 Hollis Caswell was calling for three important considerations: (1) the establishment of a consistent relationship between general goals and specific objectives to guide teachers, (2) a sound sequence of continuity in the curriculum, and (3) the provision for balance in the curriculum.[2] More recently, Haas extended these curriculum considerations to include a concern for social forces as reflected in social goals, cultural uniformity and diversity, social pressures, social change, future planning, and concepts of culture.[3]

Physical education has reached a level of sophistication at which serious thought can and should be given to a carefully reasoned and well-designed continuum for the learner, one that can replace the disjointed divisions of the past and present. The proper physical education curriculum takes into account these points:

1. It is conceived as an essential part of the total school effort.
2. It reflects the nature and needs of a democratic society, in which there is respect for the interests and capacities of individuals.
3. It is organized into an unbroken flow of experiences beginning with early childhood and extending through post-secondary education and on into later-life education.
4. It is well-balanced and affords varied experiences that will contribute to desirable outcomes for all age groups. This includes a concern for the mentally retarded and the physically handicapped.
5. It is as faithful as possible to the philosophies, discoveries, insights, major trends, methods, and materials of physical education in general.
6. It is based on rigorous criteria for content selection.
7. It is more than loosely related to the health and guidance programs of the school.
8. It promotes and encourages the professional growth of the instructional staff.
9. It is associated in a number of significant ways with the community it serves.

Building a course of study for boys and girls from kindergarten to the twelfth grade should be a challenging undertaking. It should be an "idea" occasion; an air of excitement and great expectation should prevail. If, on the

---

[1] For an historical accounting see Robert Zais, *Curriculum Principles and Foundations* (New York: Thomas Y. Crowell Co., Inc., 1976), chaps. 1 and 2.

[2] Hollis L. Caswell, "Emergence of the Curriculum as a Field of Professional Work and Study," in Helen P. Robison, *Precedents and Promises in the Curriculum Field* (New York: Teachers College Press, 1966).

[3] Glen Haas, *Curriculum Planning: A New Approach,* 2nd ed. (Boston: Allyn and Bacon, Inc., 1977), p. 6.

other hand, it is viewed as a "red-tape" procedure that is untimely, unwarranted, and painfully uninteresting, then the project is doomed at the beginning to become just another pile of printed sheets bound together into something called a curriculum guide. Moreover, the people involved in its preparation will probably show little enthusiasm for putting it to use.

Factors Affecting Program Planning

There are a number of highly important elements that either directly or indirectly influence the planning of physical-education programs. A careful study of Figure 4-1 reveals the extent to which individual and societal needs come together and how dependent they are on the local educational climate.

By surrounding the pupil in Figure 4-1 with all the elements having a bearing on the physical education curriculum, it is possible to show how many significant influences there are that must somehow be considered when a

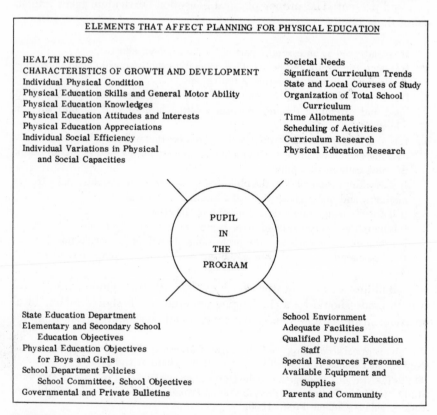

FIGURE 4-1. Elements that affect planning for physical education.

curriculum is to be developed. These elements may be grouped in three categories:

1. *Personal and group factors*—such items as growth characteristics, health status, pupil interests, individual capacities, and the general requirements of society already discussed in Chapter 2
2. *School factors*—education and physical education objectives, school department and school committee policies, local curriculum research, organization of total school curriculum in terms of specifics, such as time allotment and the scheduling of activities, and the availability of qualified staff, resource personnel, equipment, and facilities
3. *Nonschool factors*—influence of government bulletins issued by state and federal agencies, state and local courses of study, parental and communitywide opinion, and evidences of significant curriculum trends

What the community holds as its total school objectives and the attitude of school committee personnel toward the particular physical education objectives have a real bearing on the development of any worthwhile program. Moreover, the concerns of parents and community leaders cannot be taken lightly as one attempts to determine what to plan for and, eventually, what to teach. For example, the influence of a local Boosters Club can be very helpful in calling attention to real needs and current inadequacies. Such a group of people can also be overbearing in a weak system and may literally "run away" with the program by overemphasizing some pet idea. Generally speaking, the citizens of a town or city should have a real opportunity to make their feelings known about the nature and extent of physical education and recreation programs.

In Figure 4-1, another item of significance to the curriculum builder that appears is state and local courses of study. A review of state guidelines and suggested curriculum structures has much merit. In fact, in several states, the state course of study is designed especially to be followed at the local level. Very often, local guides are developed in a specific way to meet local needs but are in keeping with the major recommendations of the state guide or course of study. When state guides are developed with wide participation of physical education teachers from around the state, there is a strong tendency for local curriculum developers to want to lean heavily on the results set forth in the completed guide. In the state of Washington, several of the new guides in health and physical education involved the time and effort of over 450 individuals throughout the region.

A further look at Figure 4-1 indicates that the trends in curriculum building should be examined before local planning is carried too far. Where is the emphasis being placed in physical education at any one grade level, and what is the rationale behind this emphasis? Very much related to the question of trends is the topic of curriculum research. What effect does research in physical education have on the existing curriculum? (A more detailed discussion of this will be found in Chapter 5.)

Muska Mosston challenges the curriculum builder to put together a program that elevates people above subject matter, and of individual needs over group needs. Says Mosston, if "education is for all," then it should be designed for all. To illustrate the point that movement experiences are not so designed, he writes about the high jump as an educational experience:

> After several "innings" the rope or bar excludes most participants. If the raising of the bar continues, it soon excludes all! The design of the activity is obviously hardly congruent with the philosophy of physical education.
>
> The emphasis here is on the word "design." We have designed it! We have been teaching this design to generations of teachers, causing millions of children to be excluded from participation in this activity. Let us examine an alternative design. Place the bar at a slant, so that it represents variable height, with its intrinsic quality of *inclusion*. Experimenting with this alternative with children all over the country we have found that all children participate, including those with various physical handicaps; all children participate willingly and are motivated to begin; all children experience frequent success, for they *always* begin where they know *they* can be successful; and all children become engaged in competition. In fact, they discover that they can compete with themselves or with others, and they learn to choose for themselves the kind of competition they want. Since this arrangement never excludes the top performers and since the availability of choice provides plenty of motivation to continue, all children are always included.[4]

There are many more examples of frequently overlooked factors that have a significant bearing on program planning. Recently the President's Council on Physical Fitness and Sports felt the need to renew its commitment to physical fitness in the schools, chiefly because its research indicated that (1) physical education had suffered by the trend away from required subjects, (2) physical fitness had declined because of optional programs, and (3) when students were given wide latitude they tended to choose activities which required little physical exertion.[5]

Another critical factor affecting curriculum development deals with the extension of sports on television. Currently TV sports take up 17 percent of total programing on the three major networks. Such tremendous growth has implications for the schools. What does this do to the way people, particularly children, perceive the whole idea of sports? The National Broadcasting Com-

---

[4]Muska Mosston and Rudolf Mueller, "Mission, Omission and Submission in Physical Education," in George H. McGlynn, *Issues in Physical Education and Sports* (Palo Alto: National Press Books, 1974), p. 100.

[5]"Physical Fitness Practices and Programs for the Elementary and Secondary Schools," *Physical Fitness Research Digest* (Washington: October 1976), p. 18.

pany (NBC) paid over 80 million dollars for the TV rights for the 1980 Olympics in Moscow. It had no difficulty selling 150 million dollars' worth of advertising just to break even. However, the trend is more and more toward sports-as-entertainment—contrived shows employing sports figures and continually de-emphasizing traditional sports. Sports broadcasters are concerned that the concept of real sport and sportsmanship may suffer. This situation could be offset to some degree through the careful development of a sports-education component in the curriculum.

The Era of Major Curriculum Studies

In the last two decades, there has been an increasing awareness of the several elements that affect planning in education. Curriculum makers and reformers have been operating nationwide by updating their content, reorganizing subject matter, and introducing some fresh approaches to methodology.

So great has been the concern to restructure the curriculum and improve education in the United States that literally hundreds of separate projects have been initiated, completed, and put to use at state and local levels.

The most widely used "new mathematics" program, SMSG (School Mathematics Study Group), was funded by the National Science Foundation for almost eight million dollars. The Biological Sciences Curriculum Study (BSCS) cost approximately the same over the years 1959–1967. During this same period, the chemists revised their curriculum with the Chemical Education Material Study (CHEM); and the whole high school physics program was overhauled by the Physical Science Study Committee (PSSC) under the direction of some of the nation's finest physicists and science educators. The extent to which the concern for quality education has gone in the social studies area is well illustrated by the completion of well over forty major curriculum projects, grades K–12, in the last few years.

The School Health Education Study (SHES) was initiated in 1961 with headquarters in The American Association for Health, Physical Education and Recreation in Washington, and was supported by grants from the Bronfman Foundation until 1966, when it was taken over by the Minnesota Mining and Manufacturing Company (now 3M Company) to continue the development and publication of curriculum materials. It is an excellent example of a very complete effort to examine the status and curriculum of health instruction in grades K–12. Later the project's scope was enlarged to include the development and testing of experimental curriculum materials. Following a nationwide survey, a report was issued that clearly showed health education's low status in the school curriculum, the insufficient time allotted to it, and the students' alarming ignorance in matters of health.

The significant thing about this study was that objectives and evaluations were dealt with prior to the development of curriculum materials. Therefore, when the curriculum guides and materials were ready for experimental use, they were carefully structured to state behavioral outcomes, content, and learning opportunities for each age level. Following an experimental period in try-out schools, the new program was published and made available commercially—not as a national curriculum, but certainly as a well-developed and validated health education program of instruction.

For the most part, major curriculum studies in physical education have been limited to individual cities and towns. National guidelines are available and federal funds have been used to develop *model* physical education programs.

Sex-Integrated Planning

The separation of the sexes with the closing of the massive folding doors is a thing of the past. In fact, there are numerous instances of the dual organization of physical education programs working against the best interests of the students. Also, there is no underlying scientific basis for separate male and female programs. Men and women do more than cogitate. Celeste Ulrich makes it clear that "there are no islands anymore"—men and women do not have to be separated; the islands of sexuality should be abandoned, for a quality performance in physical education does not have a gender. There is a chance to be synergistic rather than antagonistic; after all, boys and girls can and do learn together in physical education classes. Together they should experience the joy of living of an R. Tait McKenzie and the drive of a Dudley Allen Sargent. Moreover, there is another solid dimension nicely expressed by Patricia Elliott when she states that "the flexibility inherent in having all staff members and all facilities available to students in a given class period offers exciting possibilities in terms of programs, organizational patterns, team teaching, and other creative teaching techniques."[6]

In keeping with federal government Title IX requirements, schools must integrate their classes, and girls must have the same opportunities for activity as boys. No two communities or school districts are the same in their approach to the program. In fact, in a number of schools the concept and curriculum possibilities were studied for over a year before programs were initiated.

The time factor influences coeducational activity just as it does other activities. However, in New Jersey, in which the state high school require-

[6]Patricia A. Elliott, "The Beneficial Outcomes of Required Coeducational Programs," *Journal of Health, Physical Education and Recreation*, 43 (February 1972), 35–36.

ment is that every student shall take and pass three years of physical education, and students usually take four days of physical education a week, it is possible to plan extensive sex-integrated programs. Moreover, by involving them in the planning, the students' level of motivation is raised, and they are the first to defend the programs to parents and others who sometimes do not quite understand what is taking place.

A number of schools are discarding longstanding expressions, such as "coeducation" and "co-recreation," since almost all activities involve both men and women and time has come to stop making a point of their difficulties in learning together. In some places sex-integrated teaching and playing are difficult to accomplish without some friction with some slow-to-learn teachers. For a while longer it will be necessary to work hard to achieve the equal participation of boys and girls. As a rule the problem of acceptance does not lie with the students; it lies with adults who confound the operation by adhering to past practices.

Urban Education and Inner-City Concerns

Within the last few years the wide variety of conflicts, frustrations, and unhappiness in the urban areas has been uppermost in the thoughts of leaders in government, medicine, social welfare, and education. Highly experienced people have been frustrated by their failure to solve the inner-city problems. As a big city begins to die, the inhabitants and their educational and other programs tend to die with it. Conversely, as cities like New York and Detroit show concrete signs of a rebirth, the schools tend to improve their efforts. Moreover, the homes and families from which students come influence the degree of motivation and preparation for learning which those students bring to the classroom, gymnasium, and playing field.

Focusing upon the inadequate education of essentially poor and minority children, urban education aims to discover workable solutions through the manipulation of political, social, and economic forces affecting inner cities— forces that have produced the depressed neighborhood, discrimination, inequality, indifference, and dehumanized people "holed up" in an inhuman push-button jungle. To do anything, the educator must understand racism in America and the false explanation that stereotypes people on a basis of heredity rather than environment. The problems are such that the education should be different. Middle-class programs and values frequently fail to work with children of a low socioeconomic background. Also, the myth that blacks are inherently unable to take advantage of schooling has led to a wide variety of programs that are based on the proposition that ghetto children are "disadvantaged" and therefore need "compensatory" or "catch-up" programs. The difficulty here is not that the children are disadvantaged; they certainly are.

The real difficulty lies with the teachers who have lower expectations and
thereby lower educational results. In short, there may be pathological problems at home and in the community, but these are frequently exceeded by the
social pathology in the school system.[7]

Inner-city considerations which relate to student needs and to the
effectiveness of the physical education curriculum include the following:

1. the greater need for school-sponsored physical activities—greater than in subur-
    ban areas where attention to the leisure pursuits of youth is usually better
    planned and executed
2. the special need of city students to taste defeat and success through sports and
    games—the place of athletics as a means of boosting self-awareness and leading to
    a voluntary escape from a ghetto situation after high school is completed
3. an especially prepared teacher—one who is willing to be oriented toward inner
    city schools and pupils, is familiar with inner city problems pertaining to in-
    adequate facilities, large classes, and frequently dehumanized individuals, and
    who can handle bilingual students who are unable to communicate among
    themselves or with their teacher
4. the use of particular staffing patterns in physical education, such as team
    teaching, platoon teaching, and the cycling of teachers with students in an effort
    to make activities more meaningful, which lead to a reduction in the dropout
    rate, a figure that represents 60 percent of the students in New York City
5. an awareness of cultural heritages by relating program elements to ethnic and
    minority groups—Jewish, Polish, Italian, Irish, as well as Afro-American,
    American Indian, Asian, and Puerto Rican
6. a wide variety of course offerings, some of which may take place outside of the
    school plant in another part of the community
7. greater attention to independent study
8. experimentation with the length of instruction periods
9. an examination of ways of obtaining partial physical education credit for attend-
    ance at sporting events and sport clubs
10. ways of extending the intramural experience to reach large numbers of boys and
    girls in situations in which there is a minimum of community facilities and space
    available for school use.[8]

Also, it might be valuable to consider *differentiated staffing* whereby
students are divided into groups with senior teachers and assistants or aides
who engage in a kind of team teaching that gets away from traditional rigid
structures of the school program. *Decentralization* of a school system into
smaller community units sometimes helps parents and children in urban

[7]For a full discussion of the philosophy behind "compensatory education" programs
see Atron Gentry, *Urban Education: The Hope Factor* (Philadelphia: W. B. Saunders
Co., 1972), chap. 1.

[8]For additional considerations and program suggestions, see Leonard M. Ridini and
John E. Madden, *Physical Education for Inner City Secondary Schools* (New York:
Harper and Row, 1975).

areas. So do some *alternative schools,* in which a student is provided with a choice—the more traditional pattern or the openly experimental and developmental. If there are two English or physical education departments, the student has a choice. Perhaps if two varieties of education competed with each other in a school system they would both improve. In any case, systemwide educational change is taking place today. It presupposes that there is no single school design that is the sole answer to the challenge of urban education.

Those who would teach physical education in the inner city must establish their contacts early. Student teachers must start in the freshman or sophomore year. By the senior year it may be too late to interest prospective teachers in the inner-city schools. They will not be prepared. Space problems alone will discourage them. For this reason, student-teaching experiences have been modified at such institutions as Springfield College, University of Bridgeport, Indiana University, University of Pennsylvania, and Boston University. In the latter institution large numbers of city children are transported directly to the physical education facilities where prospective physical education teachers can work with them first-hand.

Involvement in sports and athletics is a positive factor in the life of a youngster in secondary school. Boys from inner-city areas who participate in sports tend to be less involved in vandalism and are more likely to finish high school; and more of them go on to college. Frequently, they face an intense amount of pain in order to make the team. Such a demanding experience has its rewards. So do physical-education learning experiences when the class understands the objective; and students may help in the planning of experiences. Getting the pupils out of the "jungle" atmosphere of crowded conditions and into meaningful courses in swimming, bowling, tennis, and ice hockey takes planning, and has been successful in the Boston area, where city students from Roxbury and Boston English High School go to the YMCA, Boys Clubs, Harvard University, and Northeastern University for their required physical education. In such an improved atmosphere there is a much greater interest in the learning of skills.

Better utilization of the school day helps too. In some cities programs are being extended to include the time blocks from 8:00 to 8:45 in the morning, more time around the noon or lunch hour, and also the evening and the weekend. Although the logistics presents difficulties—problems of sheer numbers, busing, finances, staffing, and so forth—the payoff in terms of improved programs for people who need them most is measurable and rewarding.

Alternative Paths to Learning

For some time there has been a movement to establish alternate routes for certain hard-to-reach students. It is usually involved in a flexible situation in which the key word might be "temporary." Programs and systems are temporary, adaptive, and frequently changing. Such occurrences are in keeping with the concept that, instead of searching for some single answer, educational planning should be providing multiple options—a variety of learning environments and teaching styles.

In the *alternative school,* which is usually small, a separate facility exists in which there is a high degree of student involvement in program planning and decision making. The student makes the choice to attend. Subject-matter offerings frequently encompass the entire range of the curriculum, but they are handled in a nonconventional manner.

The *alternative program* takes place in the conventional school, and is opted by students and their parents. Sometimes within conventional programs, the opportunity exists for certain pupils to select an *alternative path*— to determine their own program of study and arrange for such undertakings as apprenticeship activity, correspondence study, independent projects, and courses given by television or community specialists. Physical education lends itself very well to the alternative-paths planning. Assigning independent work and first-hand experiences working with a golf or tennis professional in the community is quite attractive to certain students who have problems involving group learning and communicating.

Some pupils respond to motor-skill learning when they see its value and general relationship to life and lifestyles. Lawson and Lawson developed and implemented an alternative program of self-directed learnings to help students understand the "ultimate significance of their own performance."[9] The curriculum structure provided enjoyable motor learnings by employing sports and game experiences as a takeoff point for the understandings set forth as program goals. Heart rates were studied in connection with soccer; so were peer-group relationships and the mechanical bases of balance and suppport. American sport history was covered as a unit in the American history course. The more detailed look at scientific and scholarly items that support physical education activity actually awakened most sixth to ninth grade students to the underlying values attributed to human movement.

In recent years the alternative concept applied to movement experiences has moved a number of programs out of the gymnasium and off the playing fields to a challenge-adventure type of outdoor experience. Some schools have instituted a modified Outward Bound experience as a part of physical education. Others have adopted the Project Adventure program with its emphasis on problem-solving situations and environmental education. Using trees, open fields, empty lots, and buildings somewhere near the school, students have an opportunity to sample the physical, mental, and social challenges of earlier wilderness schools. Hundreds of physical educa-

[9]Hal Lawson and Barbara Lawson, "An Alternative Program Model for Secondary School Physical Education," *Journal of Physical Education and Recreation,* 48 (February 1977), 48.

FIGURE 4-2. Challenge-adventure activities—individual and group. (Courtesy, Agassiz Village, Oxford, Maine)

tion teachers have attended Project Adventure workshops to climb ropes, execute Tarzan swings, jump into cargo nets, balance on walks over mud-filled areas, and walk on wires strung between trees 50 feet above the ground.[10] The work is exhilarating, demanding, and exhausting. It serves a need; and data prove that it contributes to a raising of self-concept, with girls showing slightly greater gains in positive identity and achievement motivation.[11]

In terms of physical education goals the adventure-challenge activities make a contribution. Students do indeed stretch themselves beyond their own self-imposed limits and come to appreciate their bodies. However, these activities do not contribute to motor-skill learnings that are so much a part of physical education—individual and group sports, and quality skills to carry over into leisure-time pursuits. They should not, therefore, represent a large part of the physical education offering. Their place in the curriculum should be restricted and considered only when adequate time has been assured for such items as physical fitness assessment, general- and sports-skill development, dance and swimming proficiency, movement-exploration experiences.

While the alternatives concept is concerned primarily with the *process* that takes place within the individual of exploring and searching for ways to satisfy inner needs, the development of high-quality, self-satisfying motor skills is still a primary *product* of the physical-education curriculum.

Appraising Interests

Interests vary with the level of maturation. In this respect, much first-hand knowledge can be gained by the new teacher from watching pupils in the playground in their play activities, listening to them as they talk with one another, evaluating the stories they bring from home, and discussing them with parents, coaches, and former teachers.

Several years ago, the New York State Education Department made a concerted effort to find out what fourth, fifth, and sixth grade boys and girls like to do. What was important to them? What were their interests? This study, as well as others that have been carried out at the secondary school level, noted that there is no sudden increase or decrease in children's interests from one age to the next. Only when interests are charted over a two- to three-year period are they significant. Children's interests need time to mature, and each child must grow at his or her own speed. The interests are acquired, but they are also based upon such factors as the constitutional nature of the individual and his personality structure.

[10]Project Adventure, P.O. Box 157, Hamilton, Massachusetts 01936.
[11]Rufus Little, "Project Adventure," *Journal of Physical Education and Recreation*, 48 (June 1977) 13–16.

Figure 4-3 shows an example of a simple interest-participation checklist designed to measure the level of interest, as well as the actual amount of participation, of boys in physical education activities.[12]

Relating interests to other variables associated with educational goals and curriculum planning can be enlightening. In a study of high school girls it was determined that there was a positive relationship between attitudes toward physical education and the variables of physical fitness and personal-social adjustment.[13] In one junior high school study there was a significant positive relationship established between interests and abilities in sports and level of self-concept.[14] Moreover, there is a similarity of sports interests in parent and child that is also related to self-concept. This would seem to indicate that there is value in planning programs of sport skills that can be shared with other members of the family.

In validating the *Martinek-Zaichkowsky Self-Concept Scale for Children*, the authors employed interest-provoking pictures for children to associate with. The more positive their choices for participation, the higher their level of self-concept.[15]

There is evidence that some physical education programs have turned students off. There has to be a reason. Why do youngsters who normally and naturally look forward to their physical education classes in elementary school quickly develop a dislike for them in secondary school? Do we care what students think? Do we assess how they feel about voluntary or required-elective programs and which activities they like the least? In short, are students driven away from large-muscle activity and the satisfactions that come from movement when our avowed purpose is to encourage them?

In almost any informal survey of students, the strengths and weaknesses of the program can be ascertained. Most boys and girls are willing to suggest changes. When asked how she felt about physical education, one girl said, "It is important, but it definitely can be improved." Another girl's feelings: "It contributes to a personality that is more outgoing." However, on the negative side are such remarks as: "I've heard the same thing over and over again since the seventh grade," or "I'm a twelfth grader now and have had six years of basketball, volleyball, field hockey, and softball, but I don't know how to

---

[12]Designed by Joseph Masino of Providence, Rhode Island, and used by permission.

[13]Mary L. Young, "Personal-Social Adjustment, Physical Fitness, Attitude Toward Physical Education of High School Girls by Socioeconomic Level," *Research Quarterly*, 41 (December 1970), 593–99.

[14]Richard S. Kay, Donald W. Felker, and Ray O. Varoz, "Sports Interests and Abilities as Contributors to Self-Concept in Junior High School Boys," *Research Quarterly*, 43 (May 1972), 208–15.

[15]Thomas J. Martinek and Leonard D. Zaichkowsky, *The Martinek-Zaichkowsky Self-Concept Scale for Children* (Jacksonville, Illinois: Psychologists and Education, Inc.), 1977

Physical Education

Instructions: After the name of each activity listed, place a check mark (✓) in one of the columns in order to show "how much" you are interested. If you have considerable interest you will probably want to check "Strong Interest" or "Some Interest." If you have very little interest, you will probably want to check "Little Interest" or "No Interest." A check in the middle column would indicate that you had difficulty making up your mind.

Activity	Strong Interest	Some Interest	Indifferent (Don't Care)	Little Interest	No Interest
1. Apparatus					
2. Archery					
3. Badminton					
4. Baseball					
5. Basketball					
6. Bowling					
7. Boxing					
8. Calisthenics (Exercises)					
9. Casting					
10. Dancing					
11. Dodgeball					
12. Fencing					
13. Football (Touch/Flag)					
14. Games of Low Organization--Relays, Tag, Line, Circle, Running, and Chasing Games.					
15. Golf					
16. Handball					
17. Hiking					
18. Hockey (Ice)					
19. Horseshoes					
20. Ice Skating					
21. LaCrosse					
22. Marching					
23. Paddle Tennis					
24. Pyramids					
25. Obstacle Course					
26. Roller Skating					
27. Shuffleboard					
28. Skiing					
29. Soccer					
30. Softball					
31. Speedball					
32. Stunts					
33. Swimming & Diving					
34. Table Tennis					
35. Tennis					
36. Track & Field					
37. Tumbling					
38. Volleyball					
39. Weight Lifting					
40. Wrestling					
41.					
42.					

List here any other activity, game or sport you are interested in that does not appear above.

FIGURE 4-3. Interest-participation checklist.

II. Activities I Like To Play

Instructions: Write the Number 1 on the line in front of the activity you like to play best. Write a 2 in front of the one you like next best. Write a 3 in front of the next best, and keep going until you get to number 12. Use each number only once. If you like two activities almost the same, decide which you like just a little better.

_____ Apparatus

_____ Archery

_____ Badminton

_____ Baseball

_____ Basketball

_____ Bowling

_____ Boxing

_____ Calisthenics (Exercises)

_____ Casting

_____ Dancing

_____ Dodgeball

_____ Fencing

_____ Football (Touch/Flag)

_____ Games of Low Organization (Relays, Circle, Line, Tag, Hunting, Chasing, etc.)

_____ Golf

_____ Handball

_____ Hiking

_____ Hockey (Ice)

_____ Horseshoes

_____ Ice Skating

_____ LaCrosse

_____ Marching

_____ Paddle Tennis

_____ Pyramids

_____ Obstacle Course

_____ Roller Skating

_____ Shuffleboard

_____ Skiing

_____ Soccer

_____ Softball

_____ Speedball

_____ Stunts

_____ Swimming and Diving

_____ Table Tennis

_____ Tennis

_____ Track and Field

_____ Tumbling

_____ Volleyball

_____ Weight Lifting

_____ Wrestling

_____ Others Not Listed, List Here

_____

_____

_____

_____

FIGURE 4-3 *Continued.*

swim," or "There are no electives." Most of these comments come as no surprise. When reforming the curriculum, however, they are valuable.

The formal attitude survey can be highly indicative of the true reactions of groups of students to the physical education program and its outcomes. Students can be asked to express the degree to which they *feel* certain about physical education values. Several attitude inventories have been developed to do just this. An excellent instrument designed to evaluate the attitudes of high school girls toward the value of physical education experiences is the forty-item Mercer Attitude Inventory.[16]

An extended study of pupil interests and their motivations will not be made here. The question of motives, however, is always present. There are different personal values and motives at different age levels. Although motives change, there are a number of motives that appear to operate in physical education throughout elementary and secondary school. Cowell and France suggest the following:

POSSIBLE MOTIVES—AGES 6–12 YEARS

1. Love of activity, motion, hunting, climbing, chasing, fighting.
2. Idealizes others, wishes to emulate and be like those he loves.
3. Highly imaginative, curious. Will try many things.
4. Function pleasure. Pleasurable sensory feeling and sheer joy out of use of muscles and in testing budding capabilities.
5. Expression of independence and self-assertion. Is daring and adventurous.
6. Pride in performance. Pride in growth and development.
7. Pleasurable feeling from sense of mastery and achievement.
8. Group status and social recognition because of values placed on health, physical development, and game skills in a given culture.
9. Rational understanding of the relation of health and physical education practices to the satisfaction of many of the motives implied above. (This is a gradual progressive process starting with the nursery school.)

POSSIBLE MOTIVES —AGES 13–18 YEARS

1. Desire to understand the scientific bases (the "why") behind health and physical education activities.
2. Interest in growth and development and physiological changes of puberty.
3. Interest in impressing opposite sex.
4. Desire to be liked by classmates; sense of belonging.
5. Desire for group status and acceptance of prescribed values of the group or gang.
6. Seeking for self-discovery, self-testing, self-realization, and self-assertion.
7. Satisfaction of desire for mastery and achievement.
8. Affection for those whom one admires and respects.

[16]Developed by Emily Louise Mercer, "An Adaptation and Revision of the Calloway Attitude Inventory," (Master's Thesis. University of Connecticut, 1960).

9. Excitement, adventure, and new experiences.
10. The sheer joy of the game itself; the wholesome pleasure, richer personal contacts, and friendships it makes possible.[17]

Pupil Maturation

The question of pupil growth and development characteristics is especially germane in the curriculum-construction process. Activities need to be selected that are in keeping with the physical, intellectual, social, and emotional behavior of children at specific age levels.

Growth is a continuous process. It is difficult to subdivide the growth period into specific age levels, for the child never abruptly completes a particular stage of development and begins the next. Moreover, there is never a time when all children in a class are at the same growth stage. Chronological age and physiological age (maturation level) may be quite a distance apart (note Figure 4-4). In Part III, there is a detailed description of pupil charac-

FIGURE 4-4. Individual differences affect program planning (9th graders).

[17]From Charles C. Cowell and Wellman L. France, *Philosophy and Principles of Physical Education* (Englewood Cliffs, N.J.: Prentice-Hall, Inc., 1963).

teristics and needs set forth for the various age categories. The subdivisions employed serve only as convenient labels for periods of growth. After all, each pupil is unique and has his or her own path to follow; the pupil may behave more like the child a year or more younger or the one somewhat older. Nevertheless, a knowledge of the child's needs and general capacities at any age level is an aid to the physical-education teacher in the organization of the program of studies.

In physical education, the level of physical maturity and development may have more to do with determining what to teach than it does in any other subject-matter area. The Medford Boys' Growth Study, an intensive longitudinal growth study over many years, has produced considerable concrete evidence to show that the more active, athletic participating elementary and junior high school boys are definitely superior to their peers in maturity, body size, muscular strength, endurance, and power. There is similar evidence for girls. The significant indication here is that the *decision* as to whether boys and girls are physically ready for such participation should be determined by factors other than age or grade in school.

Student Evaluations

There is one more source of information that should be used, more than it has been, to indicate where emphasis should be placed in a local program. This is in the area of pupil evaluation. What are the results of measurement? What information can be gleaned from medical examination, physical-fitness tests, posture appraisals, nutrition surveys, general achievement tests, and tests of a number of motor skills? What may a survey of attitudes toward physical education suggest? Where are the weaknesses in a student's knowledge of games and sports? How much interest is there in intramural sports for girls? Too many evaluators limit their measurements to the determination of pupil status and the classification of pupils for instructional purposes when they should be spending a solid amount of time improving the efficiency of the teacher and the quality of the program.

Concepts in Physical Education

The concept approach offers the program planner a realistic pattern for the development of curriculum materials in physical education. The topic has been well explored, and a multitude of reliable references setting forth conceptual procedure are available. (See especially the references to Bruner, and Phenix, at the end of this chapter.) There have also been several national curriculum studies in other subject-matter fields that have used this approach quite successfully. An example close to home is the national School Health Education Study, the fruits of which became available to health and physical education personnel in late 1967.[18]

A concept is a generalization about something. It is usually built from a number of related sensations, precepts, and images. Concepts range from ideas about very simple things to high-level abstractions. Woodruff has phrased a definition for curriculum planning which states:

> A concept is a relatively complete and meaningful idea in the mind of a person. It is an understanding of something. It is his own subjective product of his way of making meaning of things he has seen or otherwise perceived in his experience. . . .[19]

To the individual pupil, a concept is a personal organization of a number of interpretations of things he or she has been exposed to. Concepts cannot be taught as such. However, teaching is directed *toward* concepts. This means that the instructor is working with pupils in terms of whole ideas, even though pieces and bits of knowledge and skills are being employed along the way. More specifically, the concept approach to learning is one in which all facts, skills, techniques, and so forth are centrally related. For too many years, teachers of physical education have taught isolated facts, stunts, and rules in about the same fashion as history teachers have taught places and dates, and health teachers have taught the many lettered vitamins. The pupil learned facts by rote memorization or repetition without seeing them as a part of a whole—a part of *his* or *her* life. Certainly, they did not become a part of the pupil's value system. The historical dates and places were soon forgotten, and the physical-education knowledge and game skills were relegated to the "growing years" and not carried over into adult life.

When men and women fail to use in their adult lives what they apparently learned during their school years, it is probably because something was wrong with the learning process. Tens of thousands of adults do not even begin to live lives that reflect a physical education. Their early physical-education experiences—the curriculum and how it was taught—did not relate to life situations. The various games, skills, and exercises were like facts that had to be learned, and were without meaning beyond the moment.

The activities that are planned for the physical education curriculum, if they are going to carry over from one grade level to another and eventually into adult life, must relate to the individual as a whole person and an expanding society. The physical conditioning exercises, the games and sports, the

[18]*Health Education: A Conceptual Approach,* School Health Education Study (St. Paul: Minnesota Mining and Manufacturing Company, 1967).
[19]Asahel D. Woodruff, "The Use of Concepts in Teaching and Learning," *Journal of Teacher Education,* 20 (March 1964), 81–99.

rhythms and dances—all of these activities must be related not only to the individual, but to the family and the community at large. Figure 4-5 is a tridimensional diagram of physical education. Each square is part of a triad. Physical education attempts to unify people physically, mentally, and socially by developing physical education behavior in the form of knowledge, attitude, and practice. In order to bring about a dynamic interaction of these components (⟵⟶) the focus of physical education is on the individual, family, and community.

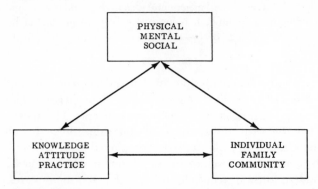

FIGURE 4-5. The physical education triad.

There is nothing spectacular about the concept approach in education. It is simply a means of helping curriculum builders put together a program that will provide students with a fuller understanding of what it is they are studying. Thus, Gallahue speaks of this approach as the means of providing "greater insight to the why and how of movement."[20] For example, when square dancing is planned for a seventh-grade class it should consist of more than the music and dance figures. Every bit as important is the planning for *discussion* relative to square dancing. What kind of groups do it in the community? Where is it being done? Can a family do it at home or on vacation? The same reasoning holds true for numerous sports skills taught through the years. Besides planning for the special techniques and practices, the unit of study must relate to the physical, mental, and social benefits to be discovered in the larger community.

Concepts and Intellectual Competency

A substantial amount of intellectual activity must accompany physical activity if physical education is to be fully understood. Intellectual competency must be planned for. Frequently, a nearby classroom can be used for

[20]David L. Gallahue, Peter H. Werner, and George C. Luedke, *A Conceptual Approach to Moving and Learning* (New York: John Wiley & Sons, Inc., 1975), p. 26.

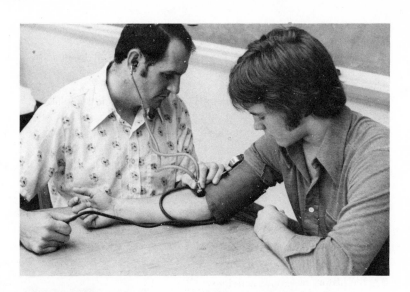

FIGURE 4-6. Examining the benefits of exercise as part of the physical education class. (Courtesy, M. C. Rhodes, Metropolitan Public Schools, Nashville, Tenn.)

discussion phases of the physical-education program. With the aid of various media such as books, magazines, charts, full-length sport and recreation films, slides, and television, it is possible to cover such areas as the following:

ELEMENTARY LEVEL

1. what we like to do
2. the rules of games
3. the current popular sports heroes and films showing their performance

4. the story of the Olympic Games
5. the reading and discussion of box scores
6. a review of the many kinds of physical activities through discussion, audio-visual aids, and role-playing
7. listening to music for dances
8. taking and talking over short tests of knowledge and its application
9. writing an explanation of an activity
10. keeping written records of squad or group activities
11. learning about seasonal and holiday activities
12. planning certain self-testing activities
13. reviewing safe practices on the playground and in the gymnasium

SECONDARY LEVEL

1. detailed rules and strategy of games
2. sports terminology
3. game equipment and playing areas
4. athletic conditioning
5. the history of various activities
6. the cultural background and dances of various ethnic groups
7. the lives of leaders in sport and dance
8. the effect of national sports on the culture and economy of the country
9. the presentation of recreational activities for use in social events
10. the role of exercise in physical performance and well-being
11. the role of diet, sleep, and relaxation in physical performance
12. the rationale behind self-testing and other measurements designed to evaluate physical conditions, sport skills, general motor skills, and social behavior
13. career fields related to sports

The framework for insuring a degree of intellectual competency will vary from school to school. The issue of how much time is considered adequate will always be valid. Perhaps 10 percent of total program time should be carefully planned to teach elementary-level boys and girls about their physical education. At the secondary level, some 15 to 20 percent of the time may be appropriate. This could mean that as much as one period in five could be devoted to a nonphysical kind of class period.[21] In most instances, however, only a part of the period would be used, with full-period meetings being reserved for special topics, in-depth study, and examinations.

When the AAHPER manual, *Knowledge and Understanding in Physical Education,* was being developed, the committee was careful to present a depth of information so that the instructor using it would get beyond pure facts to the "whys"—reasons, values, justifications. This also involves answering

---

[21]A suitable student text for middle school and junior high school that combines knowledge items with skills is Arthur T. Miller, Carl E. Willgoose, and James A. Wylie, *Your Physical Education* (New York: McGraw-Hill, 1970).

"why it happens"—principles, laws, relationships, and "what one can do about it"—application of facts, principles, and relationships. The manual covers elementary, junior, and senior levels. All concepts and descriptions of skills are very clear. Also, the content ties in with the current *AAHPER Cooperative Physical Education Tests* distributed by Educational Testing Service (ETS).

Advancing youth from the knowledge level to values and actions requires that opportunities be provided for inquiry, problem-solving, and decision-making. This too requires planning so that time spent with intellectual issues is worthwhile. By setting up behavioral objectives it should be easier to have the knowledge become a means of facilitating decision-making so that there is some feedback relative to positive individual and social action within the school and the community.

Concepts and Creativity through Movement

Because the central concepts of physical education are movement-oriented, they do not lend themselves to verbal formulation. Like the ideas of graphic arts and music, they must be expressed by doing something with the elements of space, time, body, and energy. The skills of physical education give rise to the idea of "doing a dance" or "doing a forward roll." Or they may take the form of moving something through space, as when a ball is thrown at a target. They may also be organized into the highly complex forms for games and sports that symbolize some forms of a person's interactions with the environment.

Ultimate understandings result in many specific concepts about what it means to pull, to push, to lift, to carry, to run, to jump, to swim, to exert force, to resist force, to play, to fight, to cooperate, to compete. Dictionary definitions of these concepts show how difficult it may be to express their full meaning, but they become meaningful within the context of the physical-education experiences. The concept of rhythm, for example, can be understood and acted out long before it can be verbalized. Other concepts such as balance, equilibrium, motion, up, down, circle, round, parallel, vertical, horizontal, spiral, twist, turn, and juggle can all be demonstrated by moving in appropriate ways.

Rudolph Laban described how the four elements of time, weight, shape, and flow are basic to every action. He suggested that physical education should be teaching the understanding of these elements, which underlie all movement, and the individual will become totally involved—intellectually and kinesthetically. Thus, movement education is a concept in which the student intellectualizes a performance before he or she acquires the physical skill. Creativity has its roots at this stage; exploration and discovery follow.

Piaget's theory of intelligence, Montessori's teaching methods, and Bloom's cognitive domain provide some insight into the intellectual charac-

FIGURE 4-7. Creative actions indoors—the many faces of movement.

FIGURE 4-8. Creativity through playground movements. (Courtesy, *Update,* American Alliance for Health, Physical Education and Recreation)

teristics of children as applied to physical education. Each demonstrates the link between perceptual and motor functioning with considerable interdependence. Children learn through movement because movement concepts may be readily integrated with mathematics, science, language arts, social studies, music, and art.

Curriculum Opinion

A wide variety of opinion exists among teachers of physical education as they prepare to plan a curriculum on what to include. All of the elements affecting a program (see Figure 4-1) have to be weighed by each curriculum committee member in terms of his particular philosophy and experiences.

Rothberg of Florida State University set out to analyze the opinions of selected teachers of physical education regarding curriculum concepts.[22] A large number of significant ideas having to do with the physical education curriculum were selected from the literature and developed into an opinionnaire. The curriculum opinionnaire was then administered to a national sample of physical educators, many of whom were actively engaged in the preparation of physical education teachers.

Rothberg found a significant difference of opinion among the groups of teachers surveyed in their agreement or disagreement with the selected curriculum concepts. Although there are some hazards in placing too much weight on the evidence collected by this opinionnaire technique, it is, nevertheless, helpful to note the kinds of curriculum items that professional people find it difficult to agree upon. This is as true today as when the study was completed. Some indication is illustrated by singling out several of the ideas on which opinion *differed:*

1. A program of competitive interscholastic sports should be organized at the elementary school level.
2. A rhythmics unit at the elementary school level should be taught daily, rather than once a week for a period of several months.
3. Interscholastic football competition should be organized at the junior high school level.
4. Potential dangers inherent in using the trampoline make its value questionable in the high school physical education program.
5. A well-balanced program of positive exercises and body mechanics provides the essential physical education content.
6. Emphasis on team sports and their fundamentals is the basis of a good secondary-school program of physical education for girls.
7. Slides, swings, teeters, merry-go-rounds, and similar playgound apparatus have little educational value and are not desirable on the school grounds.

[22]Robert Alan Rothberg, *An Analysis of Opinions of Selected Physical Educators Regarding Curriculum Concepts.* (Doctoral dissertation. Florida State University, 1966).

8. Wrestling is an excellent activity for boys in the fifth and sixth grades.
9. In program planning at the high school level, carry-over activities should receive more emphasis than strength and endurance development.
10. Each scheduled period of elementary-school physical education should include some time for "free play."
11. Marching has little value in the high school physical education curriculum.
12. The school physical education program and the community-recreation program should maintain themselves as two separate entities.
13. The physical needs of the highly skilled girl can be best met through an intramural program.
14. High school physical education classes should be primarily recreational in nature.
15. The basic content of physical education should stress locomotion fundamentals, or "natural" human activities.
16. The traditional team activities of football and basketball should be taught every year in the boys' high school physical education program.

Certainly a careful study of each of these not-agreed-upon concepts should lead one to realize that the planning of a physical education curriculum has its difficulties—especially when persons with varied backgrounds and opinions prepare to work together to fashion a program for all boys and girls.

Multicultural Physical Education

The dynamism of the American, Canadian, and Australian societies continues to expand, in part, because the pluralistic nature of these societies is more of an asset than a liability. In them, those who champion the rights and aspirations of minorities and ethnic groups are respected for their views. Moreover, instead of dwelling entirely on the cultural disadvantage of Mexicans, Blacks, Puerto Ricans, Indians, and Orientals, there is an effort to highlight and employ in a positive fashion the unique cultural backgrounds as they pertain to educational items such as family living practices, mores, foods, games, dances, and rituals.[23]

Physical education can be multicultural if it is oriented toward the enrichment of youth through the preservation of cultural diversities. This concept has the advantage of holding the student's interest, as well as developing stronger school and family bonds.

[23]For a wider discussion of cultural determinants see Jerry Freischlag, "Cultural Pluralism," *Journal of Physical Education and Recreation*, 48 (May 1977), 22–23. See also Thomas E. Curtis and Wilma W. Bidwell, *Curriculum Instruction for Emerging Adolescents* (Boston: Addison-Wesley Publishing Company, 1977), chap. 6.

Selection—The Essence of Teaching

Contributing to the lack of agreement upon what to put into the program is the obvious fact that there are today far more possible activities to choose from than can ever be used. As one scans the extensive list of team, individual, and dual activities from "A" for archery to "W" for water polo it becomes obvious that only those most appropriate for a given situation can be considered. The problem is further complicated by noting that there are today far more possible physical activities to choose from than there ever were in the past. Thirty years ago, coeducational instruction was rare. So were movement education and swimming. Only daredevils went skiing. Bowling was completely outside the concern of the schools. So was weight training and handball. And trampolining and circuit training were not even born.

What to select and how long to teach each selection are real questions. "Six weeks for volleyball," reads a course of study. "Eight weeks of gymnastics," reads another. How was this determined? Was there a local study made? Related to this are a number of other issues:

1. the sequence of physical education activities within a school year
2. the sequence of physical education activities over a span of several years
3. the problem of the loaded curriculum, which attempts to do a little bit of everything all in one year
4. the question of the repetitious curriculum that continues from year to year without change or innovation
5. the relationship of the curriculum parts to the whole, as, for example, how much teaching of game skills should be conducted as physical education classwork and how much should be covered in the intramural program
6. the requirements for a broad and varied curriculum

The Broad and Varied Program

How can the school provide a balanced program of physical activity amid various pressures for specialization? How comprehensive can a program of physical education be when many teachers have one or two "pet activities" they like to stress, frequently at the expense of less popular activities? How often are students heard to say, "All we have is folk dancing," or "He's the gymnastic coach so all we do during the winter months is gymnastics," or "We don't play many games; we just do exercises," or "She loves to teach field hockey; I wish we would do something else this fall"?

A condemnation of "sameness" in various physical education activities has been referred to by a number of writers, for example, Mosston:

> This is not only a matter of educational philosophy, it is a serious physiological and psychological issue. Is it not absurd to require the tall and the short, the fat

133

and the slim, the energetic and the phlegmatic to follow as one man the drive of one person—the teacher? If we recognize that individual differences exist and that these differences produce a variety of explicit or implicit needs, then should those needs not be satisfied and treated in a manner other than a communal one?[24]

Even the American Medical Association, in extolling the value of physical education, has carefully indicated that only a broad and varied program will appeal to all students. Programs are adequate when they consider the variety of interests, needs, and abilities of boys and girls. This suggests that there must be numerous individual and self-testing activities, dual games, rhythmics, adapted physical education, and a variety of team games that provide both vigorous and enjoyable experiences.

The issue of balance is as old as the species. To make full use of human resources is always a basic consideration. "Harmony," said the Greeks, "is the music of the gods." Achieving this harmony in physical eduation is not easy—especially at a time when there are powerful forces crying for more attention to such items as movement exploration or physical fitness or aquatic skills, or the preparation of physical education demonstrations and exhibitions. These activities must be put in proper focus so that there may be achieved an "orchestration of many powers."

In view of the fact that not all worthwhile physical education activities can ever be included in the curriculum, efforts must be made to *combine the concepts of those activities that have been left out of the program with the concepts and competencies of those included.* For example, the combining of several rhythmical activities in an elementary curriculum may be accomplished by selecting unifying elements from several rhythmic skills and dances to produce an adequate experience and at the same moment provide more time in the total program for something else that might previously have been eliminated. In the area of ball-handling skills, for example, there are numerous combinations that can be considered with a view toward omitting some so that another kind of physical education activity can be fitted into the block of time assigned to the program. Therefore, all kinds of ball-handling skills for a particular grade level will be reviewed in an effort to combine the common elements, and when ball skills are employed in lead-up games, careful attention will be given to select two or three. When this kind of planning is done for all parts of the program, including existing programs under revision, it will be possible to find time for a variety of activities greater than that in which touch football and field hockey are played almost exclusively from September to December, and softball is played from March to June.

[24]Muska Mosston, *Teaching Physical Education* (Columbus, Ohio: Charles E. Merrill Books, 1966), p. 32.

Unfortunately, in many parts of the country, local schools put a physical-education program together piecemeal. It is not uncommon at a middle school or junior high school level to find programs consisting of "a little of this" and "a little of that," in order to compensate for numerous inadequacies in pupils coming from different elementary school programs. These difficulties are compounded for local schools in which elementary and secondary school districts are separately organized and administered.

Broad and varied programs can be developed when local personnel and administrators appraise their current programs. Some studies have already been carried out to determine why the physical education curriculum is not as broad in scope as it might be. In his early secondary school studies, Conant found that a number of programs lacked breadth chiefly because most of the class time, staff time, budget, and energy were devoted to interscholastic sports for boys. His contention was that elementary school and girls' programs would continue to suffer as long as boys' athletics was the primary concern of the school. Although this situation has improved somewhat since the Conant report, there are still a fair number of school systems where programs are very much out of balance:

Structuring for Quality

There are at least two major considerations when *quality* programs are being discussed. They are:

1. the *kinds* of activities and the amount of exposure to them
2. the nature of the *teaching methods*

Although it is the purpose of this book to be concerned chiefly with activities and their organization in the program, it is almost impossible to steer clear of teaching methods. Ultimately, wisdom in choosing an activity and talent in teaching it go together. Keeping this in mind, therefore, is essential when quality programs are being deliberated.

To be physically educated means to be able to *use* the body efficiently. However, all too often the degree of recreation engaged in is directly proportional to the level of physical skill possessed for a given activity. This fact is vividly brought out by Cozens and Stumpf when they attest that Americans are not exclusively sports spectators but are first-degree participants when they have the abilities.[25] Furthermore, knowledge and ability in a sport produce the best kind of spectators—bright, sophisticated observers who express their judgment as a result of their experiences. Both the participants and the spectators alike seek excellence. Both are interested not only in scores, reputations, and action but also in *quality of performance*.

[25]Frederick W. Cozens and Florence S. Stumpf, *Sports in American Life* (Chicago: University of Chicago Press, 1953).

FIGURE 4-9. "The Joy of Effort" by R. Tait McKenzie (1867-1938). Taken from the face of a large medallion set in the stadium wall in Stockholm, Sweden, as a memorial to the Olympic Games.

For too long—because of short periods, loose programming, and poor teaching—thousands of schoolchildren of all ages have missed learning their general motor and game skills well enough to experience a "feeling" for them. The level of exposure and concentration in the skills has been low. The actual learning period has been so shallow that only the idea of the skill is brought up, with little opportunity provided to put muscles through their paces. The chance to practice physical skills and slowly perfect them has been treated lightly. However, today, a number of junior high schools explore a wide variety of game skills in the required program. This permits the student to elect certain games and sports in which to concentrate in a senior high school program.

When physical education skills are properly learned, the lasting value takes the form of a solid kinesthetic experience—the kind of learning that provides the pupil with a deep appreciation for the particular skills. It is this warm "feeling" for the skilled movement that furnishes the drive to engage in it again and again, perhaps throughout a lifetime.

FIGURE 4-10. A quality performance. (Courtesy, Joseph Brown, Princeton University)

QUESTIONS FOR DISCUSSION

1. Can a strong case be made for a national model program of physical education—a kind of nationwide curriculum? Where are the strengths and weaknesses? Would you follow such a model if you had one?
2. How would you react to the following statements:
   a. Planning the physical-education curriculum *with* the instructors is far superior to planning *for* them.
   b. Planning is essentially an administrative function calling for energetic leadership.

3. What procedures can be used in selecting physical-education curricular experiences?

4. Explain how you might go about amending a junior high school program of physical education that was heavily game-centered. What might be your procedure, and why?

5. Something called the "educational park" is an ideal instructional situation in which the individual pupil will have a program of studies to meet his or her particular needs. All educational resources will be in one big "super-market" kind of structure. Do you believe that such an all-encompassing structure will be helpful in achieving the goals of physical education? Explain your viewpoint.

6. How do you feel about carrying on a "pilot" study in order to improve some phase of the physical education program in a particular school?

SUGGESTED ACTIVITIES

1. Ridini and Madden (see Selected References) recommend that urban programs of physical education be more flexible and creative. Ask several inner-city teachers of physical education how they would go about following this recommendation.

2. The students' learning process, the teaching method, and the physical education course content are intricately related. Review the philosophy of Jerome Bruner relative to the "discovery method" in teaching. Review also Muska Mosston's text, *Teaching Physical Education: From Command to Discovery*. Set forth in your own words what you think is the particular influence of teaching methodology on the selection of program content in physical education.

3. Review carefully *A Conceptual Approach to Moving and Learning* by Gallahue, Werner, and Luedke (see Selected References). Note the organization of program material. List several practical ways in which this can be used by teachers. Where are the weaknesses? Are local school people generally aware of this type of book?

4. Consider the meaning of the word "innovation." Read what some general educators have had to say about it. Discuss it with your colleagues. Having done this, try responding to the following questions:
   a. Is movement education a form of innovation in physical education?
   b. Is substituting lacrosse for spring football practice an example of program innovation?
   c. Are there examples of innovation you can suggest that might be appropriate for junior high school?

5. Put together a comprehensive list of physical education activities suitable

for secondary school pupils. Choose either girls or boys. Develop a plan for deciding:

   a. which of the many activities to leave in
   b. which to eliminate
   c. which to combine with others

   This is a difficult assignment involving your consideration of activity outcomes that relate to pupil concepts as well as physical competencies.

6. Examine some behavior objectives and compare them in terms of student and teacher use, with concepts and competencies.

7. Prepare a short statement that indicates the relationship of the kinesthetic sense to quality skill performance.

SELECTED REFERENCES

ARNSTINE, BARBARA, and DONALD L. ARNSTINE, "Transforming the Curriculum," in Dwight W. Allen and Jeffery C. Hecht, *Controversies in Education*, p. 4. Philadelphia: W. B. Saunders Co., 1974.

BRUNER, JEROME S., *Toward a Theory of Instruction*. Cambridge, Mass.: Belknap Press of Harvard University Press, 1966.

CHEFFERS, JOHN, and TOM EVAUL, *Introduction to Physical Education: Concepts of Human Movement*. Englewood Cliffs, N.J.: Prentice-Hall, Inc., 1978.

COWELL, CHARLES C., and HELEN W. HAZELTON, *Curriculum Designs in Physical Education*, chap. 7. Englewood Cliffs, N.J.: Prentice-Hall, Inc., 1955.

CURTIS, THOMAS E., and WILMA W. BIDWELL, *Curriculum and Instruction for Emerging Adolescents*. Boston: Addison-Wesley Co., 1977.

DAUGHERTY, GREYSON, and JOHN B. WOODS, *Physical Education Programs* (2nd ed.). Philadelphia: W. B. Saunders Co., 1976.

FELKER, DONALD W., and RICHARD S. KAY, "Self-Concept, Sports Interest, Sports Participation and Body-Type of Seventh and Eighth Grade Boys," *Journal of Psychology*, 78 (April 1971), 223–28.

GALLAHUE, DAVID L., PETER H. WERNER, and GEORGE C. LUEDKE, *A Conceptual Approach to Moving and Learning*. New York: John Wiley & Sons, Inc., 1975.

GENTRY, ATRON, and others, *Urban Education: The Hope Factor*. Philadelphia: W. B. Saunders Co., 1972.

GLATTHORN, ALLAN A., *Alternatives in Education: Schools and Programs*. New York: Dodd, Mead and Co., 1975.

GOLUBCHICK, L., and B. PERSKY, *Urban Society and Educational Issues*. Dubuque: Kendall/Hunt Pub. Co., 1976.

HAAS, GLEN, *Curriculum Planning: A New Approach.* Boston: Allyn and Bacon, 1977.

KELLEY, E. JAMES, and CARL A. LINDSAY, "Knowledge Obsolescence in Physical Educators," *Research Quarterly,* 48 (May 1977), 463–68.

KENYON, GERALD S., "Six Scales for Assessing Attitude," *Research Quarterly,* 39 (October 1968), 566–74.

KNUTSON, MARJORIE C., "Sensitivity to Minority Groups," *Journal of Physical Education and Recreation,* 48 (May 1977), 24–26.

LAWSON, HAL, and JUDITH PLACEK, "Psycho-Physical Development," *Journal of Physical Education and Recreation,* 48 (May 1977), 26–27.

MCNEIL, JOHN D., *Designing Curriculum: Self Instruction and Modules.* Boston: Little Brown and Co., 1976.

MOHR, DOROTHY R., "Identifying the Body of Knowledge," *Journal of Health, Physical Education and Recreation,* 42 (January 1971), 23–24.

MOSSTON, MUSKA, *Teaching Physical Education: From Command to Discovery.* Columbus, Ohio: Charles E. Merrill Books, 1966.

NETCHER, JACK, *Management Model for Competency-Based Health, Physical Education and Recreation Programs.* St. Louis: C. V. Mosby Co., 1977.

NIXON, JOHN E., and ANNE E. JEWETT, *Physical Education Curriculum.* New York: Ronald Press, 1964.

PHENIX, PHILIP H., *Realms of Meaning,* New York: McGraw-Hill, 1964.

RIDINI, LEONARD M., and JOHN E. MADDEN, *Physical Education for Inner City Secondary Schools.* New York: Harper and Row, 1975.

ROBERTON, MARY ANN, "Developmental Implications For Games Teaching," *Journal of Physical Education and Recreation,* 48 (September 1977), 25–27.

RUBIN, LOUIS, *Curriculum Handbook.* Boston: Allyn and Bacon, 1977.

SCHURR, EVELYN L., *Movement Experiences for Children* (2nd ed.), chap. 3. Englewood Cliffs, N.J.: Prentice-Hall, Inc., 1975.

SIEDENTOP, DARYL, *Developing Teaching Skills in Physical Education,* chap. 4. Boston: Houghton Mifflin Co., 1976.

STRUNA, NANCY, "Teaching Movement—Our Common Goal," *Journal of Physical Education and Recreation,* 48 (June 1977), 12.

ZAIS, ROBERT, *Curriculum Principles and Foundations.* New York: Thomas Y. Crowell Co., 1976.

ZIATZ, DANIEL H., "How Do You Motivate Students to Learn?," *Journal of Physical Education and Recreation,* 48 (March 1977), 26.

Research

and

the Changing Curriculum

chapter five

The dogmas of the quiet past are inadequate to the stormy present.

ABRAHAM LINCOLN

. . . change is *necessary* because our society is changing, our students are changing, and our resources are changing.[1]

ALLEN A. GLATTHORN

Somewhere in the deep strata of human awareness breathes a voice "This is not good enough." At moments there comes to people a painful sense of the nearness of richer and broader human fulfillment—and yet a feeling that some relentless, invisible, but not quite insurmountable barrier bars the way to a vastly better life. The clearness and vividness of this sense of the better possibility varies in different minds. In many it never breaks through at all to full consciousness. But in a few minds it becomes a dominant mood. It has been called the voice of Prometheus.[2]

WILLIAM H. SHELDON

There is little question about the need for change and innovation. The only real question is, "How radical the change?"

The case for altering and developing better programs in physical education never rests completely on research and provable facts, or even on rational assessment. What gives program developers power is the Promethean voice

[1]Allen A. Glatthorn, "Continuing Change Is Needed", in Dwight W. Allen and Jefferey C. Hecht, *Controversies in Education* (Philadelphia: W. B. Saunders Co., 1974), p. 103.

[2]William H. Sheldon, *Prometheus Revisited* (Cambridge, Mass.: Schenkman Publishing Co., Inc., 1975), p. 7.

triggering the release of human energies in search of something better. It is this capacity that gives one the sense of destination and the energy to get started. This is an important concept because it deals with the degree of dedication demonstrated by individuals and groups *prior* to the initiation of any research.

Creative Thinking In Physical Education

In Shirley Jackson's eerie short story, "The Lottery," villagers hold a lottery each year to decide whom they will stone to death. One character asks why the villagers continue to carry out this inhuman ritual, but an elder quiets him with, "We have always had a lottery."

So it is with a variety of school practices, including physical education activities, gymnasium requirements, and teaching routines. We have indeed always had them, tolerated them, and we have not seriously questioned them. Under such circumstances there has been little creative thinking.

The process of creative renewal always implies an appeal from a tradition *as it is* to a tradition *as it ought to be.* The life force of a tradition is a kind of energy that seeks to improve the nature of things. The creative individual seeks a way to achieve a better curriculum without necessarily being tied to the sciences, practices, and popular views of the moment. He or she considers inventive approaches and introduces new ideas and brings to bear experimentation and research on existing programs.

Reforming the Curriculum

Frequently, curriculum reform meets resistance. Most people tend to resist change; the minority takes the leadership role in promoting innovative practices. Goodwin Watson comments that all of the forces which contribute to *stability* in personality and in social systems can be perceived as resisting change, and "from the standpoint of an ambitious and energetic change agent, these energies are seen as obstructions."[3] However, this is not all negative because, from a broader perspective, the tendencies of certain individuals to hold fast and preserve present activities and programs prevent too radical an approach to change—change that otherwise might threaten institutions and lifestyles unduly.

New curricula are being developed for physical education. Old ones are being revised and updated. Certainly, many changes have taken place since the early 1950s, but to speak of what has been happening as "revolutionary" would be overstating the case. The talk far exceeds the achievement.

[3]Goodwin Watson, "Resistance to Change", in Gerald Zaltman and others, eds., *Creating Social Change* (New York: Holt, Rinehart, and Winston, 1972), p. 610.

Curriculum reform in this country probably would have evolved much more slowly than it has if a prosperous middle class of ambitious men and women, following World War II, had not envisioned education as the means of achieving great expectations for their children. This group developed new communities and new schools and revitalized the old. The educators went along with the spirit of change and instituted school curriculum reform. In the meantime, the highly influential factors of population explosion, knowledge explosion, and the increased development of foundations devoted to education research caused every subject-matter specialist to do some soul-searching. These influences, coupled with the increasing interest of the federal government in the local schools expressed through the several programs of grants in aid, put the builders of courses of study on guard to make certain that the curricula they were planning were educationally sound and defensible.

Much of the exertion in reforming education programs, in physical education as in other areas, has been experimental. Short-term projects relative to teaching content and teaching techniques have been popular. New media have been developed; schedule changes have emerged to serve the gifted and the handicapped, and curricular sequences have been developed. Despite these changes, there is still a substantial shortage of teachers who are willing to try a new idea. Talk of curriculum reform or curriculum evaluation only irritates most people and makes them defend what they are now doing with added gusto. Unfortunately, many of these teachers feel that changes must be made all at once. This simply is not so. Pilot studies, which involve only a few students—perhaps one class of boys or girls—can be carried out in most schools without measurably uprooting classes. More pilot studies are needed so that ideas and innovations can be put to the test. After all, reform has to be based on some indication of need and practicality. This may emerge from local research or be derived from findings completed elsewhere. In any case, a rejuvenation of the experimental spirit is needed. It is as much a part of education and the school as it is a part of medicine and the hospital.

In discussing the curriculum reform movement, Goodlad suggests that it needs to become truly experimental in nature.[4] There must be vigorous trial and experimental comparisons of alternate ways of achieving goals. A word of caution, however, is necessary. Recently it has been popular to be associated with change—even to the extent of believing that change is automatically equated with the seldom-defined word "progress." Certainly there is merit in the expression "We must adapt to a changing world," but it frequently gives rise to a doctrine of over-enthusiastic adaptability which advances the asser-

[4]John I. Goodlad, "The Curriculum," *The Changing American School,* Sixty-fifth Yearbook of the National Society for the Study of Education, Part II (Chicago: The University of Chicago Press, 1966).

tion of "change for change's sake." When this happens the question is raised: Has the traditional or existing curriculum been fully evaluated in terms of its usefulness in modifying behavior, or is it being discarded simply because it is old and not subject to the seemingly new charm of "innovation" and "creativity"? Although local research is frequently given low priority, there should be some sincere effort to appraise existing programs before entirely new organizations for learning are explored. In short, it is good curriculum development practice to inquire and explore both the old and the new, with comments solicited from many sources.

Experimentation in Physical Education

There is a long history of research in physical education. For example, the *Research Quarterly* has been one of the most respected periodicals in the field of education since 1930 when it began as a scientific publication. Over the years, the national Research Council of the American Alliance for Health, Physical Education and Recreation has been extremely effective in promoting and appraising research in physical education and related areas. In fact, much of the scientific support for numerous practices and activities in the school program today stems from Research Council concern and action. This support includes curriculum items relating to evaluation materials, sports skills, physical fitness, and a large number of special program activities. Moreover, a thoroughly practical publication, *Completed Research in Health, Physical Education and Recreation,* is made available each year by the AAHPER.

FIGURE 5-1. Innovation in soccer. How long can you keep the ball up? (Courtesy, Hubert Vogelsinger)

The AAHPER has sponsored experimental clinics in which efforts to improve teaching methods, equipment, and curriculum content have been made. In many of these, the pupils are on hand to be a part of the experimentation, with considerable planning beforehand. In addition, under the sponsorship of the Division of Girls' and Women's Sports (now the National Association for Girls and Women in Sport), a wide variety of program suggestions, innovations, and research projects have been implemented for years. There is a continuing need to appraise program content to see if it is still a valid means of reaching objectives. This need for appraisal is even more acute at the local school level than it is nationally. National projects generally indicate directions, but the town or city board decides ultimately what to teach, how much, and why.

There is considerable value in reviewing physical education research. Although much of it will not relate directly to curriculum, it will, nevertheless, provide a number of implications for curriculum change. When individuals attempt to answer the old questions of what to include and how much to include in the program at any one level, they can hardly overlook research findings having to do with the peculiarities of the learner and the variety of methods to be used and time allotments to be given an activity. If at any time it can be demonstrated that shorter periods of exposure to an activity are adequate, there will be more time in the program to either increase the allotment of hours for another activity or add still another education experience to the program. Content, therefore, must always be subject to modification based on methods research as well as on an evaluation of pupil outcomes.

Consider, for the moment, the following research titles from recent issues of the *Research Quarterly.* How might each article influence curriculum reform?

"Guidelines for the Improvement of Physical Education in Selected Public Elementary Schools of New Jersey" (Koss, 36:282–88).
"Task Analysis: A Consideration for Teachers of Skills" (Robb, 43: 362–373).
"Effects of Physical Education on Fitness and Motor Development of Trainable Mentally Retarded Children" (Funk, 42: 30–34).
"Learning and Performance" (Dunham, Jr., 42: 334–336).
"Evaluation of General versus Specific Instruction of Badminton Skills to Women of Low Motor Ability" (Burdeshaw, 41: 472–477).
"Effects of Two Different Programs of Instruction on Motor Performance of Second Grade Students" (Masche, 41: 406–412).
"Practice Effects on Reaction Latency for Simple and Complex Movements" (Norrie, 38: 79–85).
"Comparative Effectiveness of Two Methods of Teaching Physical Education to Elementary School Girls" (Thaxton, 48: 420–427).
"Effect of Knowledge of Results on Attitude Formed Toward a Motor Learning Task" (McConnell, 48: 394–399).
"Decision Making in Elementary Children: Effects on Attitudes and Interaction" (Mancini, 47: 80–87).

At first glance, it might seem that only one or two of these research studies would have any bearing on program development. Yet, upon investigation, it will be discovered that each article makes a worthwhile contribution to the kind of knowledge the curriculum builder should possess. The most obvious research of practical value, perhaps, is the Koss article pertaining to program improvement in the elementary schools of New Jersey. The author developed criteria for appraising programs in philosophy, personnel, curriculum, activities beyond the in-class program, and time-space-equipment-facilities. After surveying the existing programs of 318 selected school districts, she located, visited, and further appraised the 13 districts that fulfilled the criteria most fully and the 13 districts that fulfilled the criteria least fully. The checklist data that Koss developed indicated that the community in which one lived certainly affected the scope and breadth of the physical education program. More specifically, better programs occurred where special teachers of physical education were employed. Of interest to the curriculum developer were findings that:

1. The program would consist mostly of games and relays if no special teacher were available. Programs that came closest to fulfilling the criteria were those that were conducted by the well-trained special teachers. Moreover, special teachers tended to be employed in those school systems in which the chief administrative officer "desired sequential instruction in skills and saw the socio-emotional objectives as concomitant learnings."

2. The financial and/or moral support from the board of education was a significant item.

3. The development of a local curriculum guide occurred more often in the communities with better programs (57.3 percent of the school districts had curriculum guides).

4. An extra-class program occurred more often for the older boys and girls in the school districts that fulfilled the criteria.

Let's look a little further at some of the other research articles. How does research pertaining to practice of and learning motor-skills affect curriculum planning? Do "closed" skills performed in a predictable and fixed environment require as much time to teach as "open" skills performed while one is moving through space? Will task analysis help provide an answer? Margaret Robb definitely believes in this research approach to better programing and teaching. Her article involving tasks pertains to a discussion of sensory and perceptual mechanisms and how the computer can be employed in physical education research.

The Norrie study shows that the amount of program modification needed in the learning of a single movement is small and should occur early in the practice, but for the more complex movements, there is a greater need to organize the experience and provide more practice. How might this information affect the structures of skills for learning?

Finally, the Funk study demonstrated that a planned program of physical education (30 minutes per day for 58 consecutive school days) can improve mentally retarded boys and girls in both fitness and motor development. Future research would answer the question of how much less exposure to physical activity they can take and still show growth in motor development. In this respect, the research article listed by Dunham treats the topic of learning variables which have an effect on performance. His findings, that there is a depressed motor performance attributed to the massing of practice, certainly would be germane to the study of frequency of exposure (time periods) to physical education classes.

It should be clear by now that any one of the research articles referred to above is of some value to the program builder. Moreover, every time a physical education researcher compares two or more programs for whatever variable there is an interest in, the findings are likely to be of concern to curriculum people. If, for instance, Mancini can show that young children given the opportunity to share in decision making show greater interaction with their teachers and show greater initiative, then more time should be given to decision making activities, even if it has to be taken from something more traditional.[5] Of course, care should be taken not to accept completely the results of one or two pieces of research. It is the responsibility of the physical education teacher to base the program on a wide review of research relative to growth and development, program emphasis, and methods, and a variety of behavioral studies.

Experimental studies have considerable value, especially when their results are applied to local situations. Anderson's Videotape Data Bank Project is a good example of a research study that influenced the physical education curriculum in about 83 elementary and senior high school physical education classes.[6] A substantial number of detailed videotapes of physical education classes were taken and used to analyze the effective differences among activities on a day-to-day basis. Feedback was obtained on the teacher's role in the students' selection of learning activities as well as on the percentage of time spent in everything from calisthenics to modern dance. Program adjustments came about as a result of these descriptive videotapes.

Another piece of involved curriculum research that serves as an example of something having an ultimate bearing on program reform was the Magnet Movement-Athletics Program (MMAP) of Boston University. It grew out of the desire to find a curriculum that would facilitate racial integration in the city of Boston. When the court ordered that racial integration must occur in

[5]Victor H. Mancini, John T. F. Cheffers, and Leonard D. Zaichkowsky, "Decision Making in Elementary Children: Effects on Attitudes and Interaction," *Research Quarterly*, 47 (March, 1976), 80–86.
[6]William G. Anderson, "Videotape Data Bank," *Journal of Physical Education and Recreation*, 46 (Setember 1975), 31–36.

the city schools, opposition to racial integration resulted in considerable violence.

The purpose of the MMAP was to determine the feasibility of achieving racial harmony among children through the medium of human movement. It was felt that, through the utilization of a divergent model of physical activity, racial integration could more easily be achieved. Consequently, an instructional model of activities was put together that began with the more common, more acceptable activities, such as the *popular community sports* of basketball, touch football, soccer, and baseball. Then the model was expanded to include the *lesser available activities*, such as wrestling, fencing, badminton, volleyball, skating, handball, and swimming. These activities were added to the program halfway through the school year. In the final week of the experimental program, the students went to a resident camp and participated in a living and learning situation involving *lifetime movement activities*, such as hiking, climbing, orienteering, and adventure-challenge movements.

The MMAP was a substantial undertaking. One group of students consisted of a mixture of 400 seventh and eighth graders from the city of Boston and the nearby affluent community of Brookline. In addition there was another comparable mixture of 500 students in grades 1 to 6 that was given the program. Much of the activity of this younger age group occurred in a pleasant atmosphere in which a movement-exploration approach to physical activity prevailed. In both groups there was ample opportunity for blacks, whites, Orientals, and Hispanics to mix, interact, and work and play together.

Attitudes toward physical activity were measured by the Cheffers and Mancini Attitude Scale and were found to be relatively high; the students liked the program. Their approval was an important finding, particularly in relation to the Boston children whose backgrounds of physical education experiences were slight because of inadequate city facilities. Self-concept was assessed using the Martinek-Zaichkowsky Self-Concept Scale, and there was a significant increase in the test scores.

Verbal and nonverbal behaviors and interactions between students and their teachers were measured using the Cheffers Adaptation of the Flanders Interaction Analysis System (CAFIAS). Meaningful student activity and interaction occurred as a wide number of activities that provided opportunity for close contact and personal communication were selected by the students.

Although integration cannot be hurried, the effect of this experimental research and program demonstrated some reduction in prejudices. Certainly the residential field experiences in an around-the-clock setting, coming at the end of the experiment, produced enough positive attitudinal changes and excitement to insure their potency as agents of change. Moreover, it was clearly demonstrated that a curriculum can indeed be fashioned to meet the social-cultural and physical needs of children, and promote normal relationships between ethnic groups.

Program Improvement Through Administrative Standards

A program is improved when the findings of research are evaluated and used to bring about changes. These changes occur in such specific areas as content, sequences, scheduling, time allotment, methods, supplies and equipment, facilities, personnel, and even administrative leadership. In a sense, nothing is sacred; every factor that may relate to the program is considered.

When all these factors are carefully weighed and are organized into a list of administrative standards, there is an opportunity to evaluate periodically the total physical education program. A number of acceptable standards have been employed in local studies for a number of years. Such evaluation instruments as the *LaPorte Health and Physical Education Scorecard*, the *Indiana Physical Education Scorecard*, the *Ohio Secondary Schools Evaluative Criteria for Physical Education*, the *AAHPER School-Community Fitness Inventory*, the State of Wisconsin *Standards for Physical Education, Grades One through Twelve*, the Texas Education Agency *Standards for Secondary Schools–Bulletin 625*, the State of California *Criteria for Evaluating the Physical Education Program*, the State of Missouri *Physical Education Program Review Scorecard for Secondary Schools*, and the very complete Evaluative Criteria, National Study of Secondary School Evaluation (NSSSE) *Physical Education Program* are referred to in some detail in Chapter 12.

The employment of administrative standards in a school to appraise the program is fine if a similar effort is made to consider changes following the review. At this point there should be an opportunity to consider such significant items as (1) translating research findings into gymnasium, studio, pool, and playfield learning activities, (2) curricular questions relating to required and/or elective courses, (3) modification of program content and/or course objectives, (4) the place of the multimedia approach in promoting greater individualized instructional opportunities, (5) future individual and group research, and (6) student evaluation of programs. In connection with the last item, the research shows that most students like physical education and agree that content and instruction can be improved. With them this is not a "low-priority program." In an Illinois survey, 80 percent of the students wanted physical education. Unfortunately, the public is not so well-convinced; there is a need to interpret the field and make known the fruits of research.

Institutions Influence Change

A growing number of organizations, institutions, and agencies are quite instrumental in influencing educational research and bringing about program modifications in education. Many of these are especially interested in physical education. Below are the names of some of the organizations that have always supported physical education and are interested in its overall achievements.

National Level

A great many national agencies have some interest in the advancement of optimum programs of physical education. A few of the better known groups are as follows:

** Amateur Athletic Union
 * American Academy of Physical Education
 * American Alliance for Health, Physical Education and Recreation (NEA)
 † American Association of School Administrators (NEA)
 † American Camping Association
** American College of Sports Medicine
 † American Heart Association
** American Medical Association
 † American Public Health Association
 † American Red Cross
 † American School Health Association
 † Association for Supervision and Curriculum Development (NEA)
 * Athletic and Recreation Federation of College Women
** Athletic Institute
** Boys Clubs of America
** Boy Scouts of America
 * Bureau of Health Education, United States Public Health Service
 † Department of Classroom Teachers (NEA)
** Girl Scouts of America
 * Lifetime Sports Foundation
** National Association of Secondary School Principals
 † National Education Association
** National Federation of State High School Athletic Associations
 † National Parent-Teachers Association
** National Recreation and Park Association
 † National Safety Council
** President's Council on Physical Fitness
 * Society of State Directors of Health, Physical Education and Recreation
 † United States Office of Education
 † United States Public Health Service
 * Young Men's Christian Association
 * Young Men's Hebrew Association
 * Young Women's Christian Association

*These are organizations *primarily* concerned with the promotion of all the physical education objectives. They exist as professional units dedicated to education through physical activity.

**These are organizations concerned with some part of the total physical education program. Some are interested in school athletics; others with physical exercise or recreation.

†These groups relate very often to physical education, and frequently call attention to the place of physical education in the modern school and in the community as a whole.

In addition to the major organizations interested in promoting physical education, there are a number of small but energetic national groups whose influence is highly measurable. A nationwide organization that is becoming very effective in promoting innovation and change is the Lifetime Sports Foundation. Supported by private industry, this group seeks to gain support for programs that offer opportunities to learn individual sport skills. It sets up training centers, clinics, and regional workshops and works closely with the leadership from state departments of education, coaches' associations, state recreation groups, and the National Association for Girls and Women in Sports (NAGWS) and the National Association of Sport and Physical Education of AAHPER. The Foundation has an ongoing program to support research exploring the social-psychological values of physical activity and the nature and extent of lifetime sports such as golf, bowling, badminton, and tennis.

The effect that national groups have on school programs is frequently underestimated. For example, physical education gets a real boost several times a year from such organizations as the American Heart Association and the American Medical Association. Other groups, such as the National Association of Secondary School Principals, have had much to do with the proper control of high school athletics. Then, of course, there are a number of essentially health oriented groups that indirectly advance the cause of physical education by encouraging all health-building activities in the schools.

The Federal Government

Perhaps one of the greatest boons to local research and experimentation in recent years has been the availability of federal funds. Federal aid to education has permitted hundreds of communities to try new ways of doing things. There have been numerous instances in which whole school programs have been reorganized on the basis of research findings.

For example, with money obtained under Title III of the Elementary and Secondary School Act, Topeka, Kansas made a number of significant improvements in physical education for elementary school children. Their objective was to compare techniques for educating children in health, physical education, and recreation. Pilot demonstration centers were set up in all elementary schools. The results of the program were impressive and far-reaching. There was an unusual improvement in individual physical fitness. Classroom teachers, parents, and administrators were enthusiastic about the program. A few of the accomplishments presented to the Topeka school board were as follows:

1. A total of 15 additional physical education teachers were employed to give direct instruction to over 18,000 children in 44 schools.
2. Some 570 classroom teachers were assisted by the specialists in planning and conducting physical education activities.

3. A total of 22 Saturday instructional sessions were provided, serving about 50 children at each session.
4. Almost 500 children were given physical education instruction at 7 summer school locations.
5. A course of study for physical education was produced for use by all elementary school teachers.
6. Health textbooks were purchased and instruction started for all fifth and sixth grade pupils.
7. Developmental equipment that could be used for years to come was purchased for outdoor use.
8. All specialists and coordinators were used the following year to put into effect the new course of study emphasizing team teaching.

Although this illustration reads somewhat like a fairy story as it proceeds from the pilot study stage to the implementation of a new course of study, the program is, nevertheless, entirely possible in almost any American school system today. Federal money helps measurably, but even without this financial aid, some experimentation and innovation is possible, especially when there is a strong desire to create the most creditable program of physical education.

State Level

There are several other influences for program modification in every state. One of these is the state department of education with its state director or supervisor of physical education. Most small states have one person in this position, while the larger states have several individuals assigned to assist local communities. New York, for example, has a very effective Bureau of Physical Education with several specialists for elementary programs, secondary programs, and interscholastic athletics.

State specialists cannot possibly make very many local contacts in a year. Their function, therefore, is to plan and promote group professional activities, such as conferences, clinics, workshops, and institutes. The state person is most effective when helping local physical education teachers improve their own programs.

Professional Periodicals

Over the years, the number of periodicals dealing with physical education has grown. Some of the publications pertaining to curriculum research and innovation are:

American Journal of Physical Medicine   *Camping*
American Physical Therapy Journal   *Canadian Journal of History of Sport and*
American Journal of Public Health   *Physical Education*
Athletic Journal   *Child Development*

Childhood Education	*Medical World News*
Children	*Medicine and Science in Sports*
Ergonomics	*Perceptual and Motor Skills*
Family Health/Today's Health	*The Physical Educator*
Grade Teacher	*The Physical Fitness Newsletter*
Health Education	(University of Oregon)
The Instructor	*Physiological Reviews*
Journal of Applied Physiology	*Quest*
Journal of the American Medical	*Recreation*
Association	*Research Quarterly*
Journal of Educational Sociology	*Safety Education*
Journal of Leisure Research	*Scholastic Coach*
Journal of Philosophy of Sport	*School Safety*
Journal of Physical Education and	*Science*
Recreation	*Sports Illustrated*
Journal of School Health	*Today's Education*
Journal of Sport History	

By way of summary it is pertinent to observe that ideas come from many sources. One simply has to be flexible and ready to use the fruits of discussion and research.

The Athletic Institute

In 1934 the Athletic Institute was created as a nonprofit organization to advance physical education, athletics, and recreation. This was to be accomplished by instilling a greater awareness into all levels of society through educational and public relations programs. Today the Institute is the largest producer of sports instructional films in the world as it continues to motivate both young and old to take part in some form of physical activity on a daily basis. Over the years, the Florida-based organization has assisted in the construction of new sports and recreational facilities and in the development of educational programs, guides, and other curriculum materials for the physical educator.[7] The publications are reliable, attractive, and superb in a number of ways.

QUESTIONS FOR DISCUSSION

1. Should every teacher be prepared to carry on local research? Is it possible that some teachers are better equipped to be consumers of research findings than to be producers?

[7]The Athletic Institute, 200 Castlewood Drive, North Palm Beach, Fla. 33408.

2. After reviewing several *Research Quarterly* articles, how do you feel about their use in providing suitable material with which to make changes in the physical education program?

3. There appears to be a shortage of research pertaining specifically to physical education program modification and the corresponding effect it has on pupils. Do you think that this is a true statement? False? Give your reasons.

4. Look up the meaning of the word "reform." Just how broad in scope is it? What does it really mean when applied to educational practice?

5. Those who advocate more research in developmental kinesiology theorize that changes in movement behavior occur throughout life, and not just in childhood. They feel that research into all kinds of skills—such as ball-throwing and ball-kicking—will provide information of value to curriculum specialists who must decide when certain skills are best taught. How do you feel about this?

6. Illustrate a situation in which curriculum revision can be brought about without research.

7. How would you proceed to measure the effect of a program of physical education on the dropout rate for secondary school boys and girls?

8. Illustrate how records of student progress can be of immediate use in influencing program change. Use some specific examples to illustrate your comments.

SUGGESTED ACTIVITIES

1. A number of people have said that teachers should read scholarly documents; but it is a fact that large numbers of instructors do not read the *Research Quarterly*. Moreover, if they did, many would not understand the contents. Talk with several people who have been teaching physical education five years or more. How do they feel about the *Research Quarterly* and the reading of research in general? Compare your findings with others.

2. This chapter indicated that Mary Lou Norrie completed some research that showed that more complex skills require more organization and more practice time. See if you can locate some other research articles that tend to support this viewpoint. After listing your sources and rendering some comments, see if you can suggest several ways in which learning experiences can be organized for the more complex physical education movements.

3. Interview five teachers of physical education to determine what they think constitutes the most useful program innovation in recent years.

4. Review the latest edition of *Completed Research in Health, Physical Education and Recreation,* published by the Research Council of AAHPER. Select three completed research projects that appear to be of real value in shaping a secondary school physical education curriculum for girls.
5. Look up the meaning of the word "innovation." What is its derivation? Try applying the word to a certain grade level of physical education. See if you can think of two or three ideas, procedures, or practices that, to your knowledge, have never been tried before. For example, a circuit training routine was tried with second grade children in Quincy, Massachusetts, with considerable success. It had never been attempted before.

SELECTED REFERENCES

CARLSON, E. ROBERT, "Status of Research on Children with Perceptual-Motor Dysfunction," *Journal of Health, Physical Education and Recreation,* 43 (April 1972), 57–59.

CLARK, H. HARRISON, and DAVID H. CLARKE, *Research Process in Physical Education, Recreation and Health.* Englewood Cliffs, N.J.: Prentice-Hall, Inc., 1970.

EVANS, VIRDEN, "The Humanistic Approach to Research," *Journal of Physical Education and Recreation,* 48 (March 1977), 22.

KROLL, WALTER, *Perspectives in Physical Education,* New York: Academic Press, 1971.

LOCKE, LAWRENCE F., *Research in Physical Education,* New York: Teachers College Press, 1969.

LOCKE, LAWRENCE F., "Implications for Physical Education," *Research Quarterly,* 43 (October 1972), 374–86.

MANCINI, VICTOR H., JOHN T. F. CHEFFERS, and LEONARD D. ZAICHKOWSKY, "Decision Making in Elementary Children: Effects on Attitudes and Interaction," *Research Quarterly,* 47 (March 1976), 80–86.

MORIARTY, DICK, and ANN MARIE GUILMETTE, "Change Agent Research," *Journal of Physical Education and Recreation,* 48 (February 1977), 42.

MOSSTON, MUSKA, *Teaching Physical Education,* Columbus, Ohio: Charles E. Merrill Books, 1966.

NEWCOMBE, JUDITH P., "Urban Involvement," *Journal of Physical Education and Recreation,* 48 (Nov/Dec 1977), 24–26.

NIXON, JOHN E., and LAWRENCE F. LOCKE, *Research on Teaching,* ed. R.M.W. Travers, Chicago: AERA and Rand McNally, 1973.

TERRY, JAMES W., "Changing Habits by Changing Attitudes," *Journal of Physical Education and Recreation,* 48 (September 1977), 13.

THAXTON, ANNA B., and others, "Comparative Effectiveness of Two Methods of Teaching Physical Education to Elementary School Girls," *Research Quarterly*, 48 (May 1977), 420–27.

WILBERG, ROBERT B., "A Suggested Direction for the Study of Motor Performance by Physical Educators," *Research Quarterly*, 43 (October 1972), 387–90.

ZALTMAN, GERALD, and others, *Creating Social Change*. New York: Holt, Rinehart and Winston, 1972.

ZEIGLER, EARL F., and MARCIA J. SPAETH, *Administrative Theory and Practice in Physical Education and Athletics*, chap. 1. Englewood Cliffs, N.J.: Prentice-Hall, Inc., 1975.

ZINGALE, DON, "Theory into Practice: An Inservice Approach," *Journal of Physical Education and Recreation*, 46 (November/December 1975), 31–35.

Organization
for
Instruction

chapter six

> Teachers are not good because they develop good-looking units or nicely
> detailed lesson plans. They are good when those units and lesson plans
> pay off in better instruction.[1]
>
> DARYL SIEDENTOP

Instructional planning and the organization of instructional materials
and activities cannot be viewed in isolation. Organizational efforts are a waste
of time unless they result in better teaching—the kind of teaching that
enlightens students with an understanding that learnings pertaining to human
movement are unique, yet have a connection with most other learnings. In
the end one must plan for an "orchestration of many powers," in which
curriculum content, teaching skills, and evaluation practices are harmoni-
ously arranged.

As seen by Siedentop, the problems inherent in organizing instruction
were shared to some extent by early philosopher-educators. Vergerio (1370–
1444), an ardent humanist, urged participation in games to sharpen the mind
and body, but was presented with a largely unresolved dilemma as to how to
organize youth for instruction.[2] By the eighteenth century the influence of the
old-land views and classical education was felt in America. Although Benjamin
Franklin and Thomas Jefferson helped measurably, the old difficulty of or-

---

[1]Daryl Siedentop, *Developing Teaching Skills in Physical Education* (Boston:
Houghton Mifflin Co., 1976), p. 163.

[2]Moreover, wrote Vergerio, one should be organized for recreation, for man cannot
devote his energies all day long to one particular task because "the string overstretched
will end up breaking." Translated from the Italian by Carmelo Bazzano in *The
Contributions of the Italian Renaissance to Physical Education* (Unpublished doctoral
dissertation, Boston University, Boston, Massachusetts, 1973).

ganizing and implementing one's educational philosophy prevailed. Jefferson called for a wider role for physical activity in the organizing phase of the University of Virginia, and he planned accordingly. In later years, the concern for the unity of the human personality moved Alfred North Whitehead to write about the learning experiences of the *whole* organism, and to put forth the admonition that the planning for the success of one educational effort ultimately relates to *other* educational influences. This is illustrated in physical education time and time again when a reasonably sound activity is skillfully taught but fails to "carry-over" in any appreciable way. A game of volleyball, a folk dance, or a sport like archery may have more chance of being used throughout a lifetime if teachers give some attention to historical-intellectual influences and the immediate recreational opportunities afforded locally, as well as to instructional sequences and time allotments.

Determining Scope and Sequence

The word "scope" refers to the breadth of the physical education curriculum—*what* should be taught at all grade levels. As already mentioned; the scope of a program will vary according to changes in the society and the persistent and identifiable needs and desires of boys and girls of all ages. Sequence, on the other hand, refers to the *when* of the curriculum—the grade placement of the physical education experiences. It defines the curriculum vertically, whereas scope defines it horizontally. (See a limited example in Figure 6–1.)

In determining scope, it is a good practice first to view the *total* physical education program, K–12, for both boys and girls. This view tends to put content in perspective and affords curriculum planners a chance to consider a

		ARCHERY	BADMINTON	BOWLING	GOLF	SWIMMING	TENNIS	WRESTLING
	GRADE 9							
	Advanced Skills							
	Intermediate Skills							
	Beginning Skills and Knowledges							
	GRADE 8							
	Advanced Skills							
	Intermediate Skills							
	Beginning Skills and Knowledges							
	GRADE 7							
	Advanced Skills							
	Intermediate Skills							
	Beginning Skills and Knowledges							
	ACTIVITIES	ARCHERY	BADMINTON	BOWLING	GOLF	SWIMMING	TENNIS	WRESTLING

SEQUENCE OF SKILLS AND KNOWLEDGE

SCOPE OF INDIVIDUAL SPORTS

FIGURE 6-1. Scope and sequence—vertical-horizontal organization.

broad and complete program of experiences in the life of the schoolchild. Once the spectrum of activities is clearly visible, it is proper to break it down into categories of content appropriate for organizational divisions such as primary grades, intermediate grades, junior high, and senior high. Content at these various levels will be discussed more thoroughly in Chapters 8, 9, 10, 11, and 12.

In the past, judgments as to the scope of physical education were frequently subjective and often arbitrary, engineered by influential individuals or by small selected groups. In some towns and small cities, the director of physical education may have set down the program all by himself or herself. A more recent development has been to derive content judgments from wide discussion within larger and more representative groups. The better school systems are steadily moving beyond a static course of study to a wealth of new and different physical activities that will contribute to the needs of a variety of students. In such cases, therefore, the scope of the program must be reviewed periodically in order to see what has been omitted that should be taught, or what should be omitted for something new. One way to determine scope is to lay out the content in broad categories (see Figure 6–2).

Determination of Sequence

The content of the physical education curriculum needs to be organized so that boys and girls will be able to progress toward an increasingly mature utilization of their knowledge and competency. This kind of development calls for a careful presentation of activities in sequence. Moreover, the attention must be directed to a *graduated sequence* of ideas and skills. There are too many instances today of repetitious programs, in which the same activities and the same skills are taught *ad nauseum* several years in a row. There is no graduated program of instruction in which certain activities can eventually be learned well enough to be considered adequate and the time gained can be given to the mastery of new activities. In mathematics, the student studies algebra, completes it, and goes on to geometry. But in physical education, students are too often instructed in volleyball every year from grade 4 to grade 12, with little change each year.

The chief problem facing most physical education teachers is not what to teach, but how far they should go at specific grade levels. One way to get around this dilemma is to think less in terms of stereotyped grade levels and more in terms of *skill levels*. For example, in a middle school or junior high school, it would be more efficient to build a sequence of skills and knowledge in an activity through at least three levels of expectation:

beginning level: graduated presentation of fundamental skills and knowledge
intermediate level: graduated presentation of more complicated and detailed skills and knowledge
advanced level: graduated presentation leading to development of advanced skills, understanding, and appreciation

NEEDHAM HIGH SCHOOLS
Grades: Kindergarten through Twelve
Year's Program

Grade	K	1	2	3	4	5	6	Boys 7	Boys 8	Boys 9	Boys 10	Girls 7	Girls 8	Girls 9	Girls 10	B&G 11	B&G 12
Movement Experiences:	40%	35%	35%	20%													
Ball skills	x	x	x	x													
Locomotor skills	x	x	x	x													
Movement exploration	x	x	x	x													
Body mechanics	x	x	x	x													
Development Activities:					15%	15%	15%	8%	8%	8%	8%	10%	10%	10%	5%		
Fitness testing					x	x	x	x	x	x	x	x	x	x	x		
Conditioning					x	x	x	x	x	x	x	x	x	x			
Body mechanics					x	x	x	x	x	x	x	x	x	x	x		
Movement experiences					x	x	x	x				x	x	x			
Weight training								x	x	x	x						
Rhythms:	25%	20%	20%	20%	10%	10%	10%	7%	7%	7%	7%	10%	10%	10%	7%		
Locomotor (simple dances)	x	x	x	x	x	x	x										
Rope activities	x	x	x	x	x	x	x										
Marching					x	x	x										
Square dancing				x	x	x	x	x	x	x	x	x	x	x	x		
Folk dancing				x	x	x	x	x	x	x	x	x	x	x	x		
Modern dancing					x	x	x					x	x	x	x		
Rhythm gymnastics												x	x	x	x		
Low Organization & Optional:	15%	15%	15%	15%	15%	15%	15%	10%	10%	10%	10%	13%	13%	13%	10%		
Recreational games & relays	x	x	x	x	x	x	x	x	x	x	x	x	x	x	x		
Running, tag, circle games	x	x	x	x	x	x	x	x				x					
Story plays & games	x	x	x	x	x												
Novelty activities	x	x	x	x	x	x	x	x	x	x	x	x	x	x	x		

ELECTIVE PROGRAM (Grades 11–12, B & G)

160

FIGURE 6-2. A broad content layout for physical education. (Courtesy, Needham Public Schools, Needham, Massachusetts)

ELECTIVE PROGRAM

	15%	15%	15%	15%	15%	15%	15%	15%	15%	15%	15%	17%	20%	20%	20%	20%	20%
Gymnastics & Tumbling:																	
Self-testing activities	x	x	x	x	x	x	x	x	x	x	x	x	x	x	x	x	x
Balances on floor	x	x	x	x	x	x	x	x	x	x	x	x	x	x	x	x	x
Tumbling	x	x	x	x	x	x	x	x	x	x	x	x	x	x	x	x	x
Climbing	x	x	x	x	x	x	x	x	x	x	x	x	x	x	x	x	x
Balance beam	x	x	x	x	x						x	x	x	x	x	x	x
Side horse			x	x	x						x	x	x	x	x	x	x
Rings											x	x	x	x	x	x	x
Uneven parallel bars											x	x	x	x	x	x	x
Parallel bars											x	x	x	x	x	x	x
Trampoline											x	x					
Horizontal bar											x	x	x	x	x	x	x
Horizontal ladder											x	x	x	x	x	x	x
Long box													x	x	x	x	x
Buck													x				

	45%	45%	45%	45%	50%	50%	50%	50%	50%	50%	50%	50%	37%	37%	37%	37%	50%
Sport Skills & Games																	
Basketball	x	x	x	x	x	x					x		x	x	x	x	x
Field hockey	x					x					x	x		x			x
Football	x	x	x	x	x	x			x								
Lacrosse												x					
Soccer	x	x	x	x												x	x
Softball	x	x	x	x												x	x
Speedball												x					x
Track & field	x	x	x	x	x	x	x	x	x		x	x					
Volleyball	x	x	x	x	x	x	x	x	x	x			x	x	x	x	x
Wrestling					x	x	x	x	x			x					

	10%	10%	10%	10%	10%	10%	10%	10%	10%	10%	10%	8%	10%	10%	10%	10%	8%
Class Organization																	
Opening & closing school year	x	x	x	x	x	x	x	x	x	x	x	x	x	x	x	x	x

161

TABLE 6-1. *Example:* Tumbling (Middle School-Junior High School)[3]

Level 1	Level 2	Level 3
1. Forward roll from stand	1. Backward roll with hands on ankles	1. Forward roll, dive for distances from stand
2. Backward roll from stand	2. Round-off	2. Back extension roll
3. Cartwheel from run	3. Upstart skip with hands on thighs	3. Back handspring
4. Frog handstand tip-up	4. Walk on hands	4. Front flip somersault
5. Headstand	5. Forearm balance	5. Headstand from backward roll
6. Handstand at wall	6. Headstand press-up	6. Handstand from backward roll
7. Free-exercise routine	7. Free-exercise routine	7. Free-exercise routine

By grouping students homogeneously for instruction, it is possible to concentrate the teaching at the appropriate level of individual ability. Why should a good tumbler repeat forward rolls just because it is the lesson of the day for everyone in class? Certainly, if there is more than one immediate teaching station, and either a second teacher or student leader, the boy or girl who is a skilled tumbler can begin to learn the more advanced skills. He or she may be in the advanced group for tumbling, but in the beginning group for soccer and perhaps in the intermediate group for still another activity.

One of the advantages of carefully planned skill sequences is also that they relate to a sequence in the development of ideas. Those who know the most about learning say—and they seem to agree—that a really important idea or concept does not come all at once to a person; rather it comes as a result of a long series of experiences in which aspects of the idea finally enable the individual to grasp the total idea conceptually. In health education, wanting to be healthy and understanding what it takes to be so give rise to such an idea. In physical education, knowing how to keep physically fit and wanting to do so throughout a lifetime also give rise to such an idea.

It is very easy to fall into the error of putting too much emphasis on any one curriculum factor. Failure to provide for proper graduated learnings in physical education has probably been the biggest stumbling block to quality programs. If curriculum developers and reformers will take time to develop a sequence of learning activities for all of the group, individual, and dual games, sports, and other physical education activities, the ultimate consequences might well be nothing less than spectacular. Figure 6–3 presents an example

[3]Note progression here in each level, and between levels. From Carl E. Willgoose, and James A. Wylie, Arthur G. Miller, *Your Physical Education* (New York: McGraw-Hill), p. 143.

of an ongoing activity that has been structured throughout the grades in which it will be taught.

Sequences are just as important for elementary activities as they are for the more complicated routines associated with learning to wrestle or performing in modern dance. Table 6–2 illustrates the simple sequences from the easy to the more difficult that can be organized for the fundamental locomotor skill of walking.

TABLE 6-2. Handling the Body in Relation to Locomotor Skills[4]

	K-3	
Individual Activities		*Evaluation*

WALKING
1. Develop walk   Does the pupil know the difference between an erect and stiff walk? Does he understand the effect of badly stacked blocks on balance? Do his arms swing naturally with alternation of legs?

2. Adapt it
  a. in relation to sound   Does the pupil recognize that walking is done to an even beat? Can he recognize the even beat in his foot patter, then adapt it to clapping and the use of percussive instruments? Can he identify the even beat with the use of records and walk correctly to that rhythm?

  b. in relation to tempo   Can the pupil express himself by doing different-sounding walks? Can the children beat out even rhythm showing a variation in tempo?

  c. in relation to movement   Can the pupils walk with the beat using variations in speed? Can they walk in different directions to the rhythm of the music without bumping others?

  d. in relation to others   Can each pupil adapt his step pattern to that of a partner?

  e. in relation to music   Can the pupils walk in groups and adjust their steps to those of others? Can they walk as a group with various types of accompaniment? Can they recognize the phrasing of the music and walk only to certain phrases?

  f. in relation to space   Do the pupils know that the stroll involves little upper body movement? Do they know that the rapid walk makes use of considerable leg and arm action?

[4]Adapted from *A Guide to Curriculum Building in Physical Education, Elementary Schools*, Curriculum Bulletin No. 28 (Madison, Wisc.: Wisconsin Department of Public Instruction). The "teacher-help" activities, which are well presented, are not included here.

TABLE 6-2. *Continued.*

Individual Activities	K-3	*Evaluation*
		Do they know that in a racing walk the entire body is in action?
g. in relation to moods		Can the pupils express different moods through the way they walk?
h. in relation to imaginative ideas		Can the pupils show originality in walking under various conditions?
3. Games with emphasis on walking		
a. Traffic Game		Can the pupils come to a quick stop?
b. Magic Carpet		Can they walk to the rhythm of the music?
		Can they move in a line, holding hands?
c. Posture Tag		Do they move slowly and stand tall?
4. Dances and singing games with emphasis on walking		
a. London Bridge		Can the pupils walk in time with the music while playing the singing game?
b. Oats, Peas, Beans and Barley		Can they sing and walk to the rhythm of the music simultaneously?
c. Circassian Circle		Can they fit the dance steps into the phrasing of the music?
5. Relays with emphasis on walking		

The Cycle Plan

There is a real tendency in physical education, especially at the secondary level, to teach the same major activities each year. Is there merit in a cycle plan in which certain games, dances, fitness routines, and other activities are omitted or simply reviewed every other year?

Sometimes repetition is good, particularly if it acquaints the pupil with something that he or she may have missed the year before. It may be more effective, however, in terms of both pupil motivation and ultimate retention, to teach certain seasonal activities every other year. When the total physical education program has been carefully planned, there may be real value in such a cycle plan. For example, instead of trying to teach a few lessons in several fall, winter, and spring sports each year, effort would be concentrated on only half of these one year and on the other half the following year. This has practical application in climates in which an outdoor season is quite short.

In New England, for instance, there are frequently less than two good outdoor months in the spring. It is pretty easy to spread the program quite thin by attempting to cover baseball, softball, tennis, and the numerous track and field events in such a short season. It might be far more beneficial to

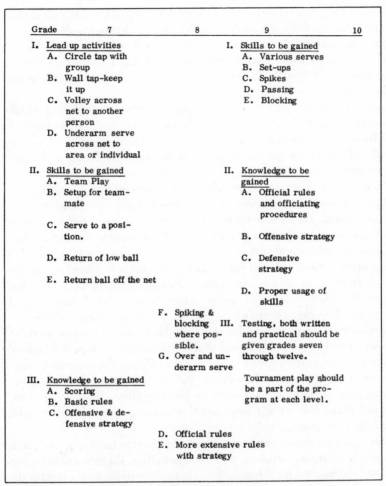

Grade	7	8	9	10

I. Lead up activities
  A. Circle tap with group
  B. Wall tap-keep it up
  C. Volley across net to another person
  D. Underarm serve across net to area or individual

II. Skills to be gained
  A. Team Play
  B. Setup for team-mate
  C. Serve to a position.
  D. Return of low ball
  E. Return ball off the net

III. Knowledge to be gained
  A. Scoring
  B. Basic rules
  C. Offensive & defensive strategy

  F. Spiking & blocking where possible.
  G. Over and underarm serve

  D. Official rules
  E. More extensive rules with strategy

I. Skills to be gained
  A. Various serves
  B. Set-ups
  C. Spikes
  D. Passing
  E. Blocking

II. Knowledge to be gained
  A. Official rules and officiating procedures
  B. Offensive strategy
  C. Defensive strategy
  D. Proper usage of skills

III. Testing, both written and practical should be given grades seven through twelve.

Tournament play should be a part of the program at each level.

FIGURE 6-3. Skill and knowledge advancement in one activity.

concentrate on these major activities every other year. This kind of arrangement means that more time can be assigned to each activity.

Required and Elective Programs

Vergerio's concern for a liberal education which "develops those highest gifts of body and of mind" is popular today. The trend is to encourage individual choice in the selection of curricula. Also, research supports the concept that students seldom continue their involvement in any activity that does not capture their interest.

For a very long while, it has been considered good practice to spell out every detail of the physical education program, kindergarten through senior high school. This has helped insure a breadth of experiences for all students. Accompanying this kind of programing has been a certain lack of flexibility. In fact, the "we-know-what's-good-for-you" approach has frequently reduced the motivation to participate of a number of students, particularly of those not especially fond of large-muscle activity.

Concerning the formative years, from kindergarten through junior high school, a strong case can be made for a required physical education curriculum that will facilitate the optimum development and understanding of a wide variety of individual, couple, and group skills, such as dance and other movement experiences, games and sports, and physical conditioning. Although this is a fixed program, there can be some room for choices, perhaps at the ninth-grade level in the form of required-electives. The student may elect to concentrate on an activity in which he or she has a fair amount of interest. Generally, it will be an activity in which the student has already had some instruction and would like more. It should not be something that will preclude learning about other physical activities. This is the chief reason for delaying electives until the later secondary years in which the individual has experimented with a number of motor activities and then begins to feel strongly about choosing activities from a wide selection made available.

Elective programs are popular today in the junior and senior years of high school. A Michigan study found that these programs appeal to school board members because they can be carried on without the expensive addition of new field houses, pools, courts, and so forth, since "off-campus" facilities are frequently employed—private bowling alleys, ice-skating rinks, ski areas, horseback riding trails, even motel swimming pools—for instruction in elective lifetime sports.

Interestingly, when secondary schools abandon the rigid required physical education and permit students to choose activities, there is a new understanding and enthusiasm for the program. This information should bolster the spirits of teachers who anticipate a falloff in enrollment when an all-voluntary physical education arrangement goes into effect in their school system. Although the voluntary program is generally undesirable (because, of those who need it, many decide not to take it), it can be made attractive to a large number of boys and girls; and the chief reason is that it ties in with the "open-school" concept and the freedom of pupils to make their own choices and decisions.

Examples:

A. *Stevenson High School*, Livonia, Michigan[5]
    The school year is divided into two semesters, with three six-week marking periods in each. During each marking period three different activities are covered. The pupils are ability-grouped in the first semester for swimming activi-

[5]See Lois J. McDonald, "An Elective Curriculum," *Journal of Health, Physical Education and Recreation,* 42 (September 1971), 28–29.

ties. During the second semester they are ability-grouped for gymnastics. A sport skill is taught in a one-week introductory unit. A second activity is presented the second week. During the remaining weeks of the marking period, the students may *decide each day* whether they will participate in sport one or sport two. Also, they may specialize in one sport the whole time. This program is an example of minimum flexibility—a beginning toward a wiser elective offering.

B. *Lexington High School*, Lexington, Mass.

The school year is divided into four quarters consisting of approximately nine weeks each. Students elect two different activities each quarter. They are not allowed to repeat activities over a single school year unless the nature of the activity requires repetition. Data-processing assignment of classes allows for sixteen periods strictly for electives in grades 11–12 combined. Class size consists of 180–200 students per class—eight teachers are assigned, thus permitting a student-teacher ratio of 25–1 maximum. Students may choose from the following in Table 6-3:

TABLE 6-3

Fall *(1st Quarter)*	*Winter* *(2nd–3rd Quarter)*	*Spring* *(4th Quarter)*
Coed	*Coed*	*Coed*
Archery I	Judo	Archery I
Archery II	Volleyball	Archery II
Tennis I	Table Tennis	Tennis I
Tennis II	Weight Training	Tennis II
Golf I	Dance	Golf I
Golf II	Fencing	Golf II
Horseshoes		Badminton
Badminton	*Boys*	Fishing
	Volleyball	Fly Casting
Boys	Basketball	
Flag Football	Floor Hockey	*Boys*
Soccer	Apparatus	Lacrosse
	Weight Training	Track & Field
Girls	Active Games	Softball
Soccer	Wrestling	
Field Hockey	Table Tennis	*Girls*
Speedball		Softball
	Girls	Track & Field
	Modern Dance	
	Self-Defense	
	Basketball	
	Volleyball	
	Tumbling	
	Modern Jazz	
	Movement For Improveme	
	Apparatus	
	Table Tennis	
	Floor Exercises	

C. *Regina High School*, Minneapolis, Minnesota

The regular physical education program was expanded to include several on-campus electives and seven others—horseback riding, golf, bowling, roller skating, swimming, skating, and skiing—which use recreational facilities throughout the Minneapolis area. To formulate a schedule, a preliminary list of electives was given to the students, with seasonal courses listed as available for all quarters; then the thirteen most frequently selected sequences of the electives were determined. A flexible modular schedule is employed.

D. In Brookline, Massachusetts, there is a modified elective program at the junior high school level, which is probably best described as a combination of required and optional activities (Figure 6-4).

BROOKLINE
PHYSICAL EDUCATION PROGRAM

GRADES 7 - 8

	ACTIVITIES		GRADE	
	Required		7	8
	Field Hockey ⎫ Soccer ⎬ 2 of these 3 Touch Football ⎭ activities		7 weeks	7 weeks
	Volleyball		3 weeks	3 weeks
	Basketball		3 weeks	3 weeks
	Softball		2 weeks	2 weeks
	Tennis		3 weeks	3 weeks
	Gymnastics		5 weeks	5 weeks
	Track and Field		4 weeks	4 weeks
	Wrestling		3 weeks	3 weeks
	Physical Fitness Testing		1 week	
	TOTAL		31 weeks	30 weeks
	Optional			
Select From:	Badminton Dance Fencing Floor Hockey Golf Lacrosse Low Organization Games Speedball Skating Weight Training		3 weeks	4 weeks
	TOTAL			34 weeks

FIGURE 6-4.

Scheduling the Curriculum

Having set forth the scope of the program and organized the content in graduated sequences, it is necessary to schedule the program as an integral part of the total school curriculum.

Scheduling is essentially an administrative procedure. No matter how "perfect" the physical education curriculum may appear on paper, in the end it is successful because of the manner in which it is implemented. This involves both teaching methods and administrative scheduling. Because so many subjects besides physical education are a part of the modern school, numerous questions arise at this point.

1. How large a block of time is set aside for physical education in a particular school?
2. Is the time block the same length each period the classes meet?
3. Is physical education scheduled twice a week, three times a week, or every day?
4. Are intramural games scheduled as part of the physical education class period or are they held at another time?
5. Is the schedule flexible enough to vary according to the nature of the activities and facilities?
6. What is the schedule when team teaching is practiced?
7. How large a block of time is provided physical education in the self-contained elementary school unit?
8. What is the schedule in the nongraded school?
9. Are such activities as programed instruction and self-testing scheduled outside the regular class period, or are they carried out during the assigned block of time?
10. Is the school exploring ways to make better use of its time?

Scheduling is a time-consuming job. Frequently a school administrator takes most of the summer months to put together a workable package of

FIGURE 6-5. Large group instruction with adequate equipment in Chicago Public Schools.

subjects. It is even more difficult to schedule when some department wants a degree of freedom to move pupils in and out of the program in order to meet individual needs. Fortunately, most larger institutions use computers today. The computer digests the data fed into it and formulates a conflict-free schedule, but the fundamental decision of what goes into it is still the responsibility of the administrator.

Scheduling is not very glamorous, but it is important to the function of required elective programs. When the computer was not helpful in Cheltenham High School, Wyncote, Pennsylvania, the 2000 students in grades 10–12 were seated in squads of 20—10 boys and 10 girls chosen on a lottery basis relative to order or selection. Squad members selected their electives and arranged themselves in groups in keeping with electives chosen. Teachers then determined the number of students in each elective and made reductions where necessary. At this point the students completed their cards for the marking period and turned them over to the instructors. This scheduling arrangement continued to work satisfactorily.

Whether the schedule is built by hand or with the assistance of a computer, the essential information needed is the same: (1) the number and kinds of students, (2) the number of instructors available, and (3) the number of teaching stations (classrooms, gymnasiums, laboratories, etc.)

To calculate the number of teaching stations needed for a secondary school, follow a plan as in Table 6-4:

TABLE 6-4

Plan	*Example*
1. Divide the anticipated enrollment by the desired average class size. This will give the number of sections needed.	$\dfrac{1{,}000 \text{ students}}{30 \text{ pupils per class}} = 34$ sections
2. Multiply the number of sections by the number of periods per week physical education is offered.	$34 \times 5 \text{ periods} = 170$
3. Multiply the resulting number by 1.25 to allow for a utilization factor.	$170 \times 1.25 = 203$
4. Divide the resulting figure by the number of teaching periods available in the school week (30 periods).	$\dfrac{203}{30} = 6.7 = 7$ teaching stations

In Table 6-4 this school of 1,000 pupils, meeting for thirty periods per week, five of which were for physical education, would need seven teaching stations to meet the space demands. To calculate the number of teaching stations required for an elementary school, proceed as in Table 6-5:

TABLE 6-5

Plan	Example
1. Estimate the enrollment by counting the number of grades and number of classes in each grade.	A school with 6 grades of 3 classes per grade = 18 classroom groups
2. Decide on length and number of class periods.	A total of ten 30-minute periods per day, or 50 periods per week
3. Decide on the number of periods per week for pupils.	5 periods per week
4. Calculate number of teaching stations: Teaching stations = 18 classroom groups $\times$ $\dfrac{5 \text{ periods per week}}{50 \text{ periods per week}} = \dfrac{90}{50} = 1.8$	

In Table 6-5, an elementary school of approximately five hundred boys and girls would require two teachers of physical education. Each would teach twenty-five thirty-minute periods a week aside from any intramural supervision and program planning.

Team Teaching

The essential requirement for team teaching is that two or more teachers be scheduled so that they will be able to work together to carry out the program more efficiently than they could if they were working by themselves. This is not a new concept in physical education. For decades, football and baseball have had special coaches who work as part of the coaching staff. In the gymnasiums and swimming pools, teachers who are well-versed in particular sport skills generally tend to concentrate their efforts where they can be the most help. Frequently, this concentration is well-planned so that both men and women instructors trade off their teaching competencies. Moreover, this kind of team teaching has been more effective when the team has been enlarged to include the assistance of energetic and skillful student leaders.

An illustration of the team-teaching technique may be observed in a number of schools, in which teachers are assigned as instructors in areas of their greatest knowledge and interest. Teachers with assignments in the same area work as a team and provide a coordinated unit of instruction that has continuity and purpose. Says one director of physical education,

> All teachers on all teams meet periodically to exchange ideas and evaluate the program along with discussions of common problems having to do with class organization, equipment, student accountability, evaluation, and discipline. Complete schedules of classes, class size, time, and place of meetings are

FIGURE 6-6. Team teaching permits a highly skilled teacher to teach a special part of an activity.

provided. Teachers assigned are responsible for the preparation and conduct of their individual class, and although a standard curriculum is utilized, each unit provides enough flexibility to allow for teacher enrichment.

The concept of teaching physical education in team fashion is sound, for it assures the new teacher that he or she is not working alone and can consult with others and employ their ideas and abilities. The team that plans and carries out a program together can also evaluate the pupils' experiences, teaching methods, facilities, and other influences that have a bearing on the curriculum.

Programed Instruction

In several areas of education, a number of booklets and texts have been prepared so that the individual student can study and learn the subject-matter materials in a series of small and related steps. As he or she proceeds, there is an opportunity to check progress. This assures students of where they stand. As they continue the program, the material gets more difficult. However, there is evidence that when the program is completed, the individual knows more about the subject than do classmates who were schooled in a more traditional fashion. Research in Chicago; Denver; Provo, Utah; and Manhasset, New York, bears this out.

Programed instruction is a supplemental activity. The technique has not been employed to any extent in physical education. It is conceivable that a series of skill sequences could be programed for a particular physical education activity for an individual pupil to follow during independent study time. Piscopo has done some of this using a videotape laboratory and setting up questions to go with selected motor skills.[6] Some other programs have been prepared for tennis, golf, badminton, and basketball; and the research indicates that they work better in the area of closed skills.[7] Gymnastic and dance routines lend themselves to programed instruction. However, the intellectual aspects of physical education are even more appropriate for programing.

Penman recognized these aspects and developed a very fine programed instruction book for college students taking physical education.[8] Most of this program could be used as is for upper-class senior high school boys and girls, especially for independent study. In 1970 a committee of the Physical Education Division of the American Association for Health, Physical Education and Recreation prepared some programed instruction material for use in physical education.[9]

The hope has always been that programed instruction materials would be the magic key to the door of *individualized* instruction—that they would liberate students from the lockstep of a mixed class and permit them to move forward at their best pace and go as far as possible.

Instructional Television

The use of television in the schools grew measurably during the 1950s and early 1960s. It was used in part to solve the crisis of quantity and quality in the schools. In many respects, it did indeed help in large group instruction

[6]John Piscopo, "Videotaping Laboratory: A Programmed Instruction Sequence," *Journal of Health, Physical Education and Recreation*, 44 (March 1973), 32–35.

[7]Lawrence F. Locke, "Prepackaged Sports Skill Instruction: A Review of Selected Research," *Journal of Health, Physical Education and Recreation*, 42 (September 1971), 57–60.

[8]Kenneth A. Penman, *Physical Education for College Students* (St. Louis: C. V. Mosby Co., 1964).

[9]Loren, Bensley and others, *Programmed Instruction in Health Education and Physical Education* (Washington, D. C.: American Association for Health, Physical Education and Recreation, 1970).

FIGURE 6-7. In depth study in an effective program.

and make a contribution to the increasing new demands in the curriculum. However, instructional television (ITV) has not had as profound an effect on American education as some of the prophets had envisioned. Wide use of ITV in the public schools in the years ahead is uncertain. Thus far, the most enthusiastic users of televised physical education programs have been elementary teachers. Larger school systems have developed their own sets of televised materials.

A number of physical education activities have been videotaped and later televised to classrooms and gymnasiums for children to react to shortly after presentation. Some have been on closed-circuit TV, and others on the regular NET (National Educational Television) network. The most effective videotaping is done as a part of the instructional effort; it has been used in team teaching and individualized teaching.[10]

Flexible Scheduling in Physical Education

One of the most influential publications to have had a bearing on educational practice in the last two decades was the 1961 report of Trump and Baynham in which the results of studies sponsored by the National Association

[10]Jerrold S. Greenberg, "How Videotaping Improves Teaching Behavior," *Journal of Health, Physical Education and Recreation*, 44 (March 1973), 36–37.

of Secondary School Principals were made available to educators at large.[11] It concentrated on basic curriculum organization with major attention devoted to *flexibility* in schedule arrangements to facilitate different class sizes at appropriate times. Of particular interest to teachers of physical education today are the following items from the report:

1. *"Some classes will be smaller."* At times there may be fewer than fifteen pupils in a class. This will aid small-group discussion and give teachers an opportunity to explore a variety of teaching techniques. For physical education, particularly, it means that pupils and instructors will get to know each other better, and instruction in such activities as badminton, handball, and bowling can be handled in small groups.
2. *"Independent study will be emphasized."* It will be possible to focus on the special interests and abilities of individual pupils. In-depth studies will be possible as the student develops a sense of inquiry. For physical education, this means a chance to "dig in" and pursue an item such as a sports topic in detail or to specialize in something like weight training by studying routines and conducting personal experimentation and library research. A member of the girls' or boys' leaders club can be encouraged to find out more about athletic conditioning, leadership techniques, and coaching. Moreover, persons in need of extra work in order to perfect certain motor and game skills can be encouraged to put in extra time in the school day.
3. *"Some classes will be larger."* Classes as large as 150 pupils may be brought together for something quite general in nature. At the start of a physical education unit, it may be desirable and efficient for a large group to view a special instructional film, watch a television production, or witness a unique physical education demonstration. In the large secondary schools, where there are several teachers to a class, such large group meetings are common. Unfortunately, in the large city schools they are too common, chiefly because there is a shortage of adequate teaching stations for small group work.
4. *"Three phases of instruction will be related."* Large group, small group, and independent study phases will be carefully organized so that the student of physical education can move from the activity of the gymnasium to the library and classroom for appropriate discussion. The Trump report (Table 6-6) suggests that a fourteen-year-old student might spend time in health and physical education as follows:

TABLE 6-6

	Large group	Small group	Independent study
Minutes per Week	40	40	80

Plus: Extra hours available for study in facilities open and supervised additional hours, days and weeks.

[11]J. Lloyd Trump and Dorsey Baynham, *Guide to Better Schools: Focus on Change* (Chicago: Rand McNally, 1961).

5. *"Teacher assistants will be used."* Team teachers will be selected for particular competencies and for specific tasks. This selection has been done in the field of men's and women's sports for a long while. Also, many high schools have specialists on the team who handle certain activities. For example, a man especially good in teaching golf may teach the girls while the girls' teacher may teach an activity she excels in, such as badminton or folk dance.

6. *"Educational facilities will reflect changes."* The buildings of tomorrow, in order to permit flexibility, will need more small group rooms, learning resources centers, and a teaching auditorium. In physical education, the requirement will be for more teaching stations and large multi-use activity areas.

7. *"Schedules will be more flexible."* Instead of six or seven class periods in the departmentalized school, there will be divisions of time into fifteen- or twenty-minute modules. At times, one module will be adequate for what is planned, and at other times two or three modules may be necessary. A number of schools in several parts of the country operate successfully on the short-time module system.

8. *"Students' individual differences will be recognized."* How to respect and do something about individual differences is always a problem. With a more flexible school day, the physical education teacher will be able to schedule pupils for adapted physical education more easily, including those boys and girls weak in basic skills and those poor in physical fitness.

9. *"Curriculum will be reorganized."* There will be a strong movement away from compartmentalized programs. Grade compartments, subject-matter compartments, and fixed-length periods have tended to stereotype education. More attention will be given to content and what the pupil knows. The nongraded school will become more popular at the elementary level. Physical education skills will be taught to those who can learn them, rather than to a particular age group. Experience here indicates, however, that physical education in the nongraded school is not without its problems. Unfortunately, pupils with too wide an age spread sometimes are put together for instruction without adequate teaching staff to handle wide differences in ability.

10. *"Evaluation will be more complete."* In physical education, not only the pupil, but the total physical education curriculum, K-12, will be appraised periodically.

The Trump report suggestions do not need to alter in any major way the preconceived scope and sequence of a given program of physical education. What the report should do is to cause the teacher to shift parts of the program about—to keep flexible—and to ask regularly these three questions:

"What can students learn largely by themselves?"
"What can they learn from explanations of others?"
"What requires personal interaction among students and teachers?"

One of the real advantages of flexible scheduling in physical education is the opportunity to vary the length of the activity period, according to the needs of the student and teacher, through the use of time blocks called *modules.* The schedule of the student is set up on the basis of 20-minute modules that permit a variety of arrangements relative to time for small- and large-group and individualized instruction. Once established, modules may be combined in almost any manner (see Figure 6-8).[12] Modular planning not only works well in the area of skills and understandings, but it fosters affective

Group	No. of 20 min. mods.	M	T	W	Th	F
A	1	Large-Group	Dress (10 min.)	Dress	Dress	Dress 40 min.
	2		40 min.	40 min.	40 min.	Indep.
			Small Gr.	Small Gr.	Small Gr.	Study
	3		Dress	Dress	Dress	Dress
B	1	Large-Group	Dress (10 min.)	Dress	Dress	
	2		60 min.	60 min.	60 min.	
	3		Small-Group	Small-Group	Indep. Study	Free
			Dress	Dress	Dress	
	4		(10 min.)			
C	1		Dress (10 min.)	Dress	Dress	
	2	Large-Group	60 min.	60 min.	60 min.	
			Small-Group	Indep. Study	Indep. Study	Free
	3		Dress	Dress	Dress	
	4		(10 min.)			

DIFFERENTIATED TIME ALLOTMENTS FOR VARIOUS GROUPS

Group A = Freshmen or beginning students
Group B = Sophomores or average ability students
Group C = Juniors and seniors or highly skilled students
Students can supplement the assigned physical education periods with additional practice during their unstructured time.

FIGURE 6-8. Twenty-minute modules permit differentiated time allotments. (Courtesy, American Alliance for Health, Physical Education and Recreation)

domain objectives by facilitating social grouping, ability grouping, interest grouping, and achievement grouping. Moreover, this arrangement helps to make differentiated staffing—in which individual teachers, team teachers, aides, and supervisors work together—an effective medium in physical education.

At the Edgewood Junior High School in Saint Paul, Minnesota, there is a Trump Model Schools Program in which large groups, small groups, learn-

[12]See AAHPER, *Organizational Patterns for Instruction in Physical Education*, p. 24.

ing packages, and paraprofessionals are a significant part of the school curriculum. The arrangements are as follows:

1. Each week students attend a large group in physical education, about 150 students each period. The presentation is to motivate students to participate in coming physical education units offered, or in others outside the program that are recreational in nature.
2. Once each week all students attend a small-group discussion. This builds group dynamics and fosters an understanding in physical education. It is a follow-up to the large-group presentation with about 15 boys and girls in each small group.
3. Each student attends three two-period sessions of physical education lab per week to learn the skills and games. Skills are presented in a learning package with clearly defined behavioral objectives and procedures to follow.
4. The instructor has a counselor role; each instructor is responsible for 25 counselees, whom he or she meets briefly before school each day, two or four times a month for one period.
5. Instructional aides (paraprofessionals) are employed to work with students under the direction of the instructor.

For most of the country, the Trump report is still way ahead of its time. In most places the traditional approach to scheduling is still practiced. It is easy to understand why school administrators are reluctant to change to a less rigid scheduling of classes. It is much simpler to divide the school day nicely into six or eight standard-length periods and assign set blocks of time to all subject-matter areas. The assumption now, however, is that a better quality of physical education can be brought to pupils when more effective schemes of organizing school time are used. Therefore, a consideration of modules, large groups, small groups, and independent study groups is especially significant.

There is at least one danger, however, in quickly adopting the "flexible scheduling" idea; it could result in a haphazard approach to the scheduling of activities, particularly if there is little planning. The so-called "open" or "free-play" type of physical education program could easily come about in the name and spirit of "flexible scheduling." This might well result in a watering-down of skills and knowledge.

Flexible scheduling, of course, takes many forms, all of which are designed to expose the student to a more effective program. Some arrangements that have been made in an effort to get away from a rigid structure are as follow:

1. Extending the school formally so that all game skills can be practiced in game situations after regular class periods are over.
2. Extending the school week to six days. For total school operation, this has not proven popular. Where community recreation departments work closely with the schools there have been cooperative efforts to extend intramurals and other physical activities into Saturday time. Perhaps classic examples of extension are in Flint, Michigan, and Lexington, Massachusetts, where school and community activities are very closely related.

3. Extending the school year. This has not proved to be at all popular. Parental activities, vacations, and so forth tend to dictate the length of the school year.
4. Assigning a large number of students to physical education in a block of time. This works only when there are a number of teaching stations and staff members available for the time block.
5. Varying the length of the time block. For certain program elements the double period has a number of advantages. It is especially valuable if a school is set up with short periods (under forty-five minutes). If fifteen minutes are allocated to undressing, showering, and dressing, only thirty minutes are available for instruction. In this case, the double period permits some depth of instruction. However, when the double period is used, it should not measurably reduce the weekly exposure to physical education. It is not recommended if there are only two periods of physical education per week, which might be combined into one double period. Five periods per week could be split into single periods on Monday, Tuesday, and Wednesday and a double period on Friday. Four periods could be split into single periods on Monday and Wednesday and a double period on Friday.
6. Assigning upper-level high school pupils to evening classes, particularly where elective activities may be practiced. Although this makes more time available for physical education, it tends to cut down on the time during which students might be doing something else at home and in the community.
7. Permitting study hall time to be used for needed instruction and practice in physical education activities when the individual pupil has a serious weakness. When carefully controlled, this practice can be very worthwhile.

Another benefit of the flexible schedule is the heightened motivation of students to learn. They can take part in activities they like with some assurance of learning the skills well. In Poway, California, the physical education instructor broke away from the traditional schedule by having an "open

FIGURE 6-9. How much activity time is there with one ball?

gymnasium" situation each day. Students came and practiced their weak skills independently. They used a performance curriculum, in which all activities were outlined by skill levels. Students moved quickly through the skill levels. They met in a large group on Monday and Wednesday of the week, and on the other three days they worked to perfect their sport skills practically by themselves.

Individualized Instruction and Learning Contracts

Acknowledging the need to reach students on a more personal basis, a growing number of schools have organized physical education so that there is greater opportunity for individualized instruction. A wide variety of activities are set up in terms of learning packages, independent study units, and learning contracts. All serve the purpose of capitalizing on students' desire to work to solve problems by themselves, individually, or in a small group. This approach is more effective with the individual and couple activities than it is with team sports, in which large groups of participants are required. It works especially well in the cognitive domain when students can do library research, survey opinions, listen to records and tapes, and view filmstrips, loop films, and videotapes.

Much of the early work of Muska Mosston has to do with individualized instruction. He discovered that once students adjust to freedom and self-direction, they become self-motivated and enjoy finding out about things themselves.[13] The same experience occurred in Omaha, Nebraska, after a new learning model program was established. There, each pupil is (1) pre-tested to determine knowledge and skills; (2) given an individual prescription based on learning needs; (3) allowed to pursue the learning task until the pupil feels that he or she has reached the objective; (4) comes to the teacher for final evaluation; and (5) picks up a new learning task.

In Omaha the new physical education looks favorably on electives and on a variety of learning strategies. Learning is enhanced by the use of self-pacing methods and self-direction. Instruction is individualized. Psycho-motor learning is advanced by first learning relevant cognitive factors and tying them in with *successful* experiences that are positively reinforced. Students help each other. The learning center is more than a gymnasium or pool. It is a place to practice, study, and observe. A prototype of a typical learning laboratory is shown in Figure 6-10. It is one possible arrangement.

Usually learning packages and learning contracts include all the directions needed to carry out an independent study project. Students are given

---

[13]Muska Mosston, *Teaching Physical Education* (Columbus, Ohio: Charles E. Merrill, 1966).

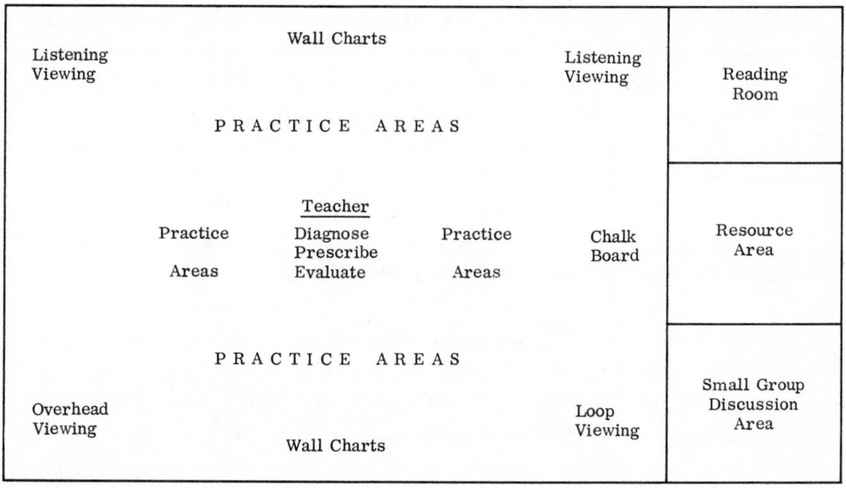

Wall Charts

| Listening Viewing | | | Listening Viewing | Reading Room |

PRACTICE AREAS

Teacher

Practice	Diagnose	Practice	Chalk	Resource
Areas	Prescribe	Areas	Board	Area
	Evaluate			

PRACTICE AREAS

| | | | | Small Group Discussion Area |
| Overhead Viewing | | | Loop Viewing | |

Wall Charts

FIGURE 6-10.

the freedom to move about the physical education area (learning laboratory) and the school. The learning package used in Table 6-7 for a wrestling unit can be printed on a small 3″ × 5″ card for student use.

TABLE 6-7

1. Behavioral Objective: On the mat you will put the Head Lever Ride on another wrestler holding tight to his wrist, driving your head into his armpit, while driving from your toes.
2. Pre-Test: Satisfy the Behavioral Objective.
3. Do at least two of the things listed:
   A. In the resource center view the loop film "Head Lever."
   B. Practice the skill on the mat with another wrestler.
   C. Ask another student for a demonstration.
4. Tell the aide of work done.
5. Post-Test:
   A. See a teacher's aide.
   B. Satisfy the behavioral objective.
   C. If you satisfy this behavioral objective, go on to another.
   D. If you cannot satisfy this behavioral objective, repeat the things listed.

Some learning contracts differ from other packaged instructions in that they carefully spell out requirements in all three of Bloom's taxonomy domains (cognitive, affective, and psychomotor). Expectations are listed and a number of learning tasks are written out in full detail. The student looks over the contract, agrees to go to work on it, signs the contract, and gets underway. In a number of secondary schools most independent study is tied up with a student contract. In this fashion the school administration recognizes students who have the privilege to move freely about the school and community to carry out their study.

The Need for Multiple Teaching Stations

It has been the experience of the author that the topic of class scheduling is highly related to facilities. If the gymnasiums and playing fields are small, there is little room for flexibility. If swimming pools, dance studios, and adapted physical education classrooms are missing, the program almost always appears inflexible, and needed activity modifications seldom take place. There are exceptions, of course, but they are in the minority, and these schools are frequently fortunate to have dedicated instructors who know how to make the most out of the least.

There is evidence to support the thesis that the finest examples of program flexibility, in both content and instruction, come about if large numbers of pupils of varying abilities are assigned to a class program in which there are multiple teaching stations—both indoors and outdoors. In this respect, the current increase in campus-type schools, consolidated schools, centralized schools, regional schools, and "educational park" schools has much to offer physical education. In some instances over 25 percent of the indoor space is assigned physical education. With vastly improved outdoor playing fields and courts, it is possible to plan large-group, small-group, and individual activities in a program that is anything but rigid.

Almost all elementary school buildings constructed in the last decade have bright, optimum-size gymnasiums and playing fields extended beyond the immediate playground. Secondary schools by the hundreds have auxiliary gymnasiums, special exercise rooms, and studios. The most promising facility, being constructed at an increasing rate in the country, is the fieldhouse, with its wide-open spaces, multi-use fixtures, and portable floors and equipment. It sets the stage for a thoroughly organized, yet flexible, program.

With the increased instructional staff assigned to large groups of students and the excellent variety of fieldhouse teaching stations, there should be no valid reason for not conducting a superior program. In the town of Medford, the new senior high school (grades 9–12) was built to permit a greatly improved program for more than three thousand boys and girls five periods each week. In the space requirement computations (Figure 6-11), note how class size has an effect on the number of teaching stations. If, for example, class size is to approximate thirty pupils, then fifteen teaching stations are needed,

Medford High School

Medford High School

Building planned to house 3008 students, grades 9-12

Space Requirement Computation

Students	Class Size	Number of Selections	P. E. Periods Each Week	Number of Sections	Number of Teaching Sections
3008	30	101	5	505/35	15
3008	*35	86	5	430/35	13
3008	40	76	5	380/35	11
3008	50	61	5	305/35	9

*Choice Selected

Preliminary Plans

1 teaching station – Weight training/ corrective 30' x 40' = 1200 square feet.

1 teaching station – Dance 44' x 48' = 2112 square feet

1 teaching station – Wrestling 44' x 42' = 1848 square feet

1 teaching station – Gymnastics 54' x 44' = 2376 square feet

2 teaching stations – Swimming pool 75' x 28', Diving Pool 32' x 34', Therapeutic Pool 32' x 34'

1 teaching station – Mezzanine 53' x 42' = 2436 square feet (over pool shower and locker area)

6 teaching stations – Cage 230' x 106' divided:
1 divisible area 64' x 104' = 6656 square feet
1 divisible area 60' x 104' = 6240 square feet
1 divisible area 84' x 104' = 8736 square feet

13 total teaching stations

FIGURE 6-11. Multiple teaching stations encourage flexibility. (Courtesy, Medford School Department, Medford, Massachusetts)

whereas if there are to be fifty pupils in the average class, the number of teaching stations required would be only nine. In the Medford illustration, thirteen stations were planned, with a corresponding class size of thirty-five pupils. Once the pupils have been assigned to the class block of time, the *actual* number at any one teaching station can be quite flexible, depending on the physical education activity to be taught.

Time Allotment for Program Elements

When a group of curriculum specialists sit down to plan a program, the topic of "how much time" eventually comes up. Agreeing on the number of days or minutes per week for physical education at elementary and secondary levels is not a difficult task. The individual states prescribe the amount. The

183

dilemma arises when time is assigned to certain parts of the program—major elements and individual activities.

Most studies show that there is a significant advantage gained by pupils engaging in daily physical education classes, particularly along the lines of reduction in body fat percentage, greater activity skills, and physical fitness levels.[14] For this reason a strong effort is being made through the professional organizations in many states to mandate daily physical education. However, the five periods of time can be allocated in a flexible fashion, as demonstrated in a seven-year study in El Camino High School in South San Francisco. There, students met only three times a week in two double periods of 100 minutes each and in one single 50-minute period. Not only did physical fitness almost double in the flexible group, but there was a six-week gain in solid instruction time annually by cutting down the time spent in the locker room dressing and undressing. This is a good point to keep in mind as one observes the increase in physical education requirements within the separate states.[15]

Once the broad and varied program has been structured in scope and sequence, how many class periods out of the total available should be set aside for an activity? For example, how much time should be allotted to rhythmics in the primary grades? If there is to be a worthwhile exposure to weight training routines in the senior high school, how many full class periods are needed at a minimum? Are three weeks of volleyball out of forty-two weeks of classes adequate to complete certain instructional sequences? Is six weeks more time than is really needed for softball?

The time allotment pattern varies considerably for the numerous physical activities taught in the country. Although certain team sports tend to dominate the seasons of the school year, schools vary widely in the time they allow for each. The author is aware of several small-city programs in which touch or flag football is taught from early September until early December as the only instructional activity beyond the five to seven minutes of calisthenics for warmup. Adjacent to these communities are schools with programs involving a half-dozen different activities covering the same period of time and the same number of days per week.

One always must raise the question of frequency. How little can one teach of an activity and still find it worthwhile? Is it worthwhile to sandwich two bowling lessons into a rather full winter program? Is it a valid move to reduce basketball fundamentals and practice from five weeks to three in order

[14]Lavon C. Johnson, "Effects of 5-Day/Week versus 2-Day/Week and 3-Day/Week Physical Education Class on Fitness, Skill, Adipose Tissue and Growth," *Research Quarterly*, 40 (March 1969), 94–98.

[15]For a breakdown of requirements, see Andrew Grieve, "State Legal Requirements for Physical Education," *Journal of Health, Physical Education and Recreation*, 42 (April 1971), 19–23.

to assign two weeks to wrestling? In short, the ideal amount of time to assign to an activity will always be difficult to agree to. It depends on local objectives and local needs. A further discussion of the time allotted as applied to the various elements of elementary and secondary programs is covered in Chapters 8 through 12.

Correlation and Integration

> There are a number of measurable trends integrating today that suggest that a health, physical education and recreation complex may be able to anticipate effectively many emerging trends of advance-education evolution, and . . . may play a far more critical part in the lives of coming generations than such categories of educational-system disciplines have played in the past.[16]
>
> R. BUCKMINSTER FULLER

Today in education there is more smoke than fire when it comes to organizing a program of instruction that provides the learner with a total view of his or her world and how to live in it. However, changes are occurring as instruction is organized away from specialization and toward increasing comprehensiveness of all educational preoccupations, and toward providing young people with a greater understanding of themselves. This reversal of educational trends from superspecialization back toward integration of the humanities and the sciences, says Buckminster Fuller, ". . . will not be confined to the purely mental categories of thought but will also involve an integration of the physical and metaphysical studies and activities." Fuller is saying that physical education has a *synergistic* role to play.[17] This role takes the form of helping the individual "comprehend the full family of generalized principles through personally experiencing with his own body all the possible coordinating capabilities to cope with all the complementary behaviors of nature." Such a Greek-like return to education, says Fuller, calls for an integrated facility that will combine the physical and the mental. More specifically, he calls for a physical education complex, a kind of field house, under one roof where one can both observe and participate in athletic activities and identify athletic experiences

> with documentaries of human organism and accelerated and slowed-down movies of internal and external physiological phenomenon . . . experiences in

[16]R. Buckminster Fuller, "A Concept for an Integrated Physical Education Facility," *Saturday Review/World*, April 10, 1973, p. 38.

[17]The word *synergy* refers to the behavior of whole systems unpredicted by the behavior of any or several of the system's parts. It is the only word that characterizes the whole of nature.

sense of size, of linear surface, and volume differentiating . . . optical, aural, tactile, and olfactory documentized experiences . . . self studies of surface tension . . . learning that the body is an automated and self-reproducing machine . . . differentiating the metaphysical self from the physical machine it employs . . . identification of self's machine with generalized principles of structure, tension, compression, action, reaction . . .[18]

Such an exciting employment of physical movement as an essential means of comprehending life in all of its manifestations is challenging to the physical educator. Yet it is a completely sound proposition, for the mind works through the body, and the body through the mind:

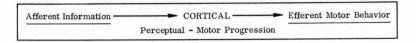

Since behavior is established on the interdependence of perceptual and motor development processes, children must be provided with numerous sensory perceptions through play and work to assist them in becoming capable sorters of information. Gallahue, Werner, and Luedke clarify this point when they write:

> Experiences involving size, speed, distance, direction, color, temperature, shape, texture, and the like are important so that each child can improve in his capacity to perceive (receive, interpret, and evaluate) increasingly more complex kinds and quantities of information. In turn, overt motor acts will come under greater control. This means that the child will run more efficiently, balance more skillfully, throw more accurately, and draw pictures with greater accuracy and more detail. Thus, we see that as perceptual-motor development progresses the child can exert more and more refined afferent control over his efferent motor behavior. We can also see that all voluntary motor acts are in reality perceptual-motor acts and that in essence physical education programs are perceptual-motor programs.[19]

In addition to the perceiving, feeling, and moving dimension in learning there is the well-known fact that when an activity is fun it will be learned more quickly. Marx discovered this when movement was used to heighten interest in poetry and to stimulate creativity in the writing of poetry.[20] Humphrey

[18]R. Buckminster Fuller, "A Concept for an Integrated Physical Education Facility," *Saturday Review/World,* April 10, 1973, p. 39.

[19]David L. Gallahue, Peter H. Werner, and George C. Luedke, *A Conceptual Approach to Movement and Learning* (New York: John Wiley & Sons, Inc., 1975), p. 272.

[20]Ellen Marx, "Poetry and Movement," *Journal of Physical Education and Recreation,* 47 (March 1976), 70–72.

found that groups that were taught concepts associated with arithmetic, science, reading, and social studies through the medium of active games made greater gains than those groups taught by traditional methods.[21] Penman, Christopher, and Wood demonstrated essentially the same with third-grade boys and girls in the state of Washington.[22]

There is a difference between correlation and integration. *Correlation involves the use of different areas within the school program through which physical education is taught.* Physical education, therefore, is correlated with science, mathematics, health, social studies, art, and music. Also, in correlation other school subjects may correlate with physical education. For example, the classroom teacher of arithmetic may have the pupils measure gymnasium court dimensions in order to illustrate a simple mathematics principle. On the other hand, the physical education teacher may take the initiative and require his class to "feel" the size of a volleyball court by actually measuring all aspects of it. This kind of interaction, at any grade level, helps motivate pupils and encourages teachers to extend their lines of communication to fellow teachers. This is most noticeable at the elementary level, in which teachers are used to correlating their activities more than they are at the secondary level. A number of fine examples of how elementary school activities can be correlated with physical education are presented by Miller, Cheffers, and Whitcomb.[23]

Physical education will be much better understood when it is correlated as often as possible with other subject-matter areas. There is hardly a subject in the modern school that does not lend itself at some time or other to the topic of physical education. The impact of sports alone is considerable. They relate to numerous social, commercial, and psychological aspects of society. They can be written about in English, humanized in geography, appraised for their beauty, symmetry, and form in the art class. Also, there is probably no more practical way to discuss mental health and desirable social behavior with children than through the medium of terms such as *fair play, equality,* and *sportsmanship.*

The general failure to engage in some form of *planned correlation* may have had much to do with producing a large number of adult citizens who simply do not understand or appreciate the unique role of physical education in their lives. Their games and sports, stunts, dances, and exercises were seen

[21]James H. Humphrey, "Active Games as a Learning Medium," *Academic Theory,* 5 (January 1969), 15–24.

[22]Kenneth A. Penman, Jon R. Christopher, and Geoffrey S. Wood, "Using Gross Motor Activity to Improve Language Arts Concepts by Third Grade Students," *Research Quarterly,* 48 (March 1977), 134–38.

[23]Arthur G. Miller, John Cheffers, and Virginia Whitcomb, *Physical Education in the Elementary School Curriculum,* 4th ed. (Englewood Cliffs, N.J.: Prentice-Hall, Inc., 1974).

FIGURE 6-12. Vertical jumping on the map of New Jersey.

as part of the growing up process only—not significant in the regimen of the mature adult. In this respect, the intellectual competency aim, set forth in an earlier chapter, needs more attention by curriculum builders than it tends to receive. There is little doubt that it will have to be planned for during curriculum development sessions.

Here are just a few examples of ways in which physical education may be correlated with other subjects:

ARITHMETIC

Measuring court dimensions, computing, and scoring
Measuring sports performance—times, distance, and heights
Making floor patterns in dance, such as circles, squares, rectangles, and parallel lines
Calculating averages from physical fitness and other performance tests
Calculating percentages—team standings, batting averages
Making use of graphs and charts to illustrate pupil progress in an activity that requires the use of numbers
Comparing European records in metric system with those of Americans
Calculating the range in such activities as archery, discus throwing, and putting the shot

ART

Reviewing scale drawings of playing fields and indoor facilities

Studying art media that can be used with stunts and tumbling activities—figure drawing, modeling media, such as clay, pipe cleaners, wood, soap.

Examining art masterpieces in painting and in sculpture that illustrate physical activity—the lines and grace of body movement, as in the early Greek friezes, Egyptian paintings and frescos, and works of the old masters

Working on school grounds beautification projects in which painting and landscaping relate to pleasant forms of recreation

Making bulletin board displays and attractive posters depicting forthcoming physical education events

BIOLOGY

Relating physical fitness in terms of muscular strength and muscular endurance to "work capacity" as measured by tests of cardio-respiratory endurance

Measuring vital capacity and correlating it with changes in physical performance

Studying reaction time and movement and how they are modified by temperature, motivation and fatigue, physical education, and sports training

Studying body function by analyzing the motor performance of individuals under different conditions

Relating constitutional endowment and genetic predisposition to such conditions as obesity, malnourishment, upper respiratory difficulties, coronary heart attacks, and performance limitations in team and individual sports activities

HEALTH AND SAFETY

Teaching rules and skills for safe physical education activities on the playground and in the gymnasium

Developing the concept that the muscular system exists to permit human activity, and that it needs daily exercise and integrated use to grow and develop ideally

Investigating the impact of inadequate diet, sleep, rest, and mental outlook on the physical capacity of the body to perform

GEOGRAPHY AND SOCIAL STUDIES

Dancing and studying the folk dances of other lands and different cultures

Researching the origins of physical education activities—pole vault, archery, basketball, the discus throw

Comparing the physical activity experiences of the ancient Greeks and Romans with those of Americans today

Watching films of the Olympic Games and learning how the modern games came into being

Discussing knighthood and the days of chivalry and tournaments

Purposely cooperating with group members to achieve a common goal

Discussing and appraising play as an activity full of meaning—a child's way of life, a therapeutic agent for the mentally ill, and an activity with powerful social, medical, educational, and recreational implications

LANGUAGE ARTS

Writing summaries of game programs from the world of sports

Writing about specific and personal physical education experiences

Reading about the origins of games, rules, and sports figures

Engaging in creative writing

Listening to and giving directions for a game

Reporting to the class on a recent sports event

Spelling sports terms and other words related to physical education

Developing dictionary skills to increase vocabulary when a new physical education activity is taught

Learning words, phrases, sentences, and stories through movement and the use of musical accompaniment

Reading literary words and classics that are concerned with physical expression and outstanding motor performances

MUSIC

Listening to music that suggests movement

Acting to music that suggests movements such as waltzing, pivoting, skipping, and the whole range of basic dance patterns

Reacting to a wide variety of rhythms—from the fundamental to the more complex

Participating in a singing game—the music to be taught initially by the classroom teacher and the game to be taught by the physical instructor

SCIENCE

Creating opportunities to relate the laws of motion to movement experiences

Understanding the application of force when hitting a ball with a bat or wrestling with an opponent

Making use of the tom-tom, piano, and records to illustrate how sounds differ from one another in pitch, volume, and quality

Using physical activities to demonstrate the laws of science, especially the laws of motion

These activities may be categorized as correlative. The integration that takes place is something that occurs in the student. From a school administrator's viewpoint, the word integration has another facet. *Integration involves an organization of learning experiences around a central objective.* It differs from correlation by relating parts to the whole. The "whole" can be anything. A well-integrated bicycle, for instance, is one in which all parts— wheels, chains, nuts, bolt, seat, handlebars, fenders—fit perfectly together to afford the rider a safe and pleasant journey. By the same token, a well-integrated child is one who has been exposed to hundreds of educational stimuli and has emerged to take his place in society as a "whole" person. He is like a giant mosaic—all the unique parts make a complete being.

The well-integrated curriculum is cooperatively planned. A definite effort is made to bring teachers together to combine many of their separate subject objectives.[24] In short, the many school activities and pupil experiences are not merely correlated with separate subject-matter areas; rather, they are part of a *joint pattern of activities*—jointly planned, understood, and implemented. This kind of integration of learning experience is difficult to accomplish at best, and therefore it is practiced more often in self-contained elementary schools than in departmentalized secondary schools.

Of particular value to the student, the teacher, and the school librarian are the many sports books that will tie the world of sport activity to the every day lives of people. A partial list of such books is as follows:[25]

Aldridge, James. *A Sporting Proposition.* Little, Brown & Co., 1973.

Allen, Maury. *Where Have You Gone, Joe DiMaggio? The Story of America's Last Hero.* Dutton, 1975.

Allen, Maury and Bo Belinsky. *Bo: Pitching and Wooing.* Dial, 1973. (Bantam, 1974)

Amdur, Neil. *The Fifth Down.* Dell, 1972.

Angell, Roger. *The Summer Game.* Viking Press, 1972.

Ashe, Arthur with Frank Deford. *Arthur Ashe: Portrait in Motion.* Houghton Mifflin, 1975.

Astor, Gerald. *". . . And a Credit to His Race": The Life and Hard Times of Joseph Louis Barrow, a.k.a. Joe Louis.* Saturday Review Press, 1975.

Axthelm, Pete. *The City Game: Basketball in New York from the World Champion Knicks to the World of Playgrounds.* Harper Magazine Press, 1970.

Barker, Robert. *Love Forty.* Lippincott, 1975.

Blount, Roy, Jr. *About Three Bricks Shy of a Load: A Highly Irregular Lowdown on the Year the Pittsburgh Steelers Were Super but Missed the Bowl.* Little, Brown & Co., 1974.

Bouton, Jim. *Ball Four.* Dell, 1971.

Bouton, Jim. *I'm Glad You Didn't Take It Personally.* Morrow, 1971.

Bouton, Jim and Neil Offen. *I Managed Good, But Boy, Did They Play Bad.* Dell, 1974.

Boyd, Brendan C. and Fred C. Harris. *The Great American Baseball Card Flipping, Trading and Bubble Gum Book.* Little, Brown & Co., 1973.

Breslin, Jimmy. *Can't Anybody Here Play This Game?* Viking Press, 1963.

Brown, Jimmy and Myrone Cope. *Off My Chest: Cleveland Browns' Star Speaks Out.* Doubleday, 1964.

Brunner, Bernard. *Six Days to Sunday: Joe Paterno & Penn State.* McGraw Hill, 1975.

Bukatta, Jim. *One on One.* Stadia Sports Pub., 1973.

Carter, Richard and Curt Flood. *Way It Is,* Pocket Books, 1972.

[24]For an example see James Bird, "Exploring The Middle Ages through Physical Education," *Journal of Health, Physical Education and Recreation,* 43 (January 1972), 21.

[25]Adapted from the list prepared by Gary Nygaard, reported in "Sport In Contemporary Literature," *Journal of Physical Education and Recreation,* 47 (November/December 1976), 20–23.

Carter, Rubin "Hurricane." *The Six-teenth Round: From Number One Con-tender to Number 45472.* Viking Press, 1974.

Chalk, Ocania. *Black College Sport.* Dodd, Mead, 1976.

Chalk, Ocania. *Pioneers of Black Sport.* Dodd, Mead, 1974.

Chamberlain, Wilt and David Shaw. *Wilt: Just Like Any Other 7-Foot Black Millionaire Who Lives Next Door.* Macmillian, 1973.

Church, Seymour. *Baseball: The His-tory, Statistics and Romance of the American National Game.* Pyne Press, 1974.

Coover, Robert. *The Universal Baseball Association, Inc., J. Henry Waugh, Prop.* New American Library, 1968.

Cosell, Howard. *Cosell.* Playboy, 1974.

Cosell, Howard. *Like It Is.* Playboy, 1975.

Creamer, Robert. *Babe.* Pocket Books, 1976.

Csonka, Larry and Jim Kiick. *Always on the Run.* Bantam, 1974.

Danzig, Allison and Peter Schwed, ed. *The Fireside Book of Tennis.* Simon & Schuster, 1972.

Davis, Mac. *Strange and Incredible Sports Happenings.* Grosset & Dun-lap, 1975.

DeLillo, Don. *End Zone.* Houghton Mifflin, 1972.

Dickey, Glenn. *The Jock Empire: Its Rise and Deserved Fall.* Chilton, 1974.

Dickey, Glenn. *The Great No-Hitters.* Chilton, 1976.

Dowling, Tom. *Coach: A Season with Lombardi.* Norton, 1970.

Dunbar, Paul. *The Sports of the Gods.* Arno, 1969.

Durso, Joseph. *The All-American Dollar: The Big Business of Sports.* Houghton Mifflin, 1971.

Frazier, Walt and Ira Beshow. *Rockin' Steady: A Guide to Basketball and Cool.* Prentice-Hall, 1974.

Gallwey, W. Timothy. *The Inner Game of Tennis.* Random House, 1974.

Gallwey, W. Timothy. *Inner Tennis: Playing the Game.* Random House, 1976.

Gallico, Paul. *Farewell to Sport.* Books for Libraries, 1938.

Garagiola, Joe. *Baseball Is a Funny Game.* Lippincott, 1960.

Gent, Peter. *North Dallas Forty.* Mor-row, 1973.

Gilman, Kay. *Inside the Pressure Cooker: A Season in the Life of the New York Jets.* G. P. Putnam, 1974.

Goldman, William. *Marathon Man.* Del-acorte, 1974.

Greenspan, Bud. *Play It Again, Bud!* Wyden, 1973.

Hackett, Buddy. *The Truth About Golf and Other Lies.* Doubleday, 1968. OP

Harris, Mark. *Bang the Drum Slowly.* Dell, 1973.

Higdon, Hal. *On the Run from Dogs and People.* Henry Regnery Co., 1971.

Hill, Dave, and others. *Roughnecks of the Fairways.* Prentice-Hall, 1975.

Hillary, Edmund, *Nothing Venture, Nothing Win.* Coward, McCann & Geoghegan, 1975.

Hoch, Paul. *Rip Off the Big Game: The Exploitation of Sports by the Power Elite.* Doubleday, 1972.

Holtzman, Jerome. *No Cheering in the Press Box.* Holt, Rinehart & Winston, 1974.

Honig, Donald. *Baseball Between the Lines: Baseball After World War II as Told by the Men Who Played It.* Cow-ard, McCann & Geoghegan, 1976.

Honig, Donald. *Baseball When the Grass Was Real: Baseball from the Twenties to the Forties, Told by the Men Who Played It.* Coward, McCann & Geoghegan, 1975.

Izenberg, Jerry. *How Many Miles to Camelot? The All-American Sports Myth.* Holt, Rinehart & Winston, 1972.

Jackson, Reggie and Bill Libby. *Reggie: A Season with a Super Star*. Playboy, 1976.

Jares, Joe. *What Happened to Gorgeous George?* Prentice-Hall, 1974.

Jenkins, Dan. *The Dogged Victims of Inexorable Fate*. Little, Brown, 1970.

Jenkins, Dan. *Dead Solid Perfect*. Atheneum, 1974.

Jenkins, Dan. *Semi-tough*. Atheneum, 1972.

Jones, Jack. *The Animal*. Morrow & Co., 1975.

Jordan, Pat. *A False Spring*. Dodd, Mead, 1975.

Jordan, Pat. *The Suitors of Spring*. Dodd, Mead, 1973.

Kahn, Roger. *The Boys of Summer*. Harper & Row, 1972.

Kaufman, Louis, Barbara Fitzgerald and Tom Sewell. *Moe Berg: Athlete, Scholar, Spy*. Little, Brown, 1975.

King, Billie Jean and Kim Chapin, *Billie Jean*. Harper & Row, 1974.

Knudson, Rozanne and P. K. Ebert. *Sports Poems*. Dell, 1971.

Kramer, Jerry. *Instant Replay: The Green Bay Diary of Jerry Kramer*. New American Library, 1969.

Kramer, Jerry, ed. *Lombardi: Winning Is the Only Thing*. Pocket Books, 1971.

Lardner, Rex. *Downhill Lies and Other Falsehoods; Or How to Play Dirty Golf*. Hawthorn, 1973.

Lardner, Rex. *Underhanded Serve; Or How to Play Dirty Tennis*. Hawthorn, 1968.

Lichtenstein, Grace. *A Long Way, Baby: Behind-the-Scenes in Women's Pro Tennis*. Morrow, 1974.

Lipsyte, Robert. *Sports World*. Quadrangle, 1975.

Lombardi, Vince, and others. *Run to Daylight*. Prentice-Hall, 1963.

McKay, Jim. *My Wide World*. Macmillan, 1973.

Malamud, Bernard. *The Natural*. Farrar, Straus & Giroux, 1961.

Matthews, Vincent and Neil Amdur. *My Race Be Won*. Charterhouse, 1974.

Meggyesy, Dave. *Out of Their League*. Ramparts, 1970.

Merchant, Larry. *And Every Day You Take Another Bite*. Dell, 1972.

Merchant, Larry. *The National Football Lottery*. Dell, 1974.

Meschery, Tom. *Caught in the Pivot*. Dell, 1973.

Michener, James. *Sports in America*. Random House, 1976.

Morris, Jeannie. *Brian Piccolo: A Short Season*. Rand, 1971.

Nack, William. *Big Red of Meadow Stable: Secretariat, the Making of a Champion*. Dutton, 1975.

Namath, Joe Willie and Dick Schaap. *I Can't Wait Until Tomorrow 'Cause I Get Better Looking Every Day*. Random House, 1969.

Namath, Joe with Bob Oates, Jr. *A Matter of Style*. Little, Brown & Co., 1973.

Newcombe, Jack. *Best of the Athletic Boys: White Man's Impact on Jim Thorpe*. Doubleday, 1975.

Noll, Roger G., ed. *Government and the Sport Business*. Brookings, 1974.

Novak, Michael. *The Joy of Sports*. Basic Books, 1976.

Oliver, Chip. *High for the Game*. Morrow, 1971.

Palmer, Arnold and Barry Furlong. *Go For Broke*. Simon & Schuster, 1973.

Parrish, Bernie. *They Call It a Game*. New American Library, 1972.

Pepitone, Joe and Berry Stainback. *Joe, You Coulda Made Us Proud*. Playboy, 1975.

Peterson, Robert. *Only the Ball Was White*. Prentice-Hall, 1970.

Piersall, Jim and Al Hirshberg. *Fear Strikes Out*. Little, Brown & Co., 1955.

Plimpton, George. *The Bogey Man*. Harper & Row, 1968.

Plimpton, George. *Hank Aaron: One for the Record*. Bantam, 1974.

Plimpton, George. *Mad Ducks and Bears*. Bantam, 1974.

Plimpton, George. *Paper Lion*. New American Library, 1974.

Ralbovsky, Martin. *Lords of the Locker Room*. Wyden, 1974.

Rentzel, Lance. *When All the Laughter Died in Sorrow*. Saturday Review Press, 1972.

Revson, Peter. *Speed with Style: The Autobiography of Peter Revson*. Doubleday, 1974.

Rice, Grantland. *The Tumult and the Shouting*. A.S. Barnes, 1962.

Ritter, Lawrence. *The Glory of Their Times*. Macmillian, 1971.

Robinson, Jackie as told to Al Duckett. *I Never Had It Made*. Putnam, 1972.

Roth, Philip. *The Great American Novel*. Holt, Rinehart & Winston, 1973.

Russell, Bill. *Go Up for Glory*. Noble, 1968.

Sample, Johnny. *Confession of a Dirty Ballplayer*. Dell, 1961.

Sanders, Doug and Larry Sheehan. *Come Swing with Me: My Life on and off the Tour*. Doubleday, 1974.

Sayers, Gale and Al Silverman. *I Am Third*. Viking Press, 1970.

Schulman, L.M. *Winners and Losers: An Anthology of Great Sports Fiction*. Macmillan, 1968.

Scott, Jack. *The Athletic Revolution*. Free Press, 1971.

Shaw, Gary. *Meat on the Hoof*. Dell, 1973.

Shecter, Leonard. *The Jocks*. Warner Books, 1970.

Shula, Don and Lou Sahadi. *The Winning Edge*. Popular Library, 1974.

Sillitoe, Alan. *The Loneliness of the Long Distance Runner*. Knopf, 1960.

Smith, Red. *Strawberries in Wintertime*. Quadrangle, 1974.

Toomay, Pat. *The Crunch*. W. W. Norton, 1975.

Twombly, Wells. *Shake Down the Thunder! The Official Biography of Notre Dame's Frank Leahy*. Chilton, 1974.

Updike, John. *Rabbit, Run*. Fawcett World, 1974.

Vare, Robert. *Buckeye: A Study of Coach Woody Hayes and His Ohio Football Machine*. Harper Magazine Press, 1974.

Veeck, Bill and Ed Linn. *Thirty Tons a Day*. Popular Library, 1974.

Whitehead, James. *Joiner*. Avon, 1973.

Wilson, Renate. *For the Love of Sport: A Guide for Parents of Young Athletes*. David & Charles, 1975.

Wolff, R. *What's a Nice Harvard Boy Like You Doing in the Bushes?* Prentice-Hall, 1975.

Student Leadership

The chief reason student leadership is referred to in this text is that it qualifies as a curriculum item. The organization of leaders' clubs and leaders' groups is not the immediate concern of this text, but acknowledging this function and planning for it in the early stage of curriculum development should not be overlooked.

There are at least two reasons for having a student leaders' corps. One, it provides an opportunity to nurture desirable personality traits such as self-confidence and dependability and to develop leadership qualities. Another reason is that a leaders' corps frequently enables the teachers to plan more efficiently a large and more varied program that will benefit additional indi-

FIGURE 6-13. The use of student leaders for spotting and other activities makes possible an extension of the program. (Courtesy, Spokane School Department, Spokane, Washington)

viduals and small groups. Without student leaders to act as assistant instructors, many overpopulated classes would simply vegetate from week to week.

A number of schools have attempted to improve programs of elementary physical education by using eighth and ninth graders to teach physical education activities to elementary school youngsters. Pioneering this development of leadership abilities, the Sarasota, Florida, Junior High School won the acclaim of the school administration and the community at large because its students were able to work with grade-school children so effectively. The Junior Teacher Program in the El Camino High School (South San Francisco) also serves children in grades kindergarten through sixth and has been very successful in motivating both those students that are taught and those who teach. Motor skills and knowledges are improved, and human relationships are developed that would be hard to experience to the same degree almost anywhere else in the educational structure. There appears to be a growing amount of enthusiasm for children teaching children, and Jerome Bruner finds that this "cross-age tutoring" not only increases performance of the tutorial children but also increases self-worth and group pride among all parties involved.[26] It seems important, therefore, to plan, organize, and schedule time for leadership experiences through physical education.

Some of the ways in which student leaders are helpful and make possible the implementation of a richer physical education curriculum are as follow:

1. They participate in teaching class activities—usually by being squad leaders, concerned with some management and routine record keeping of squad activities.
2. They assist with supplies and equipment necessary for the day's instruction. Supervising, cleaning, repairing, and keeping inventory cards for these supplies may also be a requirement of the leader.
3. They assist in laying out playing courts and fields for class use.
4. They act as area supervisors responsible for preparing an area for an activity.
5. They take part in both class and intramural officiating.
6. They help in the production of special programs, such as exhibitions, demonstrations, local clinics, and sports days.
7. They act as class monitors responsible for such items as locker room order, shower room supervision, control of lights, and keeping the class roll.
8. They assist, through individual attention, fellow students who are weak in certain skills and physical condition.
9. They participate in the measurement program by helping to test boys and girls and by keeping records, timing performances, scoring, measuring, and so forth.

QUESTIONS FOR DISCUSSION

1. Do you agree or disagree with Daryl Siedentop's view that teaching skills cannot be separated from curriculum development and organization?
2. Physical education programs should not remain static, but should be reviewed and reorganized regularly. In planning for changes, how can one decide whether to stand by the current program or make modifications?
3. Suppose your fourth grade physical education class were studying an integrated unit on "Early America." Suggest a list of physical education learnings pertaining to this kind of unit.
4. It is usually not difficult to correlate elementary school rhythms and

[26]Jerome Bruner, "Continuity of Learning," *Saturday Review*, March 1973, p. 24.

dance activities with social studies. Suggest several ways in which this might be accomplished. References such as books by Miller, Cheffers, and Whitcomb, Halsey and Porter, Dauer, and Ruth Murray should prove helpful in developing your response.

5. How did you react to the statement relative to student leaders' (Sarasota, Florida, Junior High School) being trained to work effectively with elementary school children? Are there possible weaknesses in such a plan?

6. Bryant Cratty, in *Social Dimensions of Physical Activity*, speaks of leadership in terms of a social situation, and indicates that leadership is transferable from task to task. How might you use this information when asking an administrator for a block of time in which to carry out leadership training?

7. How might one organize sports skills so that they could be programed on a card for a student to follow? Having developed the card, how might you organize the classes in order to put it to use?

SUGGESTED ACTIVITIES

1. Arrange to visit a city director of physical education and inquire about how his or her total curriculum is put together and how instructors go about carrying it out. Examine the program for seasonal content, time allotment, variety of activities, and electives available for both boys and girls.

2. Examine some of the literature pertaining to flexible scheduling in the schools. Formulate a list of advantages and disadvantages as they appear to be associated with inner-city schools. Do the same for small suburban schools. What do you find being done in physical education as it applies to small and large schools?

3. Find out where some form of team teaching is being carried on. Visit the school and investigate first-hand the extent to which the teachers feel they are effective. Are there any pitfalls in team teaching? Nicholas Polas says so in his book on *The Dynamics of Team Teaching* (Dubuque, Iowa: William C. Brown Co., 1967), chapter 4.

4. In discussing the future of physical education in the secondary school, some writers have indicated that the flexible module concept is very helpful. Locate and read articles (pro and con) on this proposition. Also, examine some courses of study for physical education in the secondary grades, and then draft a short statement either supporting or not supporting the module concept.

5. Suppose you are employed by a small-city school system as director of physical education. You have been asked to become involved in curriculum reform for the school as a whole. Indicate in several steps how

you might participate in such a project and how your participation might benefit physical education.

6. Select a game, sport, or dance appropriate for a particular level of growth and development of your choice. Make a list of the content items that seem necessary to cover in teaching the activity. Now try to put the content items in sequence from the easiest to perform and understand to the most difficult. Comment briefly on the ease or difficulty you had in attempting to do this assignment.

7. Survey the time-allotment figures from several communities pertaining to elementary and secondary physical education. Secure a copy of the course of study or curriculum guide in each of these communities. How, if at all, does course content differ in keeping with time allotted in the several communities involved?

SELECTED REFERENCES

BUCHER, CHARLES A., *Administration of School Health and Physical Education Programs* (6th ed.) St. Louis: C. V. Mosby, 1977.

DARST, PAUL W., and CAROL SEVERANCE, "Let Your Students Help You Teach," *Journal of Physical Education and Recreation*, 48 (June 1977), 48.

DAUER, VICTOR P., *Fitness for Elementary School Children through Physical Education* (5th ed.) Minneapolis: Burgess Publishing Co., 1976.

DAUGHTREY, GREYSON, *Effective Teaching in Physical Education for Secondary Schools* (2nd ed.). Philadelphia: W.B. Saunders Co., 1973.

————, and JOHN B. WOODS, *Physical Education Programs: Organization and Administration* (2nd ed.). Philadelphia: W.B. Saunders Co., 1976.

FELSHIN, JAN, "Rationale and Purposes for Physical Education," *Curriculum Improvement in Secondary Physical Education*. Washington, D.C.: American Association for Health, Physical Education and Recreation, 1973.

FROST, REUBEN B., *Physical Education Foundations: Principles and Practices*, chap. 11. Boston: Addison-Wesley Pub. Co., 1975.

GOLUBCHICK, L., and B. PERSKY, *Innovation in Education*, chap. 54. Dubuque: Kendall/Hunt Pub. Co., 1975.

GOODLAD, JOHN I., *The Changing School Curriculum*. New York: The Fund for the Advancement of Education, 1966.

HARTMAN, BETTY, and ANNIE CLEMENT, "Adventure in Key Concepts," *Journal of Health, Physical Education and Recreation*, 44 (March 1973), 20–23.

JAMES, HELEN J., "Building Reading Vocabulary in Physical Education and Health Classes," *Journal of Physical Education and Recreation*, 48 (May 1977), 56–57.

LAWTHER, JOHN D., *The Learning of Physical Skills*. Englewood Cliffs, N.J.: Prentice-Hall, Inc., 1968.

MILLER, ARTHUR, JOHN CHEFFERS, and VIRGINIA WHITCOMB, *Physical Education in the Elementary School Curriculum* (4th ed.). Englewood Cliffs, N.J.: Prentice-Hall, Inc., 1974.

NELSON, WAYNE E., "Need We Fear Voluntary Physical Education?" *Journal of Health, Physical Education and Recreation*, 43 (January 1972), 63–64.

NIXON, JOHN E., and ANN E. JEWETT, *Physical Education Curriculum*, chapters 3 and 6. New York: Ronald Press, 1964.

OLIVER, ALBERT I., *Curriculum Improvement*. New York: Dodd, Mead & Co., 1971.

PEGNIA, ANTHONY, "Helping Youngsters Read through Physical Education Experiences," in *Elementary School Physical Education*, ed. Paul A. Metzger, Jr., Dubuque, Iowa: Wm. C. Brown Co., 1972, pp. 122–24.

PISCOPO, JOHN, "Videotape Laboratory: A Programmed Instructional Sequence," *Journal of Health, Physical Education and Recreation*, 44 (March 1973), 32–35.

POLOS, NICHOLAS C., *The Dynamics of Team Teaching*. Dubuque, Iowa: W.C. Brown Co., 1967.

SIEDENTOP, DARYL, *Physical Education–Introductory Analysis*. Dubuque, Iowa: W.C. Brown Co., 1973.

——, *Developing Teaching Skills in Physical Education*, chap. 4. Boston: Houghton Mifflin Co., 1976.

STRAUB, WILLIAM, *Lifetime Sports Orientation*. Englewood Cliffs, N.J.: Prentice-Hall, Inc., 1976.

TABA, HILDA, *Curriculum Development: Theory and Practice*, chap. 22. New York: Harcourt, Brace and World, 1962.

VAN TIL, WILLIAM, *Curriculum: Quest for Relevance*. Boston: Houghton Mifflin Co., 1971.

WELSH, RAYMOND, ed., *Physical Education: A View Toward the Future*. St. Louis: C.V. Mosby Co., 1977.

WERNER, PETER, "Integration of Physical Education Skills with the Concept of Levers at Intermediate Grade Levels," *Research Quarterly*, 43 (December 1972), 423–28.

The Curriculum Guide

chapter seven

> A problem of curriculum design is . . . the problem of maintaining *balance* in the curriculum. Balance, of course, means ensuring that appropriate weight be given to each aspect of the design so that distortions due to overemphasis and underemphasis do not occur.[1]
>
> ROBERT S. ZAIS

The need to seek balance in the preparation of a curriculum guide or course of study is quite understandable as one weighs and questions the amount of emphasis to be accorded the subject matter content, on the one hand, and the learner, on the other. Setting forth carefully developed learning activities and student evaluation procedures is every bit as important as writing a detailed description of content items pertaining to particular motor skills, knowledges, and progressions from grade to grade (see Figure 7-1). For some teachers the thought of having to organize and write a course of study or curriculum guide is staggering indeed. There is little doubt that in many places developing a curriculum guide is hard, time-consuming work. Also, in a great many schools, staff and time to study curriculum change are limited.

Nevertheless, the time has never been better in this country for developing valid and useful curriculum outlines and course particulars. Parents, school board members, and other educators want to see where we are going in physical education, and they want to see it on paper. Leland Stanford used to say, "The world stands aside for the man who knows where he is going." He was 100 percent right: If you know *where* you are going, people will listen. In the past there have been too many physical education teachers—particularly

---

[1]Robert S. Zais, *Curriculum Principles and Foundations* (New York: Thomas Y. Crowell Co., 1976), Chapter 18.

200

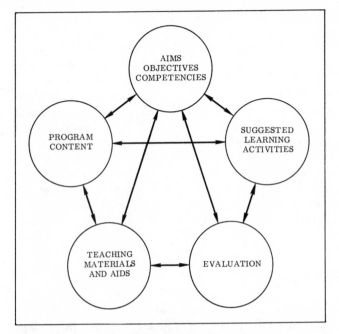

FIGURE 7-1. Curriculum components in balance.

on the local level—who have known where they wanted to go but failed to communicate with others, primarily, in writing. Fortunately, this weakness is being overcome as more and more groups of conscientious teachers band together.

At every local level, there is an opportunity to structure the physical education program on paper for all to see, to review, and in time, to modify. Moreover, one need not cause an educational explosion to get started. Simply acknowledge the necessity of written materials and ask permission to get started in a small way. Request support for a time and place to do some exploratory study. State the need. Move boldly with confidence and determination to set forth all the things you have dreamed of having in a good physical education program. Why not dream and struggle?

Curriculum Design

To cook with a "pinch of this" and a "snatch of that" in a manner reminiscent of Grandma and her baking of molasses cookies is hardly appropriate for the housewife today. A detailed recipe is required so that guesswork is eliminated. For the same reason the orchestra conductor follows a complex score, and the schoolteacher refers to a guide.

A curriculum design is a model or a pattern. It is a generalized framework which exists for teachers individually and collectively.[2] It represents in words, pictures, or both, the essence of an educational field. It is, says Raymond Muessig, "an hypothetical construct that contains many of the different components that must go into an educational program or a course of study. It is a vehicle that carries philosophies, aims, theories assumptions, cognitive and effective offerings, processes, findings, and analysis or comparisons."[3] This is a pretty full definition. From a utilitarian viewpoint, many guide builders may not desire such depth and detail in their courses of study. Their designs, therefore, may have little to do with lengthy philosophical discussion and program analysis and comparisons. This kind of written information may well appear elsewhere—perhaps as a separate statement developed for a separate publication supporting the overall purposes of physical education in the community.

Preliminary Considerations

A useful guide requires forethought and planning. At best, it will have a number of limitations. In the first place, guides and materials in physical education cannot do everything. Perhaps the effect of a curriculum guide on a program is only 5 percent beneficial. Yet, businesses fail on less than a 5 percent margin.

There are a number of preliminary considerations in developing the program and constructing the guide. These are as follows:

The Appointment of a Planning Committee. When the time is ripe for building a new curriculum guide or revising the old one, it may be advantageous to have a planning group appointed, particularly in the large school system. Such a group is an "initiating group," generally charged by the city director of physical education and the superintendent of schools to probe into practical ways of developing a comprehensive physical education program for the community (see Figure 7-2). One physical education representative from the secondary schools, one from intermediate grades, one from primary grades, and one from school administration would be a sufficient number to meet with a physical education supervisor as the official planning committee to give thought to the scope and depth of the revision to be undertaken.

There are several steps a planning group may take to initiate the curriculum project.

[2]William B. Ragan and Gene D. Shepherd, *Modern Elementary Curriculum* (New York: Holt, Rinehart and Winston, 1971), p. 164.

[3]Raymond H. Muessig, *Social Studies Curriculum Improvement: A Guide for Local Committees,* Bulletin No. 36, Washington, D.C.: National Education Association, National Council for Social Studies, 1965.

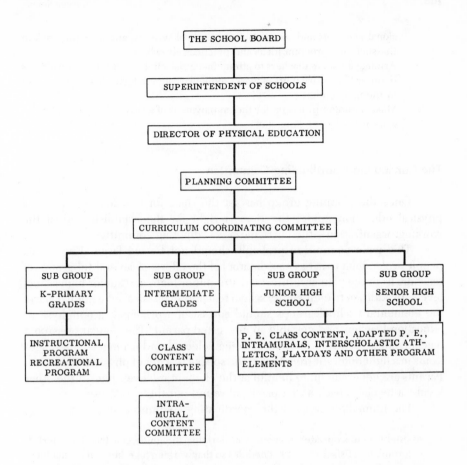

FIGURE 7-2. Organization for curriculum development in physical education.

1. Explore the expressions of dissatisfaction with the present curriculum—a logical beginning. A simple curriculum survey questionnaire can be prepared so that all members of the staff, teachers of all grades and coaches included, can respond. Each physical education teacher should be able to respond in terms of (1) the physical activities then being offered at his or her level, (2) what the teacher considers to be the strengths of that offering, and (3) what he or she considers to be the weaknesses.
2. Give some thought to categorizing learning experiences in physical education that may occur beyond the limits of the school gymnasium, pool, or playground. Later, during the guide construction stage, an effort will be made to integrate out-of-school experiences and alternative programs with in-school experiences.
3. Meet with the separate school principals and eventually with the school board in order to establish necessary administrative procedures.
    a.   Obtain released time for physical education teachers to attend some profes-

  sional meetings and visit out-of-town school systems; and to report back to the staff new program ideas and practices elsewhere.

b. Arrange for some teachers to attend in-service clinics and summer institutes in order to prepare units of work, sequences, and so forth, that may be used in the new guide.

c. Make a budget provision for the employment of a curriculum consultant to work with the teaching staff.

The Curriculum Coordinating Committee

  Once the planning group has set the stage for the development of a physical education guide, the time is right for the establishment of the working organization—the curriculum coordinating committee.

  This main committee probably should not be too large. Five or six people are enough to act as coordinators of the efforts of several subgroups of teachers from the primary, intermediate, junior high, and senior high school levels. In addition to elementary school teachers of physical education, each of the elementary school groups should consist of a principal, a nonphysical-education teacher, and possibly an interested parent. The regular classroom teacher, an asset when content is being selected and arranged, often sees items in a light different from that of the special teacher of physical education. Parents are generally quite helpful at the elementary level, too. At the other levels, a teacher-coach and a principal round out the committee.

  The immediate tasks of the coordinating committee are:

1. to establish appropriate procedures underlying the guide construction effort
2. to formulate satisfactory work schedules so that working together will be challenging for all members of the subgroups
3. to arrange stages and sequences of work
4. to prepare justifications for program proposals
5. to appoint members of the school system physical education department to subgroups. Subgroups will be necessary for kindergarten, primary, and intermediate level boys and girls. This latter level will also need an intramural subgroup. Other groups will be required for junior high and senior high boys and girls. At the secondary level, subgroups are needed for adapted physical education, boys' and girls' intramural recreation activities, and interscholastic athletics for boys and for girls
6. to organize the work of subgroups and subcommittees, and when it is completed fit it into the complete curriculum
7. to write the curriculum guide when all the information is on hand

  The work of the coordinating committee and the several specialized subgroups is time-consuming. Exchanging educational philosophies, debating personal convictions, and arriving at common goals for youth at the various age levels alone frequently take several meetings. Yet, it is worth proceeding slowly and carefully at this beginning stage in order to lay a foundation that all teachers of physical education will accept and build on when the guide becomes a reality at a later date.

The secret of group action is that if several people of different backgrounds are involved in a cooperative effort, there is likely to be some common agreement and enthusiasm for the content of the guide. In the state of Washington, about 450 people throughout the state had some worthwhile part to play in the construction of the curriculum guide over a fourteen-month period.

In defense of teachers generally, it should be pointed out that most of them take a professional attitude toward their jobs. They believe in the need for better programs and are willing to do something about them. Unfortunately, in a large number of school systems the teacher is bogged down with administrative or clerical detail and seldom has time to pursue a Utopian program.

The Role of the Administrator

As might be expected, the support of the school administrator is crucial to successful curriculum development. This person's contact with all teachers is direct; a show of enthusiasm is very often reflected in the way they carry out their teaching.

As a member of the curriculum team, the school principal has some specific responsibilities.

1. arranges for a proper place for the committee and subgroups to meet and knows which teachers can accept extra work in light of current duty assignments
2. sets forth for the committee the general goals of the total educational system and may relate these goals to physical education and vice versa
3. arranges released time for committee and group participants, including late afternoon and evening meetings and the occasional employment of substitute teachers
4. makes available numerous resources, such as instructional materials, bulletins, printed references, and, in some cases, consultant services from a nearby community or teacher-preparation institution.
5. arranges for the necessary secretarial services, equipment, and supplies
6. informs the local citizens of progress being made in developing the physical education guide, tries to make them understand why all the effort to improve physical education is necessary, as they are generally a school system's greatest asset
7. cooperates with committee personnel in raising questions and seeking answers relative to the impact of the new curriculum items on the rest of the school program
8. encourages scientific inquiry in general
9. helps appraise the results of the curriculum project

Collecting Materials

The essential task of the coordinating committee is to encourage the subgroups to perform their functions with optimism, spirit, and efficiency. The subgroups, in turn, especially in the larger school systems, will supervise the activities of the separate subcommittees that are concerned with the various segments of the physical education program.

Throughout the stages of curriculum development and guide building process, individuals and small groups of people will be gathering data. Initially, these data will pertain to physical education philosophy and general aims. Shortly thereafter, they will narrow down to lists of specific-grade-level objectives and behavioral objectives, to be followed in depth by content items and teaching suggestions. At this stage the subcommittees will be working the hardest. Their task will be to create blocks of material in the form of specific lesson plans that represent the results of a careful selection of activities and a graduated sequence of instruction. In the elementary grades, for example, a classroom teacher and the physical education instructor may prepare a sequence of fundamental rhythms that will later be fitted into the instructional program by the subgroup. For example, a music teacher might be added to the subcommittee of two who would be interested in defining what is essentially music education, what is physical education, and what can be correlated in organizing the topic of basic rhythms for boys and girls. In secondary schools a number of subcommittees will be at work. Two instructors may work to develop an appropriate basketball unit for the junior high school. Where they initiate the program and how far they develop it will have to be related to elementary and senior high school basketball skills; this may create the need for two or three basketball subcommittees to work together, so that when basketball content is considered by the subgroup, it will represent the combined thought and effort of personnel at several instructional levels.

Fitting all the reports of subcommittees into one perfectly balanced program will require some elaborating and some cutting. A great motion picture is made the same way. In every respect a report is a cooperative effort capable of providing a rich professional experience for the participant.

Constructing the Guide

With most of the curriculum materials collected and with some thought given to writing the guide, it is a good idea to look at several recent guides or courses of study. The libraries of most teacher-preparation institutions carry examples of local curriculum guides in physical education. They include manuals from large cities, small towns, rural areas, and suburban regions. Helpful is the annual listing of curriculum guides contained in the publication of the Association for Supervision and Curriculum Development (ASCD). Another ASCD publication, *Curriculum Materials,* may be of value. Also useful are the guides and units of work prepared at the state level.

In reviewing several of the better guides for the various grades, it is interesting to observe that a number of them have roughly the same format and table of contents. Outlines are generally prepared either for the total school program or separately for the elementary and secondary levels. In considering the total program, a format such as the following might be employed:

  I.   Title of Guide
 II.   Introduction
III.   Philosophy of Physical Education
     Physical Education Defined
     Why Physical Education?
     Movement and Sports in Education
 IV.   Physical Education Program Aims
     Long-Range Goals
     Objectives
       Behavioral Objectives or Competencies by Grade Level
       Concepts by Grade Level
  V.   Program Content
     Time Allotments
     Broad Layout Plan—Elementary
     Broad Layout Plan—Secondary
     Elementary
       Learning Activities
       Resource Aids and Materials
     Secondary
       Learning Activities
       Resource Aids and Materials
 VI.   Evaluation in Physical Education
     Elementary
     Secondary
VII.   Selected References
     For Students by Level
     For Teachers by Level

Of course, there are many excellent curriculum guides now being used all over the country. The organization of content is similar in the larger systems. A review of guides in cities such as Philadelphia in the East; Gary, Indiana, in the middle states; and Salem, Oregon, in the West, reveals numerous points of agreement. Perhaps because they have less staff to build the guides, many rural and smaller communities present outlines that lack detail. This is understandable. The town of Lexington, Massachusetts, is an exception. Its guides are regularly revised and are limited in scope to certain ages. At the elementary level, for example, the Level I guide is for pupils five to eight years of age; Level II is for pupils seven to ten years of age, and Level 3 is for children nine to twelve years of age.[4]

The following illustration is that of a state department of education curriculum guide. Because most state guides are constructed with the assistance of local people working in committees, it is not strange to find that they do not differ essentially from those written by a town or city staff. State guides, such as New York State's, are usually developed to help school administrators and physical education teachers plan well-balanced programs.[5] Very often teachers use the state guide as a model and construct their own courses of study.

[4]*Physical Education Elementary Guide, Level III, 9–12 Years of Age*, Lexington, Mass.: Lexington Public Schools, 1973.
[5]*Curriculum Guide, Physical Education in the Secondary Schools*, Albany, N.Y.: State Education Department, updated.

Organization of the Program
   Class Instruction
   Adapted Activities
   Extraclass Athletic Activities
The Scope of the Program
Content of Program
A Sample Physical Education Curriculum, Grades 7–12
Administration of the Program

Usually, the curriculum guides with greater depth are the ones that set forth a number of helpful points relative to the learner and the learning process, as well as including suggestions for the various program elements.

How to Use a State Guide

In many respects, a state guide is a stepping-off point for local school teachers. Frequently, it sets forth a variety of methods of approach to the development of challenging programs. The New York State Guide points out:

> The guide is not meant to be a comprehensive development of a complete program of physical education for children, rather it is expected that teachers may use the examples as a model in developing similar plans for teaching other basic motor activities and to work out developmentally progressive units of work important in the total movement education experience of the child.[6]

The curriculum guide from the state frequently serves as a flexible resource for planning lessons. To use such a guide properly, the State Office of Public Instruction in Olympia, Washington, made four fine suggestions to district teachers:

1. Appoint a curriculum committee to review the entire guide.
2. Ascertain how the program items may best be taught—integration, correlation, or direct instruction.
3. Designate teachers to develop more detailed teaching units.
4. Develop in-service programs.

QUESTIONS FOR DISCUSSION

1. Since the design of the program is set forth in the curriculum guide, is there a danger that the program may become too rigid?
2. What are some of the circumstances that might occur to prevent you from teaching units of a program as they appear in a guide or course of study?

[6]Ibid., p. 13.

3. One of the reasons given for having a planned program of physical education is that it helps the instructor avoid monstrous repetition. Try defending this statement. Also, try to attack it as misleading.
4. To what extent should elementary classroom teachers become involved in planning the physical education curriculum? Explain your viewpoint in detail.
5. Having examined several curriculum guides, what do you find to be the common elements? Why do the guides have common elements?

SUGGESTED ACTIVITIES

1. Organize a plan for a summer workshop for teachers who will gather to construct a curriculum guide for secondary physical education.
2. In one of his studies of teachers and institutions (*The Education of American Teachers* [New York: McGraw-Hill, 1963], pp. 153–54) Dr. Conant suggests that elementary teachers should have familiarity with a variety of subjects, and should have depth in a single subject or combination of related subjects. In your opinion, could this depth be in physical education? How do you think elementary teachers feel about this? Run a brief survey in which ten or a dozen teachers are questioned on this point. What are your findings?
3. Visit a school system that is developing or revising its physical education program. Find how teachers are organized, how the guide content is being gathered, and how the guide will be prepared.
4. Review several curriculum guides. Compare content as set forth by large communities with that developed by small towns in rural areas.
5. Suppose you were a city director of physical education with a staff of men and women teaching in twenty-three elementary schools, five junior high schools, and two senior high schools. Your task for the school year is to examine the present curriculum content and how it is being implemented. Where would you begin? How would you organize curriculum committees? Set up a hypothetical plan of operation.
6. Examine several curriculum guides in areas other than those of physical education. Note how they differ and how they are like many of those in physical education. Do there appear to be any major weaknesses? Discuss these.

SELECTED REFERENCES

Eisner, Elliot W., ed, *Confronting Curriculum Reform*. Boston: Little, Brown and Company, 1971.

GRIEVE, ANDREW, "Try It—You'll Like It—Format for Curriculum Guide," *Journal of Health, Physical Education, and Recreation,* 43 (May 1972), 34–35.

HASS, GLEN, *Curriculum Planning: A New Approach* (2nd ed.). Boston: Allyn and Bacon, 1977. Section 6.

MCNEIL, JOHN D., *Designing Curriculum.* Boston: Little, Brown and Company, 1976.

OLIVER, ALBERT I., *Curriculum Improvement.* New York: Dodd, Mead & Company, 1971.

part three

IMPLEMENTING

THE CURRICULUM

The Elementary Program,

Grades K-6

chapter eight

> . . . In teaching children, train them by a kind of game, and you will be
> able to see more clearly the natural bent of each.
>
> PLATO, *THE REPUBLIC*

When composing his poetry and song Carl Sandburg gave thanks for the laughter of children ". . . who tumble barefooted and bareheaded in the summer grass." Like others, he was impressed by their naturalness, innocence, and lack of sophistication—the essential characteristics that make it possible to accept the words of Plato relative to obtaining a valid observation of how children feel about an activity and each other while at play. In a more profound dimension, Gesell was concerned with group play as an activity that "taps the deeper springs of personality which are not reached by sedentary and restricted indoor schooling" and renders "a beneficial effect upon the organization of the emotions."[1]

From the disciplines of the classics and archeology, and from the antiquities of civilization come support for the concept that children's play is as old as the culture. From Rousseau to Piaget it has been called priceless—the children's way of life. Through play the children learn about themselves and the people and the world around them. Children, as well as animals, have not waited for people to teach them their playing. This they have done themselves, in a manner that is serious and full of meaning. John Denver, the Aspen lyricist, sings elegantly about "the wisdom of the children."[2] There is much to be learned from them.

[1]Arnold Gesell, *The Child from Five to Ten* (New York: Harper and Row, Publishers, 1946), p. 363.
[2]From the lyrics set forth by Gerald B. DeFries, "Will I Ever Catch Another Butterfly?" *Journal of Health, Physical Education and Recreation*, 41 (November-December 1970), 41–43.

The Kindergarten Pupil

It is difficult to structure a program of physical education that is perfect for the kindergarten child. It is much safer to think in terms of activities satisfactory for the longer time from nursery school to first grade. There is a solid reason for this. Variations in maturation, coupled with the many other differences among boys and girls, require that the curriculum provide a variety of experiences for students to enjoy.

The attention given to enjoyment is not to be taken lightly. For young children the need to have fun and thoroughly enjoy an activity is very important. The kindergarteners are alive and alert. They are not going to submit to lecturing and reasoning as to why they perform certain physical activities. They are simply going to act and *feel*. This characteristic is well expressed by Dorothy Gardner in her book, *Feelings and Learning*, when she says, "The basis of learning is emotion . . . there is no intellectual interest which does not spring from the need to satisfy feelings."[3]

Clark Hetherington had these five- and six-year-olds in mind over a half-century ago when he stressed the need for sympathetic teachers who can provide a nondominating kind of leadership and for the type of physical education content that will fit the developmental characteristics of the pupil.

This child craves activity, has an imagination that outruns skill and judgment, and has a short span of attention. Large muscles are better developed than the small ones. He and she can run, jump, skip, climb, speak and act spontaneously, brag often, yet be capable of self-criticism. The age group is "mother-centered" and self-centered, proud of possession, curious, and usually healthy (except for occasional colds).

This is the pupil who needs:

1. to experience basic body movements involving the arms, legs, and trunk, with and without music and rhythms
2. to participate in games with simple rules and boundaries
3. to engage in vigorous physical activities
4. to have periods of quiet activity and rest periods
5. to eat mid-morning food, milk, or juice
6. to gain confidence as a person
7. to take turns and to share
8. to love a warm, friendly, reassuring teacher of physical education

The Kindergarten Program

Much of the play activity suitable for the five-year-old is set forth in the many curriculum guides as proper for primary graders as well. A circle game, for example, is just as beneficial for a kindergarten child as it is for a second-

[3]Dorothy E. M. Gardner, "Emotions, a Basis for Learning," in *Feelings and Learning*, Washington, D.C.: Association for Childhood Education, 1965, p. 34.

grader. The choice of games, story plays, and creative activities depends upon the depth of attention and detail the students can handle. Therefore, simple tag games, ball-handling activities, and individually centered fun games, such as "Fox and Geese," "Squirrels in the Tree," and "Magic Carpet," are quite appropriate.

There are a number of desirable physical activities for kindergarten children that can be organized under the following headings.

1. ball activities
2. circle games
3. exploring games
4. imaginative play
5. drawing and modeling
6. story plays
7. fundamental skills of running, jumping, climbing, balancing, hopping, and skipping
8. rhythmical activities
9. singing games

Take a moment to review the selected references at the end of this chapter that deal primarily with specific games, dances, and other activities. Note that it would not be difficult to formulate a list of desirable physical activities for five-year-olds.

The question of how to distribute the time assigned to physical education will depend on the program emphasis. A play-instruction period of twenty minutes per day permits time enough to organize a regular course of study. Fait prefers thirty minutes, with an emphasis on movement-exploration skills and rhythms that may total 30-60 percent of the allotted time.[4] It is quite possible that with the increasing attention being given to the "guided discovery technique" of teaching, the Fait figures are wholly reasonable. It does take time to explore—especially if the teacher is extremely careful not to tell the answers. Mosston makes this point very clear in his discussion of the "discovery method."[5]

Kindergarten children need playground experiences also. They should learn how to use essential playground equipment correctly—not only for enjoyment but for personal safety. It is also a time to plan for free play, in which the pupils can do as they like. The free play should be preceded by the learning of a number of interesting activities from which pupils tend to make their free-play selections.

[4]Hollis F. Fait, *Physical Education for the Elementary School Child,* 3rd ed. (Philadelphia: W. B. Saunders Co., 1976), p. 68.
[5]Muska Mosston, *Teaching Physical Education* (Columbus, Ohio: Charles E. Merrill Books, 1966), p. 145.

The Primary Grade Pupil
(early childhood, ages six to eight years)

Both program planning and effective teaching require a familiarity with the signs of growth and development—especially in physical, social, and emotional behavior. In this connection, it is better to group children over a three-year span than it is to subdivide the growth period and try to pinpoint behavior at any one particular year. Moreover, there is never a time when all boys and girls in a class are at the same growth stage. In Table 8-1 the subdivisions used serve only as convenient labels for periods of growth. A thorough understanding of these general characteristics and needs will make it easier to pass judgment on the nature of elementary physical education content and the amount of time that should be assigned to each activity.

At this age level, the effect of physical prowess on personal feelings of adequacy is significant. During the elementary years children place definite values upon their own abilities and those of their peers. The level of skill attainment is closely associated with social prestige. By the third grade, children who are superior in gross motor skills are by and large better adjusted than the children who exhibit poor ability in these skills.[6] This indicates that quality is significant in the teaching of a wide variety of skills and requires more attention than it gets in some places.

TABLE 8-1. Ages Six to Eight Years

General Characteristics	Needs
1. *Physical Characteristics* Growth is relatively slow during this period as compared to the early period. Large muscles of the trunk, legs, and arms are more developed than the smaller muscles.	To experience many kinds of vigorous activities involving many parts of the body. This will increase heart action and respiration and help build endurance. To improve skills of body control—speed, stopping, starting, dodging, turning, balancing.
Hand-eye coordinations are incomplete, but developing. Eyes are slow to focus and usually farsighted at start of this period.	To experiment with many kinds of movements. To catch, throw, run.
Bones are hardening. Heart and lungs are small in proportion to body weight and height.	Relaxation periods to follow periods of physical activity.

[6]Lawrence Rarick and Robert McKee, "A Study of Twenty Third Grade Children Exhibiting Extreme Levels of Achievement on Tests of Motor Proficiency," *Research Quarterly*, 20 (May 1949), 142–52.

[7]The characteristics and needs were taken in part from Carl E. Willgoose, *Health Education in the Elementary School*, 5th ed. (Philadelphia: W. B. Saunders Co., 1979), chap. 6.

TABLE 8-1. *Continued.*

General Characteristics	*Needs*
Endurance may be poor.	Continued emphasis on proper body mechanics and posture in all school activities.
Fatigue is "enemy of childhood," but recuperation from fatigue is usually good.	To receive instruction in swimming skills.
Reaction time is about half that of an adult.	To have approximately twelve hours of sleep a night. To know how to play safely.
Accidents are leading causes of death, especially for boys.	To have the chance to express himself through numerous activities that stimulate physical, social, and mental-emotional growth.
The five- to eight-year-old usually has great vitality and radiates exuberance and enthusiasm for most physical activities.	To play favorite games, often, with no emphasis on score.
Becomes restless when he cannot be active.	To engage in a number of physical education activities, all of short duration.
2. *Mental-Emotional-Social Development* Individualistic and possessive; egocentric after age six.	To learn to share with others, to play alone and with small groups, and to play as an individual in larger groups. Needs recognition for his personal abilities and to shift gradually to more group activities.
Dramatic, imaginative, and highly imitative. Curious about things in general.	To create and explore, to "try out his muscles," to perform new stunts, and to identify himself with persons and things.
Wide variety of emotional reactions. Enjoys rhythm and rhythmic sounds.	To receive guidance in social developments through game experiences.
When approaching age eight, he wants a chance to act on his own and is sometimes annoyed with conformity. More sensitive to judgment of other children with a slowly decreasing concern for adult opinion.	To win without boasting and to lose without an alibi. To respond to rhythmic sounds such as drums, rattles, musical beats, voice, etc.
Generally eager to learn new physical education skills and please the instructor.	To cooperate at school and home in play and other group activities.
Boys and girls tend to form separate play groups.	To participate in some corecreational games and dances to foster a degree of mutual understanding.[7]

The Intermediate Grade Pupil
(middle childhood, ages nine to eleven years)

The experienced teacher will appreciate that most of the characteristics of the intermediate grade child are not new. They are only modified and represent a gradual maturation of the primary grader from the more negative to the more positive qualities. Again, children are following their own paths, and the characteristics of growth and needs in Table 8-2 are representative of the average rather than of any one individual:

TABLE 8-2. Ages Nine to Eleven Years

General Characteristics	Needs
1. *Physical Characteristics* Muscular strength is behind physical growth; postural habits vary.	To have instruction in body mechanics, causes of fatigue, nutrition, and factors influencing growth in height and weight.
A noticeable growth spurt takes place at end of period which continues into adolescence. This differs with individual levels of maturation.	To engage in strenuous activity that taxes the muscles, heart, lungs, and other organs to the limit of healthy fatigue.
Sex differences appear, with girls more mature and taller. Rough-and-tumble activities highly enjoyed, often by the girls.	To engage in wholesome corecreation and coeducational relationships, both in the classroom and on the playing field.
A few girls begin menstruation by ages eleven and twelve.	To participate in those physical skills that properly utilize elements of roughness to build motor skills and physical fitness.
Some girls may be more developed in motor skills than some boys.	To be recognized as different individuals. To have a chance to appraise self through self-testing activities.
Coordinations are good. Many physical skills are now automatic. Reaction time is improved.	To relate success in motor skills to personal well-being and health habits.
Interest in food and appearance increases.	To discuss personal grooming and the nature of physical fitness.
2. *Mental-Emotional-Social Development* Longer span of attention and greater interests in a wide variety of activities.	To take part in a wide range of physical activities involving several methods of presentation and teaching aids.
Noticeable craving for recognition; a strong sense of rivalry.	To experience success in a number of physical activities—and to do so with some degree of cooperative effort.

TABLE 8-2. *Continued.*

General Characteristics	*Needs*
An increasing attitude of independence coupled with a desire to help.	To have a chance to formally plan, lead, and carry out certain projects and to check progress made. To assist the instructor with supplies, records, etc.
Sex antagonisms gradually appear. Sexual modesty is observed.	
Strong sense of loyalty to groups, teams, or "gangs." Greater concern over group approval than teacher approval.	To gain respect and approval of others. To engage in activities in which achievement is recognized by one's peers.
	To compete fairly with others, obtaining an understanding of the place of personal cooperation in the process.
Enjoy competition, whether physical or essentially mental, but may become angry when tired, or easily discouraged.	To work coeducationally in the physical activities that broaden social relationships and obtain answers to questions involving the opposite sex.
Interest in opposite sex indicated by teasing, hitting, chasing, etc.	
Interests shifting from the immediate environment to the wider world.	To become aware of games and sports from other lands, and what they mean in everyday living.
Adventuresome; interested in all kinds of experimentation; critical enough to need to be shown why.	To take part in challenging physical education activities and begin to learn a number of these in detail.

Curriculum Content for the Elementary Grades K–6

Figure 8-2 indicates the scope of the physical education curriculum for the whole elementary school. It presents a kind of overview that would probably fit the pattern of most localities that enjoy the six-year elementary school organization. It could be adjusted and extended without much effort to embrace a middle-school plan.

In Figure 8-2, the primary grades have some concern with the activities of all ten major areas. Having reviewed a good many curriculum guides, the author finds the information within this overview quite in line with present practice. Of course, some schools that are pressed for time do less in each of the major areas than others do.

Another overview category employed sometimes is social-recreational activities. School-community activities are highlighted, and pupils plan recreational games for parties and other social affairs. If there is an adequate time allotment for the physical education curriculum, there is room for this social-recreational emphasis.

FIGURE 8-1. Program in space go together. Fifteen boys playing a game of head tag.

Middle Schools

More than 80 percent of middle schools indicate a grade 5-through-8 or 6-through-8 pattern. In these situations there is no junior high school, so the middle school has the responsibility of helping the students make a satisfactory transition from the child-centered philosophy of the elementary school to the subject-centered high school curriculum. This "bridging-the-gap" experience between elementary and secondary has been growing in popularity, with the number of schools quadrupling in a recent five-year period. In Middle Schools the program is student-centered with flexible student schedules which can vary daily, and planning is done by a team of teachers directly responsible for the activities of a group of students. However, in most instances the physical education program has not been modified to any significant degree. In short, the grade 4 to 6 program is simply extended to seventh- and eigth-graders with perhaps a little more attention given to depth of instruction.

OVERVIEW OF ACTIVITIES SATISFYING GROWTH DEMANDS

GRADES 1 - 6

MAJOR AREAS	1	2	3	4	5	6
I. MIMETICS						
Mimetics	X	X	X			
Story Plays	X	X	X			
Athletic Game Actions				X	X	X
II. MOVEMENT EXPLORATION	X	X	X	X	X	X
Movement Fundamentals	X	X	X			
Creative Movements	X	X	X	X	X	X
III. RHYTHMS AND DANCES						
Basic Rhythms	X	X	X			
Creative Rhythms	X	X	X	X		
Singing Games	X	X	X			
Folk Dancing	X	X	X	X	X	X
Social Dancing						X
Novelty (Tap, Clog, etc.)				X	X	X
Marching	X	X	X	X	X	X
IV. GAMES						
Group Games	X	X	X	X	X	X
Team Games				X	X	X
Lead-Up Games				X	X	X
Relay Games			X	X	X	X
Dual Games						X
V. SELF-TESTING ACTIVITIES						
Tumbling	X	X	X	X	X	X
Miscellaneous Stunts	X	X	X	X	X	X
VI. APPARATUS						
Balance Beam	X	X	X	X	X	X
Playground Equipment	X	X	X			
Ropes and Rope Jumping		X	X	X	X	X
Gymnastics					X	X
VII. PHYSICAL CONDITIONING	X	X	X	X	X	X
Posture Training			X	X	X	X
VIII. SWIMMING	X	X	X	X	X	X
IX. INTRAMURALS				X	X	X
X. MISCELLANEOUS						
Adventure - Challenge Activity			X	X	X	X
School Camping				X	X	X
Recreation	X	X	X	X	X	X

FIGURE 8-2. The scope of an elementary school program of physical education.

FIGURE 8-3. Fun plus challenge on the playground.

224

Time Allotments

After seeing the number of major activities that are taught to some degree throughout the country, one might legitimately inquire where the emphasis is to be placed. The answer, in part, depends on where pupils are in skills and knowledge at any grade level, and on what experiences they have had during preschool and kindergarten years.

The most common practice is to give more attention to the movement education and rhythms areas at the primary level, and to games at the intermediate level. Numerous communities have developed excellent guides just for these two categories. It is generally felt that if more communities had swimming facilities and a swimming program, swimming would command a large share of the total time available. Unfortunately, there is still a long way to go before swimming becomes an important curriculum item.

The time allotted to elementary school physical education varies from state to state. The range is from 45 to 150 minutes per week. In New York State, it is 120 minutes per week exclusive of time necessary for dressing and showering; the time may be divided between morning and afternoon.[8] The standard of the American Association for Health, Physical Education and Recreation is 30 minutes per day of instruction activity for all children; this is in addition to time allotted for free and/or supervised play.[9] In several cities, 40 minutes per day is allocated for instruction—20 minutes in the morning and 20 minutes in the afternoon.

Even a few minutes can provide for a variety of physical education activities. In the Brookline, Massachusetts, kindergarten and primary grades lesson plans that follow, the particular 20 minute and 30 minute time allotments are effectively broken down.

Emphasis on Major Activities

The most pressing question asked in every curriculum conference and workshop is: "How much time shall I give to a major physical education activity?" What percentage of the time should be allotted to games? To self-testing activities? To dance? Do we assign more or less time to an activity as we progress from the kindergarten to the sixth grade?

A close look at the amount of time allocated to the major elements of the

[8]George H. Grover, "New York State's New Regulations Governing Physical Education," *Journal of Physical Education and Recreation*, 46 (September, 1975), 29–30.
[9]American Association for Health, Physical Education and Recreation, "Essentials of a Quality Elementary School Physical Education Program," *Journal of Health, Physical Education and Recreation*, 42 (April 1971), 42–46.

```
┌─────────────────────────────────────────────────────────────────────────┐
│                      SAMPLE LESSON PLAN FOR K-3                            │
│                                                                           │
│  Model for Kindergarten — 20 minute period                                │
│                                                                           │
│      5 minute   GROUP ACTIVITY:   Active-type movement (i.e. parachute    │
│                 play).                                                     │
│                                                                           │
│      5 minute   RHYTHMIC ACTIVITY:   Singing Game (i.e. Shoemaker's        │
│                 dance).                                                    │
│                                                                           │
│      6 minute   INDIVIDUALIZED ACTIVITY: Ball skills (i.e. throwing and    │
│                 catching).                                                 │
│                                                                           │
│      4 minute   GAME:   Incorporating ball skills taught (i.e. call ball   │
│                 or circle toss).                                          │
│                                                                           │
│     20 minute   TOTAL                                                      │
└─────────────────────────────────────────────────────────────────────────┘

┌─────────────────────────────────────────────────────────────────────────┐
│  Model for 1 - 3 — 30 minute period                                        │
│                                                                           │
│      2 minute   READINESS OR WARM-UP:   Run, jumping jacks, sit-ups and    │
│                 toe touch.                                                 │
│                                                                           │
│      5 minute   INDIVIDUALIZED ACTIVITY:   Mat stunts (i.e. forward roll,   │
│                 tripod and headstand).                                     │
│                                                                           │
│      3 minute   COUPLE ACTIVITY:   (i.e. wring the dishrag, twister,        │
│                 Chinese get-up).                                           │
│                                                                           │
│     10 minute   RHYTHMIC ACTIVITY:   Simple locomotor patterns to music,   │
│                 drum, or no accompaniment.   (i.e. step-step-hop-step)     │
│                                       (i.e. skip-skip-run-run-hop)         │
│                                       (i.e. slide-step-turn-slide-step-turn)│
│                 *Allow children to create their own movement patterns      │
│                 and show to class (include a forward roll).                │
│                 *Play "corners." Who can go from the center of the gym     │
│                 to a corner by using 3 different ways of moving and using  │
│                 your feet?                                                 │
│                                                                           │
│      6 minute   GROUP ACTIVITY:  Parachute play over mats while individual │
│                 children and small groups of children create their own     │
│                 patterns as they go under and across parachute.  (i.e.     │
│                 step-hop-step-hop-forward roll-jump).                      │
│                                                                           │
│      3 minute   BRIEF DISCUSSION:  How does your body look when you do a    │
│                 forward roll? What do the two people have to do in trying   │
│                 the Chinese get-up?  Why? What shape do your hands and head │
│                 make on the mat when you do a tripod?                       │
│                                                                           │
│     30 minute   TOTAL                                                      │
└─────────────────────────────────────────────────────────────────────────┘
```

FIGURE 8-4.

physical education program by the various guides and authors reveals a number of common trends:

1. Games and basic sport skills grow considerably in importance from the primary level to the intermediate. Most curriculum guides show games getting increasingly more attention until by grade 6 they frequently command 50 percent of the physical education program.
2. Mimetics and story plays decrease with the child's age.
3. Time for rhythms and dances is usually reduced slightly between grade 3 and grade 6.
4. Movement education tends to receive less attention in the intermediate grades.

226

TABLE 8-3. Miller, Cheffers, and Whitcomb[10]

Sexes	Boys and Girls			Boys			Girls		
Grades	1	2	3	4	5	6	4	5	6
Types of Activities	Percentages¹			Percentages			Percentages		
1. Movement exploration	25	25	20	10	10	10	10	10	10
2. Low organization activities	35	35	20	20	20	15	25	20	15
a. Running and tag games	(20)	(10)	(5)	(5)	(5)	(5)	(15)	(5)	(5)
b. Ball games	(15)	(20)	(10)	(10)	(10)	(5)	(5)	(10)	(5)
c. Relays	(5)	(5)	(5)	(5)	(5)	(5)	(5)	(5)	(5)
3. Team Sports	0	0	20	40	40	45	35	35	40
a. Sport skills	(0)	(0)	(5)	(10)	(15)	(15)	(15)	(15)	(15)
b. Lead-up games	(0)	(0)	(5)	(15)	(10)	(5)	(15)	(10)	(5)
c. Athletic team games	(0)	(0)	(0)	(5)	(15)	(25)	(5)	(10)	(20)
4. Dance activities	20	20	20	10	10	10	15	15	15
a. Creative rhythms and dance	(10)	(10)	(10)	(5)	(5)	(5)	(10)	(10)	(10)
b. Singing games	(5)	(5)	(0)	(0)	(0)	(0)	(0)	(0)	(0)
c. Folk dances	(5)	(5)	(10)	(5)	(5)	(5)	(5)	(5)	(5)
5. Apparatus, tumbling, stunts	15	15	15	15	15	15	15	15	15
6. Individual and couple activities	5	5	5	5	5	5	5	5	5
Totals	100±	100±	100±	100±	100±	100±	100±	100±	100±

Notes

Parentheses indicate partial scores under the respective types of activities.
¹Percentages are given here to illustrate trends and should not necessarily be considered unchangeable.

[10]Arthur G. Miller, John Cheffers, and Virginia Whitcomb, *Physical Education in the Elementary School Curriculum*, 4th ed. (Englewood Cliffs, N.J.: Prentice-Hall Inc., 1974).

5. Activities such as stunts, tumbling, apparatus, and self-testing routines, tend to increase slightly with age and cut across both primary and intermediate levels, appealing to both extremes of the age groups.
6. Relay racing begins gradually at about grade 2 and commands about 5–10 percent of the total elementary school time.
7. Swimming, although considered desirable, is generally omitted because of unavailable facilities.
8. Lead-up games become a significant element of the program in grades 4–6.

In Tables 8-3, 8-4, 8-5 are some illustrations of time allocated to the major physical education areas.

TABLE 8-4. Fait Time Allotments[11]

A. Activities	Nursery School, Kindergarten, and Primary Grades			
	N1 3 yrs.	N2 4 yrs.	K–1 5–6 yrs.	2–3 7–8 yrs.
Basic skill or low organized games		10–20%	20–30%	15–25%
Rhythms (70% movement exploration type)	40–60%	30–50%	25–45%	25–45%
Stunts and tumbling and self-testing activities	10–20%	10–30%	10–30%	10–30%
Basic skills of activity			5–10%	5–15%
Fundamental skills (50% movement exploration type)	10–30%	10–30%	10–30%	10–30%

	Upper Grades					
	4–5	4–5*	6	6*	7–8	7–8*
Basic skill games or low organized games	5–10%	10–15%	5–10%	10–15%	2.5–5%	5–15%
Rhythms and dance	15–20%	20–25%	10–15%	15–20%	2.5–5%	5–15%
Stunts and tumbling and self-testing activities	15–20%	20–25%	15–20%	20–25%	20–25%	25–30%
Basic skills of sports	10–15%	10–15%	10–15%	10–15%	10–15%	10–15%
Fundamental skills	5–10%	5–10%	5–10%	5–10%	5–10%	5–15%
Aquatics	20–25%	–	20–25%	–	20–25%	–
Team activities	25–30%	30–35%	30–35%	35–40%	35–40%	40–45%
Physical fitness or developmental activities†	5–10%	5–15%	5–10%	5–10%	10–15%	10–15%

(Classroom games not included in total percentage)

*Time allotment when swimming is not available.
†Many activities overlap; nearly all make some contribution to physical fitness. The category here is restricted to those activities in which the chief contribution is to physical fitness such as pull-ups.

[11]Hollis F. Fait, *Experiences in Movement: Physical Education for the Elementary School Child,* 3rd ed. (Philadelphia: W. A. Saunders Co., 1976), p. 68.

TABLE 8-5. Dauer[12]

Primary Grades	K	Grades (Percent) 1	2	3
Movement Experiences and Body Mechanics	40	35	35	20
Fitness Routines, Activities				10
Rhythmic Activities	30	25	25	20
Apparatus, Stunts, Tumbling	15	20	20	20
Simple Game Activities and Relays	15	20	20	20
Sports Skills and Activities				10
Swimming and Water Safety				(a)

Intermediate Grades	4	5	6
Movement Experiences and Body Mechanics	5	5	5
Fitness Routines, Activities, Testing	20	20	20
Rhythmic Activities	15	15	15
Apparatus, Stunts, Tumbling, Combatives	15	15	15
Simple Game Activities and Relays	20	15	10
Sports Skills and Activities	25	30	35
Swimming and Water Safety	(a)	(a)	(a)

(a) Swimming and Water Safety is a recommended area of instruction for elementary schoolchildren. The amount allocated to this area would depend upon the facilities and instruction available. If swimming is included in the school program, it should proportionately reduce the percentage of time allotted to other activities.

TABLE 8-6. Third Grade Time Allotment

Activity Type	Percentage (year)	Periods (days)
Movement Exploration and Body Mechanics	20%	36
Rhythmical Activities	20	36
Stunts, Tumbling, Apparatus	20	36
Fitness Routines	10	18
Simple Game Activities and Relays	20	36
Sport Skills and Activities	10	18
Totals	100%	180 days

[12]Victor P. Dauer, *Dynamic Physical Education for Elementary School Children*, 4th ed. (Minneapolis: Burgess Publishing Co., 1971), p. 18.

FIGURE 8-5.   Explorations begin early with easily moved equipment.

TABLE 8-7.   Third Grade Planning for Seasons

| | | Seasons | | | |
Activity Type	Year's Periods	Fall	Early Winter	Late Winter	Spring
Movement Exploration and Body Mechanics	36	5	13	13	5
Rhythmical Activities	36	0	16	15	5
Stunts, Tumbling, Apparatus	36	8	10	10	8
Fitness Routines	18	6	2	5	5
Simple Game Activities and Relays	36	16	2	2	16
Sport Skills and Activities	18	10	2	0	6
Total	180	45	45	45	45

Implementing the Allotted Time

Structuring the program elements comes next. Although the percentages assigned to an activity can be translated into an effective physical education program in a number of ways, the manner in which Dauer does it is

230

relatively easy and practical.[13] He suggests seven steps. This may be illustrated with a third grade program:

1. The major activities are selected and the time to be assigned to each is determined.
2. The number of whole class periods devoted to an activity is calculated from the percentage assigned. For example, suppose we assign movement exploration 20 percent of the total third grade time. Therefore, 36 periods are assigned to movement exploration because this is exactly 20 percent of a total of 180 school days for the year.
3. The activities are scheduled by seasons. In a nine-week season there would be 45 school days. How might the 36 periods assigned to movement exploration be spread over the year? As indicated below, most of it (32 periods) comes during early and late winter when classes are usually indoors. Simple games, however, are concentrated in the fall and spring when classes can enjoy the greater space of the outdoors. Note, too, that most rhythmical activities are scheduled during the winter months.
4. For each season of the year a weekly program is made. This reflects both the activity and the time element already determined.
5. Chosen next are the specific activities to be taught each day of the week.
6–7. Outlines and lesson plans are constructed for each lesson in the week.

Curriculum Content

A number of comments should be made regarding the major areas of emphasis. A quick glance at Figure 8-2 will serve as a review of the content.

I. Mimetics

To overlook this area for the more spectacular ones is to miss one of the greatest opportunities to see children performing as their true selves. From the nursery school through the primary grades, "all the world is a stage," and the boys and girls—beautifully immature and uninhibited—are the actors and actresses. Moreover, the laws of science mean nothing to them at all, for they can be flying humans at one instant and lumbering elephants the next. Living the part of the elevator operator or even being the elevator itself is an illustration of play in its fullest sense. It is serious and full of meaning. It is imaginative and loaded with opportunities for creativity. Freedom and lack of regimentation prevail. Probably more often than suspected, mimetics in their several forms are capable of providing pleasant relief from the anxieties and mental workout of the classroom—the true re-creation.

Simple mimetics, in which boys and girls demonstrate how leaves fall,

[13]Victor P. Dauer, *Fitness in Elementary School Children Through Physical Education* (Minneapolis: Burgess Publishing Co., 1962), pp. 19–20.

Movement education, therefore, may be simply defined as a means of achieving body management through an understanding of movement factors and the ways in which they affect the body in motion. In this case *body management* refers to the control of the body as it moves. *Movement exploration* is the general term given to the method employed: guided discovery and problem-solving.

To know the body—its capabilities and its limitations—is the objective in movement education. Seymour Fisher makes it clear that individuals experience their bodies more often and in far greater depth than any other object in the environment, but their perception of this frequently remains distorted throughout life.[19] Moreover, there is research to suggest that a number of learning difficulties and behavioral problems may be improved by giving children a more realistic image of their bodies, especially their spatial dimensions. Studies carried on in selected New York City schools indicate that children lacking in experiences using their bodies are often at a disadvantage in the classroom; there is an improvement when individuals become involved, not only in manipulative skills, but in controlling the body in space and discovering how the different parts of the body move.[20] It is clear that early motor experiences are more important than ever for young children because they relate so closely to such items as self-discovery, environmental discovery, freedom, safety, communications, enjoyment and sensuous pleasure, and acceptance. Furthermore, classroom teachers have volunteered that "movement exploration improves listening habits, creativity, and confidence. . . ."[21]

Body management activities contribute to the development of laterality and directionality, which are fundamental to perceptual-motor skills. In the Dayton, Ohio schools there are seventeen full-time teachers working under James C. Wheeler in a body-management program that serves both brain-damaged children and those with perceptual-motor problems relating to underachievement. In Ocilla, Georgia, the body-management efforts of Martha Owens have resulted in a model program in which movement readiness through listening and awareness activities is employed prior to physical activities taking place.

Hackett and Jenson have contributed considerably to the concept of "movement exploration" as a major area in the physical education curriculum.[22] They present movement experiences in relation to time, space,

[19]"Experiencing Your Body: You Are What You Feel," *Saturday Review*, July 18, 1972.

[20]Theresa Rizzitiello, "Movement Education Challenges an Inner-City School," *Journal of Health, Physical Education and Recreation*, 43 (January 1972), 35–37.

[21]Elsie Werra, "Movement Education: Play with a Purpose," *Instructor*, 80 (October 1970), 84–88.

[22]Layne C. Hackett and Robert G. Jenson, *A Guide to Movement Exploration*, (Palo Alto, Calif.: Peek Publications, 1966).

FIGURE 8-6. Moving and taking a position is perceiving. (Reprinted from *Instructor*, copyright © October 1972, The Instructor Publications, Inc., used by permission.)

force, and what Rudolf Laban refers to as "flow." Their curriculum items and progressions are especially well-presented, and their sample lesson plans could be used in almost any elementary school with little modification. Schurr's analysis of basic movements and detailed learning activities is also very helpful.[23] Excellent progressions are available in loop films from The Athletic Institute, Holt/Ealing, and Encyclopedia Britannica Films.

The movement education focus, as Mosston admirably points out, must be on the structure.[24] Paramount to the success of this experience is the guided discovery concept—a well-documented technique of teaching employed in other fields of education. Guided discovery differs fundamentally from other styles of teaching in that the teacher prepares the pupil for learning *but never tells the answers.* By following this rule, the teacher stimulates inquiry. The physical education pupils are motivated to *find out* for themselves how a movement feels in its many variations. Problem-solving is part of the discovery process. It occurs when they seek answers entirely on their own. For example, they may be given a clue from the teacher that a ten-inch ball has certain qualities they might want to examine. They seek an answer or answers. How many ways can the ball be bounced? How many ways can it be used? How does it feel to bounce it several ways, or use it otherwise?

Since movement exploration activities were started in the English schools over a quarter-century ago, they have increased measurably in popularity both in America and abroad. Supporters of the "movement movement" have made it clear that:

1. Individual development of each pupil is the chief concern.
2. Successful movement experiences contribute to self-confidence and enhance the self-image.
3. Movements are introduced in the form of a challenge appropriate for the age of boys and girls.
4. Pupils figure out their own movements in ways that mean something to them.
5. Creativity is encouraged; all possible patterns are open for investigation.
6. Progression from the simple to more complex movements is structured into the daily class period and over the course of the total unit of study.

For the most part movement exploration activities have been concerned with the basic skills. In some of the British elementary schools, however, a variety of apparatus skills—referred to as modern educational gymnastics— are taught as movement experiences. Pupils are given a free choice as to how they use the apparatus, and they are encouraged to move continuously. Howard tells how the students are directed "toward supporting and suspending their bodies on different parts of the apparatus and toward developing a variety of ways for mounting, dismounting, and moving on the apparatus. The teacher then further structures problems by specifying the path of the movement, the types of movement, or the quality of movement."[25]

[23]Schurr, *Movement Experiences for Children*, chapter 9.

[24]Mosston, *Teaching Physical Education*, p. 2.

[25]Shirley Howard, "The Movement Education Approach to Teaching in English Elementary Schools," *Journal of Health, Physical Education, and Recreation*, 38 (January 1967), 31–33.

FIGURE 8-7. Limited by a rope circle, what can I do? (Courtesy, Marjorie Blaufarb, American Alliance for Health, Physical Education and Recreation)

Lorena Porter has had considerable experience with Rudolf Laban's principles of movement. She illustrates this by building her themes for lessons around five fundamental questions:

1. *Why* do we move? (purpose)
2. *Where* do we move? (space perception)
3. *How* do we move? (quality control)
4. With *what* do we move? (body action)
5. With *whom* do we move? (relationship)[26]

The teaching of exploratory movement can be simplified under the following categories:

1. *Body Awareness:* Learning to control and move the body as a whole, or different parts of it, in many different situations.
2. *Space Awareness:* Discovering the ways in which the body can move through space, and learning to control those ways.
3. *Time:* Movements can be varied and made more interesting by changing the speed at which they are performed.
4. *Force:* Movements require different amounts of effort to be performed efficiently, and the force with which a person moves results in highly varied activities.
5. *Flow:* A movement may be freely flowing and unable to be arrested or bound in flow and under control at all times.
6. *Continuity:* Whether a movement is continuous and flowing or broken and staccato makes an important difference.

[26]Elizabeth Halsey and Lorena Porter, *Physical Education for Children,* rev. ed. (New York: Holt, Rinehart and Winston, 1963), pp. 174–76.

To illustrate the principles listed above, the teacher prepares the class for an exploration of movement with a question such as "How far to the right can you reach without falling over?" or, with the pupils in a standing position, "Can you sit down on the floor without touching either hand to the floor?" Note that the use of such phrases as "Can you . . .?" and "Show me . . ." are particularly useful in challenging a group of students to move creatively and individually. In the area of fundamental movements a number of experimental activities are possible.

WALKING

1.   Can you walk with the toes pointed straight ahead and the arms swinging freely from the sides?
2.   Show how you walk very fast and change to another direction when the whistle blows.
3.   Walk in a large circle without running into anyone.
4.   Can you walk to a black object in the gymnasium, touch it, and return to where you started without touching anything else?
5.   Show how a person walks through wet snow that is over one foot deep.

RUNNING

1.   Can you run all about the gymnasium without hitting anyone?
2.   Try running quickly and quietly on your toes.
3.   Can you run by bringing the knees up to the waist?

HOPPING

1.   Hop on one foot in a small circle.
2.   Stand with both feet together and hop forward into the air, landing on both feet. Can you repeat this six times in a straight line without falling over or hitting anyone else?
3.   Can you hop into the air using both feet and clap your hands twice before you land?
4.   Show how a rabbit hops.
5.   Can you hop backwards in a small circle?

SLIDING

1.   Step sideward to the right with the right foot; slide the left foot to the side of the right foot; shift body weight to the left foot.
2.   While sliding to the left, swing your arms to the opposite side.
3.   Try to slide with two other people in a circle.
4.   While sliding to the right, place hands behind the neck and look to the left. Can you do this in reverse?

SKIPPING

1.   Step out with the left foot; hop on it; step forward with the opposite foot; repeat. Can you do this with the right foot?

2. Can you skip around the gymnasium and change direction when the whistle blows?
3. Skip backward holding hands over head.
4. Find a partner and skip together in a small circle.

DODGING

1. Can you move quickly in any direction—sideways, forward, backward, down and up?
2. Show how you run quickly around the gymnasium dodging classmates.

LEAPING

1. Show how you leap.
2. Show how you would leap over a toy wagon left in the driveway to your house.
3. Leap very high into the air.
4. Leap forward to gain distance.
5. Hold hands with a partner and leap together several times for the length of the gymnasium.

CLIMBING

1. Can you make believe you are climbing a ladder?
2. Show how you would climb the ropes (nearby).
3. How do you climb when one hand is carrying an object, such as a book?

OTHER FUNDAMENTAL MOVEMENTS

(Each of these movements can be varied. Pupils can be challenged to perform them forward, backward, up, down, around, and as they might be executed in certain occupations and sports.)

Swinging–A pendulumlike movement executed by the arms, by the legs, or by the body as a whole.
Bending and Stretching–Movements that bring parts of the body closer together or farther apart.
Pushing and Pulling–A strong movement away from the body or a strong movement toward the body.

In the Londonberry, New Hampshire elementary schools, a fair amount of attention is devoted to the concept of movement and self-imagery as a way of perceiving one's self in the general environment. For example, in grade 2 a question is raised that leads to the activities in Figure 8-8.

It should be made clear that in the process of exploring the fundamental movements, the pupil should eventually arrive at the happy state of knowing how to execute basic skills properly. For example, he may have experimented with several ways of walking and running, but should emerge from these activities with a walking position that is erect and relaxed and a running gait

```
┌─────────────────────────────────────────────────────────────────────────┐
│          QUESTION:    CAN YOU SEE AN ACTIVITY IN YOUR MIND                │
│                       BEFORE YOU DO IT?                                    │
│                                                                            │
│                       ACTIVITIES - GRADE 2                                 │
├─────────────────────────────────────────────────────────────────────────┤
│                                                                            │
│   CAN YOU SEE ANIMALS?    Lions, Tigers, Bears,                            │
│                           Snake, Turtle, Chicken                           │
│                                                                            │
│   CAN YOU SEE MACHINES?   Jet Plane, Rocketship, Crane,                    │
│                           Typewriter                                        │
│                                                                            │
│   CAN YOU SEE PEOPLE?     King, Knight, Soldier,                           │
│                           Policeman, Fireman, Doctor                       │
│                                                                            │
│   CAN YOU SEE BODY POSITION?   Swinging and Swaying    With Reference To:  │
│                                Bending and Stretching  Space, Quality, Quantity │
│                                Rising and Falling                          │
│                                                                            │
│                           Back to Back, Scooter Games, Wheelbarrow Relay,  │
│                           Red Light, Jump Rope, Tunnel Ball, Keep Away,    │
│                           Crab Tag, Posture Tag                            │
│                                                                            │
│   CAN YOU SEE:  yourself preparing to return to school                     │
│                 someone taking a long hike through the woods               │
│                 the farmer picking apples                                  │
│                 the Pilgrim going into the woods to shoot a Thanksgiving turkey │
│                 someone throwing snow balls                                │
│                 trees in a storm                                           │
│                                                                            │
│   CAN YOU SEE A LETTER OF THE ALPHABET - Now make it with your body:       │
│                                Group Activity - forming words,             │
│                                such as:                                     │
│                                - Walk, Run, Skip, Hop -                     │
│                                                                            │
└─────────────────────────────────────────────────────────────────────────┘
```

FIGURE 8-8.

that is rhythmical and flowing. In all of the fundamental movements it is good to contrast very quick and very slow movements. This is the way to understand the impact of time, force, and flow on the body. But before leaving the lesson completely, the teacher should be certain that each student knows how to walk, run, hop, jump, skip, gallop, and leap in good form.

Although the fundamental game skills may be taught through movement education activities, there is evidence to indicate that the traditional teaching methods may be more effective, especially when the game skills are combined in group play. One study of elementary school girls showed that in all of the activities, except basketball, the movement exploration group was significantly better than the traditional group.[27] Probably a combination of the traditional and movement education methods is warranted, depending on the type of activity taught and facilities available.

It seems reasonable to expect a number of values to be obtained when the growing child has an opportunity to experience a wide variety of move-

[27]Anna B. Thaxton, Anne L. Rothstein, and Nolan A. Thaxton, "Comparative Effectiveness of two Methods of Teaching Physical Education to Elementary School Girls," *Research Quarterly,* 48 (May 1977), 420–27.

ment that he or she gives some thought to and acts on directly. The human organism is a unity. Its adaptive behavior involves all parts, organs, and special structures. Mind and physical processes are subject to the same principle of integration. Every activity that encourages a close association between thinking and acting is educationally sound. Moreover, it tends firmly to link the kinesthetic or "muscle sense" with the higher domain of the central nervous system, therefore cultivating an early appreciation for skilled movements.

III. Rhythms and Dances

There is a rich social inheritance embodied in rhythms and dance. In all lands, for centuries, dances have been a part of the lives of people. They have been executed formally as an art form, and as a means of self-expression for religious worship, war, death, birth, marriage, and funerals. They have been performed spontaneously for pure joy and to communicate feelings and ideas.

One of the wonders of the dance experience, says Nancy Smith, "is its changing, amorphous, and quicksilver nature. It is process, not permanent fixed product. The same is true of the child, a human changeling hung between being and becoming, suspended in being for a very brief and special time. It is beautifully apparent that dance and the child are natural companions."[28]

The social value of singing games and folk dances is unquestioned, for they relate to the customs, interests, and traits of peoples everywhere. To the young person who is awakening to an era of adventure and challenge, what a wonderful stimulation lies ahead as he or she prepares to dance "Bonnie Dun Dee" with the Canadian lumberjacks or the French Colonial Minuet, the Hungarian Czardes, the English Hornpipe, the Polish Polka, the Russian Cossacks' dance, the dances of Israel, or the dances of the American pioneers from the great Southwest.

For the child, dancing can be a constant delight, for childhood is the one time in life when children are uninhibited—when they can relax, be creative, and be themselves. Every movement and succession of movements they make to rhythm are a form of dance. Even two elemental movements a boy or girl puts together may be called dance. Dance, like art, is a composition. It is expression in movement. Teachers working closely with children are quick to point out:

> Don't be afraid of dance—it's just simple when you let your mind move your body with imagination.
>
> I create a situation for the group to interpret. . . . I use a turbulent piece of

[28]Araminta Little, "The Meaning of Dance for Young Children," *Journal of Physical Education and Recreation*, 48 (May 1977), 35–39.

music suggesting that they are in a storm seeking shelter. In another, the students portray miners trying to escape after being trapped in a mine cave-in. To Western music, the children are pioneers pulling oxen, going through deserts, and wading through mud. . . . In all selections, I try to have them interpret and experience as many human emotions as possible—grief, great pain, love for one another, hatred, jealousy and isolation (loneliness).[29]

As our work with dance progressed I found the children following directions, listening, thinking, solving problems, and inventing. I felt that they were feeling better about themselves, and were sensing and responding; they felt accomplishment.

The (dance) experiences provided for these children included combining locomotor and nonlocomotor movements in various ways, using a problem-solving approach, using percussion to accompany original movements, and using the body to move to original interpretations of words, phrases, sentences, haiku, and other poetry.[30]

We asked:

Can you move one part of your body fast and another slow to music?

Can you freeze like an icicle, then thaw and drip from the sunshine?

To a slow, steady beat can you twist yourself like a dishrag and then shake out again?

Survey data reveal that dance and dance-related activities in early and middle childhood have been sadly neglected. Programs in grades 3 through 6 appear limited insofar as rhythmic activity is concerned, and little emphasis is given to creative activities and the relationship to literature, creative dramatics, science, or social studies. Because of this the Task Force On Children's Dance set forth the following guidelines:[31]

MOVEMENT–CENTERED DANCE ACTIVITIES

The following movement-centered activities are basic to children's dance development and, when adapted to age level, should form the major part of the dance curriculum from early through middle childhood and beyond. It is upon the success of these experiences, especially the first four, that satisfactory and satisfying dance learnings will depend.

Experiences evolving from the use of the movement element of space, time, force, and the development of an awareness of sequential changes in body shape.

[29]Monica Prendergast, "Creative Dancing," *Instructor,* 80 (March 1971), 62–63.

[30]Marie Louise Sterne, "Dance in the Creative Arts Curriculum," *Journal of Health, Physical Education and Recreation,* 42 (October 1971), 33.

[31]Task Force on Children's Dance, I. *Status of Dance In The Elementary School,* AAHPER, *Journal of Health, Physical Education and Recreation,* 42 (June 1971), 14–23.

Movement exploration, improvisation, investigation, and invention, using dance ideas such as those evolving from experiences with movement elements, from imaginary and literary sources, from properties of various kinds, or from music and other types of sound accompaniment.

Experiences with movement, which help to synchronize it with musical structure, such as pulse, accent, phrasing; the development of sensitivity to the quality of musical sounds and the ability to relate to them in many different ways.

Experiences with basic locomotor and nonlocomotor movements; making combinations of these movements; discovering and learning traditional dance steps.

The organizing of movement into dances of various complexities.

The relating of dance movement to other curriculum experiences, such as art, music, science, social studies, and language arts—wherever and whenever appropriate.

Of the many kinds of "learned" dances, certain ones help to motivate movement in early childhood. Some of these are known as action or movement songs, others as singing games or song dances. These should be included in a comprehensive dance curriculum.

Traditional folk dance patterns are best left for the middle childhood years, where they will be learned quickly and danced with satisfaction if based upon earlier learnings. Further experiences which might be included in the dance program for the middle childhood years are the following.

Experiences with movement, arrived at through exploration, which can be used to increase body strength, flexibility, and precision.

Experiences in ethnic and popular "fad" dance patterns.

Opportunities for performing dances for schoolmates other than regular classmates and possibly for outsiders, such as parents.

In the primary grades, the teacher of music and the physical education instructor frequently work together. Both are equally interested in fundamental rhythms. Musicians seek a response to or "feel" for sound—the tempo and strength of the beat. The physical education teacher seeks the same through a muscle reaction. Both, therefore, build their early grades curriculum on rhythmical responses: marching, running, hopping, and so forth, to the beat of a drum, and other appropriate sounds.

Rhythmical activities are an excellent means of socializing. They furnish vigorous, strong, and free movements that allow children to express just about every emotion that can be isolated. Furthermore, rhythms and dances tend to lead boys and girls away from self-consciousness and timidity into confidence and poise. Needless to say, these joyous undertakings are most effective when selected on the basis of age, maturity, background, ability, and interest of children. Moreover, there should be a gradual progression of rhythmic activities from the kindergarten through the school years.

The rhythmical curriculum for the primary grades may be divided into four areas: (1) basic rhythms; (2) creative rhythms; (3) singing games; and (4) folk dancing.

1. *Basic rhythms* are not altogether different from the locomotor activities associated with movement education. The primary distinction is that the activities are performed rhythmically. Activities such as walking, running, hopping, skipping, jumping, sliding, galloping, and leaping are done to an accompaniment of rhythm sticks, tom-tom, hand clapping, piano, tone block, triangle, and appropriate records. For certain movements, a particular accompaniment is quite effective. The slow clanging of a gong or cymbals is excellent for leaping movements. The triangle is perfect for setting a clear beat for rhythmical skipping. Band music is hard to surpass when it comes to marching. It makes children *feel* like marching and performing other movements to music. It is difficult to keep from tapping a toe when the music is played. Quick-time marching and double-time marching are popular activities. Changing from the slow tempo to the fast is also fun.

There is a value in responding rhythmically with different parts of the body and in portraying how various things feel. Progressions move from experiencing contrasting dimensions, such as high and low, heavy and light, hard and soft, to responding to even and uneven rhythmic patterns, high and low level sounds, and the flow of music and movement.

Bouncing rubber playground balls to a musical beat is an activity that can be a part of almost any primary grade curriculum. Throwing, catching, passing, and dribbling different-sized balls can be done to the musical beat.

Rope jumping can be done to several kinds of musical accompaniment. The waltz, the polka, and quick march music are appropriate for jump-rope activity. The chance to create new patterns of movements employing balls and jump ropes is ever present.

2. *Creative rhythms* permit some freedom of choice in rhythmical movements. Young children enjoy dramatizing, suggesting new rhythmic movements, and creating patterns. English, social studies, and other subjects are filled with possibilities for self-expression that may take the form of rhythmic movements created by children. With a little help, at Thanksgiving time, a basic Indian war step or canoe dance step can be used by pupils to establish several patterns of movement.

Creative exploration through rhythms and dance may be accomplished in a number of ways: creating an exercise routine in time to music, a rhythm beat, or the reading of a poem; performing a movement from a stimulus given by a phrase of music; making up a simple dance routine to the music of a familiar song; and illustrating an innovative swimming routine to music and beat. The main elementary school thrust, as Torrance has pointed out, is not to leave creative development to chance. Instead, teachers should encourage

FIGURE 8-9. What am I doing right now? (Courtesy, Marjorie Blaufarb, American Alliance for Health, Physical Education and Recreation)

curiosity, be respectful of unusual ideas, recognize original creative behavior, ask questions that require thinking, build onto skills that the pupils already have, and give opportunities for learning in creative ways.[32]

3. *Singing games and folk dancing* have much in common and probably should be considered together. In singing games, the children learn the words to a song. Sometimes the words tell what to do in the dance that follows, such as in the traditional Mulberry Bush tune in which the children chant and act, "This is the way we wash our clothes, wash our clothes, wash our clothes. This is the way we wash our clothes so early Monday morning." At other times, the old nursery rhymes are sung but have little to do with telling the movement; examples are "The Muffin Man" and "Baa Baa Black Sheep."

Although the folk dance is defined as traditional dance, over the years many variations have developed. Primary grade children usually take part in simple actions such as walking, skipping, sliding, and side-stepping, in their singing games and dances, reserving the more specialized steps, such as the polka, waltz, and schottische, for the intermediate grades.

In both the primary and intermediate grades, the folk dances have much to offer. They usually have a history that children should know. They frequently use a distinct musical tune that is associated with the country they come from. At the intermediate level, they include the American square

[32]E. Paul Torrance, "Seven Guides to Creativity," in Paul A. Metzger, Jr., ed., *Elementary School Physical Education* (Dubuque, Iowa: William C. Brown Co., 1972).

dances and contradances as well as the more complicated couple dances from various sections of the United States and abroad. Every elementary dance curriculum should include the traditional dances from other lands, for they are part of the American heritage and contribute admirably to the cultural objectives. A few examples of the more appropriate dances from other lands are:

FOLK DANCES OF EUROPE

Bulgarian–Tropanka
Czechoslovakia–Tancij, Kanafaska
Denmark–Created Hen, Ace of Diamonds, Shoemaker Dance, Nixie Polka, Little Man's in a Fix
England–Maypole Dance
Estonia–Jamaja Labajalg
Finland–Martin Wappa
France–Corsican Dance, Jibido-Jibido, La Soyothe
Germany–Come Let Us Be Joyful, Brummel Schottische, Broom Dance
Holland–Dutch Couples, Little Dutch Girl
Hungary–Csebogar, Czardes
Ireland–Irish Lilt, Six-Hand Reel
Italy–Tarantella, Italian Danza
Lithuania–Kalvelis
Norway–Norwegian Mountain March
Poland–Kujawiak
Scotland–Highland Schottische, Rye Waltz
Serbia–Kolos
Sweden–Lassie Dance, Gustaf's Skoal, Hi, Little Lassie, Swedish Clap Dance, Tantoli, Snurrebocken
Switzerland–Swiss May Dance, Swiss Weggis, Grandma Dance
Yugoslavia–Kola
Wales–Old Welsh Dance

FOLK DANCES OF LATIN AMERICA

Argentina–Palapela
Brazil–Fado Blaquita
Chile–Si Senor
Mexico–La Cucaracha, La Bamba, La Raspa, Chihuahua, Los Viejitos
Panama–Tamborito
Peru–Huyano (Inca), Marinera
Venezuela–El Llanero

There are many excellent rhythmic activities for elementary school children. Here are a few, from the less difficult to the more difficult. They are listed by grade level, with a suitable record source.

GRADE 1

Bluebird (Bowman 1519B)
Broom Dance (Victor 20448)
Chimes of Dunkirk (Victor 45-6176)
Danish Dance of Greeting (Folkraft 1182)
Did You Ever See a Lassie (Victor 45-5066)
Farmer in the Dell (Folkraft 1182)
Hickory, Dickory, Dock (Folkraft V22760)
How D'ye Do My Partner (Victor 21685)
A-Hunting We Will Go (Victor 22759)
Jingle Bells (Folkraft T1068B)

Jolly is the Miller (Victor 20214)
London Bridge (Victor 20806)
Looby Loo (Victor 20214)
Muffin Man (Folkraft F1188)
Mulberry Bush (Victor 20806)
Oats, Peas, Beans (Victor 20214)
Old Roger Is Dead (Victor 45-5066)
Rig-A-Jig-Jig (Bowman 1521A)
Round and Round the Village (Folkraft F1191)
Sing a Song of Sixpence (Victor 22760)
Thread Follows the Needle (Victor 22760)

GRADE 2

Ace of Diamonds (Victor 456169)
Bow, Belinda (Burns and Evans # 1)
Brummel Schottische (Victor 45-6177)
Carrousel (Victor 45-6179)
Dutch Couples (Derlaterbacher) (MH1020)
Gustaf's Skoal (Folkraft F 1175)

Hansel and Gretel (Victor 45-6182)
Paw Paw Patch (Victor 45-5066)
Seven Jumps (Methodist 101)
Shoemaker's Dance (Victor 20450)
Skip to my Lou (Decca 18224)
Ten Little Indians (Bowman 1522)
Yankee Doodle (Bowman 1522B)

GRADE 3

Bleking (Victor 45-6169)
Broom Dance (Victor 20448)
Captain Jinks (Victor 2291)
Circassian Circle (Windsor 782)
Cshebogar (Victor 45-6182)
Green Sleeves (Victor 45-6175)

Jolly Is the Miller (Decca 18223)
Klappdens (Victor 45-6171)
Minuet (Victor 45-6181)
Narcissus (Imperial 1006)
Pop Goes the Weasel (Victor 45-6180)
Shoo Fly (Folkraft F1102)
Virginia Reel (Victor 45-6180)

GRADE 4

Badger Gavotte (Decca 26052)
Dutch Couples (Victor 45-6123)
Irish Reel (Victor 21616)
May Pole Dance (Victor 20990)
Military Schottische (Decca 25062B)
Minuet (Victor 45-6181)

Norwegian Mountain March (Victor 45-6173)
Oklahoma Mixer (Imperial 1122)
Patty Cake Polka (Imperial 1117)
Teton Mountain Stomp (Windsor A783)
Troika (Kismet loy A)
Waves of Tory (Methodist 102)

GRADE 5

Bingo (Victor 45-6172)   Sailor's Hornpipe (Victor 21685)
Chain Schottische (Decca 45059)   Soldier's Joy (Folkraft)
Highland Schottische (Victor 45-6179)   Ten Pretty Girls (Windsor 7613)
Hula Blues Mixer (Dot 1012A)   Wooden Shoes (Imperial 1007)
Lili Marlene (MacGregor 310)   Gay Gordons (Folkraft)
Oh Johnny (Ascap 10-769)   Spanish Cavalier (Victor)

GRADE 6

Canadian Barn Dance (MacGregor 631)   La Raspa (Imperial 1084)
Cielito Lindo (Imperial 1085)   Red River Valley (Windsor A-752)
Cotton-Eyed Joe (MacGregor 604)   Rustic Reel (Victor 45-6178)
Five Foot Two (Rondo 186)   Sicilian Circle (Windsor A 784)
Kanafaska (Imperial 1089)   Tarantella (Victor 17083)
La Cucaracha (Imperial 1082)   All-American Promenade (Windsor A
                                                  784)

IV. Games

Games are to physical education what reading, writing, and arithmetic are to an academic education. They have significance in the program—not only in popularity with children of all ages but also in total potential value to the individual participant. Their contribution to social, physical, and recreational objectives make them subject to close scrutiny at times, particularly when they are improperly taught or built into the curriculum pattern at an inappropriate grade level.

Children fully enjoy games when they have mastered the game skills and learned the essential rules. Each game that is taught, therefore, must contribute to some objective; it must be taught with an eye on quality. This means participation for all class members, correction of outstanding faults, taking turns, and requesting pupils to ask questions.

There are *group games* for every grade level, from Animal Tag in grade 1 to Soccer in grade 5. Group games differ from *team games*. Even the most individualistic and self-centered first-grader can play a group game such as tag ("me for me"), whereas he or she would not be ready for a team game. In about the third or fourth grade, boys and girls begin to want to form small groups to work together and compete with other groups. Instead of the word "I," the word "we" appears. Before this period team games are difficult to keep going. The author has witnessed teachers having trouble with kickball at the primary level, as those pupils actively kicking and throwing are interested, and those out in the field are gazing at the clouds or watching a bug crawl along the ground. The same reasoning applies to *relay games* that are commenced too early. When a teacher has to work hard to get kindergarteners and first graders to run in relay fashion "down to the nearest tree and back," or "to go to the end of the line," and so forth, it is time to give up the activity and try something less complicated.

Dual games are usually saved for the late middle grades and junior high school years, not because children cannot learn to play badminton, tennis, and golf, and bowl at an early age, but because there simply is not time enough in the curriculum to explore and test one's self in a wide variety of physical activities and have time left for dual games. However, dual activities such as Indian hand, arm, and leg wrestling, Greco-Roman wrestling, Push-Push, and Chinese Get-Up, can be sandwiched in at the end of almost any free exercise or calisthenics formation.

After-school games and sports are a major part of the intermediate physical education curriculum. Children need the vigorous activity. All games can be adapted to the ability of the pupils.

Several of the instructional games that are particularly challenging and appropriate for the various grades are listed here in progression from the less difficult to understand and play to the more difficult. The individual teacher, however, will want to modify these lists slightly in order to take into account the actual level of maturity and skill of the boys and girls.

GRADE 1

Animal Tag

Bean Bag in the Triangle

Bean Bag Passing Game

Brownies and Fairies

Cat and Rat

Charlie over the Water

Drop the Handkerchief

Duck, Duck, Goose

Fox and Geese

Hill Dill

One, Two, Button My Shoe

Scatter

Skip Tag

Squirrels in Trees

Tag Games

Where's My Partner

GRADE 2

Animal Chase

Back to Back

Circle Stride Ball

Circle Elimination

Club Snatch

Fox and Hound

Hopscotch

Midnight

Pop Jack in the Box

Red Light

Red Rover

Ring Toss

Stop and Start

Stoop Tag

Two Deep

Water Sprite

TEAM GAMES

Dodge Ball

Kick Ball

Kick the Can

Red Rover

Line Soccer

Capture the Flag

GRADE 3

Beat Ball
Back to Back
Bean Bag Target Toss
Bronco Tag
Chinese Tag
Center Base
Circle Soccer
Crows and Cranes

Jump the Shot
Poison Circle
Maze Tag
Scat
Three Deep
Triple Change
Wastebasket
Weathervane

TEAM GAMES

Circle Team Dodge Ball
End Ball
Newcomb
Circle Kick Ball
Bounce Tag Ball

Circle Baseball
Softball
Keep Away
Line Soccer
German Bat Ball

LIMITED SPACE AND CLASSROOM GAMES

Artists
Cat and Mice
Catch Basket
Change Seats
Chair Ring Toss
Corner Spring
Dead Ball

Do This, Do That
Overhead Relay
Jackstones
Magic Numbers
Musical Chairs
Musical Arms
Simon Says

SIDEWALK GAMES

Block Shuffle
Checker Shoot
Chinese Chicken
Hop and Balance
Irish Hopscotch
Ladder Hopscotch

Pitch for Twenty
Poison-Wrestling Circle
Target Toss
Zig-Zag Tag
Baltimore Shuffleboard

GRADE 4

Bat Ball
Black Tom
Box Ball
Cageball Kick-Over
Corner Change
Four Squares

One O'Cat
Fox and Geese
Norwegian Ball
Streets and Alleys
Steal the Bacon
Volley Ground Ball

TEAM GAMES

Dodge Ball
Line Soccer
Soccer, Simplified

Running Dodgeball
Basketball, Simplified
Mass Volleyball

GRADE 5

Battle Dodgeball
Basketball Twenty-One
Bombardment (with Indian Clubs)
Captain Ball
Circle Tug-of-War
Pin Baseball
One Old Cat

Mass Soccer
Octopus
Prisoner's Base
The Ocean is Stormy
Shipwreck
Two Square
Tether Ball

TEAM GAMES

Captain Ball
Dodgeball
Speedball
Bound Ball

Basketball, Simplified
Deck Tennis
Soccer Baseball
Soccer, Modified

GRADE 6

Bird, Beast, or Fish
Chain Tag
Circle Captain Ball
Fox and Geese
Memory Run

Odd and Even
Fish and Net
Prisoner's Base
One Base Dodgeball
Team Tag

TEAM GAMES

Line Soccer
Line Basketball
Speedball

Flag Football
Softball
Scatter Dodgeball

Lead-up games deserve special attention. There is a definite place in the curriculum for these modified team games that "involve one or more of the fundamental skills, rules, and procedures used in a major team game."[33] They permit pupils to go beyond the drill of isolated skills and to play a version of the game at a level in which success and personal enjoyment may go hand in hand. They are a means by which children link the simple with the complex. An extensive list of lead-up games can be developed for a number of sports.

One of the advantages of the lead-up game is that it is possible for the instructor to plan a number of basic skills for classes and groups of pupils in need of special attention. If, for example, dribbling skills are weak for basketball, a game of Target Ball or a dribble contest in the form of a relay may be chosen. In an effort to help the instructor, Blake and Volp have constructed charts of the basic skills used in several team games.[34] Table 8-8 is a chart for volleyball.

[33] O. William Blake and Anne M. Volp, *Lead-Up Games To Team Sports* (Englewood Cliffs, N.J.: Prentice-Hall, Inc., 1964), p. 1.
[34] Ibid., p. 168.

TABLE 8-8. Lead-up Games Designed to Develop Volleyball Skills

Basic Skills Involved

Lead-Up Game	Throwing	Catching	Volleying	Setting up	Serving	Blocking	Spiking
Hot potato	x	x					
Mass deck tennis	x	x					
Net ball	x	x					
Battle ball	x	x					
Newcomb	x	x					
One-bounce volleyball			x		x		
Fabric volleyball			x	x	x	x	x
Leader ball			x	x			
Zig-zag volley			x				
Target ball					x		
Keep it up			x				
Pass placement			x	x			
Backboard set-up			x	x			
Volleyball, modified			x	x	x		
Spike and block			x	x		x	x
2-3-4 man volleyball			x	x	x	x	x
Three-pass volleyball			x	x	x	x	x

In a child's social world, competition and cooperation are important. Aggression, alliances, and coalitions are other social behaviors that occur. Cratty finds that cooperative behavior is more difficult for children than are competitive behaviors.[35] His program, therefore, requires the playing of a cooperative game at the elementary school level—this to be followed by a discussion in which questions, such as the following, are raised:

1. In the game played, with whom did you cooperate best?
2. Can you cooperate with someone you don't like?
3. Is "teamwork" the same as cooperation? If different, how?
4. How are competition and cooperation similar to and yet different from each other?

V. Self-Testing Activities

Greater glory hath no man than that which he wins with his own feet and hands.

HOMER

It is not uncommon to hear the modern elementary school criticized because children spend so much of their time working directly on teacher-

[35]Bryant J. Cratty, *Learning About Human Behavior Through Active Games* (Englewood Cliffs, N.J.: Prentice-Hall, Inc., 1975), p. 139.

prepared activities designed to present more and more information. This activity is not necessarily harmful, provided that boys and girls become *involved* in the process by taking a real part in it. They have to *do* something *with* something. What they do—in physical education or anywhere in school—has to be related to themselves in a personal way.

One cannot underestimate the significance of the children's own immediate appraisal of an activity. Given the opportunity, they will evaluate themselves by: (1) how they compare themselves from performance to performance and (2) how they compare with their peers. It is not uncommon, therefore, to find boys and girls anxious to discover how they measure up to others in speed, strength, balance, agility, and coordination.

The numerous motor activities that test the self have great appeal because the children in our culture, as well as the adults, want recognition. There is a craving for a degree of prestige and status in the group, which to a large extent is contingent on such items as good body poise, game skills, and courage. Aware that they possess these characteristics, pupils tend, according to research, to develop feelings of adequacy, security, and acceptance. Elementary children with the greatest development of physical skills are the best adjusted. Therefore, setting aside a definite amount of time in the

FIGURE 8-10. Lightweight equipment encourages play activity. (Courtesy, Raven Industries, Inc.)

curriculum for the self-testing activity is a sound practice. Self-testing is especially valid if it is not used solely to obtain a grade, but is done for fun and personal enlightenment.

The number of self-testing activities that can be done with and without equipment on the playground or in the gymnasium is considerable. They include all kinds of stunts, tumbling, conditioning exercises, and creative dramatic skills.

Listed here are several examples of activities that are appropriate for self-testing. The methods employed to present the activities and the time assigned for pupil appraisal are matters for the individual instructor to resolve. The activities progress in difficulty.

GRADES 1-3

On the Jungle Gym	Stunts
Speed climb to the top	Log roll
Climb with hands only	Jump and click heels once
"Skin the cat"	Jump and turn (a quarter)
Climb the long way around	Backward jump landing on one foot
	Frog handstand
	Front somersault
	Jump and reach
	Crab walk
	Duck walk
	Mule kick
	Frog leap
	Cartwheel
	Camel walk
	Elephant walk
	Kangaroo leap
	Single leg dip
	Greet the toe
	Hand push
	Head stand

GRADES 4-6

Individual	Dual or Group
Turk stand	Pull across
The top	Chinese get-up
Seal crawl	Indian leg wrestle
Stork stand	Indian arm wrestle
Measuring worm	Double knee-bend walk
Kneeling jump (on mats)	Pull stick
Standing broad jump	Angle balance
Jump and reach	Hobbyhorse
Corkscrew	Walking chair
Cup stunt	Skin the snake

General Characteristics	*Needs*
Jumping Jack	Chain forward roll
Human ball	Double forward roll
Jump through the stick	Double backward roll
Ankle jump	
Ankle toss for distance	
Folder leg walk	
Seal slap	
Heel click, double	
Forearm stand	
Nest hang	

VI. Apparatus

It is probably less than logical to assume that self-testing activities and apparatus work are completely different topics. In reality, a large part of apparatus work in the elementary grades is an example of self-testing activity.

The apparatus classification includes curriculum items requiring equipment: rope skipping and rope climbing, the balance beam, and other gymnasium and playground activities requiring equipment.

Rope Skipping.   In the early grades, rope skipping is more popular today than it ever was in the past. Several new records have appeared that present a full routine of rope movements together with a cheerful musical score. Jumping skills are basic to all games and sports and to the rhythmic area of physical education. They promote balance, coordination, and physical fitness. Pupils are challenged to test themselves for speed, timing, and accuracy and to create new jump patterns. Rope jumping can be done to all varieties of music, from the march to the minuet. In the latter case, the long rope is used; it can also be used for ball passing, mat rolling, the rope-within-a-rope stunts as it continues to be turned.

Rope Climbing.   From about the second grade up, children are fascinated with ropes. They are an essential part of every elementary school gymnasium. Dauer makes this clear in his text, in which he presents a selection of several excellent rope-climbing skills.[36] The success of this activity probably stems from the fact that most children like to hang suspended or climb something at one time or another.

Balance Beam.   Primary grade children find the balance beam a continual source of amusement. It presents a natural way to satisfy the often overwhelming desire to walk the railroad rails or the back fence. The number of challenging movements possible on the balance beam is almost without

[36]Victor P. Dauer, *"Dynamic Physical Education for Elementary School Children,"* (1971) pp. 165–67.

limit. Although the Department of Public Instruction in Springfield, Illinois, at one time published a list of sixty-six activities, it was still possible to add several more without too much effort. Here are a few examples of the more difficult items that encourage balance, flexibility, and coordination:

Walk forward to middle of beam; turn, and return to start
Walk backward to middle of beam; continue to opposite end
Alternate leg-raising and walking forward
Alternate knee-bending and walking forward
Knee-bending and walking forward
Move one step forward and one step backward
Walk on all fours forward
Walk on all fours backward
Walk forward in duck-walk position
Progress forward executing full turns
Progress backward executing full turns
Step over obstacles placed at intervals on the beam

Gymnastics. In the well-equipped elementary school, the intermediate graders may have a chance to learn basic approaches and skills on the traveling rings, buck, and horizontal ladder. For the most part gymnastics are a secondary school item to be taught when the arms and shoulder girdle are strong enough. Moreover, if the program is loaded with gymnastics during the elementary years, a pretty good chance exists that a number of the especially worthwhile activities for the lower grades will be omitted. This would be unfortunate. Therefore only a sampling of heavy apparatus activities should be considered in grades 1 through 6 and gymnastics should be pretty much concerned with stunts, tumbling, pyramid building, and trampolining. The latter activity has become very popular in the larger schools in which several teaching stations are available and supervision is adequate.

VII. Physical Conditioning

It seems hardly necessary to single out the area of physical conditioning for separate attention. After all, most of the items in the physical education curriculum contribute in some fashion to the development and maintenance of physical fitness. Moreover, since the formation of the President's Council on Physical Fitness in 1956, there has been a vigorous cooperative effort in this country to raise the physical capacity of youth.

As long as men and women need the physical capacity to perform a day's work and have a reserve for recreation and emergencies, the school will have to be seriously concerned with the topic of physical fitness. Physical fitness can be carefully structured through free exercise, self-testing activities, stunts and gymnastics, and a number of vigorous games appropriate to grade level. This approach presupposes, of course, a proper concern for other components of good physical condition, such as nutrition, rest, and mental-emotional health.

Measuring the level of physical fitness is a significant part of the program. It should be provided for periodically by employing any one of a number of valid and reliable tests (Chapter 12). Moreover, following the testing, certain program changes should be made for individuals in need of special help. When regular test records are kept, it is possible to know whether an activity is sufficient to maintain a satisfactory level of condition. Thus, for some boys and girls the program will need modifying in favor of more vigorous activities.

In addition to the activities already discussed, several others make a major contribution to physical condition.

Free exercise or calisthenics is the all-time favorite means of developing physical condition. Exercise serves nicely as a warm-up routine for the need of something vigorous, especially when a particular daily lesson requires that pupils observe and listen more than usual.

Traditionally, *stunts and gymnastics* have played a strong role in the physical fitness program. Besides the ropes and the trampoline, schools have employed *isometric exercise, cage ball drills, circuit training,* and *obstacle course running*.

Even the discarded parachute has been used successfully to attract boys and girls to vigorous, fun-filled movements. Parachute play can actually begin at any level, but it is more exciting for elementary children, and it uses the muscles of the entire body. In parachute play, large numbers of children can become involved at once on the playground or gymnasium. A whole class can spread out around the edges of the fully opened chute (see Figure 8-10). By pulling outward together, everyone experiences a firm isometric exercise involving the muscles of the shoulders, arms, and back. Then, by turning about, gripping the parachute once more, and pulling outward, everyone brings into play the opposite set of muscles in another isometric exercise. A distinct variety of exercises has been developed and carried out with children for some time.

Gaining popularity is the *mini-Olympics.* This activity has been very successful in the 170 elementary schools of the Houston, Texas, Independent School District. In Newton, Massachusetts, the Olympic Games have been limited to the fourth, fifth, and sixth grades. There students are first grouped according to physical fitness levels. This is followed by a self-appraisal and in-depth discussion routine, after which students are placed into top, middle, and low categories for competition. Equality between teams is assured. The teams (countries) consist of two boys and two girls. With the exception of the relay race, competition is between members of the same sex in all events. There follows several lessons in which the game activities are reviewed and practiced, with the most difficult events being taught first. These Olympic Games are the most popular activity of the school year.

FIGURE 8-11. Tug-of-war with Jayfro rope. (Courtesy, Jayfro Corporation, Montville, Connecticut)

In recent years, some elementary teachers have set up *circuit training* routines for young children. These not only serve to promote physical fitness, but they frequently become an excellent self-testing activity. In Quincy, Massachusetts, the activities are pictured on large cards and set around the playroom or gymnasium at stations. Pupils work at an assigned station, then move on to the next station around the circle. In grades 1, 2, and 3 the emphasis is on skill rather than speed. In grades 4, 5, and 6, however, there is a greater concentration on physical fitness. Directions are included with the picture cards at each station. The events for the Quincy Circuit Training routine can be done with a 15-inch bench and two to three mats, as in Table 8-9.

One should not underestimate the value of *playground devices* in the development of physical fitness. Many towns and cities have installed unique and novel types of play devices that allow children to use their imagination as well as their muscles. Slides, swings, horizontal ladders, horizontal bars, traveling rings, and balance beams are the most common exercise items. However, there are other pieces of equipment that command much attention, such as play logs, pipe tunnels, rope ladders, and steps and platforms.

It is not difficult to single out a particular community for its special efforts with children. For over ten years Project Broadfront in the school district of Ellensburg, Washington, has operated to improve the physical fitness of elementary age children. Particular attention has been given to development programs for boys and girls below accepted standards. The

TABLE 8-9.   Circuit Training

Repetitions

Event	Girls or Beginners	Boys or Advanced
1. Bench Step	10	15
2. Windmill	4	6
3. Sprinter	4	8
Jog one lap°		
4. Sit-Ups	9	14
5. Squat Thrust	4	8
6. Side Saddle Hop	6	10
Jog one lap°		
7. Push-Ups	5 (kneeling)	4
8. Trunk Twister	5 (each way)	5 (each way)
9. Side-Winder	5 (each way)	5 (each way)
Jog one lap°		

° Where area is small, jog in place.

physical fitness tests employed are the Washington Motor Fitness Test for the first three grades and the Oregon Simplification of the Rogers Physical Fitness Index for grades 4 through 10. Case studies are conducted for pupils who do not improve appreciably through the physical conditioning programs. Parents and classroom teachers are also very much involved. Because of the attention afforded this dimension of the elementary physical education curriculum it is rare to have a student who continues from one year to the next in a special development class; usually pupils who are new to the Ellensburg schools now make up these classes.

VIII. Swimming

In cities in which swimming pools are available, many fully developed programs are in operation. Instruction is provided from the level of preswimming skills to the level of lifesaving and small craft safety. The progressive programs recommended by the American National Red Cross or the Young Men's Christian Association are frequently employed as the acceptable curriculum.

The need for aquatic instruction is great; more than four-fifths of accidental drownings are associated with swimming, wading, playing in the water, or falling into the water. Also, 50 percent of all pool drownings occur during the first eight years of life. As a result, many elementary schools have developed a water safety program—generally by using an available community pool. The trend is to reach lower-grade children early. In one community the program was expanded to include second grade pupils with excellent results in skills learned, and with very strong public support. Other schools provide an inexpensive portable "learner's pool." Such a facility receives full usage because it can be employed to teach adapted physical education and special learning activities for the physically and mentally handicapped.

IX. Adventure-Challenge

In recent years, a category of activity has been added to the physical education curriculum that concerns the provision of alternative paths to learning body control and advancing self-concept and social efficiency.

Individuals need adventure and a degree of risk in their lives to develop self-confidence and independence. Yet, most school programs and educational subjects stay clear of almost everything that is risky. Even the parents frequently caution their offspring against climbing a tree or walking on a fence. In an effort to provide the thrills of accomplishing, of overcoming obstacles, and of succeeding against seemingly impossible challenges, a number of schools are adding an Outward Bound or Project Adventure type of program to the physical education curriculum.[37] Students become members of teams that set out to solve problems—problems such as figuring out how to get the whole team over a ten-foot high wall, how to use ropes to cross a crocodile infested stream, how to move across an imaginary high voltage electric fence, how to trust a friend while blindfolded on a walk over rough terrain, and how to survive in orienteering with map and compass in challenging hills and gullies.

For most intermediate level and middle school students, a rare and exciting experience is to be in the hands of others whom they must trust completely. Before long, in such group involvement almost everyone is concerned about the success of almost everyone else. In a sense, everyone turns out a winner in these problem-solving, body-management activities.

X. Relaxation For Fun

Elementary school children will take relaxation seriously if given a chance. They will also employ their imaginations to relax. Lying on the gymnasium floor or playing field they can imagine that they are "floating" on a cloud or "melting" like new snow in the noonday sun. They can imitate the looseness of a rag doll or spread themselves out on all fours, arch their backs, and stretch like cats. They will respond to Jacobson's method of progressive

---

[37]See *Adventure Curriculum: Physical Education*, Project Adventure, 775 Bay Road, Hamilton, Mass. 01936. See also, Charles D. Smith and Samuel Prather, "Group Problem Solving," *Journal of Physical Education and Recreation*, 46 (September 1975), 20–21.

relaxation, in which one body segment becomes thoroughly relaxed and other segments follow in order.

XI. Intramurals

Intramurals provide the place to practice the skills learned in the physical education classes. They are particularly suitable for grades 4, 5, and 6, if they are organized as after-school games (see Chapter 11 for more detail).

XII. Miscellaneous

This category includes all those activities not listed under other headings. They qualify for inclusion in this chapter because they relate to the elementary physical education curriculum. Three examples follow:

1. *School Camping.* This activity has gained wide acceptance in recent years, especially in such pioneer states as Michigan, Georgia, Missouri, and New York. Each year additional communities schedule upper elementary classes for a school camping experience, during which they live and observe in the outdoors for a week or more. Obviously, the opportunity for several physical education activities is close at hand in a camping situation. Moreover, usually, the physical education department is responsible for the organization of the camping program and for the physical recreation experiences. In planning a full year's course of study, it is desirable to have camp time in which to expose children to supplemental activities not covered in regular school time.
2. *Winter Sports.* In the northern areas of the country there is an opportunity to organize an after-school program involving winter activities, such as ice skating, figure skating, skiing, and winter tournaments and carnivals. In New York State alone dozens of communities teach skiing and ice skating all winter long as an extra elementary school activity. Lake Placid is probably the most famous for its school-run annual winter carnival, in which all pupils assist in some way or participate as contestants. These kinds of activities fall somewhere between intramural and recreational experience.
3. *Social Recreational.* As boys and girls mature they begin to be especially interested in doing things together. Noon-hour or after-school parties can be fun, and physical education teachers are frequently the best fitted to plan them.

Stimulating after-school programs can be fashioned for almost any elementary school in the land. Such programs should be broad and varied in their offerings. Whether they are essentially cultural, social, artistic, or physical, they must be diversified enough to tickle the interests of a large number of children. What one child likes, another may not. The thrill of mastering a crafts project or developing a photograph in the darkroom may be far more stimulating to the inventive and imaginative boy and girl than music or even a game of ball. A good elementary program, however, should provide an opportunity for the searching and feeling neophyte to try·many activities.

Wide experiences during the formative years set the stage for richer understanding and practices in the later years. Research indicates that game, sport, and hobby skills developed before the age of twelve tend to carry over to adult life.

To paraphrase Jay B. Nash, the happy child and the busy child are one, busy but not cramped, able to paint, sing a song, study the stars, see a great play, and dream of sagebrush and snow-capped peaks—active but with sufficient lapse of motion for recuperation.

QUESTIONS FOR DISCUSSION

1. Arnold Gesell, writing in *The Child from Five to Ten,* spoke about the need for free, unregimented play activities for children. His feeling was that this kind of activity "taps the deeper springs of personality." How do you feel about this? Is there a difference between "aimless play" and "organized play"? Also, are there values in both kinds of play for K–6-level boys and girls?

2. How would you explain "movement education" and "movement exploration" to a parent? How would you employ such descriptive terms as creation, invention, discovery, and feelings?

3. What is the essence of creativity in education; and what are the factors that seem to foster it? Does the creativity approach to learning aid or hinder the development of high quality motor skills for games and sports? Elaborate.

4. Having read about child development and the needs of growing children, how do you view symbolic play? See if you can formulate a rather thorough answer to this question by referring to the work of Jean Piaget, Margaret Mead, or Lawrence Frank.

5. If the music teacher and the physical education teacher come together to discuss rhythms, what might they talk about?

6. Find out about play in other cultures. Are games of low organization about the same everywhere? What did Margaret Mead find out in the Samoan culture? (See Selected References.)

7. It has been said that the development of motor performance in primary grade children can be advanced more effectively through a program of specific skills instruction than it can through low-organization play and movement exploration. How might you ascertain the truth of this statement? What kind of experiment might you set up? (See Kathleen Masche in Selected References.)

SUGGESTED ACTIVITIES

1. Examine several loop films designed for the teaching of swimming. Especially helpful are those distributed by Holt/Ealing, The Athletic

Institute, and Encyclopedia Britannica Film Corporation. Put together an intermediate-level swimming lesson and show how you would use the loop film as part of the instructional method.

2. Collect a number of definitions of play. Note how play differs from work. Set up a list of play activities that might be listed by the recreational therapist. Contrast these activities with those that appear appropriate for primary grade school pupils.

3. Review a number of sources dealing with movement education, movement exploration, or both. From your reading, formulate your own definition of movement exploration. Especially helpful in your study of movement will be the writings of individuals such as Wessel, Cratty, Jenkins, Broer, Metheny, Mosston, Laban, and Halsey.

4. Formulate a progressive sequence of folk dances appropriate for grades 4, 5, and 6. To do this properly you may want to talk with some teachers of elementary physical education to see why, for example, they prefer a certain dance in grade 4 instead of grade 3.

5. Observe children walking on the balance beam for a while. Then prepare a list of different things that can be done on the balance beam. In one course of study, sixty-six activities were set down on paper. How many can you think of?

6. Develop the concept that dance is indeed a "basic educational technique." The Frederick Rand Rogers and Ruth Murray references will be particularly helpful.

7. Set up several practical situations that would be suitable for the "problem-solving" method of physical education. See if you can obtain an answer to the question of why this kind of method is not used more often in physical education.

8. Survey a number of elementary schools (class project) to determine the extent of the games and sports program. List the lead-up games employed.

SELECTED REFERENCES

ANDERSON, MARIAN H., MARGARET E. ELLIOTT, and JEANNE LA BERGE, *Play with a Purpose*. New York: Harper and Row, 1972.

BARRETT, KATE R., "Physical Education is Movement Education," *Instructor*, 82 (January 1973), 47–49.

BOORMAN, JOYCE, *Creative Dance in the First Three Grades*. New York: McKay, 1969.

BROER, MARION R., *Efficiency of Human Movement* (3rd ed.). Philadelphia: W. B. Saunders Co., 1973.

BUCHANAN, HUGH T., JOE BLAKENBAKER, and DOYICE COTTON, "Academic and Athletic Ability as Popularity Factors in Elementary School Children," *Research Quarterly*, 47 (October 1976), 320–24.

The Secondary Program,

Grades 7-12

chapter nine

> If you treat an individual as he is, he will remain as he is, but if you treat
> him as if he were what he ought to be and *could be,* he will become what
> he ought to be and could be.
>
> JOHANN GOETHE

In the secondary schools, the great masses of adolescents and young adults should have the opportunity to experience a full curriculum—one that challenges them—and to be taught by teachers who accept them for what they are and what they could be. Goethe would agree, for there is the chance to capture the curiosity, idealism, energy, and adventurous spirit of a new generation that is ready to grow in a number of ways—health, motor, social, and cultural—through the medium of the physical education curriculum.

Past efforts at the secondary level have left much to be accomplished in numerous communities. Physical educators are aware of certain program shortcomings. So are observant educators in general. In fact, Curtis and Bidwell, after studying the secondary schools concluded that "education has failed in the main in the production of well-developed bodies on the part of high school youth and adults, and in addition has not developed concepts which would lead to a later correction of such problems."[1] This kind of criticism, unpleasant as it is to hear, is not without foundation. It does, however, provide the needed stimulus for many teachers of physical education that will result in a more careful scrutiny of existing programs.

[1]Thomas E. Curtis and Wilma W. Bidwell, *Curriculum and Instruction for Emerging Adolescents* (Boston: Addison-Wesley Pub. Co., 1977), p. 135.

The Secondary School Organization

In terms of pure logic it is easy to separate the junior high school years from the senior high school years. All one has to do is to treat them distinctly. The difficulty, however, is that by studying the two programs in an isolated manner, the significant ingredient of *continuity* is apt to be slighted or ignored altogether. Viewing the curriculum, grades 7 through 12, as a continuum, it is possible to appreciate the need for activity progressions and to observe and appraise pupil progress effectively. Moreover, there are a number of activities in the junior high school program of physical education that are repeated in greater depth in the later secondary period; these activities should be studied in terms of their total effect over the span of the several years.

There are two-year (grades 7 and 8) and three-year (grades 7, 8, and 9) junior high schools throughout the country. They prepare children for four-year (grades 9, 10, 11 and 12) and three-year (grades 10, 11, 12) senior high schools. There are also the traditional grammar schools, K–8, which prepare students directly for the high school years. Although these are the common patterns, there are also an increasing number of so-called "middle-schools." These middle schools subscribe to the concept that seventh- and eighth-graders have more in common with upper elementary pupils than they have with ninth-graders. Therefore, the middle school includes grades 5 through 8 or 6 through 8. There the upper elementary pupils gain the advantage of departmentalization and special teachers. In physical education, frequently, they have an earlier opportunity to take showers following vigorous activity, and they are taught by fully qualified teachers.

The Secondary School Years

Someone has said that "we have the darndest programs in the name of physical education in our secondary schools." There is some degree of truth in the statement. There is everything from disorderly free play to a highly organized and inflexible routine. There are programs in which sport skills and conditioning activities are kept in the background, as games are played period after period, and there are programs in which little is done to fire the imagination or to teach activities that could be fun to play for years to come.

The worst part about such conditions is that we do not fool anyone. Secondary-school boys and girls are already mature enough to spot a weak program or a weak teacher. These are the years in which pupils are being prepared either to go on to higher education or to terminate their education at grade 12. Because it is not possible to determine early enough who will go on

267

to college and who will finish his or her formal education, we have to prepare everyone as if this were the last exposure to physical education. Moreover, college physical education programs differ widely in scope and depth, so it is almost impossible to know how far to go and when to limit instruction in order to tie in with a particular college curriculum. One valid reason higher education programs vary so much is that they attempt to meet the needs of their freshmen—students who come to college from all kinds of programs, some of which prepared students poorly in physical education skills and knowledge.

The colleges and universities will continue to have this problem as long as secondary schools are so inconsistent in their offerings. It is time to stop debating whether the emphasis should be on physical fitness, games for fun, skill teaching, carry-over sports, or corecreation. It should be on all these activities and lead to purposeful, graduated schooling from the junior high through the senior high.

The Junior High School Student, Grades 7, 8, and 9

There is a time in the lives of young people when they are curious and when the iron is hot for discovering and trying new things. That is the "teachable moment" in which to strike home with solid experiences. The junior high school period is such a time. The age level is wonderful to instruct, for boys and girls are capable of extensive physical activity; they have not yet begun to slow down and become semisedentary in an affluent and ultrasophisticated society. Instead, they are willing to struggle and perspire and really concentrate on game skills, conditioning routines, and vigorous dances. They will try things, enjoy things, and work on quality performance. It is the time for the able teacher who is knowledgeable and will set standards, post results, and challenge the pupils to give their best.

In order to plan a properly functioning school program, one must activate it not only by the demands of society, but by a recognition of the learner's characteristics and needs. These physical, mental, emotional, and social requirements of adolescent boys and girls tend to be similar, but pupils vary considerably. For the most part, the immature pupils at one end of the scale are balanced by the more mature pupils at the other end, with the great mass of pupils falling somewhere in the middle.

The Senior High School Student, Grades 10, 11, and 12

As indicated earlier, the whole secondary school span should be viewed as a continually evolving period of growth and maturation that gradually comes to fruition in the later years in the form of the young adult ready to take

FIGURE 9-1. Innovation and fun: cargo net tug-of-war.

his or her place in the collegiate environment or in the world of earning a living. Therefore, some of what has been listed as characteristic of the junior high school student will still apply at the senior high school level. The characteristic may have changed only in degree. Boys in grade 10, for example, will be even more interested in their physical strength and motor skills than they were previously; and girls will still be interested, more so, in some instances, in the opposite sex, how they look to others, and how to win approval of their peers. All through these years, therefore, the opportunity should be present to guide and encourage individual and group participation in the kinds of curriculum items that foster personal security. Pupils should come to the final year in school satisfied that physical education has indeed helped them understand themselves, and that it is something to be carried into the adult years with family and friends.

Basic Considerations, Grades 7-12

In the earlier chapters program planning and organization were discussed in detail, to show that curriculum content is directly related to specific grade level objectives. Because of the characteristics and developing needs of secondary school boys and girls, the following (Table 9-3) specific objectives will need to be highlighted in order for appropriate program items to be selected. Note that the objectives change very little, but the *degree of emphasis* may change considerably.

TABLE 9-1. Characteristics and Needs—Ages 12–14

General Characteristics	Needs	Suggested Activities

1. Physical Characteristics Both Sexes

Growth rapid and uneven; long bones of arms and legs grow rapidly. The lateral types (mesomorphs) mature earlier than the linear type (ectomorphs).	Frequent health examinations and physical fitness screening tests with effective follow-up.	Group and individual games, stunts and tumbling. *Girls* need body control skills used in walking, running, standing, sitting, and relaxing.
Rapid muscular development that may result in periods of relatively poor coordination and the appearance of awkwardness.	An opportunity to develop skill and coordination.	Body conditioning, self-testing activities including those for flexibility, wrestling, track, and field. For *girls*, trampolining.
Motor ability continues to increase, but at a slower rate than in middle childhood and in later adolescence.	Activities to develop strength and flexibility. To learn new motor skills with form being stressed.	
In some cases posture is poor.		Developmental and remedial classwork related to posture.
Acne period may begin.	Attention to body mechanics and general posture.	Participation in wide variety of team and individual sports; those demanding great endurance should have frequent rest periods.
Youngsters appear to have unlimited sources of energy, but much of this energy is expended in growth process.	Vigorous activities interspersed with rest periods. *Boys* need protection from overloading.	
Exuberant, outgoing, boisterous.		
	Instruction on how to relax.	Knowledge of body limitations and capabilities.

Boys Stronger than girls.	Environment of supervision to avoid bone and joint injuries.	Properly equipped and supervised contact sports with body conditioning activities prior to participation.
Growth spurt in width of shoulder girdle.		
Ossification of skeletal system still incomplete. Injuries to growth plates may occur.	Opportunity to appreciate variations in growth among boys and girls.	Classroom discussion of the role of diet, rest, and exercise in personal effectiveness in physical activity and other things.
Voice changes and pubic hair on average of about 13.5 years of age.	To participate in activities that do not call attention to awkwardness.	

TABLE 9-1. *Continued.*

General Characteristics	Needs	Suggested Activities
Sexual maturity reached in most cases.		
Girls About 1½ to 2 years ahead of boys in maturation.	Chance to talk about figures and appearance.	Participation in co-educational activities through discussions and active games and sport participation.
Height increases rapidly, size increases, and secondary sex characteristics develop.	Opportunity to appreciate growth variations in sexes.	
Menstrual cycle irregular.		Square, folk, and social dancing.
More concerned with personal appearance and posture than boys are.		Discussion and films depicting normal growth, the menstrual cycle and exercises for menstrual pain.

2. Mental-Emotional-Social Development Both Sexes

Desire for independence. Adults are seen as old-fashioned. May rebel against parental and school authority.	Opportunities for the development of a sense of responsibility and qualities of leadership.	Assignment or election to duties as squad leaders, class timers, equipment and sport managers and intramural officials.
Great loyalty to group leaders.	Need and want many friends. Need varied activities so that they can discover at least one sphere in which they can achieve.	
Intense interest in self-improvement in basic skills.		Varied activities.
Interest in impressing the opposite sex.		Tests of achievement and motor ability.
Reality begins to hold sway over imagination. Fantasy and day-dreaming, for some, give way to intellectual analysis.	Chance to improve skills in self-appraisal through a variety of activities.	Coeducational dancing, volleyball, etc.
Advanced ability to follow directions.	Chance to develop social poise and confidence.	Classroom discussion to see how skills and understanding can be applied.
A desire for clothes, movies, and parties.	To understand why physical education is	

TABLE 9-1. *Continued.*

General Characteristics	Needs	Suggested Activities
	important in their lives now and in the future.	
	To plan and take part in school recreational affairs.	
Boys		
Sometimes self-conscious because of physical inadequacies.	Opportunities to observe normal growth patterns and individual differences.	Encouragement in all team and individual sports plus correct body mechanics.
Concerned about losing status because of small size.		
Fighting tendency is strong.	Develop confidence through guidance in overcoming physical and emotional problems.	Learn to play coeducational sports such as tennis, badminton, and swimming.
May have love attachment with girl of about same age.		
Think physical prowess is very important. Intense desire for competition as age increases.	Sympathetic guidance and understanding by parents, teachers, and other adults.	Measure personal performance against posted achievements standards. Participate in supervised competition against others of similar physical capacity and ability.
	To develop strength, speed, agility, balance, and endurance in a wide variety of activities.	
Girls		
Interested in grooming and personal appearance. Fears are concerned with wearing the wrong clothes and relationship with others of same and opposite sex.	Continued guidance in healthful living with particular attention given to the maintenance of personal fitness and body mechanics.	A wide variety of exercises before full-length mirrors for body observations, and vigorous movements that can be enjoyed.
Peer acceptance very important.		
Interested in boys and dancing.	Chance to develop poise, grace in movement, and personal confidence in ability to work and play with opposite sex.	Coeducational experiences in the pool and gymnasium, and on the playground.
May show short, explosive outburst of temper. May cry easily when things go wrong.		

272

FIGURE 9-2. Movement as an art form develops lifelong kinesthetic appreciations.

TABLE 9-2. Characteristics and Needs—Ages 15–18

General Characteristics	Needs	Suggested Activities
1. Physical Characteristics Both Sexes		
Improve in motor coordination.	Continued vigorous physical activity, especially in communities where early sophistication tends to limit physical expression.	Exercise for flexibility, agility, stunts, fundamental movements and supervised competition in all phases.
Boys continue to grow muscularly; girls taper off.		
As period progresses, the bones complete most of their growth, coordination is refined, the puberty cycle is completed, and both boys and girls know how to handle personal grooming.	Stress on form and skill in sport activities, especially those of a carryover variety.	Separate boys and girls classes, but provide chance to participate in many coeducational activities.
Maturity in height and weight is almost achieved, but some sex differences exist in timing of physical growth.	Prolonged activities, but with fewer and extended periods of rest.	Refined skills and knowledge in such activities as archery, badminton, tennis,
Pupils relatively free from infection.	Continued attention to the role of enjoyable skills in the maintenance of personal appearance and condition.	bowling, golf, social and folk dancing, and numerous aquatic activities.
Large appetites continue for both sexes, but some girls continue to restrict intake of food.		

273

TABLE 9-2. *Continued.*

General Characteristics	*Needs*	*Suggested Activities*
Interest centers on personal development: girls because of weight and figure, boys because of the need for athletic condition.		
Boys Strength is doubled.	Stress on form and quality skills in the intramural and inter-scholastic sports activities.	Basketball, soccer, speedball, track and field, flag football, tackle football, wrestling, and weight training.
Motor coordination and strength greatly increased.		
Physical coordination and dexterity equal or exceed that of most adults.	To learn how to control body weight through choice of food, exercise, and periodic medical advice.	Classroom instruction in the role of exercise, diet, and emotional well-being in the maintenance of optimum body weight.
Most boys finally catch up to girls in physical growth, and some pass by them in height and weight.		
Secondary sex characteristics now complete.		
Rapid increase in weight toward end of secondary period.		
Girls Increase in weight as basal metabolic rate slowly decreases.	More vigorous and prolonged physical activities.	Team and individual sports of all types, both in class and in an after-school sports program.
Endurance usually increases.	Guidance in developing proper attitudes toward sex.	Menstrual education and sex education discussions that pertain to boys' and girls' recreational interests and activities.
Poise, grace, and grooming are more pronounced.		
Sexual maturity is reached by end of secondary school period.		
Interested in excitement and adventure; adult drives are strong.		
2. Mental-Emotional-Social Development Both Sexes		
Intensely emotional and complex.	Experience in accepting defeat and victory in a wholesome manner.	Both vigorous and moderate physical activity.

274

TABLE 9-2. *Continued.*

General Characteristics	*Needs*	*Suggested Activities*
Sensitive to limitations in early years.		Relaxation-type exercise coupled with gymnastics, free exercise routines, and folk and social dance; modern dance for girls.
More cheerful, friendly, outgoing, and well adjusted to school and community life.	Understand the need for and value of rules.	
Attempt to gain status through social activities.	Periods of rest, knowledge of ways to relax, as well as vigorous activities to release tension.	Class leadership duties; leaders club and intramural assisting.
Conformity to peer group standards is a dominating influence.	Experiences in working on many committees to plan social activities.	Membership in a homeroom or class team that competes at noon or before or after school.
Highly critical of both adults and peers.		
Dating becomes common.	Opportunity to work with peers and peer groups for a common goal.	
Social activity extends beyond home and school.		Social-recreational activities such as shuffleboard, table tennis, archery, and softball.
Broadening of social attitudes and personal philosophies.	Opportunities in co-educational activity to develop wholesome boy-girl relationships.	Individual sports such as badminton, golf, bowling, tennis, and dancing.
	Experiences in activities that one may enjoy alone or with a few friends.	Discussion of the importance of proper attitudes toward game results. Mixers in dancing, and changing squad membership will help.
	To accept official's decisions and to appreciate real differences in individuals.	
Boys Mild to strong interest in girls.	To participate in mixed activities, and acknowledge the masculine and feminine roles as social circles are broadened.	Dancing—folk, square, social; tennis, badminton, volleyball, archery, swimming, bowling, table tennis, etc.
Fighting tendency is strong in some boys.		
Emerge from a short period of roughness and rudeness to all females to a period of overt interest in girls.	To learn to understand the opposite sex.	Wrestling, speedball, tackle football, and strength contests such

TABLE 9-2. *Continued.*

General Characteristics	Needs	Suggested Activities
	To learn and take part in combative activities under supervision.	as Indian leg wrestling and tug-of-war. Corecreational activities at the several levels—physical, intellectual and social.
Girls Strong interest in boys Narrowing interest in sports, with a trend toward specialization. Strong interest in personal appearance.	Chance to develop skill in activities they prefer. To develop poise, grace, and skillful use of body in a number of common situations.	Advanced units in a variety of activities with chance to concentrate on skills preferred. Fundamentals of body movements in walking, sitting down, getting up, picking up items, performing household tasks—in proper postural attitude and with movement flow.

When it understands the values of a first-class physical education program, a community is ready to support a secondary school curriculum that consists of three parts: class instructions, adapted activities, and extraclass activities.

Class instruction is that in which prescribed experiences are provided for all boys and girls during regularly scheduled periods.

Adapted activities are those experiences designed to meet the needs and interests of students unable to take part in the regular class instruction period or who require additional instruction. Some special education students will require these programs to a degree commensurate with their abilities.

Extraclass athletic activities are that part of the program carried on beyond the regularly scheduled school periods to provide enrichment opportunities, essentially through practice and competition.

Intramural activities are that part of the physical education program which are organized and conducted within one school, and include only those pupils enrolled in that school.

TABLE 9-3. From Junior High School Through Senior High School

Junior High	Senior High
1. Optimal physical development through vigorous physical activities adapted to the individual.	Continued.
2. Exploration and experimentation in many activities so that valid choices can be made.	Continued to a lesser degree, but with an opportunity to become proficient in choices selected.
3. Development of physical skills, coordination and abilities useful in work and play, including team sports.	A finer development of these same skills to yield a greater satisfaction, and greater attention to individual and couple activities.
4. Promotion of social skills, poise, and proper boy-girl relationships through combined classes and other activities.	Continued to a greater degree through promotion of social activities.
5. Learning of cooperative democratic living through experiences in followership and leadership.	Continued to a greater degree.
6. Promotion of an understanding of sports and other physical activities.	Continued to a far greater degree, and involving attitudes and appreciations sufficient to affect post-school physical education choices.
7. Development of self-confidence, self-direction, initiative, and feelings of personal worth and belonging.	Continued to a far greater degree by programing pupils into intramural and interscholastic games and contests.

Extramural activities are events that are participated in as play days and sports days on which pupils from two or more schools compete, and do not involve a season-long schedule, league competition, or championship.

Interscholastic athletic activities are those that permit the more gifted students to represent a school in competition with representation from other schools and that involve seasonal schedules, organized practices, competition, and sometimes championships.

Related activities are those in clubs, councils, and associations of pupils, which are conducted for enrichment of the program.

There are a number of *guiding statements* that should be adhered to in carrying out the several parts of the physical education program.

1. Both boys and girls should be exposed to a well-rounded program.
2. The means of progression of instruction in each activity area should be validated. This means that the procedure of moving from the lesser skills to the more advanced skills shuold be pretested and found sound.
3. Five class periods of physical education each week are recommended, including the adapted program. Three class periods is the minimum if one is to come at all close to gaining the depth in teaching that secondary school students require.
4. A large number of activities, because of their contribution to personal skill and physical condition, should be continued from grade 7 through grade 12 in order

for the student to progress efficiently from the elementary to the advanced skills.

5. Nearly all activities should be introduced at the junior high school level, so that students may become acquainted with them, explore the field, and be able to participate in intramurals and in games with their parents and friends with some degree of effectiveness.

6. In grades 8 and 9, team sport activity is the heaviest for both boys and girls. It should thereafter begin to decrease in order to allow more time for dual and individual sports in grades 11 and 12.

7. Schools organized on other than the traditional schedule should provide physical education experiences for each pupil comparable in time to that allocated to other major courses.

8. The instructional program should be scheduled to allow for maximum participation and adequate time for each pupil to have an opportunity to gain the satisfaction that comes from achievement.

9. All students should be enrolled in physical education classes. Time should be scheduled in the physical education program for special education pupils and others handicapped by functional or structural disorders and those who find it difficult to adjust to the regular program.

10. Assignment to physical education classes should take into consideration sex, skill, maturation, grade level, and health status.

11. The pupil/teacher ratio for physical education classes should not be constant, but should vary depending upon the activity.

12. There should be no substitute for the instructional program.

13. The teacher's schedule should allow time for preparation and planning.

Title IX Considerations

The Education Amendments Act, Public Law 92-318, was passed by Congress in 1972. Title IX of this act clearly pertains to the need to program equal opportunities for men and women carefully:

> No person in the United States shall, on the basis of sex, be excluded from participation in, be denied the benefits of, or be subject to sex discrimination under any education program or activity receiving Federal financial assistance.

The primary purpose of the Act was to insure that girls and women would have every bit as much attention given to their welfare and physical education experiences as is provided for boys and men. It was intended to remedy a situation that had been out of balance for decades—a situation in which women frequently received less of the total physical education instructional dollar, supplies, facilities, and general program opportunities.

Although class instruction in physical education and interscholastic programs have been functioning in keeping with Title IX for several years, there are still numerous pockets of resistance to the concept of equal opportunity for men and women. However, Kroll's findings indicate that four years after the start of the Act there was more agreement than disagreement, as well as a reduction in the adversary-like atmosphere and intense debates about the Title IX issues.[2] Less than a year later Arnold found that most schools had carried out a self-evaluation of their programs and were grouping students for physical education and competition, choosing instructional strategies, selecting activities, evaluating student performances, and conducting coeducational classes.[3] In short, program modifications have been occurring rapidly throughout the country in an effort to meet the original deadline date of July 1978, established by the Act. In order to speed up the integration process several states issued guidelines. In Florida, for example, the Department of Education set forth particulars indicating that all classes should be coeducational, be taught coeducationally, have students assigned without regard to sex, be grouped on the basis of ability without regard to sex, and be assigned instructors without regard to sex.[4]

Appropriate staff training, curriculum planning, class scheduling, and formulating program requirements and options take time to initiate, try out, and live with. Obviously sex-integrated classes lend themselves to a variety of teaching methods, including individualized instruction, learning packets, contract teaching, and performance-based activity. Helpful coeducational ideas may be found in *Ideas for Secondary School Physical Education*, published by the American Alliance for Health, Physical Education and Recreation. Published by the same organization is the public information film, *An Equal Chance Through Title IX.*

Title IX legislation stresses self-evaluation as a means of arriving at an operational state in which *equal opportunity* for each sex, though not necessarily equal programs exist. Significant, therefore, is the need to combine the best of men's and women's philosophical positions as they pertain to goals for men and women, standards and program quality, and their acceptance by the general public. To do otherwise is to miss the opportunity to examine the status and roles of men and women in contemporary society, and to educate participants in physical education in the meaning of basic human equality.

Planning and Organizing the Content, Grades 7-12

There are at least two major considerations to be dealt with in discussing the mechanics of organizing curriculum content. One has to do with the percentage of time assigned to the major content areas, and the other relates

[2]Walter Kroll, "Psychological Scaling of Proposed Title IX Guidelines," *Research Quarterly,* 47 (October 1976), 548–53.

[3]Don E. Arnold, "Compliance with Title IX in Secondary School Physical Education," *Journal of Physical Education and Recreation,* 48 (January 1977), 19–25.

[4]Barbara J. Kelly, "Implementing Title IX," *Journal of Physical Education and Recreation,* 48 (February 1977), 27–29.

to the selection of and time allotted to the subactivities in junior and senior high schools.

In establishing a structure for the secondary school physical education program, it is generally advantageous first to organize the major content areas into large blocks of time according to the amount of emphasis considered appropriate through the grades. After this has been accomplished, a further breakdown of time can be determined for the several activities selected in each major content area. The breakdown, of course, will depend on other variables, such as the number and length of classes per week, staff, and teaching stations.

An indication of time allotments for content areas is shown in Tables 9-4, 9-5, and 9-6. Although the emphasis varies a small amount for boys and girls the opportunity for coeducation instruction is not limited in any way. Also, the practice of selecting electives in the upper grades is encouraged within the recommended time allotments.

Activity Selection and Time Assigned

In the selection of activities for the major content areas, most school systems tend to follow what others have done. This could be a real mistake or a genuine blessing, depending on what the other school system used for guidelines and how thoroughly it fashioned its curriculum. There is some validity, however, in making a list of the names of the schools with the better programs of physical education and examining their courses of study in some detail to ascertain what they have in common. With a list of the major program elements on hand, staff should be able to determine how well these elements agree with local philosophy and meet local needs. Everything from wrestling to modern dance must be carefully evaluated in terms of its appropriateness locally.

Very often the validity of a program is determined by referring to the experts—individuals who are in a position to judge the worth of a proposition. In this respect, being able to turn to a state department of education for assistance should not be undervalued. State supervisors of physical education who have been working with curriculum guides and problems for several years have much to offer. The curriculum recommendations of states such as Michigan, California, Kansas, Maryland, Virginia, and New York are especially worth reviewing before any local endeavor is completed.

The author holds considerable respect for the program recommendations of the New York State Education Department. The following physical education program, for boys and girls in grades 7 to 12 is adapted from the New York State Curriculum Guide.

A close study of the sample program from New York State indicates a number of suggestions relative to grades 7 through 12.

1. Synchronized swimming is introduced for the girls along with life-saving and skin and scuba diving for both sexes at the ninth grade level.
2. Self-testing activities remain throughout the total period to challenge individual performance.
3. Weight training units for boys and girls are taught each year.
4. Little time is spent on low-level group games so that more attention can be given to individual, dual, and team games. However, this does not prohibit the use of certain lead-up games in the teaching of team sports.
5. Archery and badminton are introduced in the early years, and then given much greater attention just before graduation from high school. Note also that tennis, golf, and bowling are introduced in the seventh grade and given double the instruction time in grades 11 and 12.
6. Wrestling is a solid subject for the six-year period.
7. Soccer and speedball are played chiefly in grades 7 and 8; after that, other team sports take the time—particularly field hockey for girls and lacrosse for both boys and girls. In many parts of the country the lacrosse time would be assigned to soccer. However, lacrosse is an excellent team activity not to be slighted in the least.
8. Touch football or flag football does not dominate the curriculum; in fact very little time was allocated to it in the last two years.
9. Basketball and volleyball are taught each year to both sexes with a slowly diminishing amount of time through grade 12.
10. Rhythms and dancing command a fair amount of time each year, with the girls spending about twice as much time on them as the boys do.
11. A scheduled amount of time is assigned to the evaluation of the students.
12. All pupils have the opportunity for daily physical education, upon request.

There is far more attention being given today to *elective* activities—especially in the later secondary years when the student may pursue an in-depth experience through the avenue of independent study. In addition to exploring the activity in the gymnasium, he or she may seek out information in the library and the media or learning center as well as within the community at large, and in so doing contribute measurably to cognitive, affective, and motor learnings to a degree sufficient to bring about personal decision-making.

Another secondary-level happening is the allocation of more and more time to a study of human movement fundamentals, as applied especially to sports and gymnastic activities. Therefore, the Ohio Curriculum Guide Committee's calling for the mastery of basic motor patterns applicable to most sports comes as no surprise.[5] This concept is developed by sequential move-

[5]The *Ohio Guide for Girls' Secondary Physical Education* may be obtained without charge from Margaret Love, 606 State Office Building, Columbus, Ohio, 43210.

TABLE 9-4. New York–The State Education Department Sample Physical Education Curriculum Suggested Time Allotment for a Physical Education Program*

Boys and Girls, Grades 7–12

Periods Per Year

Major Area	7 Boys	7 Girls	8 Boys	8 Girls	9 Boys	9 Girls	10 Boys	10 Girls	11 Boys	11 Girls	12 Boys	12 Girls
CONDITIONING AND BODY MECHANICS												
Calisthenics, fundamental movement, and posture training	3	5	3	5	3	3	1	2	4	5	2	2
AQUATICS												
Swimming, diving and water safety	35	35	35	35								
Swimming, synchronized swimming, diving, and water safety					25	25	25	25	25	25	25	25
Lifesaving, skin and scuba diving					10	10	10	10	10	10	10	10
SELF-TESTING ACTIVITIES												
Gymnastics: Tumbling, stunts, apparatus	10	15	10	20	10	5	10	10	5	10	5	10
Track and field	10	15	15	10	15	15	10	10	10	10	10	10
Weight training	10		10		10		10		10		10	
GAMES												
Group games	4	8	2	4	2	5	2	2	2	3		
Individual and dual sports: Archery, horseshoes, fly and bait casting	10	10	10	5						20	20	5
Badminton, table tennis, shuffleboard and quoits	10	10			4	6	15	15	5	5	20	20
Tennis and golf (plus handball above grade 10)	10	10		5	10	5	5	10	20	10	20	20

Major Area

Periods Per Year

Major Area	7 Boys	7 Girls	8 Boys	8 Girls	9 Boys	9 Girls	10 Boys	10 Girls	11 Boys	11 Girls	12 Boys	12 Girls
Bowling, deck tennis, and fencing	4	4		5			10	10	5	10	7	12
Ice skating and skiing	2	2		5		5	1	10	7	5	5	5
Wrestling	8		15		15		15		15		10	
Team sports												
Soccer	5	5	9	10							8	
Speedway or speedball	5	5	5	10		5						
Softball	7	7	5	10	10	10	10		5	5		5
Touch football	10		15		10		10		5		7	5
Basketball	10	10	15	10	15	10	5	5	5	5	5	5
Volleyball	5	7	10	15	5	5	15	10	15	5	5	5
Field hockey						15	15	10		10	10	5
Lacrosse					10	10		10	10	10		10
RHYTHMS, MARCHING, DANCING	10	20	10	20	15	25	10	25	10	20	10	20
EVALUATION, SKILL AND												
KNOWLEDGE TESTS	7	7	6	6	6	6	6	6	7	7	6	6
Physical fitness tests	5	5	5	5	5	5	5	5	5	5	5	5
Total	180	180	180	180	180	180	180	180	180	180	180	180

*The suggested number of periods assumes a daily schedule. If less than a daily period or fewer facilities are available, appropriate adjustments in the schedule will be necessary.

ment patterns that are refined into specialized skills. Hartman and Clement nicely illustrate progression and sequence as follows:[6]

Progression	*Sequence*
Fundamental movement	Jumping-hitting
Combination of movements	Running, jumping, hitting
Motor patterns	Overarm throw as a method of applying impetus to a ball above shoulder height
Specialized sports skills	Volleyball spike
Sport, game, or activity organization	Volleyball

TABLE 9-5. Arkansas—State Education Department Secondary School Time Allotments

Type of activity	Seventh grade		Eighth grade		Ninth grade		Tenth grade		Eleventh grade		Twelfth grade	
	Boys	Girls	Boys	Girls	Boys	Girls	Boys	Girls	Boys	Girls	Boys	Girls
Rhythmic activities	15%	30%	15%	30%	15%	30%	10%	30%	10%	30%	10%	30%
Team activities (highly organized team sports)	30	25	30	25	30	30	35	30	35	30	35	30
Individual activities (individual sports and recreational activities including aquatics)	20	20	20	20	20	20	30	30	30	30	30	30
Self testing activities (including gymnastics)	15	10	15	10	15	10	20	5	20	5	20	5
Games and relays	15	10	15	10	15	5						
Body mechanics and conditioning activities	5	5	5	5	5	5	5	5	5	5	5	5

There appears to be little reason why the program for boys and girls cannot be combined into one structure. No substantial research is available to indicate otherwise. Therefore, a suggested time allotment suitable for everyone might appear as in Table 9-6.

Arranging the Content

It is possible that both the traditionalist and the innovator would accept the programs of activities that have been outlined above. These programs leave room for a fair amount of freedom for local manipulation. However, a

[6]Betty Hartman and Annie Clement, "Adventure in Key Concepts," *Journal of Health, Physical Education and Recreation*, 44 (March 1973), 20–21.

TABLE 9-6

| | Grade | | | | | |
	7	8	9	10	11	12
Dance	20	20	20	20	15	15
Team sports	30	30	30	25	25	25
Individual sports	20	20	20	30	35	35
Gymnastics	20	20	20	15	15	15
Aquatics	10	10	10	10	10	10

number of individuals would like to give the secondary school student a greater choice of activities. They believe that a person will not necessarily make an intelligent choice of recreational activity in later years unless he or she does some choosing during the school years. Does a formal presentation of the many skills develop this ability?

Diversified programs with variable scheduling and a wide choice of sex-integrated classes and electives have rejuvenated many secondary school programs. In the Woodstock Community High School in Woodstock, Illinois, teachers moved away from the traditional locked-in periods and courses and found that both teachers and students were enthusiastic about the flexibility and offerings. Moreover, there was a solid movement of youth toward lifetime and individual sports. This kind of surge toward lifetime sports was noticed also in a demonstration school in Jacksonville, Florida, in which these particular sports were made coeducational.

In some communities the "open campus" has caused problems dealing with the quality of instruction in physical education. By having "free play" and "open gym" periods, it is sometimes difficult to handle varying numbers of students who arrive at particular periods. However, most places are able to create a structure that will channel the interests of pupils and make the department offerings attractive. In the Needham High School, Needham, Massachusetts, elective program for juniors and seniors, the students can choose eight activities over the course of 40 weeks of instruction (see Table 9-7).

Individual projects in the school library may be assigned during the five weeks of class activity. One of the eight activity spots is reserved for evaluations held each year. Thus, in the course of two years, the upper secondary student is exposed to fourteen different activities of his or her own choosing. Encouragement is given to balance group and individual activities. Also, any activity a group of students wants will be scheduled if at all possible. Then a workshop is run for the teachers who will teach the activity. Independent study is available for a student who has had an accident or illness. Rather than be excused, he or she does essential library work and research into a physical education topic.

In Braintree, Massachusetts, the core program is offered to grades 9 and

TABLE 9-7. Needham High School Elective Program

Juniors & Seniors

Fall—I	Fall—II	Winter—III
Archery	Badminton	Apparatus I (B)
Badminton	Flag Football (B)	Basketball (B)
Golf	Flag Football (G)	Modern Dance
Lacrosse (B)	Games (Outdoor)	Rhythmical Gymnastics (BG)
Lacrosse (G)	Lacrosse (B)	Self-Defense
Soccer (B)	Lacrosse (G)	Social Dance (BG)
Soccer (G)	Speedball (B)	Tumbling I
Spin & Fly Casting	Speedball (G)	Weight Training
Tennis (B) (G) (BG)	Tennis	
Volleyball & Cageball	Volleyball & Cageball	

Winter—IV	Winter—V	Winter—VI
Apparatus I (G)	Apparatus I (B)	Apparatus II
Basketball (G)	Basketball (B)	Basketball (G)
Games Indoors	Modern Dance	Slimnastics
Slimnastics	Games Indoors	Square & Folk Dance
Square & Folk Dance (BG)	Rhythmical Gymnastics (BG)	(BG)
Weight Training	Self-Defense	Street Hockey (B)
Street Hockey (B)	Social Dance (BG)	Street Hockey (G)
Wrestling (B)	Street Hockey (G)	Tumbling II
Yoga (BG)	Tumbling I	Weight Training
	Weight Training	Wrestling
		Yoga (BG)

Spring—VII	Spring—VIII	
Testing—A.A.H.P.E.R.	Archery	
50-Yard Dash	Golf	
Long Jump	Handball	
Pull-Ups (B)	Softball	
Arm Bent Hang (G)	Spin & Fly Casting	
Shuttle	Tennis (B) (G) (BG)	(B)—Boys Only
	Track & Field	(G)—Girls only
	Volleyball & Cageball	(BG)—Coed

10. The elective program, with dance being the only core activity, gets underway in grades 11 and 12. Major activities, most of which are sex-integrated, are as follows in Table 9-8.

At both secondary and college levels a growing body of professionals feel that the "why" approach is necessary in order to make a person intellectually competent to choose between an active and an inactive life. Perhaps a true laboratory experience has value. Some upper secondary schools have de-

TABLE 9-8

	Grades 9 and 10 *Activity*	Grades 11 and 12 *Activity*
FALL SEASON	General Orientation Fitness Testing Field Hockey Speedball Tennis Volleyball Lacrosse Touch Football Soccer Cross Country Team Handball Recreational Games Basketball Golf Weight Training	Football Archery Golf Jogging Tennis Field Sports Volleyball
WINTER SEASON	Gymnastics (Tumbling & Apparatus) Indoor Track Basketball Folk, Square, Modern Dance Slimnastics—Jogging Wrestling Weight Training Volleyball Table Tennis Recreational Games	Self Defense Yoga Basketball Fistball Volleyball Weight Training Folk Dance Floor Hockey Modern Dance Team Handball Recreational Games Indoor Golf Wrestling Indoor Track and Field Square and Social Dance Bowling Table Tennis Badminton Recreational Gymnastics Winter Sports (Skiing, Skating) Tap Dance
SPRING SEASON	Golf Archery Tennis Track and Field 1, 2 Softball Badminton	Archery Golf Tennis Softball Track and Field Football Lacrosse Handball Basketball Volleyball Recreational Games Table Tennis

veloped laboratory blocks in which the student concentrates on one or two activities during the semester, applying the physiological and kinesiological principles. The size of the school and the ability of the staff limit the number of laboratory blocks or modules that are offered. These sessions provide for considerable discussion as the student searches for an answer to "What happens to me when I engage in certain physical activities?"

This text does not intend to become involved in teaching methods, yet to discuss the nature of program content is almost impossible without making several references to how it is taught. In this respect, the *contract program* is worth mentioning. Of particular significance is the opportunity for the student to organize his or her time toward goals and performance objectives. In Cedar Rapids, Iowa, the high school boy or girl elects a unit of study and sets a performance objective. Once this is met he or she may advance to a higher level of skill or change units. The work need not be done in the school, but may be practiced at any suitable location. In the Needham illustration, Table 9-8, seniors on contract are encouraged to work outside the school day in essentially nonschool physical activities, such as scuba diving, ballet, African dance, "Y" swim team, figure skating, yoga, horseback riding, and so forth. This "extra class" program is particularly suitable for alternative high schools. Full knowledge of what is expected is the primary concern when the contract program is organized (see Figure 9-10). An excellent example of how this is spelled out for the student is shown in the Hillsborough County Public Schools illustration (see Figure 9-3). Note the clarity of performance objectives, strategies, and instructional aids.

Related to both program content and teaching method is the topic of *progression*. If the secondary physical education offering is on a continuum from grade 7 through grade 12, then the manner in which activities and skills progress from grade to grade is important. There must be purpose and order. Too often pupils have simply repeated the same skills year after year. This is particularly true in those systems in which all junior high or all senior high grades are thrown together for physical education, and there is no division of classes by skills, ability, and experience. These "exercise them" and "shower them" programs are frequently so haphazard in organization that they create an unfavorable image of physical education. Fortunately, however, an increasing number of schools have given considerable thought to graduated sequences for every activity. When sequences are written into the curriculum guide or course of study, or both, instructors and administrators know where the program is going.

Progressions can be set up in the guide with a minimum of detail so that readers of the program can see at a glance what is planned for each activity. This is nicely illustrated in the following (Table 9-9) single apparatus activity in one guide.

Progression may also be scheduled in terms of beginner, intermediate, and advanced skill levels. In Brookline, Massachusetts, all activities are blocked as in the archery example in Figure 9-4.

HILLSBOROUGH COUNTY PUBLIC SCHOOLS
Tampa, Florida

I. Course Title:
   Golf I

II. Course Number:
    542

III. Course Description:
     Provides a series of development skills that will assist the student in necessary knowledge, attitudes, skills and in making desirable value judgements concerning the use of this activity throughout life.

IV. Course Content:
    a. Golf is being offered because of the increasing need for students to aquire a sport of a lifetime nature. Because of the shorter work week and earlier retirement age, students will need to acquire skills in activities of a lifetime nature that will enable them to take an active part in their retirement years.
    b. The course will cover all of the basic skills in a sequential manner relating to golf. The rules, playing surfaces and golf etiquette will also be part of the course content.

V. Goals:
   a. Students will develop techniques and skills in golf that will enable them to become a better golfer.
   b. Students will develop positive attitudes toward golf that will enable them to become more effective golfers.
   c. Students will become aware of the possible potential of making golf a career.

VI. Performance Objectives:
    a. Given a series of trouble situations. The student will select the club to be used in each situation.
    b. Given an extremely difficult situation, the student will not lose self composure while solving it.
    c. The student will, on his own, practice his game in order to assess his own potential of the sport.

VII. Strategies for Achieving Objectives:
     a. Some of the skills to be taught are grip, stance, swing, approach, driving, putting, trouble shots. Some of the activities are squad competition in putting, distance, accuracy, and driving for distance.
     b. Plan one for objective 1:
        Situation: The ball is imbedded in the sand in a trap.
        Plan #1. Show the students a Super 8 loop film on how to get out of a trap. Have each student try it.
        Plan #2. Teacher demonstrate the technique.
        Plan #3. Have student assistant demonstrate.
        Plan #4. Have professional come and demonstrate.

VIII. Instructional Aids:
      a. Basic text - Physical Education for Life. (McGraw-Hill Book Co.)
      b. Supplementary text: How to Improve Your Golf, published by Athetic Institute.
      c. Books, periodicals, etc. to be used as teacher resources.
         Hillsborough County teaching guide on "Lifetime Sports".
      d. Super 8 loops from depository.
         1. stand and address
         2. the full swing
         3. swing with different clubs
         4. pitching and chipping
         5. putting
         6. trouble shots
         16 mm film from depository, lifetime sports in education.
      e. Field trips: On April 15 all classes will be bussed to Lock-Low par three course and play one round. On April 22 all students will be bussed to Palm Golf Club and play the front nine.
      f. Resourse personnel: On April 10 Mr. Sam Jones, club professional at Palm Golf Course has been invited to speak to the class on why golf as a lifetime sport.

IX. Evaluation:
    Written and skill test will be given at the conclusion of the course.

FIGURE 9-3. Student program. (Courtesy, Hillsborough County Public Schools and Warren J. Littell)

TABLE 9-9. East Syracuse-Minoa Central School*

Uneven Parallel Bars	7	8	9	10	11	12
Mounts						
Jump support	x	x				
Thigh rest	x	x				
Straddle	x	x				
Rear mount	x	x				
Brief review of above			x	x	x	x
Single cut			x	x		
Crotch seat			x	x		
Pendulum			x	x		
Push-stem			x	x		
Knee circle			x	x		
Oblique					x	x
Cast					x	x
Running kip					x	x
Hip circle					x	x
Moves						
Hip roll	x	x	x			
Scissor circles	x	x	x			
forward						
backward						
Hip circle	x	x	x			
Swan support	x	x	x			
Riding seat	x	x	x			
Forward extension seat	x	x	x			
Layout seat	x	x	x			
Front support	x	x	x			
Leg circle turn	x	x	x			
Reverse riding turn	x	x	x			
Front seat turn	x	x	x			
Thigh rest handstand	x	x	x			
Scale	x	x	x			
Brief review of above				x	x	x
Hip circles				x	x	x
lower to higher bar						
higher to lower bar						
Forward roll to layout position				x	x	x
Knee circle backward and uprise				x	x	x
Piko thigh rest				x	x	x
Crotch seat				x	x	x
Knee circle bac'ffall uprise				x	x	x
Backfall hip				x	x	x
Rear and front swing				x	x	x
Cast swing				x	x	x
Double leg circles				x	x	x
Angel balance				x	x	x
Arabesque knee hook balance				x	x	x

*Adapted from the *Physical Education Guide for Girls, Grades 7–12* (East Syracuse, N.Y.: East Syracuse-Minoa Central Schools, 1965).

TABLE 9-9. *Continued.*

Uneven Parallel Bars	7	8	9	10	11	12
Dismounts						
Rear	x	x				
Front	x	x				
Arch cast	x	x				
Hip circle	x	x				
Brief review of above			x	x	x	x
Knee hang			x			
Handstand layout			x	x		
Forward layout				x	x	x
Back tuck				x	x	x
Pivot squat				x	x	x
Flank	x	x	x			
Rear (kehre) over high bar				x	x	x
Squat					x	x

	SKILLS	ACTIVITY: ARCHERY		
		BEGINNING	INTERMEDIATE	ADVANCED
Shooting	Finger Shooting	X		
	Bracing and Unstringing Bow	X		
	Stance	X		
	Nocking the Arrow	X		
	Drawing	X		
	Anchor Point	X		
	Aim – Point of Aim	X		
	Sight on Bow		X	
	Release	X		
	Follow Through	X		
	Perfection of Shooting			
	Skill and Form		X	
	Twenty Yards	X		
	Thirty Yards		X	
	Forty Yards			X
Retrieval of Arrow	From the Target	X		
	From the Ground	X		
Advanced Shooting	Clout Shooting		X	
	Tournament Shooting			
	Columbia Round			X
	Double Round			X
	Hereford Round			X

Performance Objectives:

1. At the 10th grade level the students should be able to execute 11 of 12 beginning skills.

2. At the 11th grade level the students should be able to execute all beginning skills and 3 out of 4 intermediate skills.

3. At the end of the 12th grade level all beginning skills should be executed and all intermediate skills.

FIGURE 9-4.

A Closer Look at Content

One reason that curriculum planning is so difficult is that each of the major areas of content has to be carefully organized, yet kept in balance with the other areas, and set up so that there is opportunity for flexibility, modifications, and innovations. Under such demanding circumstances it would be relatively easy simply to set up a number of suggested activities under each of the major areas of content and leave the rest to the instructor when the time comes to teach the particular activity. This is precisely what has been done in the past, and has resulted in programs that are too open, too indefinite, and almost impossible to defend in terms of achieving desired program outcomes. A far sounder practice is to structure a rather firm and detailed course of study that is thorough and balanced in coverage, and then allow some departure by capable instructors who desire to try new ideas.

There are a number of comments to be made regarding the major areas of emphasis.

FIGURE 9-5. Attractive way to develop physical fitness in junior high school. (Courtesy, Marjory Blaufarb, AAHPER)

1. Conditioning and Body Mechanics

A unique goal of physical education is the development and maintenance of an optimum level of physical condition. This kind of "capacity for activity" has been the concern of physical education teachers for centuries. In fact, long before games and recreational activities were generally considered educational, the doctors of medicine and teachers in Greece, Rome, Germany, and Sweden were proclaiming the virtues of personal exercise as a contributor to good physical condition and well-being. Since those early days a great variety of activities designed to promote physical fitness have been proposed.

The answer to the question of what kind of activity to include in a secondary school physical fitness routine must always relate to whether the activity does indeed build the elements of physical fitness—muscular strength, muscular endurance, and cardiorespiratory endurance. Periodic testing with an acceptable test of physical fitness will help provide an answer.

Fortunately, many activities that build physical fitness also develop high levels of motor ability—speed, explosive power, agility, balance, reaction time, kinesthetic awareness, and certain psychological capacities. Thus, it is possible to develop motor coordination, together with a wide variety of sport, dance, and game skills, and at the same time gradually develop a satisfactory level of physical condition. Although this is true, the individual development of physical condition cannot be left entirely to game and sport participation. Other more specific activities will be needed in many cases.

Calisthenics and free exercise routines are traditional curriculum standbys for class "warm-up" and general body conditioning and body mechanics. They have the advantage of not taking up the whole physical education class period. Most of these exercises are of the isotonic variety, but in recent years it has been popular to introduce a few isometric exercises, mostly for variety and fun.

At this point it must be emphasized that strength-building activities are very much a part of the girls' program. Experience shows that many girls are unaware that basic strength and endurance are prerequisites to the desired qualities of proper weight level, grace, poise, pleasing posture, and a generally attractive appearance. Girls are frequently not motivated to build strength as boys are, but they are interested in gaining some skills that result in pleasurable activity. To achieve these goals, girls perform some very vigorous routines. Research shows that both aquatics and modern dance can be extremely vigorous. In the Houston secondary schools, the girls have an aerobics program which includes jogging. Ribbons for jogging are awarded for 1 to 250 miles of running. Participants jog the mile within a time limit without stopping, and the totals are cumulative. In bad weather the girls do rope-skipping routines.

The secondary school girl should be exposed to a series of *menstrual exercises* designed to help relieve menstrual pain. Thanks to the efforts of physicians such as Golub, Mosher, and Billig, many women can keep the abdominal and pelvic region musculature firm over the years, a condition that will reap benefits in improved comfort during menstruation as well as in reduced tendency toward low-back pain in later life.

Weight training has gained in popularity to such an extent that hundreds of junior and senior high schools own complete sets of weights, enough to service a full class of thirty students working in pairs. The pupils keep their own records of progress.

Sandbags have also been used satisfactorily in place of the traditional disc weights. They lend themselves well to certain exercises, and they are made in a wide variety of sizes and shapes. The instructional emphasis is on body conditioning rather than on weight lifting for competition. In one school there was so much real interest in weights and conditioning that the instructor started a One Hundred Ton Club. A certain number of pounds are achieved each workout period. The amount of weight times the number of repetitions determines the number of pounds credited to the club score. (Example: 100 pounds × 10 repetitions = 1000 pounds toward the goal of 100 tons.) No more than five workouts a week are permitted, and each week the total pounds earned are posted on a huge chart in the locker room for all to compare.

Several secondary schools have introduced *running* or *jogging* for fun and conditioning. The activity has much in its favor as a builder of condition. It challenges the circulatory and respiratory systems. Moreover, says Vermont's renowned cardiologist Wilhelm Raab, it is "the best of all physical exercises" because it is "strenuous and enduring . . . and rhythmical." Obviously, this activity has great carryover value—especially when we have experienced what it feels like to achieve good running condition. Perhaps we should envy the runner, for he is probably one of those *bon vivants* of the athletic world who is completely happy while jogging the streets and byways. Unfortunately, most schools do little cardiovascular training. Cooper has shown that as little as 6–14 minutes of jogging as a part of the regular physical education class can increase cardiovascular endurance over 17 percent, and an entire school can become involved.[7] A number of instructors now have their boys and girls run-walk continuously on a running track for 12 minutes and keep a record of the distance run on each occasion. This serves as a measure of progress in the conditioning program.

Circuit training is another significant fitness activity worth program-

[7]Kenneth H. Cooper, and others, "An Aerobic Conditioning Program for the Fort Worth, Texas School District," *Research Quarterly*, 46 (October 1975), 345–50.

ing for both developmental and adapted classes. Its chief advantage in the conditioning of pupils is that it applies the principle of progressive loading. It enables large numbers of students to train at the same time by employing a circuit of consecutively numbered exercises through which each performer progresses, carrying out a prescribed amount of work at each station and checking their progress against the clock.

Although the basic exercises in the circuit remain the same for each student, the intensity at each station may differ according to the fitness of the individual pupil. Therefore, boys and girls of all levels of condition can work on the circuit at their own degree of intensity.

In some schools, pupils are tested to determine their maximum performance in a circuit exercise. Their training then is to do only half this amount, repeated three times, by repeating the total circuit three times each workout period. In at least one junior high school (Table 9-10) the circuits are set up with specific requirements for four levels of physical conditioning.[8]

TABLE 9-10. Circuit Program for a Junior High School

Station°	Circuits			
	Green	Red	Blue	Gold
Squat thrusts	8x	10x	12x	Max.
Pull-ups	3x or max.	5x	7x	Max.
Bench steps	15x	20x	25x	Max.
Rowing	5x, 30 lbs.	5x, 35 lbs.	5x, 45 lbs.	Max. 50 lbs.
Sit-ups	10x	15x	20x	Max.
Rope climb	½ way	¾ way	all the way	Max.
P-bar dips	3x or max.	5x	7x	Max.
¾ squats	5x piggy back	7x piggy back	9x	Max.
Standing press	4x, 30 lbs.	5x, 35 lbs.	6x, 40 lbs.	Max. 60 lbs.
Push-ups	8x	6x hand clap	10x hand clap	Max.
Curls	4x, 30 lbs.	5x, 35 lbs.	6x, 40 lbs.	Max. 45 lbs.
Wrist-rolls	1x, 5 lbs.	1x, 10 lbs.	1x, 15 lbs.	Max.

°All stations are to be performed for 30 seconds.

After studying the Europeans' "outdoor exercise path," the Alabama Commission on Physical Fitness set up a statewide Olympic Fitness Circuit—a three-mile jogging track, which rolls over hills and winds through beautifully wooded areas. Spotted along this jogging path are exercise stations at which participants execute various types of calisthenics. Instructions are written on metal plaques at each station. The more strenuous exercises are

[8]Frank F. Gambelli, "Circuit Training in the Junior High School," *Journal of Health, Physical Education and Recreation*, 38 (March 1967), 93–95.

located in the middle third of the circuit; and relaxation exercises come near the end.

The *obstacle course* is another physical conditioner of long standing. However, because of its usual space requirements, it is often omitted from the program in the larger cities. However, a very good obstacle course will afford a measure of general motor ability as well as physical conditioning that can be set up around a gymnasium. Moreover, only a small amount of time is needed each physical education period to run through the course. In Los Alamos, New Mexico, junior high school pupils work in an outdoor area and use exactly eight minutes per period to scramble through an eight-obstacle, 400-yard course. The improvement in AAHPER Youth Fitness scores was considerable after they worked out on the following course obstacles:

1. hand walking through the parallel bars
2. going over and under six hurdles
3. mounting the climbing wall
4. running the zig-zag log run
5. duck-walking a tunnel
6. going up and down a series of four-foot mounds
7. hand walking the horizontal ladder
8. rope swinging across the mud pit

When the President's Council on Physical Fitness and Sports set up its Varsity Club Program for the average community in 1972, the Council suggested a very fine fitness-building routine. The exact specifications for this are worth reviewing.[9]

The last example of a valuable conditioning activity, particularly for senior high school pupils, is *neuromuscular relaxation*. Relaxation is a neuromuscular accomplishment that results in a reduction of tension in the skeletal musculation. In today's world, it is practically impossible to attain a state of "zero activity" in the voluntary motor apparatus by simply deciding to do so, unless the individual has had some training to learn how. In this connection Hatha Yoga, which concentrates on a physically relaxed body, is an appropriate activity. Meditation, biofeedback routines, and Jacobson's progressive relaxation are alternative practices that could be adapted to physical education class involvement.

II. Aquatics

There is little that can be added to what has already been said about the need for swimming, survival skills, and other water-related activities. Although a pool may not be available, or even in the planning stage, a good

[9]Write to President's Council on Physical Fitness and Sports, Washington, D.C., 20402.

practice is to include aquatic activities for boys and girls in the course of study for both junior and senior high school pupils. This inclusion keeps the topic alive and reminds instructors and others that they must be continually seeking a way to realize this part of the total physical education experience.

Fundamental swimming and water safety skills should be taught at advanced levels throughout the secondary school years. Swimming for fun can be coupled with competencies in aquatic survival. Wetmore maintains that no swimmer is safe in the water until he or she has learned to swim long distances and to float long periods in rough water fully clad without suffering from fatigue; to swim when afflicted with cramps or injury to limbs; and to cope with panic-provoking situations.[10] Moreover, the application of Lanoue's downproofing skills—subsurface floating and travel stroke—is facilitated by an understanding of body buoyancy, control of breathing, conservation of energy, and emotional adaptation to the water environment.

FIGURE 9-6. An efficient organization of space permits self-testing through apparatus skills. (Courtesy, Chicago Public Schools)

[10]Reagh C. Wetmore, "Teaching Aquatic Survival," *Journal of Health, Physical Education and Recreation,* 44 (March 1973), 77–78.

III. Self-Testing Activities

As with elementary-age children, the desire to measure personal progress against previous performances and the accomplishments of peers is ever present with most junior high school students. The boys are eager for a challenge, and the girls have not yet become so sophisticated that they need special motivation. Stunts, tumbling, apparatus work, weight lifting, obstacle course running, and the several track and field events are especially vigorous, difficult, and fun to perform. In many situations, all it takes to get self-testing rolling is a bulletin board chart of "items to do" and a willing teacher.

IV. Games

In the junior high school some time should be allotted to group games, such as cageball, keep-away, tug-of-war, and numerous running and dodging relays. Although they are not highly organized, they do permit a collective enjoyment and lead up to the more complex activities. In this respect, lead-up games for all team sports require serious consideration. There are many of these, such as line soccer, circle kickball, kickpin baseball, basketball dribbling and shooting relays, and soccer dribble relays. An excellent collection of lead-up games may be found in the Blake and Volp book listed at the end of this chapter.

FIGURE 9-7. Teaching stations and good equipment enhance the program. (Courtesy, Jayfro Athletic Supply Co.)

The place of *individual and dual sports* is well established in secondary education. These are activities which permit a person to compare performance with a standard, a record, or with that of another individual. They also involve two individuals in competition with one another.

For purposes of classification, the following activities may be considered individual and dual sports

Archery	Deck tennis
Golf	Table tennis
Badminton	Horseshoes
Tennis	Quoits
Handball	Skiing
Fencing	Ice skating
Bowling	Shuffleboard
	Wrestling

At the secondary school level, an allotment of a generous amount of time to these kinds of activities seems advisable. The progressive development and perfection of the skills and knowledge involved in these games provide a wholesome, enjoyable, and physically satisfying form of recreational activity that is important in a culture characterized by shorter working hours, automation, and the tension syndrome.

Those schools that are geographically located to take advantage of a winter season of snow and ice should have skiing and skating instruction as a part of the regular midwinter curriculum.

The need for a combative activity during the winter season is real in a number of communities. Wrestling satisfies this requirement very well. It supplements other individual and team activities, develops strength, agility, and physical condition, and prepares a number of pupils for interscholastic competition. In the small schools, wrestling fills a void during the winter months and fits well with interscholastic competition.

V. Team Sports

The need for sports education has been eloquently stressed. Cozens and Stumpf point out that "common interests, common loyalties, common enthusiasm . . . are the great integrating factors in any culture. In America, sports have provided this common denominator in as great a degree as any other single factor.[11]

Simply stated, team sports are learned and played in the junior and senior high schools for something more than recreation; they are played in order to develop in the participants a quality of social efficiency—the ability to get along with others and to exhibit desirable standards of conduct. There is abundant research to validate the positive relationship between motor performance on teams and the character traits of leadership and cooperation.

[11]Frederick W. Cozens and Florence Stumpf, "American Sports from the Sidelines," *Journal of Health, Physical Education and Recreation*, 23 (November 1952), 12–14.

During the adolescent period, physical conditioning and the development of sports skills come together to provide a *capacity* to understand others.[12] This capacity leads to greater social acceptance. Team sports, therefore, should be taken more seriously than they are in many instructional programs.

Too often team sports are engaged in with a bare minimum of instruction. Skills are poorly learned, as pupils rush onto the fields and courts to play the game. Skills and knowledge need to be properly taught if sports experiences are to leave their mark of value. Moreover, the teams need to be as equal in ability as possible if sportsmanship is to be developed. When activity groups and teams are purposely set up so that none has an unfair advantage and when equality between players is the rule, then there is opportunity for sportsmanship in play, with the corresponding development of personal adjustment and optimum group behavior.

The cognitive aspects of a sports education can be advanced by relating to the world of art. The alliance of art and sport is a natural one. Certainly the agile, disciplined, and rhythmic movements of the athlete are expressions of a different form of the beauty of a piece of sculpture or fine painting. In this connection the AAHPER filmstrip, *Art and Sport,* is especially appropriate for secondary level classes. It is available from the national office in Washington.[13]

There should be a concentration of team sports in grades 7 through 10, with a distinct tapering off after this period in order to make room for instruction in those activities that tend to have a greater degree of carry-over value into adult life. The team sports most frequently taught in the instructional program are as in Table 9-11.

TABLE 9-11

Boys	Girls	Sex-Integrated
Flag football	Field hockey	Field hockey
Soccer	Lacrosse (girls' rules)	Soccer
Speedball	Soccer	Speedball
Basketball	Basketball	Volleyball
Volleyball	Volleyball	Softball
Softball	Softball	Track and field
Captain ball	Track and field	
Lacrosse		
Ice hockey		
Track and field		

VI. Rhythms and Dance

Much of what has already been said about the value of rhythms and dance in elementary education could be repeated here. This would serve the purpose of tying in the elementary level experiences with those of the secon-

[12]Carl E. Willgoose, *Evaluation in Health Education and Physical Education* (New York: McGraw-Hill, 1961), p. 346.

[13]See also Annie Ingram, "Art and Sport," *Journal of Health, Physical Education and Recreation,* 44 (February 1973), 24–27.

dary period, for we are dealing here with a total package of movements, grades K–12. The upper-grade activities should be an extension in both depth and scope of what was experienced in the lower grades.

In planning a secondary program, therefore, first we should become familiar with what has been offered to the boys and girls in the earlier years. For example, frequently we assume that students entering the junior high school have had instruction in the fundamental rhythms, singing games, and folk dances. Unfortunately, in many instances this is not the case, and the junior high school instructor must run quickly through the various fundamentals of walking, running, jumping, skipping, galloping, sidestepping, leaping, and marching to several kinds of audible accompaniment. Because of the nature of singing games, if they have not been taught previously, there is little point in struggling with them in the secondary school.

Marching. Marching has always been an enjoyable kind of rhythmic when coupled with various kinds of accompaniment and made challenging by the introduction of special steps, intricate maneuvers, and changing tempos. Gymnastic marching, done for the sake of "discipline" or "attentiveness" has little value. It must serve a purpose that students subscribe to. Marching and exercising to music, somewhat in the Danish fashion, frequently have great appeal to both secondary school boys and girls and can be especially fine coeducational activities.

Dance

. . . to give poise to the nerves, schooling to the emotions, strength to the will, and to harmonize the feelings and the intellect with the body which supports them.

G. STANLEY HALL

FIGURE 9-8. Innovative dance movements with ropes. (Courtesy, Dorothy P. Stanley)

In 1905 Hall declared that the need for dancing was acute in education because it had the potential of harmonizing body, mind, and feelings in a unique fashion that is quite uncommon in other subject-matter areas. Many decades later educational researchers like Benjamin Bloom called for more attention to the affective and action domains; and Charles Silberman expressed the view that if the scales have to be tipped toward any domain, they should be tipped toward the affective. And this, says Mary Ella Montague, is where dance has one of its strongest potentials—"to release human feelings in ways which are significant to the doer, enabling him to make a personal statement of what 'life feels like.' "[14] It is this sorting out of impressions and sensations by first internalizing them and then externalizing them in movements that matters.

It is the objective of the National Dance Association to make dance a part of every individual's experience from early childhood to old age, for it is through the medium of dance that everybody is offered the opportunity for self-expression and aesthetic development. Already good programs exist in such places as East High School, Salt Lake City, Utah; New Triar High School, Winnetka, Illinois; George Washington High School, Denver, Colorado; and in Detroit, Michigan, and Orlando, Florida.

Dance as a means of expression, as an art form, and as a way of physical conditioning and recreation is a very big order to fill in physical education. In the total curriculum, how much time can be given to folk, square, modern, and social dance? Are time allotments varying from 10 to 25 percent adequate? Should dance as an art form be left solely to those interested students and teachers who establish a school dance club? Should not the young man or young woman compare the well-conditioned and moving body of the modern dancer with that of the athlete? Is it not true that athletics and dance have at least two things in common—both are art education and humanistic education?

Modern Dance is one of the finest educational experiences that the school has to offer. Movement is explored without adherence to the kinds of set patterns found in social, folk, and square dancing. It is a vigorous group and total-body activity bringing into play every conceivable complementary and reciprocal combination of the muscles, senses, and mind. Dancing, says Martha Graham, "is movement made significant." The key word is movement. With a growing consciousness of the "movement meaning" in physical education, new insights relative to the value of the dance curriculum in an integrated education will need structuring. Fraleigh makes this unmistakably clear when she speaks of physical education in terms of the "arts of move-

[14]Mary Ellen Montague, "Dance Is Affective and therefore Effective Education," *Journal of Health, Physical Education and Recreation*, 43 (March 1972), 87–88.

ment."[15] So does the educational philosopher, Philip Phenix, when he defines physical education:

> The arts of movement are the foundation for the learnings which take place under the broad heading of "physical education" . . . all intentional activities, undertaken for aesthetic purposes, in which the desired expressive effects are communicated by the movement of the human body.[16]

Not only is dance a reflection of the culture, it is a revelation of the individual as it requires carefully timed and qualified movements—movements that illustrate a certain style and evoke a particular state of feeling. Laban was aware of this factor when he initiated his Effort/Shape Analysis for English factory workers a number of years ago.[17] This awareness and feeling for movement is well understood by dance therapists who are able to identify particular characteristic movement profiles exhibiting certain emotional and personality conflicts. The mentally ill, says Marion North, ". . . always reveal in their movements characteristics and habits very definite variations and distortions from the range of 'normality.' "[18]

Modern dance is not exclusively a girl's activity. Because women's departments have been noticeably separated from the men's, boys know little about it. Sexism need not exist in dance; the joy of the activity can be shared. It must be taught coeducationally by men as well as women. Dennis Fallon nicely sets the stage:[19]

> But what does a society think of a boy's performance in dance? Does a boy dance gracefully or does he dance effeminately? In a society where his performance in physical activity is measured quantifiably, man has received little encouragement to express himself aesthetically in movement. There are few Bannisters in the athletic world who run with an awareness of self and universe that produces harmony with nature and satisfaction from a race run well regardless of victory or defeat. While it may be unproductive and therefore unlikely for the athlete, male or female, to strive for aesthetic expression, such expression is

[15]Sondra H. Fraleigh, "Unity of Design: Modern Dance in Physical Education," *Journal of Health, Physical Education and Recreation*, 42 (November-December 1971), 31–33.

[16]Philip H. Phenix, *Realms of Meaning* (New York: McGraw-Hill, 1964) pp. 165–66.

[17]Anatomical function was analyzed with the body parts in action. Scrutinized was the movement origin, shape, size, direction, counterdirection, clarity of form, and opposites, such as sudden and sustained; also, motion factors, such as time, space, flow, and weight.

[18]Marion North, *Personality Assessment Through Movement*, (London: McDonald and Evans, Ltd., 1972), p. 19.

[19]Dennis Fallon, "A Man Unchained," *Journal of Physical Education and Recreation*, 48 (May 1977), 43–45.

the essence of dance. And in dance, where performance is motivated by intrinsic satisfaction, a young man without orientation to creative, spontaneous expression stands barren and ignorant of his own body. With no apparent alternative, he shamefully rejects his bodily impulses to become the ultimate athlete.

Currently, more and more boys are becoming active participants in high school dance organizations. To learn how Ted Shawn felt about the effect of predance training on man, how Jan Veen (Hans Wiener) built good dancers, and how Hanya Holm teaches controlled movements, I recommend that the Rogers text be reviewed, for it is a classic and stimulating treatment of the topic.[20]

Folk and square dancing.   Although some dances can be taught separately to boys and girls, the most successful programs will be presented coeducationally. If the folk and square sequences are scheduled for both sexes at the same time, this form of recreational activity can be learned well enough for immediate carry-over to other school and community settings. A full unit of class instruction and practice should occur in grade 7 and again in the senior high school period. This should be supplemented by shorter review units during the in-between years.

Dance skills should progress from the more fundamental steps and patterns to the more intricate as pupils get older and require a greater challenge. An indication of the level of difficulty of some folk and square dances appears in Table 9-12.

In *modern square dancing*, which has been growing in popularity, there is room for creative calls, patterns, and adaptation of movement to a variety of musical scores, as well as to tempo and rhythms. The basic research in square dance patterns done by Patricia Phillips (Bridgewater State College, Bridgewater, Massachusetts) is especially significant.

Social dance.   The newer forms of social dance, in which the individual or the couple follow their own leadership, are here to continue and slowly evolve into something else. Over the years social dancers have gone from the "Charleston" to the "Funky Chicken" and beyond. Still other dances are to come as long as people get together and express themselves to rhythm and music. Although the move in social dance has been away from partners and toward individual and group dances, there is today a slow return to an interest in dancing with partners in the secondary schools. For this reason there is value in teaching the basic steps, such as the fox trot, slow rhythm and blues, waltz, jitterbug, and the South American rhythms of the tango, rumba, samba, and cha-cha.

Jazz seems to broaden a student's interest in dance—not only in terms of

[20]Frederick Rand Rogers, *Dance: A Basic Educational Technique* (New York: McGraw-Hill, 1941).

TABLE 9-12

GRADES 7–8 (BEGINNING)	GRADES 9–10 (INTERMEDIATE)	GRADES 11–12 (ADVANCED)

Folk Dance

GRADES 7–8 (BEGINNING)	GRADES 9–10 (INTERMEDIATE)	GRADES 11–12 (ADVANCED)
Badger Gavotte	Horah	Czardes
Bingo	Irish Lilt	Hambo
Circle Schottische	Italian Quadrille	Highland Fling
Crested Hen	Kalvelis	Hopak
Green Sleeves	Korobushka	Mexican Waltz
Heel and Toe Polka	La Cucaracha	Sailor's Hornpipe
Irish Two-Step	Mexican Mixer	Sicilian Tarantella
Narcissus	Norwegian Polka	Swedish Varsovienne
Tantoli	Rye Waltz	Tivoli Hambo
Tropanka	Spanish Circle	Ukrainian Ohorodnik
Wooden Shoes		

Square Dance

GRADES 7–8 (BEGINNING)	GRADES 9–10 (INTERMEDIATE)	GRADES 11–12 (ADVANCED)
Review of Fundamentals	Arkansas Traveler	Ladies Grand Chain
Alabama Jubilee	Back to Back	Lady Walpole Reel
Buffalo Gals	Birdie in the Cage	Paul Jones
Dive for the Oyster	Darling Nellie Gray	Push Her Away
Divide the Ring	Forward Six	Rose of San Antone
Grand March	Girl I Left Behind	Sashay Partner Half Way
Honolulu Baby	Indian Style	Round
Marching Through Georgia	Ocean Wave	Sides Divide
Oh Johnny	Lady Around Lady	The Route
Oh Suzanna	Sally Goodin	The Basket
Pop Goes the Weasel	Solomon Levi	Three Ladies Chain
Two Ladies Cross Over	Teton Mountain Stomp	Whirlpool Square
Turkey in the Straw	Texas Star	
Yankee Doodle	Waltz Promenade	

attracting men to modern dance, but in the recreational or social dance setting. Danced somewhat individually in the gymnasium or ballroom, recreational jazz dance makes use of jazz movements in various styles including "old jazz," "Latin," "rock," and others which permit the flexibility of axial movements that are fun to perform. For this reason, a number of secondary schools schedule social dance instruction as part of the regular physical education curriculum.

VII. Evaluation: Skill and Knowledge Tests

Every complete curriculum outline should contain a scheduled time in which to measure pupil progress toward the goals of the physical education program. Experience indicates that if evaluation is not thought of as a curriculum item, a strong possibility exists that no specific time will be provided,

and evaluation soon becomes haphazard. Tests of achievement and knowledge should go along with the instructional units. Tests of physical fitness
should be scheduled periodically (see Chapter 12). The student-parent contract may also serve as an evaluation toll (see Figure 9-9).

VIII. Intramurals

No program of class instruction in the foreseeable future can hope to
meet the need for full and vigorous group competition completely. This will
only come when appropriate time is set aside for intramural participation. A
course of study, therefore, is incomplete if it fails to make mention of kinds and
extent of intramural play. Certainly, the objective is to get a high percentage
of boys and girls to take part in intramural competition each season. Not
unrealistic is the aim for 100 percent student participation sometime during
the school years in extraclass activity—75 percent in intramurals and 25
percent in interscholastics and sports days. See Chapter 11 for additional
details.

IX. Interscholastics

Extraclass participation in games and sports should be encouraged in
both junior and senior high schools. The opportunity to train and compete
under proper supervision should be available to all boys and girls. Generally
speaking, however, the emphasis at the junior high level is on learning the
fundamentals and engaging in a shorter season than at the senior high level.

X. Adventure-Challenge Activities

Youth, large, lusty, living—youth full of grace, force, fascination

                                                                         WALT WHITMAN

For many secondary school boys and girls an attractive *alternative path*
is needed if they are to attain the goals of physical education. Ways other than
the traditional means of obtaining body management and kinesthetic experiences must be found. In this respect adventure-challenge programs have
applied the words of Whitman and have succeeded noticeably, especially
when the programs are viewed as a part of the *total* curriculum and combined
with the more common physical education activities.

The adventure-challenge activity explores the numerous ways in which
the body can be used to serve the individual by confronting the student with
exciting problems that have to be solved. Moreover, the problems generally
have to be solved to the satisfaction of the group. (See Chapter 8, p. 260 for
elaboration). Evidence is increasing that these programs are very well ac-

NEEDHAM HIGH SCHOOL

Department of Physical Education

Extra Class Program

Student – Parent Contract

The Physical Education Department provides an opportunity for the student to extend his physical education beyond the school walls and to pursue on an individual basis a course of instruction of interset to him. The course of instruction must be at an advanced level or an activity which is not offered presently at Needham High School.

To take part in this program a student must accept definite responsibilities and abide by the rules governing the program.

The student must be certain the he satisfies the requirements necessary for receiving course credit stipulated by the Physical Education Department.

The student and parent will make provision for transportation and are responsible for course fees involved in this program.

The student agrees to be in regular attendance in his course of instruction.

The student agrees to observe all rules and regulations set down by the agency rendering the course of instruction.

The student agrees to discuss with the advisor, in advance, before deciding to drop the course of instruction.

The parent will assume liability for the student when he or she is participating in the course of instruction.

- -

Date ____________

________________________ has my permission to participate in this
(Student's Name)

program and receive instruction in ________________________ for
(Activity)

____________ class hours at ________________________.
(Agency)

We have read the statements on this form.

____
Parent/Guardian Signature

____
Student's Signature

____
Advisor's Signature

FIGURE 9-9. Evaluation can be improved with a contract plan. (Courtesy, Needham Public Schools, Needham, Massachusetts)

cepted by older children—children who will voluntarily tell how their self-reliance and self-confidence were raised by overcoming mental and physical obstacles, winning the respect of others by contributing to the group effort, and by succeeding in seemingly impossible challenges.

This Outward Bound variety of risk and challenge activities has given some otherwise ineffective physical education programs a real boost in popularity and worth. Although this is to be desired, there is the danger of assigning an undue amount of attention to this relatively new activity area at the expense of skill-development practices in such fundamental lifetime pursuits as aquatics and team and individual sports. This is an especially important consideration when electives are offered. At this time the concept of the balanced curriculum should prevail as students are guided in making their choices.

QUESTIONS FOR DISCUSSION

1. How well are Title IX practices going in your area. Where are the strengths? Problems?
2. Explain how time allotment, class size, and the number of teaching stations have a bearing on the scope of the secondary school program of physical education.
3. Seasonal programs and daily schedules frequently list marching as a secondary school activity. Is this justified today, or is it an activity that has "hung on" from a bygone era when formal gymnastics and gymnastic marching went hand-in-hand?
4. Where, in your opinion, does social dance fit best in the secondary school physical education program? Back up your answer with the viewpoint of at least one reference.
5. Is risk-taking an essential ingredient in secondary physical education? Explain your view.
6. Is there any purpose to be served by carefully developing an aquatics curriculum on paper if there are no swimming facilities in the community?
7. What are some of the content weaknesses in junior high school programs for girls? For boys? Try answering the same question for the senior high school level.
8. If you were the city director of physical education, how might you go about correcting imbalances in the program of studies?
9. What can you discover relative to the amount of time assigned to a particular part of the program by studying curriculum guides for several similar towns or cities?

SUGGESTED ACTIVITIES

1. Observe two or three junior high school physical education classes. Note the nature of the pupils—their enthusiasm, general attitude, and performance. Note also the lesson content. Record the highlights of what you were able to see. Compare your findings with those of your classmates. Are there observations you share in common?

2. Arrange a visit to a school setting in which adventure-challenge programs are in operation. Talk with students and instructors relative to the value of this activity as a part of the total physical education curriculum.

3. Review two or three references having to do with the problems of the young adolescent. Set down on paper five or six of these problems and proceed to show how physical education may contribute to their partial solution.

4. Examine the literature relative to "extra class programs," "alternative schools," and "learning contracts." What do you find to be the advantages and disadvantages of these programs in secondary education? What can you discover relative to physical education? Are local schools involved in this kind of innovation?

5. Survey the recreational facilities in a particular community—both commercial and noncommercial. To what extent does the curriculum in physical education in the junior and senior high school provide the appropriate skills and stimulate interest in the use of these facilities?

6. Select a teaching topic, such as a team sport, dance, or physical conditioning, and set up what you believe to be a logical sequence of learning experiences, grades 7–12. Do not try to include all of the instructional detail, just the highlights.

SELECTED REFERENCES

ALEXANDER, RUTH, and DOROTHY A. SHIELDS, "Aquacies in Florida," *Journal of Health, Physical Education and Recreation*, 44 (January 1973), 83–84.

ANNARINO, ANTHONY A., *Developmental Conditioning for Physical Education and Athletics*. St. Louis: C. V. Mosby Co., 1972.

BAIN, LINDA L., "Description of the Hidden Curriculum in Secondary Physical Education," *Research Quarterly*, 47 (May 1976), 154–58.

BENT, RUDYARD K., and HENRY H. KRONENBERG, *Principles of Secondary Education*. New York: McGraw-Hill, 1967.

BLAKE, WILLIAM, and ANNE VOLP, *Lead-Up Games to Team Sports*. Englewood Cliffs, N.J.: Prentice-Hall, Inc., 1964.

BROER, MARION R., ed., *Individual Sports for Women*, (5th ed). Philadelphia: W. B. Saunders Co., 1971.

BUSCH, JO ANN, "Everybody Teaches, Everybody Learns," *Journal of Physical Education and Recreation*, 47 (February 1976), 53–54.

COOPER, PHYLLIS, *Feminine Gymnastics* (2nd ed). Minneapolis: Burgess Publishing Co., 1973.

CREW, LOUIE, "The Physical Miseducation of a Former Fat Boy," *Saturday Review*, February 1973, p. 11.

DAUGHTREY, GREYSON, *Effective Teaching in Physical Education for Secondary Schools*. Philadelphia: W. B. Saunders Co., 1973.

————, and JOHN B. WOODS, *Physical Education Programs: Organization and Administration*. (2nd ed). Philadelphia: W. B. Saunders Co., 1976.

GROVER, GEORGE H., "New York State's New Regulations Governing Physical Education." *Journal of Physical Education and Recreation*, 46 (September 1975), 29–31.

HENDERSON, JAMES G., "Synchronized Swimming for Men," *Journal of Physical Education and Recreation*, 48 (October 1977), 24.

HULT, JOAN, "Equal Programs or Carbon Copies?" *Journal of Physical Education and Recreation*, 48 (May 1976), 24–26.

HYPES, JEANNETTE, "Dance Production as an Educational Experience," *Journal of Health, Physical Education and Recreation*, 43 (November-December 1972), 49–54.

LOCKHART, AILEENE, and ESTHER E. PEASE, *Modern Dance—Building and Teaching Lessons*. Dubuque, Iowa: W. C. Brown Co., 1973.

PIERCE, ELIZABETH THAMES, "Dance: Let's Take Time," *Journal of Physical Education and Recreation*, 48 (March 1977), 46.

RAE, CAROLE, "Dance Commentary: Educational and Performing Art," *Journal of Physical Education and Recreation*, 47 (November/December 1976), 50.

RESICK, MATHEW, BEVERLY L. SEIDEL, and JAMES G. MASON, *Modern Administrative Practices in Physical Education and Athletics* (2nd ed). Boston: Addison-Wesley Pub. Co., 1975.

SMITH, CHARLES D., and SAMUEL PRATHER, "Group Problem Solving," *Journal of Physical Education and Recreation*, 46 (September 1975), 20–21.

ULRICH, CELESTE, "Education for a Dynamic Lifestyle," *Journal of Physical Education and Recreation*, 48 (May 1977). 48.

VANNIER, MARYHELEN, and HOLLIS F. FAIT, *Teaching Physical Education to Secondary Schools* (4th ed), Philadelphia: W. B. Saunders Co., 1975.

VITALE, F., *Individualized Fitness Programs*. Englewood Cliffs, N.J.: Prentice-Hall, Inc., 1973.

WALKER, JUNE, CHARLES C. COWELL, and HILDA M. SOHWEHN, *Modern Methods in Secondary School Physical Education* (3rd ed). Boston: Allyn and Bacon, 1973.

WILLGOOSE, CARL E., *Health Teaching in Secondary Schools*, pp. 99–105. Philadelphia: W. B. Saunders Co., 1977.

ZIEGLER, EARLE, *Physical Education and Sport Philosophy.* Englewood Cliffs, N.J.: Prentice-Hall, Inc., 1977.

The Adapted Program:

Individualizing

Physical Education

chapter ten

We know what we are but not what we may be.

WILLIAM SHAKESPEARE

The long history of education demonstrates that a common practice for many years has been to impose unfairly inactivity on the handicapped individual. This practice has been especially true for students without a portion of their physical well-being, students prone to weaknesses in emotional control, and students classified as mentally retarded. In most of these instances there has been an unrealized potential—a potential that Shakespeare recognized when he referred to individuals not knowing *what they may be*. These young people have not benefitted from motor experiences that boost self-esteem and self-reliance. Also, careful examination of overall personal and social rewards associated with learning a motor skill at a self-satisfying level of performance has not been possible.

This chapter emphasizes a curriculum that concentrates on flexibility and innovation in meeting individual weaknesses. Thus, the word *adapted* is the key word. It sets the stage for a program that seeks an active participation of all students who cannot safely or successfully take part in the unrestricted activities of the regular physical education program. This includes much more than the youngster with minor orthopedic difficulties, postural problems, and low levels of physical fitness. The complete adapted program provides opportunities for *all* students who need individualized and specialized help, including the visually handicapped, hearing-impaired, overweight, emotionally disturbed, socially maladjusted, mentally retarded, convalescing, neurologically impaired, brain-damaged, those with special health problems (such as cardiac abnormalities, muscular dystrophy, multiple sclerosis, and so forth) and individuals with specific motor deficiencies

312

and motor perception problems. Moreover, the program is a diversified one of developmental movement activities, games, sports, and rhythms suited to the interests as well as the limitations of students.

The Mandate for Adapted Physical Education

A physical education curriculum that does not plan specifically for individual differences is incomplete. Merely excusing children who are unable to take the full program is to sidestep a clear responsibility. In reality there is something in physical education for everyone. What is required is a clinical dimension—a humanistic dimension that Warren Johnson writes about.[1] Also required is an attitude toward flexible placement based on how the individual can perform in the activities of the time. His or her medical and psychological diagnosis will be one of the several factors considered in determining placement for each activity.

The National Education Association and the American Medical Association have long been aware that good physical education programs offer the student a chance to take part in a wide variety of activities with differing degrees of intensity, and that the physician and special education teacher have a responsibility to guide the student with a handicap into a program of physical education adapted to his or her individual needs. To do otherwise is to "hamper personal development and interfere with group acceptance of a student."[2]

In view of the strong support for adapted physical education programs, one would expect to find provisions for this special area of concern in most of the curriculum guides across the country. There have been a great number of communities, from small towns to large cities, which have a very well-developed program for normal school children in all grades but give little or no attention to screening out those pupils who can profit from a special program. These communities have complained that there is no time, facility, or staff to work with individuals to any serious degree, so the pupils are either excused from participation or struggle through what is being offered the best they can. Teachers do try to work with individual differences in these situations, but it is a haphazard and poorly planned kind of effort. Simply working with a few students who "need help" is certainly not a good example of an adapted program in operation.

[1]Warren R. Johnson, "A Humanistic Dimension of Physical Education," *Journal of Health, Physical Education and Recreation*, 43 (November–December 1972), 31–33.

[2]Committee on Exercise and Physical Fitness, American Medical Association, *Classification of Students for Physical Education, Journal of the American Medical Association*, 199 (January 23, 1967), 4.

The *need* for adapted physical education is greater today than ever before. Children with all kinds of handicaps and inadequacies are attending the nation's schools for longer periods. Because of sedentary existences there are large numbers of substrength boys and girls in need of special physical fitness efforts as well as relaxation routines. Leading pediatricians, cardiologists, psychiatrists, and specialists in physical medicine and orthopedics continually call attention to the schools' responsibility to work with the less than normal youth—a cooperative effort involving the school health service personnel, the special education teacher, the instructor of physical education, the parents, and the family physician.[3] In short, everyone wants the schools to help youths obtain their fullest development. Who needs physical fitness more than the cripple? Who needs development of ego more than the disabled youth? Who needs game experiences and social development more than the frustrated or withdrawn pupil?

Exceptional Children and Special Education

There are a number of ways of classifying children as exceptional and in need of adapted physical education. Generally they are exceptional "where they are so different in mental, physical, emotional, or behavioral characteristics that in the interest of equality of educational opportunity special provisions must be made for their proper education."[4]

As instructional intervention has occurred and curricula have been developed in most subject matter areas it has become acceptable to refer to handicapped children as exceptional children who require a special education and have a special education teacher to guide their activities. The term "special education" applies to physical education, for it is referred to specifically in the federal legislation governing the education of the handicapped:

> (16) The term "special education" means specially designed instruction, at no cost to parents or guardians, to meet the unique needs of a handicapped child, including classroom instruction, instruction in physical education, home instruction, and instruction in hospitals and institutions.[5]

---

[3]Moreover, scientific measurement has shown repeatedly that almost any handicapped person can improve his maximum oxygen uptake, vital capacity, and forced expirating volume in exercise programs. Endurance improves as well as does the increased ability to participate in physical activities.

[4]Arthur S. Daniels and Evelyn A. Davies, *Adapted Physical Education*, 3rd ed. (New York: Harper and Row, Publishers, 1975), p. 4.

[5]Public Law 94—142, December 30, 1976.

The Education of All Handicapped Children Act

Back in 1973 Congress enacted the Rehabilitation Act in which Section 504 guaranteed civil and personal rights of handicapped persons in all programs for which sponsoring groups received federal funds. The section prohibits "handicapism" in the same fashion as racism is prohibited in Title VI of the Civil Rights Act.

The rules pertaining to the implementation of the Rehabilitation Act were set forth in December 1976 as part of The Education of All Handicapped Children Act (Public Law 94-142) which had been signed into existence the year before. This act is designed to ensure that all handicapped children have available to them a free, appropriate public education that includes special education and related services to meet their unique needs. In addition, the law ensures that the rights of handicapped children and their parents are protected, gives assistance to states and localities in providing for the education of all handicapped children, and requires assessment to ensure the effectiveness of efforts to educate these children. Recreation is identified as one of the specified related services.

The curriculum is to be fully operational by 1980. Student needs are to be met by:

1. Conducting a needs assessment program which will establish realistic goals for each learner. Individual testing will determine the extent to which he/she has attained the goals. The "gaps" between the established goals and the level of the learner will be identified and put in statement form.

2. Planning and initiating an Individualized Educational Program (I.E.P.). As carefully defined in the regulations, the term "individualized education program" means a written statement for each handicapped child developed in any meeting by a representative of the local educational agency or an intermediate educational unit . . . who shall be qualified to provide or supervise the provision of, specially "designed" instruction to meet the unique needs of handicapped children, the teacher, the parents or guardian of such a child, and, whenever appropriate, such child, which statement shall include (A) a statement of the present levels of educational performance of such child, (B) a statement of annual goals, including short-term instructional objectives, (C) a statement of the specific educational services to be provided to such child, and the extent to which such child will be able to participate in regular educational programs, (D) the projected date for initiation and anticipated duration of such services, and appropriate objective criteria and evaluation procedures and schedules for determining, on at least an annual basis, whether instructional objectives are being achieved. Long range goals must be set up for each learner with short range objectives, i.e., measurable activities which reflect degrees of goal attainment.

3. Evaluating learner progress at least once annually.

4. Placing each learner in the "least restrictive environment".

5. Keeping parents advised at periodic intervals as to the progress of their child.

For the purposes of this Act, physical education includes special physical education, adapted physical education, and motor development. It includes the development of physical and motor fitness, fundamental motor skills and patterns, body mechanics, individual and group games, and sport skills such as intramural and lifetime sports, and dance and movement education. Also, each handicapped child must be afforded the chance to participate in the regular physical education program available to nonhandicapped children, unless the child is enrolled full-time in a separate facility. If specially designed physical education is prescribed, the public agency responsible for the education of that child must provide services directly or make arrangements for them through other public or private programs.

Cooperative Planning:
Physical Education and Special Education

It is obvious that any worthwhile program that meets the legislative requirements for the handicapped learner must involve a close working arrangement between those who instruct in physical education and the special education teachers. Curriculum planning will make it possible to provide a number of supportive and challenging physical activities involving both group and individual experiences. Such cooperative planning is time-consuming, but it is not an out of the ordinary happening for people who work with individuals requiring additional attention, warmth, and understanding.

Classification and Organization

The individual requirements of youth with handicapping conditions can best be met through classifying students into several categories of participation in physical education. This can be accomplished when school and family physicians work together. The school has an obligation to acquaint the family physician with the various activities in the program. In turn, the physician has an obligation to encourage the school to set up the type of program that meets the individual needs of the boys and girls. The American Medical Association has established groupings as follows:

1. *Unrestricted activity*—full participation in physical education and athletic activities.

2. *Moderate restriction*—participation in designated physical education and athletic activities.
3. *Severe restriction*—participation in only a limited number of events at a low level of activity.
4. *Reconstructive or rehabilitative activity*—participation in a prescribed program of corrective exercises and adapted sports.

The first three categories apply to youths convalescing from illness who need a gradual return to activity, students in whom certain muscle groups need strengthening, the handicapped who will benefit from physical activity, and those with postural deviations or other conditions medically determined as subject to improvement through prescribed activities. A program of reconstructive physical education is possible when medical supervision is available.

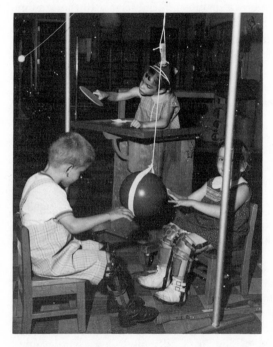

FIGURE 10-1. Individualized educational programs have special rehabilitative activities at all age levels.

The selection of pupils for the adapted program is accomplished through the usual measurement and observation procedures. Tests of physical fitness, general motor ability, perceptual-motor condition, posture and body mechanics, and social efficiency help instructors discover pupils in need of some special consideration. Frequently overlooked are those pupils who score poorly in skill tests and other similar tests of motor achievement. The person with "two left feet" or one who cannot seem to learn skills very well needs help every bit as much as the person with poor posture. Schedules should be modified to provide more time for people who require a greater exposure to a physical activity skill in order to master it at a satisfactory level of performance.

Students are also selected on the basis of medical examination. The obese, the handicapped, the mentally retarded, and the emotionally disturbed students require close school-home cooperation. Family physicians, together with parents who understand what the school is trying to do, are in a position to be partners in the adapted physical education program. In the following examples of letters to family physicians (Figures 10-2 and 10-3), the approach is positive and makes clear that anyone who can attend school can take part in some way in physical education. In the example from Albion, Pennsylvania, there is a wide choice of activities for the physician to look over. In this instance boys and girls have separate referral forms. In the example from California, the physician has to consider also the time it may take for the patient-student to be in a modified program. Note also the classification card of the Worcester Public Schools (Figure 10-4).

Programing Adapted Physical Education

In arranging the adapted program it is important to think in terms of a number of potential accomplishments and behaviors:

1. Develop physical capacity and joint function within the limits of individual disabilities.
2. Acquaint the student with his or her limitations by arranging a program tailored to physiological and psychological tolerance.
3. Develop skills in recreational sports and games within the limits of individual disabilities.
4. Achieve a state of adjustment of the student when the disability is permanent.
5. Foster personal pride in overcoming handicaps and weaknesses.
6. Generate an appreciation of individual differences and the ability to accept limitations without withdrawing from the group.

In the past, a number of impaired, disabled, and handicapped youngsters who could participate and compete to some degree with regular-class children have been kept in special adapted classes with little opportunity to venture out. Homogeneous grouping prevailed over heterogeneous grouping. For this reason, the integration of the moderately handicapped and the nonhandicapped students is now mandated. This is the practice of *mainstreaming*. Mainstreaming is not new but it has proven valuable. Mainstreaming permits handicapped individuals to socialize with their peers, and

NORTHWESTERN HIGH SCHOOL
Albion, Pennsylvania

Name_____

Date_____

Department of Physical Education for Girls

The Physical Education program at Northwestern High School is so planned that every pupil able to be in school should be able to derive benefit from some phase of this program.

After allowing time for undressing, dressing and showers, the actual amount of time left for activities is about 25-30 minutes. All girls are enrolled in two physical education classes per week.

Please check (X) either generally or individually the type of Physical Education which you would recommend for this student.

MILD ( )	MODERATE ( )	STRENUOUS ( )
( ) Badminton Practice	( ) Table Tennis	( ) Basketball
( ) Corrective Exercise	( ) Girls' Volleyball	( ) Cageball
( ) Throwing - Catch	( ) Folk Dance	( ) Tumbling
( ) Throwing at Target	( ) Corrective Exercise	( ) Apparatus (P-Bars)
( ) Table Games - Chess, etc.	( ) Softball	( ) Trampoline
( ) Golf Practice	( ) Apparatus (Horse)	( ) Soccer
( ) Tennis Practice	( ) Relay Races	( ) Field Hockey
( ) Archery	( ) Golf	( ) Speedball
( ) Mild Folk Dance	( ) Tennis Practice	( ) Speedaway
( ) Shuffleboard	( ) Badminton	( ) Relay Races
( ) Table Tennis	( ) Rhythmic Exercises	( ) Tennis - Game
( ) Marching	( ) Indian Club Drills	( ) Badminton - Game
	( ) Marching	
	( ) Bowling	

NOTE:
    If strenuous exercise is recommended, it is taken for granted that the mild and moderate are permissable unless exceptions are specifically stated; if moderate activities are recommended, again it is taken for granted that mild activities are permissable. Should you feel that generally the student should take only mild activity, but find that you feel one or two of the moderate activities such as bowling or golf should be included, simply check them.

COMPLETE REST: If the condition of this girl is such at the present that complete rest (recumbent position in bed) is desirable during her physical education period, please indicate this and give the number of days she should continue these supervised rest periods.

Up to the date of_____please restrict this girl's activities as indicated above. She is under my care for_____.

_____

Signed_____Examining Physician

COMMENTS: _____

_____

FIGURE 10-2. Adapted physical education referral form.

STATE OF CALIFORNIA

REFERRAL FORM

PHYSICIAN'S RECOMMENDATION FOR PHYSICAL EDUCATION AND OTHER PHYSICAL ACTIVITIES

Dear Physician:

All pupils enrolled in the public schools participate in physical education activities which are designed to meet the growth and developmental needs of boys and girls. In addition many pupils participate in other types of physical activity such as intramural programs, interschool athletics, band, drill team. To identify specific needs of each pupil, the physician, parents, and school personnel must work cooperatively. Will you please provide us with the information listed below so that we can provide appropriate activities for:________________________
(Pupil's name)

FINDINGS AND RECOMMENDATIONS TO THE SCHOOL

I have examined________________________and find the following handicaps,
(Pupil's Name)
if any:____
____

I recommend the following: (check appropriate item or items)

____ 1. No restriction on any type of activity.

____ 2. Participation in all activities (intramural and other activities in addition to physical education) with the exception of interschool athletics.

____ 3. No restriction on activities in physical education.

4. Adaptions in physical education to fit individual needs:

____a. Little running or jumping

____b. No running or jumping

____c. No activities involving body contact

____d. Exercises designed for rehabilitation

____e. Strenuous conditioning exercises

5. Other adaptions: (specify)________________________
____

I recommend the adaptation for: ____2 weeks, ____1 month, ____3 months, ____6 months

Date________________________ Signature________________________

Address:________________________

Please mail this form to: (Name and address of school should be given here)

Form approved in compliance with Education Code section 11906, Superintendent of Public Instruction, State of California 10/25/62.

FIGURE 10-3. A letter to the family physician.

(FRONT)

WORCESTER PUBLIC SCHOOL
MEDICAL CLASSIFICATION CARD
DEPARTMENT OF HEALTH, PHYSICAL EDUCATION & SAFETY

PUPIL'S_____   DATE_____
    Last Name   First Name   Middle Initial

THE ABOVE PUPIL HAS COME TO YOU FOR A PHYSICAL EXAMINATION AND ADVICE CONCERNING HIS
(HER) PHYSICAL EDUCATION PROGRAM. PLEASE INDICATE THE GROUP INTO WHICH YOU DESIRE THIS
PUPIL PLACED. (CIRCLE THE LETTER AND CHECK OFF ACTIVITIES ON BACK OF CARD.)

GROUP "A" — UNRESTRICTED: PUPIL MAY ENGAGE IN STRENUOUS ACTIVITY AND COMPETITION.

GROUP "B" — MODERATE: PUPIL MAY ENGAGE IN INDIVIDUAL EXERCISES AND QUIET GAMES.

GROUP "C" — REST: PUPIL MAY NOT ENGAGE IN PHYSICAL ACTIVITY.

DATE OF CLASSIFICATION_____.

DATE OF RE-EVALUATION
  OF CLASSIFICATION_____

SIGNED:_____M.D.

(OVER)

NO. P.E. 1

(BACK)

PLEASE CHECK THE ACTIVITIES BELOW IN WHICH THE PUPIL SHOULD **NOT** PARTICIPATE.

ARCHERY	SKIING
BADMINTON	SOCCER
BASKETBALL	SOFTBALL
BOWLING	SPEEDBALL
CONDITIONING DRILLS	SQUASH RACKETS
DANCE	SWIMMING
FIELD HOCKEY	TABLE TENNIS
GOLF	TENNIS
GYMNASTICS, TUMBLING, TRAMPOLINING	TOUCH FOOTBALL
HANDBALL	TRACK & FIELD
LACROSSE	VOLLEY BALL
PHYSICAL FITNESS TESTS	WEIGHT LIFTING
SHUFFLE BOARD	WRESTLING

FIGURE 10-4. Classification card for instructor. (Courtesy, Worcester Public Schools, Worcester, Massachusetts)

contributes to higher academic and social achievement.[6] Also, there is evidence of better results in coping with the real world when grown if they have had nonsegregated experiences in the early years. The stereotype of the handicapped is also diminished.

Julian Stein states that mainstreaming is not practiced simply to cram children into programs that do not fit:

> If individuals can be mainstreamed in just one activity, they must be; special programs should be reserved only for those activities for which they are really necessary. An unemphasized benefit of mainstreaming stems from its refutation of rigid categories. . . . Some activities lend themselves more readily to mainstreaming than others. For example, exploratory, tumbling, gymnastics, and most parallel play activities are excellent for the process, since success or failure does not depend on the performance or ability of others.[7]

As Jansma points out, mainstreaming is here to stay, and in order to better prepare teachers for the process, in-service training is necessary.[8] The physical education teacher will need to have more knowledge and experience in such areas as behavior management, handicapping conditions, the assessment of perceptual-motor ability and physical fitness, the use of special equipment, knowledge of resource materials, and a multidisciplinary orientation toward adapting content to the limitations of the students.

One of the most successful large-city programs of adapted physical education in the country is carried on in the Philadelphia public schools. Pupils requiring a restrictive or modified program are classified for *vigorous, moderate,* and *mild* activities.

Category I—Vigorous Activity

Pupils in this category engage in the regular physical education program and are allowed certain exceptions in keeping with their condition, as approved by the school medical examiner and communicated to the physical education instructor. The pupil with the chronic knee defect, for example, takes the regular program except that in high jumping or broad jumping the level of participation may be simply to assist the teacher in measuring the jumps of classmates. A pupil who should not run or dance vigorously does so with restraint, so does not have to be eliminated from the program.

[6]Glen Haas, *Curriculum Planning: A New Approach,* 2nd ed. (Boston: Allyn and Bacon Co., 1977), p. 257.

[7]Julian Stein, "Sense and Nonsense About Mainstreaming," *Journal of Physical Education and Recreation,* 47 (January 1976), 43.

[8]Paul Jansma, "Get Ready For Mainstreaming," *Journal of Physical Education and Recreation,* 48 (September 1977), 15–17.

Category II—Moderate Activity

Pupils in this category take part in a wide variety of activities but need an entire modified program in which the intensity and duration of the activities is reduced and in which certain highly vigorous activities are eliminated.

Category III—Mild Activity

Pupils in this category take part in activities that are considerably less vigorous than those found in the moderate category. Some students may have to perform actions in a sitting or lying position. Very few pupils are in this category in the Philadelphia schools. Some examples of program elements follow:

Moderate	Mild
MODIFICATIONS: PHYSICAL CONDITIONING	
Decrease in number of repetitions. Slower rhythms. Omission of movements of certain body parts.	Less vigor and fewer repetitions.
RHYTHMS AND DANCE	
Decrease in number of repetitions. Substitute alternate rhythmical activity such as walking or sliding for running.	No vigorous marching or turning. Rhythmic walking substituted for vigorous movements in singing games, folk dances, and contemporary social dances.
SELF-TESTING ACTIVITIES	
Decrease vigor of activity. Take fewer turns. Competition with others may be limited or prohibited. Substitute a different but *related* activity, i.e., a short throw for accuracy may replace a distance throw. Stunts are self-limiting.	Measure self carefully against own progress. Rope climbing, jump rope work likely to be too vigorous. May be self-limiting by nature of disability.
APPARATUS AND TUMBLING	
Simple exercises of short duration; involve only moderate expenditure of energy. Omit certain vigorous stunts, or do them only one or two times a period. Substitute a *related* activity that will be less taxing.	Limited number of repetitions. More full rest periods. Solicit opinion of physician relative to student activity.

Moderate   *Mild*

GAMES AND INDIVIDUAL SPORTS

Limit the number of times the pupil may run during a certain physical education period.

Restrict the length of time a pupil may be "It."

Take turns at bat, but have another pupil run the bases.

Engage in recreational activities, such as:
    modified bowling
    quoits
    shuffleboard
    table tennis
    target throws
    accuracy throws
    archery
    croquet
    roller skating
    hopscotch

Keep the pupil from participating in the role of a runner. May play in circle game, but do no running or dodging.

Practice individual skills.

Engage to a mild degree in some part of the following activities:
    throwing bouncing, rolling balls
    stilt walking
    pogo stick
    deck tennis
    tether ball
    table tennis
    marbles
    bicycle riding
    playground swings, slides, ladders, and jungle gyms.

TEAM SPORTS AND RELATED CONTESTS

Decrease duration of playing time.

Play a position requiring less activity, i.e., centering the football instead of running after a pass.

Avoid sudden spurts of effort and limit rought body contact.

Take periodic rests between short repetitions of the activity.

Assist with timing and scoring in the more vigorous sports, such as soccer, lacrosse, football, field hockey.

Omit rough body contact.

The value of *aquatics* in the curriculum cannot be overemphasized. Numerous programs have to do without it because of the lack of appropriate facilities. A long history of successes indicates that whenever efforts are made to remedy weaknesses and adapt programs to individual shortcomings the use of aquatic activities is recommended. Not only are swimming and various hydrogymnastic movements helpful in increasing the range of motion, elevating strength and endurance, and restoring disabled or limited body parts, but the fun and freedom found in the water environment may foster motivation toward becoming socially competent. Moreover, the more one approaches aquatic instruction from the normal expectations, the greater the response will be.[9]

[9]William T. Muhl, "Aquatics for the Handicapped," *Journal of Physical Education and Recreation,* 48 (February 1976), 42–43.

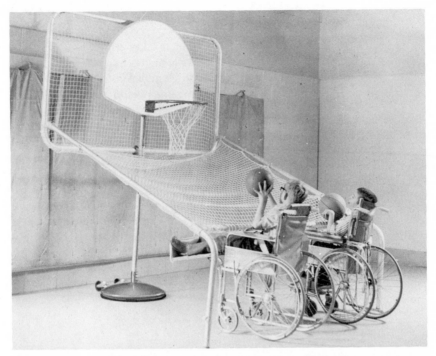

FIGURE 10-5. Controlled basketball unit combines fun with development of upper extremities. (Courtesy, Jayfro Corporation, Waterford, Connecticut)

Scheduling Adapted Physical Education Classes

The scheduling of classes depends upon the availability of a teaching station, the available instructors, and the nature of the handicapping conditions. The "block assignment" held in connection with the regular class program appears to be the most effective, for it nails down a specific time for the instruction. Although handled individually in the physical education facility (pool, dance room, gymnasium, remedial laboratory), a variety of conditions can be grouped together. In many schools the mentally retarded and sometimes the emotionally disturbed attend a special physical education class. Although such a homogeneous arrangement may be efficient in terms of fundamental skill development and body management, it should be used sparingly, or there will be little opportunity to join in selected activities with other students in the regular class program. Vodola finds this to be important if self-image is to be enhanced, especially in the "eyes" of the peer group.[10]

[10]Thomas M. Vodola, *Individual Physical Education Progress for the Handicapped Child* (Englewood Cliffs, N.J.: Prentice-Hall, Inc., 1973), p. 29.

When the intent is clear to help the pupil in need of individual attention, a way will be found. A half-dozen pupils can always be fitted into some space somewhere during or after school hours, but not large numbers. If staff is available and there are at least two teachers assigned to a class period, one should be able to work primarily with the remedial group or with those requiring a modified program. If there is only one person handling the class, the use of student leaders partially frees the teacher to direct some attention toward pupils who can profit from individual, adapted physical education.

Although noon hours, after school time, and study periods have been used, the most efficient programs are those preplanned and taught during the regular school day. In order not to upset an established school schedule, it is advantageous, if possible, to appraise students in June before classes are suspended for the summer. At this time, it is determined which pupils will profit most from an adapted physical education program starting in September. Then, when school administrators and computers go to work in the summer months to build a workable schedule for the total school curriculum, extra class time will be included. At the same time questions relative to staff, class size, and teaching stations can be resolved to the satisfaction of principal and teachers alike.

Project Active

There are several ways of programing adapted physical education so that it meets government concerns relative to providing an efficient combination of (1) individualized attention; and (2) the heterogeneous grouping of the handicapped with the nonhandicapped. These practices are not difficult to combine if adequate staff and space is available. In Oakhurst, New Jersey, for example, the Project Active program under the direction of Thomas Vodola received state-wide and national recognition because it focused on these concerns in admirable fashion.

In Project Active pupil goals are planned while teachers are trained in a forty-hour course to teach in a *personalized* fashion the mentally retarded, the learning disabled, the orthopedically handicapped, the post-operative convalescent, the visually or auditorily handicapped, and the pupils with breathing problems, postural abnormalities, nutritional deficiencies, and low physical fitness.

Students with handicapping conditions and various motor problems are taught by the teachers who have received the special instruction in adapted physical education. These teachers write individualized prescriptions, prepare information on individual strengths and weaknesses, and carry out appropriate tasks and activities commensurate with student needs. Since 1974, there has been an ongoing evaluation of the effectiveness of the project.

Results have been so positive that plans for national dissemination have been undertaken.[11]

The Perceptual-Motor Program

Children with specific learning disabilities exhibit a disorder in one or more of the basic psychological processes involved in understanding or in using spoken or written language. These may be manifested in disorders of listening, thinking, talking, reading, writing, spelling, or doing arithmetic. They include conditions that have been referred to as perceptual handicaps, brain injury, minimal brain dysfunction, dyslexia, developmental aphasia, and so forth. They do not include learning problems which are due chiefly to visual, hearing, or motor handicaps, to mental retardation, emotional disturbances, or to environmental disadvantage.[12] The motor development view suggests that the dynamics of learning are involved in movement and body management.

Research indicates that perception is multisensory and that all modes of perception are dynamically tied to the neuromuscular system and the movements of the body. Moreover, the role of motor activity in perceptual processes is significant in both directing and correcting perception, in relating kinesthetic information to essential changes in visual orientation, in influencing cognitive development through a sophisticated link with language and communication skills, and in advancing self-concept.

Perceptual-motor training activities can make a real contribution to adapted physical education programs because of the numerous associations with handicapping conditions. For example, the improvement in laterality and directionality in the gymnasium tends to advance reading and arithmetic skills and boost auditory and visual perception, especially in young children.

In recent years a fair amount of attention has been given to perceptual-motor development. Because the best instruction is individually prescribed and each child moves through a program at his or her own rate, an adequate amount of exposure to instruction and practice needs to be scheduled. Such scheduling depends on the kinds of sequential activities, the age of the pupils, and the availability of paraprofessional personnel.

In the Alameda Unified School District (Alameda, California), the perceptual-motor program meets the needs of children in the kindergarten through the third grade and special education classes by concentrating on the

[11]For additional details, contact Thomas M. Vodola, Project Active Director, Township of Ocean School District, Dow Avenue, Oakhurst, N.J. 07755.

[12]Janet W. Lerner, "Learning Disabilities: A School Health Problem," *Journal of School Health*, 42 (June 1972), 320–24.

acquisition of efficient movement, sensory functioning, and the development of a positive self-image. This is accomplished through the programing of (1) balance skills; (2) locomotor skills; (3) hand-eye coordination; and (4) body and space awareness.

In the Dayton, Ohio, Public Schools, the program operates for the primary grades under the direction of the body-management instructor in the physical education department. Research in Dayton showed that students participating in the program made gains well above those not in the program in the areas of academic achievement, self-image, self-concept, sense of worth, and peer acceptance (see Figure 10-6).

FIGURE 10-6. Alternate foot hopping. (Courtesy, Nissen Corporation)

In the Riverside County Schools in California, a high degree was attained in working with perceptually handicapped children by exposing them to carefully selected movements that were designed to develop individual competencies in (1) laterality; (2) body rhythm; (3) balance; (4) hand-foot coordination; (5) upper-lower extremities awareness; and (6) attention-concentration span. Much of this is accomplished through the programing of clever exercises and stunts that are fun to do.

The Mentally Retarded

Mental retardation "refers to sub-average general intellectual functioning which originates during the developmental period and is associated with impairment in adaptive behavior."[13] The schools' concern is chiefly with the mentally retarded that are educable. Kirk describes the educable mentally retarded child as one who has potentialities for development in academic subjects at a minimum level, in social adjustment "to a point where he can get along independently in the community" and can later on "support himself partially or totally at the adult level."[14]

In physical education programs, common practice in the past has been to excuse mentally retarded children altogether, or to relegate them to some kind of "free-play" activity in which they merely wander aimlessly from wall to wall and person to person, or run wildly about "blowing off steam" so that they will be a little quieter in the subject-matter period that follows. Moreover, the physical education teacher has, for the most part, not wanted to work with these pupils, for they are usually more difficult to teach than the regular student body, and not all teachers have the patience and understanding required to teach them effectively. It has been easy, therefore, to release these children from the responsibility of the physical education department and let the special education teacher handle them and provide whatever recreational activity might seem necessary. This practice is fast changing as new governmental regulations and field experiences indicate how the mentally retarded can be helped.

The Physical Activity Potential of Mentally Retarded Children

The United States Office of Education estimates that 83 percent of the retarded are educable. Another 12 percent are trainable, and can live happily and usefully at home or in a sheltered workshop. What this means is that there is a large task ahead for physical education and recreation specialists who want to develop the *potential* of the mentally retarded child.

Research of recent origin indicates that the lack of intellectual ability resulting from arrested mental development need not affect the levels of motor development and physical fitness of retarded pupils. Stein makes it clear that "the mentally retarded respond and progress as much as normal boys and girls when given specialized training or instruction in a systematic

[13]H. J. Grossman, *Manual on Terminology and Classification in Mental Retardation,* (*American Association on Mental Deficiency,* 1973), p. 5.
[14]Samuel A. Kirk, *Educating Exceptional Children* (Boston: Houghton Mifflin Co., 1972), p. 186.

and progressive physical education."[15] The key words here are *systematic* and *progressive;* the program has to be carefully planned and implemented. When it is, the results are sometimes most rewarding, for the total behavior of the individual is frequently altered. As retarded children gain new skills and physical control over themselves, they develop a sense of security. Moreover, the individual improves in the means of physical expression, which tends to counterbalance the disturbing lack of verbal expression. Evidence suggests that this improvement fosters an educational climate in which defeatism, lethargy, and general rebellion over personal inability to cope with school learning situations are less.

The physical educator who works with the mentally retarded discovers, somewhat as Schiller did years ago in Germany, that a human being is at his or her best in play. It is play that extends the self. In play the retarded individual struggles to new attainments and new contacts with persons and things. The struggle is therapeutic.

When physical education programs have been modified or created especially for the mentally retarded, some dramatic results have occurred. In the Howe studies, some relatively complex skills were mastered by retarded boys and girls after only ten days of instruction.[16] The mentally retarded show

FIGURE 10-7.   Balance contributes to a sense of security.

[15]Julian V. Stein, "The Potential of Physical Activity for the Mentally Retarded Child," *Journal of Health, Physical Education and Recreation*, 37 (April 1966), 25–27.

[16]Clifford Howe, "A Comparison of Motor Skills of Mentally Retarded and Normal Children," *Eceptional Children*, 25 (April 1959), 352–54.

the same pattern of improvement in the AAHPER Youth Fitness Test as do the normal pupils. Hayden has demonstrated that even the severely retarded boys and girls show significant improvement in muscular fitness and endurance through participation in a program involving intensive muscular activity that stresses the development of organic fitness.[17] Earlier, Oliver found the same in England; he also learned that a ten-week daily period of physical education will improve athletic achievement, emotional stability, and personal adjustment and raise significantly the aptitude for learning.[18] Corder duplicated Oliver's research design at George Peabody College.[19] A daily one-hour period of planned physical education lessons was presented. They were progressively more difficult and challenging. After only four weeks, improvements were recorded in the intellectual development of educable mentally retarded boys.

In discussing the importance of motor skills for the mentally retarded, Dunham makes it clear that a genius can afford to be a "motor moron," but a person with an IQ score of 50 cannot.[20] Being able to perform motor skills generally relates directly to the degree of social competence and acceptance by peers. Evidence is plentiful to show that the early appraisal of motor capacity, coupled with individualized practice sessions sprinkled with verbal praise, is an effective physical education undertaking. However, it is frequently necessary to engage in overlearning in order to promote retention of gross motor skills.[21]

At this point, keep in mind the fact that *all effective motor learning* depends upon certain conditions present in the learner, and the teaching method. If carefully worded explanations, proper demonstrations, and adequate conditions for practice are essential for the development of high-quality skills and other motor learning for the average pupil in class, they are even *more* important for the mentally retarded. An extra effort along these lines can be provided when

1. Programs are carefully planned, structured, and staffed.
2. Skills to be learned are set up in sequence from the less difficult to the more

[17]Frank Hayden, *Physical Fitness for the Mentally Retarded* (Toronto: Metropolitan Association for Retarded Children, 186 Beverley Street, 1964).

[18]James N. Oliver, "The Effect of Physical Conditioning Exercises and Activities on the Mental Characteristics of Educationally Sub-Normal Boys," *British Journal of Education Psychology*, 28 (June 1958), 155–65.

[19]W. O. Corder, "Effects of Physical Education on the Intellectual, Physical and Social Development of Educable Mentally Retarded Boys" (unpublished special project, George Peabody College, Nashville, Tennessee, 1965).

[20]Paul Dunham, Jr., "Teaching Motor Skills to the Mentally Retarded," in Paul A. Metzger, Jr., *Elementary School Physical Education* (Dubuque, Iowa: W. C. Brown Co., 1972), p. 139.

[21]William C. Chasey, "Motor Skill Overlearning Effects on Retention and Relearning by Retarded Boys," *Research Quarterly*, 48 (March 1977), 41–46.

difficult. Among other things, this will provide children with goals with which they can have some measure of success.

3. Pupils with similar strengths and weaknesses are grouped together for controlled instructional purposes. At other times, such as in certain game situations, they should mix with other pupils. For the most part, however, they should be taught pleasantly in small groups and individually in order to be sure of developing the numerous nonverbal skills that physical education has to offer.

4. Teaching techniques and practices reflect the need to progress slowly, exercise a firm and patient approach, permit some choice of activities, and encourage the learning of activities that can be used after school hours and later in life. The theories of reinforcement, as they relate to learning, and the presentation of semi-concrete materials as opposed to those of an abstract nature appear to be all-important when dealing with this type of youngster.

The Program

Probably, no one program is "just right" for a given community. However, a number of effective programs have been set up for the mentally retarded. Those that have gained acceptance make an effort to combine physical conditioning, skills development, and confidence-building activities. Work, challenge, and fun are in the program—areas frequently missing in the home, where mentally retarded children are often overprotected by cautious parents, and where they are too sheltered to taste life-enrichment activities.

Experimentation over a two-year period at the University of Bridgeport determined that programs should include a large number of locomotor skills, such as walking, running, turning, and jumping, in relation to balance and visual focusing. Much of this was done on the trampoline and balance beam.[22] Along with this were hand-foot-eye coordination activities in which there was a large measure of throwing and catching. Also, there were many opportunities to creep, crawl, roll, and move bodies in a number of ways on a mat and through hula hoops, automobile tires, and around bowling pins and other objects to promote an improved body management, greater self-awareness, and an increase to some degree of self-sufficiency.

One of the most extensive studies undertaken in recent years to structure physical education for the educable mentally retarded was done by Goheen. He developed three different types of programs—skill-oriented, play-oriented, and free play. Each was evaluated before and after an instructional period of thirteen weeks (thirty-nine class hours) in terms of achievement levels in physical fitness, motor ability, and social adjustment.

In this study, the student population, ages ten to fifteen, came from three institutional schools for the mentally retarded. A jury of experts deliberated on the programs that were developed, and a number of revisions were

[22]Martin L. Zwirin, "Mental Retardation: How Can We Help," *Journal of Health, Physical Education and Recreation,* 43 (October 1972), 79–80.

made before pilot studies were carried out. Following the pilot studies, the main study was conducted to determine which kind of program seemed to work best.

In all three programs, Goheen realized that definite guidelines should be established and followed relative to locker room and gymnasium facilities, and that all students would benefit the most from their kind of program if concrete rather than abstract proposals were presented, if nearly everything discussed could be carefully demonstrated, and if constant motivation and praise were a part of the instructor's teaching and supervising routine.

The Programs[23]

A. Skill-oriented program.   This program was set up on the premise that more could be gained by the educable mentally retarded individual if *the major emphasis were placed on basic and progressive skill development.*

1. Each class hour was carefully organized in terms of content and teaching techniques.
2. The specific skills included during a given class hour were carefully explained and demonstrated. Organized practice, drill-type activities, or both followed.
3. Activities other than skill learning per se were presented as culminating or evaluative measures or both.
4. The following limitations were observed on time allotment during the organizational and instructional portions of each class hour.
   a. Roll-call and personal inspections: 2–4 minutes
   b. Warm-up activities: 4–6 minutes
   c. Instructional class: 28–32 minutes
      1. Skill learning: 22–28 minutes
      2. Culminating activity: 4–6 minutes
   d. Showering and dressing: 18–22 minutes
5. Class content was progressively planned on a daily basis; it was presented in three divisions as follows:
   a. Progressive basic movement skills relative to fundamental motor development.
   b. Progressive skills and skill sequences leading up to participation in modified games of soccer and volleyball.
   c. Progressive skills involving individual stunts and elementary tumbling and apparatus.

The three divisions of class content were broken down as in Tables 10-1, 10-2, 10-3.

[23]Royal L. Goheen, "The Development and Evaluation of Three Types of Physical Education Programs for Educable Mentally Retarded Boys" (Doctoral Dissertation, Boston University, 1967). Dr. Goheen is department chairman and professor of physical education at the University of Maine, Presque Isle, Maine.

TABLE 10-1. Division I: Progressive Basic Movement Skills

Day	Objectives	Specific Skills	Culminating Activity
1.	a. To introduce formal class organizational procedures. b. To present fundamental skills relative to basic motor development.	Walking forward, backward and on low balance beam Balance	Tight Rope Relay
2.	a. To continue emphasis on formal organizational procedures. b. To enlarge the scope of activity relating to basic movement skills.	Walking forward, backward and on low and inclined beam Balance	Tight Rope Relay
3.	a. To reinforce techniques relative to organizational procedures. b. To slightly increase the complexity of basic movement skills.	Balance Walking on inclined and raised beam Running	Reverse and Run Relay
4.	To continue presentation of basic movement skills which are slightly more difficult.	Walking on beam Running forward and backward Dodging while running	Balance and Turn Relay
5.	To introduce techniques which generally represent more advanced fundamental skill development.	Running and dodging Hopping one foot two feet	Dodge-Hop Relay
6.	To further develop more advanced fundamental movement skills.	Standing Brd. Jump Hopping variations Leaping	Follow the Leader
7.	To introduce variations of a multiple-movement type skill.	Jumping over moving object and moving rope	Crossing the Brook
8.	To continue class participation with specific emphasis on multiple movement type skills.	Jumping over moving object with ind. ropes	Last Man Out
9.	To introduce skills involving the use of a large circumference ball.	Passing with one and two hands Dribbling	Pepper Squat
10.	To emphasize further, selected fundamentals involving simple ball skills.	Passing-enrichment Bounce pass Dribbling Pivoting	Dribble-Volley-Pass-Relay
11.	To introduce simple skills involving the use of a small circumference ball.	Throwing underhand overhand Catching	Minute Drop

TABLE 10-1. *Continued.*

Day	Objectives	Specific Skills	Culminating Activity
12.	To emphasize further, selected skills related to simple ball activity.	Throwing variations Catching flyballs and ground balls	Pepper Squat
13.	a. To determine to what extent the students will achieve in a selected battery of skills. b. To determine the reaction of the students to a challenging but somewhat complex situation.	Beam walking Running-dodging Leaping Throwing and retrieving Dribbling and passing Standing Brd. Jump One-foot hop	Obstacle Course

TABLE 10-2. Division II: Progressive Skills and Skill Sequences Leading up to Modified Games of Soccer and Volleyball

Day	Objectives	Specific Skills	Culminating Activity
1.	To introduce basic skills relative to soccer.	Passing Trapping Dribbling	Hot Ball
2.	To increase individual student understanding and skill development relative to basic soccer skills.	Passing with direction Trapping Dribble-Pass	Dribble-Pass Relay
3.	To reinforce basic soccer skills as they are utilized in a more complex manner.	Passing-Trapping Dribbling and passing ahead or laterally	Touch It If You Can
4.	To improve upon individual performances involving multiple-type soccer skills.	Passing ahead or laterally Dribble-Shoot	Touch It If You Can
5.	To introduce, further, coordinated movement techniques which demand a greater development of fundamental soccer skills.	Dribble-Shoot Goalie Blocking Passing laterally two boys on move	Simple Soccer
6.	To allow for continued development of selected fundamental soccer skills which have been previously presented.	Dribble-Shoot Goalie Tech. Passing laterally	Simple Soccer
7.	a. To introduce formal counting where applicable concern-	Volleying individually as a group	Keep It Up

TABLE 10-2. *Continued.*

Day	Objectives	Specific Skills	Culminating Activity
	ing warm-up activities. b. To present basic skills relative to volleyball.		
8.	To continue with emphasis on selected fundamental volleyball skills.	Volleying individually as a group	Keep It Up
9.	To continue reinforcement of skills basic to fundamental volleyball.	Volleying Passing with and without net Service-closed palm	Keep It Up
10.	To strengthen individual student development of basic volleyball skills.	Passing variations Service-fist	Pepper Squat Relay
11.	To promote continued development of volleyball skills which are generally more difficult.	Enrichment** Team passing Wall Volley	Simplified Volleyball
12.	To continue development of more difficult volleyball skills.	Enrichment Team Passing	Simplified Volleyball
13.	To formally evaluate the students concerning selected skills in soccer and volleyball.	Service accuracy Individual volley Soccer shooting accuracy	

**Enrichment denotes review

It is not possible here to give all the details for each class lesson. However, the outlines above do indicate a progression that should prove helpful in other situations. Goheen spells out very carefully just how the separate skills are to be taught. For example, in the very first lesson (Division I, Class No. 1) four activities (walking forward, walking backward, walking forward on the balance beam, and the tight-rope relay) are explained as follows.

2. *Explanation-Demonstration*
   A. Walking forward
   B. Walking backward
   C. Walking forward on low balance beam
3. *Participation-Practice of Skills*
   A. Walking: Form three squads which run parallel to one another. The first in each group walks normally toward the other side of the gymnasium under the watchful eye of the instructor. This is repeated for each and individual instruction should be given where necessary to aid in correcting obvious faults.

TABLE 10-3. Division III: Progressive Skills Involving Individual Stunts and Elementary Tumbling and Apparatus

Day	Objectives	Specific Skills	Culminating Activity
1. To introduce stunts relative to subsequent development of basic tumbling and apparatus skills.	Crab Walks, Dog Run, Lame Dog, Seal Crawl, Heel Click, Heel Slap Jump-Turn (1/2), Mule Kick, Coffee Grinder	Skin the Snake Relay	
2. To continue participation in individual and/or couple stunt-type activities which modify basic skills relating to developmental tumbling and apparatus.	Enrichment°³ Chicken Walk Frog Leap Rocker Chinese Get-up	Animal Walk Parade	
3. To present selected skills basic to fundamental tumbling.	Enrichment Forward Roll Two's Over and Under	Follow the Leader	
4. To continue emphasis on class participation relating to fundamental tumbling skills.	Enrichment Backward Roll	Follow the Leader	
5. a. To further develop basic tumbling skills. b. To introduce fundamental balancing skills.	Enrichment Squat Stand Squat Balance	Follow the Leader	
6. To present tumbling skills of a semi-intermediate level.	Enrichment Dive and Roll	Log Rolling Relay	
7. To continue presentation of fundamental tumbling and balancing skills which are increasingly more difficult.	Dive and Roll Doubles Balances Balance and Roll	Forward Roll Relay	
8. To cause the boys to become more proficient in individual and couple oriented skills.	Doubles Balances Dive and Roll Head Stand	Backward Roll Relay	
9. To cause the students to become familiar with fundamental skills involved with selected apparatus.	Beam walking forward, backward, and side Bar, hang and drop, rail walk, and leg-raisers	Pyramid Building	
10. To continue presentation of skills basic to fundamental apparatus work.	Enrichment Beam, walk on all fours Bar, rail hop and balance hang Climbing Rope, lying	Pyramid Building	

TABLE 10-3. *Continued.*

Day	Objectives	Specific Skills	Culminating Activity
		to sit, then to stand, hanging, footlock and climb	
11.	To present somewhat more difficult skills fundamental to selected apparatus.	Beam, squat walk Bar, inverted hang Climbing Rope, limited swinging	Follow the Leader
12.	To continue to promote individual development in selected fundamental apparatus skills.	Enrichment Bar, pull-ups	Follow the Leader
13.	To evaluate the students through a sequential course of events which involves selected fundamental skills.	Walk raised beam Dog Run, zig zag Dive and Roll Log Rolling Rope Swinging Jump and Turn Backward Roll and Crab Walk	Follow the Leader (optional)

°°Enrichment denotes review

B. Backward walking: Utilizing the same lines, practice the backward walk. Begin with one at a time in each line and then progress to the entire group moving simultaneously. (⅓ available time.)

C. Beam walking: Utilizing these same groups, the pupils practice walking forward on low balance beams. No more than two should be on a beam at the same time. (⅓ available time.)

4. *Culminating Activity*
Tight Rope Relay: The groups form three relay columns. Each player walks heel and toe the length of the line and back, tags the hand of the next player, and goes to the end of the line. If a player should step off the line, that player must stop momentarily and then continue.

B. Play-oriented program. This program was set up on the premise that more could be gained by the educable mentally retarded individual if major emphasis were placed on play-type activity that would encompass a number of developmental skills. The emphasis here (Tables 10-4, 10-5, and 10-6) was on the less formal and more permissive activities.

C. Free-play program. This program was set up on the premise that more could be gained by the educable mentally retarded individual if the major emphasis were placed on the free selection of and participation in play-type activities.

TABLE 10-4. Division I: Games and Play-Type Activities of Low Organization That Include Fundamentals of Motor Development

Day	Objectives	Play-Type Activities	Related Fundamentals
1.	a. To introduce class organizational procedures.	Tight Rope Relay	Walking
	b. To present organized play-type activities which involve techniques basic to fundamental movement.	Club Snatch	Running Dodging
2.	a. To reaffirm class organizational procedures.	Club Snatch Backward Walk Relay	Walking a. backwards b. low bal. beam
	b. To introduce play-type activities which are based on simple variations of fundamental movement.	Beam Walk Relay	Running Dodging
3.	To continue participation in play-type activities which modify fundamental movement.	Beam Walk Relay Backward Walk Relay	Walking variations Running Dodging
4.	To present play-type activities which modify a larger scope of fundamentals basic to movement.	Strike and Chase Circle Weave Barrel Break Skip Tag	Walking-Running Running-Dodging Crawling and Skipping
5.	To introduce activities which are based on fundamental movement of a more difficult nature.	(Walk, Run and Skip Circle Weave) Cowboys and Indians	Walking and Running Skipping Hopping Variations
6.	To continue play-type activities which provide for further development of more difficult fundamental movement techniques.	Cowboys and Indians Magic Spots Crossing The Brook	Hopping a. one foot b. two feet Skipping and Leaping
7.	To reinforce student development relative to more difficult fundamental movement.	Crossing The Brook Jump The Shot	Leaping and Jumping Standing Brd. Jump
8.	To continue play-type activity which is basic to greater individual development.	Jump The Shot Jump Over Rope	Jumping a. over moving rope b. over moving object
9.	To introduce play-type activities which are based on simple techniques involving a large circumference ball.	Hot Spuds Circle Ball Wall Ball Relay	Passing a. two-hand chest b. baseball c. shovel
10.	To continue utilization of play-type activity which provides enrichment relative to the development of simple ball fundamentals.	Wall Ball Relay Target Pepper Squat	Passing variations Dribbling Simple Pivot

TABLE 10-4. *Continued.*

Day	Objectives	Play-Type Activities	Related Fundamentals
11.	To present play-type activities based on the utilization of a small circumference ball.	Pepper Squat Wall Volley Relay	Rolling ball Tossing ball Throwing ball Catching ball Fielding grounders
12.	To further enhance student development in simple ball handling techniques through organized play-type activities.	Pepper Squat Hot Ball Cross Over Relay	Enrichment (above)
13.	To evaluate the students concerning a number of selected fundamentals which have been inherent in the organized play-type activities presented in this division.	Obstacle Course	Walking Beam Running-Dodging Leaping Throw and Retrieve Dribble and Pass Standing Brd. Jump One-foot Hop

TABLE 10-5. Division II: Related Play-Type Activities and Modified Games Based on Fundamentals of Soccer and Volleyball

Day	Objectives	Play-Type Activities	Related Fundamentals
1.	To introduce play-type activities which involve fundamentals of soccer.	Hot Ball Pepper Squat Circle Soccer	Passing inside of foot Trapping
2.	To provide experiences in a more difficult play-type activity which is based on fundamental soccer techniques.	Line Soccer Dribble-Pass Relay Hot Ball	Passing Trapping Dribbling
3.	To present activities that generally require at least a minimal sufficiency in selected fundamental soccer techniques.	Soccer Goal Kick Baseball Soccer	Dribbling-Shooting Toe Kick Long Pass
4.	To continue with play-type activities which reinforce the opportunity to learn and/or develop fundamentals of soccer.	Soccer Goal Kick Baseball Soccer	Dribbling-Shooting Toe Kick Long Pass Limited Blocking
5.	a. To present play-type activities which provide further developmental opportunity in fundamental soccer techniques. b. To provide opportunity for concentrated team play.	Touch It If You Can Simple Soccer	Passing Trapping Shooting Dribbling Limited Blocking

TABLE 10-5. *Continued.*

Day	Objectives	Play-Type Activities	Related Fundamentals
6.	To further enrich and reinforce student development of soccer fundamentals through the medium of organized play-type activity.	Wall-Volley Relay Simple Soccer	Passing Trapping Shooting Dribbling Limited Blocking
7.	To introduce play-type activities which involve fundamentals of volleyball.	Keep It Up Fist Fungo	Volleying a. above the waist b. below the waist Serving (closed palm)
8.	To continue involvement in play-type activities which include selected volleyball fundamentals.	Keep It Up Fist Fungo Touch It If You Can	Volleying Serving a. closed palm b. fist
9.	To foster further development of volleyball fundamentals through organized play-type activity.	Touch It If You Can Volley Baseball	Volleying Passing Serving variations
10.	To continue participation in play-type activities which generally require more efficient development of volleyball fundamentals.	Volley Baseball One Bounce Volleyball	Serving variations Passing Volleying
11.	To present play-type activity, the success of which depends to a large degree on the achievement level of the individual students.	Wall Volley Relay Pepper Pass Contests One Bounce Volleyball	Directed passing Serving variations Volleying
12.	To introduce play-type activities which demand greater versatility of performance.	Pepper Pass Contests Wall Volley Relay Simple Volleyball	Continual Volley Directed passing Serving variations
13.	To present play-type activities which also allow opportunity for evaluation of student achievement.	Serving Into Hole Big Eye Individual Volley	Serving Soccer Kick Volleying

In these free-play periods no organized instructional programs were adhered to other than roll-call procedures, personal inspection, and warm-up activities. One of the students was permitted to choose the activity within the limitation of available facilities, equipment, and supplies. Each student in the class took a turn at making a selection. The selection had to meet with majority approval or another choice had to be made. The instructor offered at least three choices concerning possible activities when a student requested them. Skills and techniques of play were not discussed or demonstrated, and the instructor acted only as an official during team games or as a mediator at other times.

TABLE 10-6. Division III: Play-Type Activities Based on Various Fundamental Stunts, Tumbling, and Apparatus

Day	Objectives	Play-Type Activities	Related Fundamentals
1.	To present organized play-type activity which modifies selected basic stunts.	Animal Walk Parade Crab Walk One Base	Crab Walks Dog Run Seal Crawl Frog Leap
2.	To continue participation in basic stunts, within a play-type setting which involves the individual student.	Animal Walk Parade Seal Crawl Circle Weave Animal Walk One Base	Enrichment Lame Dog Run Chicken Walk
3.	To increase the emphasis on individual performance and initiative in play-type activities which involve basic stunts.	Animal Walk Parade Chinese Get-up Wheel-Barrow Relay	Enrichment Chinese-Get-up Wheel-Barrow
4.	To further develop individual initiative through play-type activities based on individual stunts.	Follow the Leader Chinese Get-up Log Rolling Relay	Enrichment Heel Click Jump and Turn Mule Kick Rocker (ind.) Flat Rolling
5.	a. To continue emphasis on individual initiative. b. To introduce play-type activity based on fundamental tumbling techniques.	Follow the Leader Last Group Out Log Rolling Relay	Enrichment Heel Slap Coffee Grinder Jumping and Rolling
6.	To present further, tumbling and balancing techniques applicable through selected play-type activity.	Last Group Out Shoulder Bal. Contest Forward and Backward Roll Circle Relay	Shoulder Balance Forward Roll Backward Roll
7.	To introduce more difficult fundamental balancing techniques through an organized play-type activity.	Forward and Backward Roll Circle Relay Squat Stand Circle Doubles Bal. Race	Enrichment Squat Stand Sitting Balance Horizontal Balance
8.	To increase emphasis on play-type activities based on generally more difficult tumbling and apparatus techniques.	Squat Stand Circle Doubles Bal. Race Dive and Roll Relay	Enrichment Dive and Roll
9.	To present experiences in semi-balancing and tumbling techniques which require more effective group interaction.	Doubles Bal. Get-up Pyramids: Can You Match Us Dive and Roll Relay	Enrichment Pyramid variations
10.	a. To provide further opportunity for individual leader-	Pyramids: Can You Match Us	Beam variations Bar variations

TABLE 10-6. *Continued.*

Day	Objectives	Play-Type Activities	Related Fundamentals
	ship and responsibility. b. To introduce fundamental apparatus techniques through organized play-type activity.	Follow the Leader	Rope Climbing lying to sit lying to stand hanging
11.	a. To continue provision of opportunity for leadership. b. To further enhance individual development of techniques relative to selected apparatus.	Pyramids: Can You Match Us Follow the Leader	Beam variations Bar variations Rope Climbing
12.	To reinforce student development of selected apparatus techniques.	Follow the Leader	Beam variations Bar variations Rope variations
13.	To evaluate students through a competitive activity which involved selected fundamental techniques.	Obstacle Course	Walk Raised Beam Dog-Run-Dive and Roll Log-Roll-Rope Swing Jump and Turn-Backward Roll-Crab Walk

FINDINGS

1. The group of students who participated in the skill-oriented program showed a significant improvement in a greater number of physical fitness and motor ability test items than either of the other groups.
2. There were no significant differences between the three groups when social adjustment scores were compared. However, the play-oriented group showed a higher percentage of improved performance in individual subtests. It appears that the play-oriented kind of physical program offers a greater opportunity for the development of social efficiency.

After a careful review of the Goheen research and observation of varying degrees of formal and less formal physical education classes for the mentally retarded, a combination program of skill-oriented and play-oriented activities seems advisable. This program will permit the student to work on skill and fitness details, yet be able to have leadership and followship experiences and communication with peers.

QUESTIONS FOR DISCUSSION

1. How do you view the relationship between overlearning and the retention of a gross motor skill?
2. In the Cratty and Drowatzsky references at the end of this chapter, the conditions having a bearing on effective motor learning are discussed. How do these conditions relate to the teaching of physical education to the mentally retarded?
3. Auxter and others make a strong plea for building the curriculum for the mentally retarded around homogeneous and heterogeneous experiences in order to ensure optimum development through physical education. What are the advantages and disadvantages in such planning?
4. Why is the word *adapted* a better term to use today than *remedial* or *corrective*?
5. What do you think of units of work dealing with relaxation exercises? Should they be designed strictly for the chronically fatigued and hypertense boys and girls, or for everyone?
6. What are the several obstacles to overcome in establishing an adapted physical education curriculum in a school system that has never had this kind of program before?
7. Dysmenorrhea, painful menstruation, may be relieved or cured in 75 percent of the sufferers through Mosher, Golub, or Billig techniques. What are these techniques? Do you think they belong in the physical education program? Read what Mueller and Christaldi have to say about them (see Selected References).

SUGGESTED ACTIVITIES

1. Prepare a statement that will support the premise that a proper program of physical education will provide an opportunity for the development of physical skills and physical expression to counteract the lack of verbal expression in mentally retarded children.
2. Survey several large schools to determine the extent of adapted physical education programs. Find out their objectives, schedules, and content. Compare your findings with those of your classmates.
3. Examine several physical education curriculum guides in a college or university library. Find out to what extent a program for the mentally retarded has been developed in these guides.
4. Talk with some teachers of special education. Determine their views relative to the value of a progressive kind of physical education as compared to a free-play period.

5. Examine the extensive programing activities of Vodola (see Selected References), Chapter 7, in which a "prescriptive list of skills" is set forth so that the teacher can appraise motor ability and body management. Indicate how you might use this material in a school of your own.
6. Describe what you believe to be the most effective kind of relationship between the school physician and the teacher of physical education. Support your viewpoint with at least one book and one periodical reference under five years old.
7. Read several reviews of mainstreaming activities both in and out of physical education. Note the successes as well as the questionable results.

SELECTED REFERENCES

American Alliance for Health, Physical Education and Recreation, *Adapted Physical Education Guidelines*. Washington, D.C., 1977.

ARNHEIM, DANIEL D., DAVID AUXTER, and WALTER C. CROWE, *Principles and Methods of Adapted Physical Education*, 3rd ed. (St. Louis: C. V. Mosby Co.) 1978.

BALL, EDITH, and others, "The Need for Lesiure Education for Handicapped Children and Youth," *Journal of Physical Education and Recreation*, 47 (March 1976), 53–55.

BRENTON, MYRON, "Mainstreaming the Handicapped," in Glen Haas, *Curriculum Planning: A New Approach*, (2nd ed.), p. 255. Boston: Allyn and Bacon, Inc., 1977.

BUELL, CHARLES, "Physical Education for Visually Handicapped Children," *Journal of Health, Physical Education and Recreation*, 42 (April 1971), 63–64.

CALLAN, LAWRENCE B., and ANDREW McCRAY, "Case Studies on Remediable Health Defects," *Journal of School Health*, 42 (November 1972), 528–30.

CHADWICK, IDA F., "Historical Aspects of Dance Therapy," *Journal of Physical Education and Recreation*, 48 (January 1977), 46–47.

COUSENS, CHRIS, "Adapted Sports and Recreation for the Handicapped Child," *Journal of Health, Physical Education and Recreation*, 43 (November–December 1972), 53–54.

CRATTY, BRYANT J., *Active Learning: Games to Enhance Academic Abilities*. Englewood Cliffs, N.J.: Prentice-Hall, Inc., 1971.

CROWE, WALTER C., DANIEL D. ARNHEIM, and DAVID AUXTER, *Laboratory Manuel in Adapted Physical Education and Recreation*. St. Louis: C.V. Mosby Co., 1977.

CRUICKSHANK, WILLIAM M., ed, *Psychology of Exceptional Children and Youth* (3rd ed.). Englewood Cliffs, N.J.: Prentice-Hall, Inc., 1971.

DANIELS, ARTHUR S., and EVELYN A. DAVIES, *Adapted Physical Education*
    New York: Harper and Row, 1975.
DROWATZSKY, JOHN N., *Physical Education for the Mentally Retarded.*
    Philadelphia: Lea & Febiger, 1971.
DUNN, LLOYD M., ed., *Exceptional Children In The Schools*. New York:
    Holt, Rinehart and Winston, 1973.
FAIT, HOLLIS F., *Special Physical Education: Adaptive, Corrective, Develop-
    mental* (4th ed.). Philadelphia: W. B. Saunders Co., 1978.
GALLAHUE, DAVID L., PETER H. WERNER, and GEORGE C. LUEDKE, *A Concep-
    tual Approach to Moving and Learning*, chap. 12. New York: John Wiley
    and Sons, Inc., 1975.
HIRST, CYNTHIA, and ELAINE MICHAELIS, *Developmental Activities for Chil-
    dren in Special Education*. Springfield, Ill.: Charles C. Thomas Co.,
    1972.
KIRK, SAMUEL A., *Educating Exceptional Children*. Boston: Houghton Mif-
    flin Co., 1972.
KOLSTOE, OLIVER P., *Teaching Educable Mentally Retarded Children* (2nd
    ed.), New York: Holt, Rinehart and Winston, 1976.
KRAUS, RICHARD, *Therapeutic Recreation Service,* (2nd ed.), Philadelphia:
    W.B. Saunders Co., 1978.
LOGAN, GENE A., *Adaptations of Muscular Activity*. Belmont, Calif.:
    Wadsworth Publishing Co., 1964.
MCCLENAGHAN, BRUCE A., and DAVID L. GALLAHUE, *Fundamental Movement:
    A Developmental and Remedial Approach*. Philadelphia: W.B. Saun-
    ders Co., 1978.
MOUROUZIS, ANN, and others, *Body Management Activities: A Guide to
    Perceptual-Motor Training*. Cedar Rapids, Iowa: The Nissen Co., 1970.
MUELLER, GROVER W., and JOSEPHINE CHRISTALDI, *Remedial Physical Educa-
    tion*. Philadelphia: Lea & Febiger, 1966.
RARICK, G. LAWRENCE, and others, *The Motor Domain and Its Correlates
    in Educationally Handicapped Children*. Englewood Cliffs, N.J.:
    Prentice-Hall, Inc., 1976.
ROWAN, RUTH I., *Helping Children with Learning Disabilities*. Nashville:
    Abington Press, 1977.
SHORT, FRANCIS X., "Team Teaching for Developmentally Disabled Chil-
    dren," *Journal of Physical Education and Recreation,* 46 (October,
    1975), 45–46.
SIEDENTOP, DARYL, *Physical Education: Introductory Analysis,* (2nd, ed.),
    chap. 8. Dubuque: W.C. Brown Co., Pub., 1976.
SINGER, ROBERT W., *Motor Learning and Human Performance*. New York:
    Macmillan, 1968.
VANNIER, MARYHELEN, *Physical Activities for the Handicapped*. Englewood
    Cliffs, N.J.: Prentice-Hall, Inc., 1977.

VODOLA, THOMAS M., *Individualized Physical Education Program for the Handicapped Child.* Englewood Cliffs, N.J.: Prentice-Hall, Inc., 1973.

WAGGONER, BERNICE E., "Motivation in Physical Education for Emotionally Handicapped Children," *Journal of Health, Physical Education and Recreation,* 44 (March 1973), 73–75.

WEBB, WELLINGTON, "Physical Education Classes for the Emotionally Disturbed Child," *Journal of Health, Physical Education and Recreation,* 43 (May 1972), 79–80.

WEHMAN, PAUL, *Helping the Mentally Retarded Acquire Play Skills: A Behavioral Approach.* Springfield, Ill.: Charles C. Thomas, Publisher, 1977.

WICKSTROM, RALPH L. *Fundamental Motor Patterns,* (2nd ed.). Philadelphia: Lea and Febiger, 1977.

Intramural

and Interscholastic

Programs

chapter eleven

He who wins of a sudden, some noble prize
In the rich years of youth
Is raised high with hope; his manhood takes wings,
He has in his heart what is better than wealth.

PINDAR

Samuel Johnson used to say that sport is "play . . . and tumultuous merriment." Perhaps it should be; and perhaps it was in the eighteenth-century world of Johnson. Today, however, there is some question whether sport is much more than slightly related to merriment. There is evidence to suggest that as school sports are conducted in a more serious and businesslike fashion closely resembling the professional scene, the cherished values may exceed the grasp of many participants, and a significant number of boys and girls will miss tasting "in the rich years of their youth" what Pindar the poet wrote about so long ago.

Interestingly, in the days of the early Greeks, both the Spartan and Athenian philosophers focused on the dangers inherent in overemphasis and specialization in athletics. The intellectuals tolerated sports chiefly because sports prepared the male citizen to defend the land from external aggression or internal revolution, contributed to the advancement of physical condition, and fostered national unity as teams came together from all over the country to take part in national athletic festivities. Although such major sport and game activities were accepted by the Romans, the concern persisted that they could get out of control and defeat the sportsmanship objective. As a critic of his society, Cicero saw in sport some real value, but it also symbolized in a general

348

way the moral degradation of the society of Rome. In discussing Cicero's views, Fielding relates them to the twentieth century:

> He was talking to a society that needed desperately to learn how to use its leisure. A leisure similar to our own, in that for the few it was partly earned, while for the many it was imposed. A leisure that had markedly political overtones and which could be used as an opiate to lull the masses into passivity. At the center of the leisure Cicero saw competitive sport, oriented to the spectator and impoverished of ethical overtones. He saw all too clearly what might happen to a society which becomes seduced by its pursuit for pleasure, particularly when this pursuit of pleasure becomes divorced from the desire for good and results in the view that pleasure is the sole object of existence.[1]

There is some concern that many youth programs today are imperfect copies of professional sports with which their organizers and coaches are familiar and in which the business is to win at almost any cost. Under these circumstances, the ennobling contribution of sport to education that Vergerio wrote about during the Renaissance would be weakened considerably.

Fortunately, in a great number of school situations the athletic goal sights are set high, so that the student engaging in sports not only becomes very much aware of his or her limits and concept of self, but also takes from the experience a real appreciation of a quality performance—in terms of both lasting skills and the essence of fair play. Therefore, encouraging appropriate extraclass athletic activities for everyone makes sense. This part of the curriculum is a well-tested experience consistent with the broad purposes of education.

No wonder then that the private schools usually insist that their students take part in sports—from the mildest to the most vigorous in nature, from the competitive to the noncompetitive, and from team to individual. Where else is the potential for actualization as prevalent as on the playing field? The sense of purpose, commitment, and self-discipline has more lasting value than the outcome of the competition. Moreover, says Konrad Lorenz, "sport educates man to a conscious and responsible control of his own fighting behavior . . . [and insists on the] value of restrictions imposed by the demands for fairness . . . which must be respected in the face of the strongest aggression-eliciting stimuli."[2] Youths require a testing ground that places real demands upon them. After climbing Mt. Everest, Jim Whitaker was asked how it felt to

[1]Lawrence W. Fielding, "Marcus Tullius Cicero: A Social Critic of Sport," *Canadian Journal of History of Sport and Physical Education*, 8 (May 1977), 16–27.

[2]Konrad Lorenz, *On Aggression*, transl. Marjorie Kerr Wilson (New York: Harcourt, Brace and World, 1966), pp. 280–81.

conquer the mountain. He replied, "We didn't conquer the mountain; we conquered ourselves."

Genuine satisfactions gained during the upper elementary and junior high school years do indeed carry over to adult life. Therefore, the skilled, the unskilled, and the handicapped all must have some opportunity to participate in the extraclass program, through intramurals, extramurals, or interscholastics. Moreover, school committees should be reminded to give more credit to these activities on the *revenue* side of the budget, not always on the expense side.

Balance in Extraclass Programing

In order that all boys and girls may have equal opportunity to participate in a variety of activities, a careful balance must be maintained between offerings in intramurals, extramurals, and interscholastics, as defined in this list:

1. intramural activities—conducted within one school, and include only those pupils enrolled in that school
2. extramural activities—conducted as sports days, play days, or other approved interschool activities without involving a season-long schedule, league competition, or championship
3. sports days—occasions when pupils from two or more schools engage in one or more activities retaining the identity of the school
4. play days—occasions when pupils from two or more schools participate in one or more activities without retaining the identity of the school
5. interscholastic athletic activities—enrichment opportunities offered the more highly skilled pupils to represent the school in competition with representatives from other schools, which involve season-long schedules, organized practices, league competition, and championships.

If a proper balance between the extraclass activities at both junior and senior high school levels is not maintained, possibly program emphasis will center primarily on interscholastic games and contests. This is a natural occurrence in any locality where school and community spirit run high and people take pride in their teams. This is where the pressure is. A normal reaction, therefore, is for teachers and coaches to prepare their teams diligently for the spectators who come to see intense competition in which, hopefully, their school will emerge a winner. Unfortunately, however, this causes one part of the program to overshadow the rest.

Perhaps 15 to 20 percent of the pupils take part in interscholastic activities, whereas 80 to 85 percent of the students need encouragement and a chance to participate in an extraclass activity that is suited to their ability and interests.

Probably, intramural team experiences are capable of promoting lasting values. The fact that they are completely voluntary and the participants work hard together to achieve a common objective is by itself reason enough for these sports activities to be included in an educational program. Furthermore, when pupils are properly motivated to win a contest fairly, they call upon all of their mental and physical powers, their cooperative abilities, and their individual perseverance to see it through.

Frequently critics of intramural and interscholastic programs state that there is too much emphasis on competition and the winning of events. Curriculum planners must make it clear that in order for sports to be a testing ground for all of the accepted processes of interaction there must be a cooperative process. Games make use of both the competitive and cooperative processes. "Competition cannot occur without cooperation between opponents with regard to rules and tactics, and without cooperation among teammates with regard to task and responsibility."[3] In addition, athletics may help to control violence. It makes little sense to condemn not only the violence of youthful spirit but also the most important existing surrogate for actual violence—competition.

Planning Extraclass Activities

Like anything else, an extraclass program must be planned carefully if it is to yield good results. This is especially true in the large school systems today. After-school business is big business. The co-curricular activities are extensive in number and quality. Moreover, they tend to compete with each other for the pupil's free time, each requiring such a concentration of effort that to participate fully in more than one or two experiences is almost impossible. The member of the band, for example, can hardly engage in varsity football. Nor can the cross-country aspirant give much attention to an afternoon hobby group.

Despite the fact that there are many other interesting after-school activities in elementary and secondary schools, it is possible to build an extraclass physical education experience that will be able to reach most of the students. This kind of planning takes place when curriculum studies are being initiated and guides are being prepared. The task of the planning committee is to structure the extraclass program so that it supplements the development and adapted activities of the class instruction period.

In the elementary grades, because of adequate staff and facilities, to encourage as much as 100 percent participation in intramurals and play days is

---

[3]See Celeste Ulrich, *The Social Matrix of Physical Education* (Englewood Cliffs, N.J.: Prentice-Hall, Inc., 1968), pp. 86–87.

desirable. Certainly, at some time during the school year, each pupil in grades 4 to 12 should have this kind of group experience. The content should be worked out on paper through the combined efforts of the department planning committee, the respective school principals, and the teachers involved.

In the secondary schools, the programs have to be especially attractive and well-organized or the students will head elsewhere when formal classes end for the day. Loosely run intramural programs tend to attract only a few students—and these are usually students who would like to see more of their friends take part. Today, unfortunately, a number of urban and suburban schools find themselves with the kind of supersophisticated pupils who frequently shy away from vigorous after-school activities. Once they are motivated to participate, however, they stand to reap the same kind of benefits as anyone else.

Leadership is required. In each school, there should be a person designated responsible for extraclass activity. In this way, boys and girls with a wide variety of interests will be encouraged to take part in physical education offerings. In some cities, up to 75 percent of the secondary school students are expected to take part in at least one intramural or extramural activity during one of the three seasons of the school year. Also, a number of school systems try very hard to get this kind of participation during *each* of the seasons. They hope that the other 25 percent of the student body will take part in interscholastic athletics and sports days. This is possible only when staff and facilities are available to permit varsity, junior varsity, and freshman teams for both boys and girls.

Failure to plan a full program of extraclass activities so that all energetic pupils can find a place to play may be far more serious than heretofore realized. Recent studies having to do with delinquent children have indicated that time spent in school "blowing off" energy and aggressive tendencies may satisfy the juvenile so that he doesn't have to "explode" and work off this energy somewhere else in the community. Glueck and Glueck have shown that the active mesomorphic boy becomes the delinquent.[4] However, generally the extreme mesomorphs are not the ones who cause the trouble, for they have the body build and power to make the first or second team. Glueck's opinion is that the lesser mesomorphs (the 3 and 4 variety), the "also-rans," become the juvenile delinquents. What do we do for these people? When 100 energetic students turn out for the junior high school basketball team, what do we do? We keep twenty-five and tell the rest to play intramural basketball, and hope that they follow the advice.

[4]Sheldon and Eleanor Glueck, *Physique and Delinquency* (New York: Harper and Row, 1956).

The Elementary School Program

It has been said that "a child is tuned to activity." The child likes movement. In the past children had the chores to do, or they ran through the fields, climbed hills, and skated on the pond. But today's boys and girls are victims of an "easy" society, one in which the natural opportunities for physical movement are becoming fewer. Only an adequate physical education program of after-school games and sports with playrooms, gymnasiums, and playing fields can hope to compensate for the loss of open spaces and movement opportunities of the past.

Intramural and extramural activities may be played directly after school, during noon hours, on weekends, and during the vacation periods when associated with community recreation programs. An individual in each elementary school should be designated to head this activity for boys and girls, grades 4 and up. The numerous particulars relative to the role of the classroom teacher, the kinds of facilities required, and organizing and teaching suggestions will not be covered here.

Interschool Activity

In its concern for the physical and emotional health of younger boys and girls, the American Alliance for Health, Physical Education and Recreation conducted a survey of 528 school districts to ascertain the kind of athletic competition engaged in by elementary school-aged children. About 37 percent of the sample had some form of organized interschool athletic competition sponsored by the school. The figure was higher in the central and northwest areas of the country and lower in the east. School size was a significant variable; in the smaller school systems where a K-8 pattern existed there was more apt to be interschool competition than in the larger systems in which the K–6 pattern prevailed. Throughout the country basketball, followed by track and softball, led the list of interschool activities. In view of the fact that the percentages for K–6 were based on the 26 percent with interschool activities, it is apparent that the large majority of school systems were not promoting interschool athletic programs.

In 1968 the *Policy Statement on Competitive Athletics for Children of Elementary School Age* was approved and given wide distribution by the American Academy of Pediatrics, American Medical Association Committee on Medical Aspects of Sports, American Association for Health, Physical Education and Recreation.[5] It acknowledged the benefits of competitive

[5]See report, *Desirable Athletic Competition for Children of Elementary School Age* (Washington, D.C.: American Association for Health, Physical Education and Recreation, 1968).

sports, and set forth a number of items for local consideration having to do with the conduct of the sports, grouping of participants, protective equipment, well-maintained facilities, adequate medical appraisals, and qualified leadership. Moreover, the statement called for participation limited to upper-grade elementary children, parental permission, and activities limited to a neighborhood or community basis without play-offs, bowl contests, or all-star contests. To be avoided are high-pressure practices involving excessive publicity, pep squads, commercial promoting, the "grooming" of players, elaborate recognition ceremonies, and the exploitation of children in any form. Generally speaking, this policy statement has been well received nationally, and for the most part followed in the spirit in which it was written.

Intramural Play

Games and sports suitable for intramural participation are learned through class instruction. The rules are simplified, and sometimes the games are modified to coincide with the abilities of younger children. For the most part, the activities selected should be of the noncontact variety. Although there are exceptions, most research indicates that because of the possibility of damage to immature bodies, contact sports, such as tackle football, should be reserved for a later period. There are other physical activities that will effectively serve the competitive and social needs of upper elementary school children.

Appropriate games and sports that are interesting and foster participation for all are as follows.

BOYS AND GIRLS—GRADES 4, 5, AND 6

Activity: Softball
Modified forms: Kick and Run   Beat Ball
                 (Foot Baseball)   Hit Pin Baseball
                 Kick-Beat Ball   Two Pitch
                 Throw and Run   Regulation Kickball
Activity: Basketball
Modified forms: End Ball   Line Basketball
                 Captain Basketball   Pin Basketball
Activity: Soccer
Modified forms: Modified Soccer   Soccer Kickball
                 Soccer Dodgeball   Line Soccer
Activity: Volleyball
Modified forms: Newcomb   Keep It Up
                 Modified Newcomb   One Bounce Ball
Activity: Floor (Street) Hockey

Activity: Track and Field[6]

      Running Events: 30, 60, 100,   Field Events: broad jump, high jump,
      220, 440, and 880 relay   softball throw

Organized intramurals are far more effective in many schools when boys and girls assist in the planning of the sports and contests. Moreover, there is greater interest and anticipated fun when some kind of "club" or "color" system is employed. Cowell and Hazelton have suggested the following arrangements.

1. Each class would have two units or "houses" called, say, Blue and Maroon (named after the two school colors).
2. Each boy and girl would belong to one of the two "houses" and every effort would be made to keep these two groups equal in general playing ability.
3. Theoretically assuming a class of thirty (fifteen boys and fifteen girls), teams for the Blues and for the Maroons would be available in grades 4, 5, and 6.
4. Each grade would have its own participating units; activities could be planned in terms of the interests and maturity level of each class, yet each student would feel a sense of affiliation with students in the other two grades of the school.
5. A boy would become interested in what the girls do because he would have common membership in the "house" (either Blue or Maroon) with certain of his girl classmates as well as boys. Specific coeducational activities would be planned so that the Blue (boys and girls) would be participating in activities against the Maroons (boys and girls).
6. In an event such as an all-school track and field day, there would be events suitable for boys and girls of all three grades. Furthermore, a classification scheme that accounts for differences in maturity and body structure would place all children in some class such as A, B, C, D, or E depending on their exponent number resulting from the scheme. This equalizes competition and gives every boy and girl a chance for success.
7. In an all-school event such as a field day or play day, each boy and girl would contribute to his "house" (Blue or Maroon) since, if desired, all points for the three grades could be added.
8. In an event like a swimming meet for the boys and girls, a similar arrangement may be made and a variety of events chosen accordingly.[7]

Play days, in which pupils from neighboring schools join local boys and girls for an afternoon of active recreation, are especially suited to this elemen-

---

[6]In recent years track and field as an intramural activity has commanded considerable attention. Interest may be heightened by conducting exhibition races, all-school meets, and all-city meets. Records kept year by year further strengthen student motivation. See detailed account by Larry B. Yazel, "An Elementary Intramural Track Program," *Journal of Health, Physical Education and Recreation,* 43 (April 1972), 63.

[7]Adapted from Charles C. Cowell and Helen W. Hazelton, *Curriculum Designs in Physical Education* (Englewood Cliffs, N.J.: Prentice-Hall, Inc., 1955).

tary school level. Among the activities offered would be dances, all kinds of relay races and running games, and a selected number of individual and team games. The emphasis is on participation for all, with activities scheduled throughout the day, and friendly rivalry rather than defeat of another school stressed.

Sports days may also be held at this age level. When the several teams from other schools gather, the participants represent their own school. One or more sports may be played. Interest is usually high, and any pressure to win is minimized by including social activities and refreshments in the program with the competitive sports.

Postal or telephone meets may be held while the team remains at home and competes against the team of another school. Scores are exchanged by letter or telephone and winners determined accordingly.

Working through intramural activities in studying sportsmanship and moral reasoning, Horrocks found that fifth and sixth grade students were quite aware of sportsmanship and leadership qualities. He exposed them to (1) class discussions in order to advance their awareness of moral reasoning and (2) a rating system for identifying and exhibiting sportsmanlike behavior. Each student employed the rating scale to rate peer group members while engaged in game play. By introducing these two items in the curriculum a noticeable cooperative interaction occurred among his grade school children.[8]

The Secondary School Program

At both junior and senior high school levels the extraclass program may include intramurals, play days, sports days, and interscholastic games and sports. There is little doubt that these physical activities at the secondary level are frequently the very lifeblood of the after-school program. When properly organized and supervised, they become an essential part of a full and effective curriculum.

Intramural Play

The "golden age" of intramural sports could be just around the corner. Interest appears to be higher than ever. Today, large numbers of students prefer to be involved in actually participating rather than merely watching from the stands. Local school statistics support this view. In Norfolk, Virginia, intramural bowling alone attracts 5,000 pupils on 1,000 teams each week after school. In the Clark County School District of Nevada, systemwide table tennis tournaments involved 1,995 boys and girls in grades 7 to 12. Badminton

[8]Robert N. Horrocks, "Sportsmanship," *Journal of Physical Education and Recreation,* 48 (November/December 1977), 20–21.

drew 1,475 entrants, and archery over 500 more. The same story is repeated many places as the emphasis is directed toward giving everyone a chance to participate in physical activities.

The voluntary intramural program succeeds in the secondary schools if it is properly organized and implemented and if the following points are considered.

1. Intramurals should supplement and not replace required physical education and interscholastic athletics.
2. The games and sports selected should afford individual and team experience for both boys and girls, and should be broad enough in scope to interest and attract most of the students.
3. No pupil should be denied opportunity to take part in intramurals because of low academic or poor sports skill ability.
4. Competition should be arranged between those of equal skill, whenever possible.
5. Opportunities for individual and team practice should be provided.
6. Officials should be well-trained.
7. Individual and group instruction should be given when requested by students.
8. The program should be conducted according to a regular schedule.
9. Complaints and protests must be handled in a fair and democratic manner.
10. Tournaments that offer continuous participation should be preferred to those that permit only occasional participation.
11. Intramural records must be kept, not only for publicity and display purposes, but for making evaluations of the program.
12. The intramural program should not be thought of as a proving ground for varsity candidates; those students with exceptional ability should be encouraged to advance to the varsity team.

The availability of teaching stations has much to do with the extent to which an intramural program can be developed. In the list that follows, there is a great variety of suggested activities for boys and girls to be played separately or corecreationally. Archery, golf, tennis, bowling, and track and field are especially good corecreational sports for intramural play.

Generally, seasonal sports such as soccer, basketball, and softball are scheduled according to available facilities. There will be times, however, when the number of facilities is limited. On these occasions it may prove helpful to schedule an activity like intramural badminton during the afternoons in the fall and again during the late spring. This will permit access to the gymnasium courts at those times of year when most extraclass activities are being held outdoors. The same reasoning holds true for softball. Because of too few ball diamonds and too many team entries, it may be possible to hold some competition in the fall and some in the spring.

In the following list of suggested intramural sports activities, no distinction is made as to which activity is especially appropriate for the junior high

school or senior high school student. At some time, all of these activities have
been used at both levels. Ordinarily, field hockey for girls and wrestling and
gymnastics for boys are reserved for high school pupils. The final choice of
activities should be based on local needs and facilities.

SUGGESTED INTRAMURAL SPORTS ACTIVITIES

FROM SEPTEMBER TO NOVEMBER

Archery	Modified-games
Bicycling	Paddle tennis
Cross country	Quoits
Field hockey	Soccer
Flag football	Speedball
Golf	Swimming
Hiking	Tennis
Horseshoes	

FROM DECEMBER TO MARCH

Aerial darts	Modified-games
Badminton	Riflery
Basketball	Shuffleboard
Basket-shooting	Swimming
Bowling	Table tennis
Deck tennis	Volleyball
Fencing	Water games
Gymnastics	Wrestling

FROM APRIL TO JUNE

Archery	Roller skating
Baseball	Sailing
Golf	Softball
Horseshoes	Tennis
Modified games	Track and field
Paddle tennis	Swimming
Quoits	Surf casting
Relays	

Sports days and play days are a part of the extramural program of
competition between schools. They are an extension of the intramural activity, a broadened athletic experience that is free of any high-pressure concentration on winning. In the sports days events, the several competing schools
maintain their identity, scores are kept, and winners are determined. The
play days are more informal, school identities are not distinguished, and the
emphasis is on friendly competition and fun.

Careful preplanning and effective game day management have much to do with the success of these kinds of sport gatherings.

Participation in most intramural activities can be increased. The Moyer study found that minority pupils needed extra encouragement, and girls at all grade levels tended to have a low rate of participation.[9] However, by offering these students several options for engaging in intramural play there was a 25 percent increase in minority participation, a 50 percent increase in girls' participation, and an overall school system increase of 50 percent. One playing option was designed to serve only seventh and eighth grade boys and girls with varsity players excluded. Another was for junior high school boys only. Another was for homeroom competition, but with no playoffs. Another option was for intramural competition only among the physically gifted—an "All-Star" option.

Suitable activities for sports days and play days include:

Team Sports	*Individual/Dual Sports*
Soccer	Tennis
Flag Football	Badminton
Speedball	Archery
Basketball	Horseshoes
Softball	Table Tennis
Volleyball	Shuffleboard
	Golf

Noncompetitive Activities	*Track and Field Events*
Folk and Square Dance	Relays
Social Dance	Dashes
Stunts and Tumbling	Distance Throws
Swimming	Distance Kicks
Skating and Skiing	Free Throws

Women in Sports

In 1972 the American Academy of Physical Education recognized the long-time discrimination against females in athletics, and voted for equality in athletics by calling for "teams for women . . . in a variety of sports, and that the opportunity and the option exist for the students to participate on mixed teams."[10] Obviously, this is quite a change from past practices of limiting the number of varsity sports for girls and the sexes to their own areas.

[9]David H. Moyer, "Increasing Participation," *Journal of Physical Education and Recreation,* 48 (February 1977), 36–37.
[10]*The Academy Papers* (Iowa City, Iowa: The American Academy of Physical Education, 1972), p. 19.

Programs for girls and women today have a wide number of activities available. Girls take part in crew, lift weights, and compete with boys in other noncontact sports. Experimentation in 100 high schools in New York State as far back as 1970 indicated that girls could participate very well on mixed teams—specifically golf, tennis, swimming, skiing, gymnastics, track, bowling, cross-country, riflery, and fencing. Moreover, parents, school administrators, and physicians felt that participation was a successful experience. Two years later the Division of Girls' and Women's Sports (AAHPER) set forth a position paper indicating that teams should be provided for all girls and women who desire competitive athletic experiences. It cautiously indicated that although positive experiences for the exceptional girl or woman competitor may occur through participation in boys' or men's competitive groups, these instances "are rare and should be judged acceptable only as an interim procedure for use until women's programs can be initiated." This serves to indicate that women do not want to copy men's programs. They want their own. Playing on all-school teams is desirable, but they also want their own interschool competition. This view was fostered in New York State where the regulations of the Commissioner of Education were amended to permit girls on the same noncontact sport team with boys, provided the school attended by a girl wishing to participate does not maintain a girls' team in the sport.

Under Title IX of the Educational Amendments of 1972, all sex discrimination in American education has to end. The effective deadline for secondary school compliance is July 21, 1978. The first step calls for self-evaluation of policies, practices, and programs to be completed by 1976. Remedial steps are to follow such evaluations in every community. Physical education and athletic programs for one sex and the use of facilities exclusively by one sex are no longer tolerated. Regulations call for a curriculum and standards of conduct that apply equally to both sexes.

Intramural and interscholastic competition must accommodate the interests and abilities of both girls and boys. Schools may offer separate teams in contact sports and in those sports in which selection is based upon competitive skill. Separate teams are to be offered only when sponsorship of primarily girls' and boys' teams is the only way to accommodate effectively the interests of both sexes. If a school sponsors separate teams, selection of members must be based on competitive skill. Thus, members of one sex may be allowed to try out for the team sponsored for members of the opposite sex. This provision rejects the separate but equal position, a concept declared unacceptable by the courts.

When a school sponsors one team in a sport open to both sexes, the coach has to employ objective criteria to select who competes. A performance-based criterion is a logical item to employ. The most satisfactory arrangement will generally be to sponsor a wide variety of activities for boys and girls separately, as well as boys and girls together, with equal attention given to the needs of each sex.

Some school boards have found it difficult to balance budgets, so additional funds are not likely to be available for increased coaching staff, facilities, and equipment for the broader interscholastic program that adds a number of girls' sports and boy-girl activities. In most instances, programs will be planned with existing personnel and facilities. Training programs for women coaches have been necessary in most communities.[11] This law has stimulated the reexamination of status and roles in contemporary society and promoted fundamental practices of equality.

National Association for Girls and Women in Sport

For over two decades the Division of Girls' and Women's Sports of the American Association for Health, Physical Education, and Recreation gained considerable respect in the area of intramural and extramural play. When the AAHPER became an alliance, the National Association for Girls and Women in Sport (NAGWS) was formed in order to continue improving sport and physical education programs for the female participant. To meet the interests of women and to tie in with the spirit of Title IX, the following seven divisions in NAGWS were formed:

Affiliated Boards of Officials
Association for Intercollegiate Athletics for Women
Organization of Athletic Administrators
National Intramural Sports Council
National Coaches Council
Athletic Training Council
Organization of State and District GWS Chairpersons

These organizations continue to reach most of the communities in the country through state contacts and AAHPER publications. Their concern for curriculum content and teaching practices continues at a high level. That their concern for intramurals has not been overlooked is especially significant because in some areas the measurable increase in interscholastic sports competition for women has resulted in a drop-off in intramural play. A reasonable balance should exist between intramurals and interscholastic opportunities.[12]

[11] For a discussion of some of the problems involved, see Donna Cleland reference at end of chapter.

[12] See Dana E. Clark, "Intramurals: A Casualty of Title IX?" *Journal of Physical Education and Recreation*, 48 (May 1977), 66–67.

Interscholastic Athletics

In most communities, the crowning point of the physical education program is the opportunity afforded the gifted students for interscholastic competition in several team and individual sports (see Figure 11-1). Certainly, the school personnel who have been responsible for a full curriculum for grades K–12 that is well-constructed and implemented should be able to think of the athletic programs as excellent for going beyond the limits of an intramural activity to a more competitive, more demanding, and more concentrated group experience.

FIGURE 11-1. There is no substitute for a competitive program in secondary education.

Organized competition between school teams that is properly controlled can make a valuable contribution to the aims of education, and more specifically to the aims of physical education. Because of the emotional atmosphere surrounding a contest and the desire of the players to win the game, athletic activities are more subject to manipulation than other education experiences. Overemphasis, coaching pressures, exploitation of players, and other abuses sometimes creep into an athletic situation and threaten the security of the entire physical education curriculum.

Values and benefits from interscholastic athletics do not come automatically from participation. They have to be well planned under the leadership of knowledgeable and dedicated school officials. In most of the larger communities today, athletic policies are written with the full understanding and support of the school board, superintendent of schools, junior and senior high school principals, athletic director, and head of the department of physical education.

Program planning should take place at both the junior high school and senior high school levels, and relate to:

1. the total number of team and individual/dual sports the particular school can offer for both men and women
2. reasonable schedules with opponents
3. length of season and number and frequency of games
4. the division of available facilities, staff, and equipment between intramural and interscholastic athletics for both men and women
5. financing the program
6. relationship to leagues and the state high school athletic association and the National Federation of State High School Athletic Associations

The appropriateness of junior high school athletics for pupils in a transitional stage between elementary school and high school has been discussed for a number of years. The effects of contact sports and undesirable pressures from intense athletic competition have been debated for some time, but the evidence is not significant enough to ban properly controlled and supervised athletic programs for junior high school students. In fact, Louis Alley, who headed a national committee to determine desirable athletics for this age group, concluded his studies by pointing out that a number of students with superior athletic ability need an opportunity to develop and utilize their talents fully.

By far, the most comprehensive review of junior high school research was completed by Bucher for the New York State Education Department in 1965.[13] He indicated that programs may be harmful or beneficial depending upon their *conduct and administration.* More specifically, summarizing this extensive report, he made it clear that athletic programs may have education value when

1. Purposes and philosophies of the junior high school athletic program are fully understood.
2. Growth and development of the students is considered.
3. Game rules and facilities are adapted to pupil needs.
4. Health and medical supervision is frequent and thorough.
5. Previous conditioning and sound training in the fundamentals of the sport are assured.
6. Competition is with equals in maturity, age, weight, and skill.

[13]Charles A. Bucher, *Interscholastic Athletics at the Junior High School Level* (Albany, N.Y.: The State Education Department, 1965).

7. Protective equipment is purchased as part of the program.
8. Facilities that are safe and adequate are provided.
9. Consideration is given to the removal of undesirable pressures such as all-star contests, too many contests, awards of high material value, post-season games, commercial promotions, and so forth.

Much of what has been written on the subject of athletic competition for this age group can be summed up in two words: leadership and supervision. When these qualities are present there is a better chance of obtaining ethical behavior consistent with societal approval. In New York, a code of ethics has been developed and given wide publicity by the New York State Public High School Athletic Association (see Figure 11-2).

<u>Code of Ethics</u>

It is the duty of all concerned with high school athletics:

1. To emphasize the proper ideals of sportsmanship, ethical conduct, and fair play.

2. To eliminate all possibilities which tend to destroy the best values of the game.

3. To stress the values derived from playing the game fairly.

4. To show cordial courtesy to visiting teams and officials.

5. To establish a happy relationship between visitors and hosts.

6. To respect the integrity and judgment of sports officials.

7. To achieve a thorough understanding and acceptance of the rules of the game and the standards of eligibility.

8. To encourage leadership, use of initiative, and good judgment by the players on the team.

9. To recognize that the purpose of athletics is to promote the physical, mental, moral, social, and emotional well-being of the individual players.

10. To remember that an athletic contest is only a game -- not a matter of life or death for player, coach, school, official, fan, community, state, or nation.[14]

FIGURE 11-2.

The Selection of Activities

The selection of athletic activities for secondary school students might well come from the list of school games and contests presently sponsored throughout the country. This is rather extensive because local needs, facilities, and interests vary somewhat according to geography, climate, and

---

[14]Charles E. Forsythe and Irvin H. Keller, *Administration of High School Athletics,* 6th ed., (Englewood Cliffs, N.J.: Prentice-Hall, Inc., 1977).

traditions. The total number of interscholastic sports offered in any school depends on the school budget and student interest. Moreover, there is evidence that athletic programs become more elaborate as the population swells.

One may determine the kinds of sports being engaged in by reviewing the results of a national survey, as has been done from time to time by the National Federation of State High School Athletic Associations. State surveys, however, are generally more meaningful because they pertain to a geographical area that is likely to be more consistent than considering the whole country. In Eastern Massachusetts, for example, a very thorough survey of boys' and girls' sports participation was published in late 1972 by the *Boston Globe.* Three-and-a-half times more boys than girls engaged in athletics. This was because the boys were provided more opportunity for participation by almost a 3-to-1 ratio. Many schools were very much over-balanced in favor of the boys. A rare equality of opportunity was achieved in a few small schools. Football continued to be the major sport for boys, with basketball and baseball following. Surges in soccer and ice hockey were apparent, and there was more and more wrestling, skiing, and softball; while gymnastics, volleyball, and tennis continued to grow.

Figures gathered by the Athletic Institute also show where the participation is (see Table 11-1).

TABLE 11-1

Rank	Sport	Participants
1	Football (11-Man)	822,681
2	Basketball	674,938
3	Track and Field	509,687
4	Baseball	355,053
5	Wrestling	140,719
6	Cross-Country	120,096
7	Tennis	86,247
8	Golf	73,700
9	Swimming	64,720
10	Volleyball	55,743

These figures pretty much indicate a seasonal pattern:

fall: football, cross country
winter: basketball, wrestling, volleyball
spring: track and field, baseball, tennis, golf

Apparently, swimming is popular in any season of the school year that facilities are available. In certain sections of the country, gymnastics are prevalent during the winter season, but they are not strong enough nationally to rank with the first ten sports. The same can be said for soccer, which accounted for fewer than 35,000 participants in the schools studied. Within the last several years, however, soccer has grown measurably in popularity at both junior and senior high school levels. It is still played intramurally and in physical education classes to a far greater extent than it is played interscholastically.

There are a number of undeveloped sports in the high school program that the United States Olympic Development Committee is trying hard to develop nationally; women's track and field events, for example. Among these sports, for boys, are competitive boating, cycling, fencing, gymnastics, ice hockey, judo, skiing, volleyball, water polo, weight lifting, and wrestling. These sports are the ones in which United States teams have not been generally successful in comparison with other countries. Although there is a limited number of teams in these sports, their popularity is increasing as more and more competition in the individual/dual activities is being scheduled.

Wide sports participation and a concentrated effort to improve human performance must be planned if local, regional, national, and Olympic records are to be challenged. The fabulous world-record long jump of Beamon at Mexico City (29 feet, 2½ inches) may possibly be the greatest single feat in the recorded history of athletics. It could never have been done in an intramural or purely recreational atmosphere during Beamon's early years of training and competing. *The joy of excelling—achieving a hard-won goal through sport— is attributed to those who planned interscholastic programs as well as to the athlete himself.*

Since exercise is no longer considered "unladylike" and girls and women are finally being accorded an equal opportunity to engage in athletic competition, an appropriate selection of activities is necessary. Most individuals are motivated to participate in a sport only when they know something about it. Heretofore a number of girls have been somewhat shielded from the physically demanding skills, risk-taking sports, and from the challenging movements frequently associated with running, jumping, catching, and throwing. In many schools, therefore, successful program planning will require student-teacher and peer-group discussion sessions in which athletic events are explained, films are shown, special sport skills are demonstrated, and the value of participation in advancing health status, carry-over skills, and aesthetic and kinesthetic feelings are made clear.

There is every indication that there will be more athletic activity in the years ahead. Program planning, therefore, will become more important than ever. Already there are thirty sports being offered in the nation's secondary schools. These activities will need coordinating with nonschool athletic programs—which are also on the increase. Moreover, the nonschool organizations have initiated national meets in baseball, golf, tennis, track and field, swimming, and wrestling for secondary youth. Athletes are being asked to specialize in year-round competition in a single sport. Numerous communities in states such as Iowa and Minnesota continue regular interscholastic athletic schedules among high schools throughout the summer months. This movement is growing. All in all, more boys' and girls' competition in sports calls for greater care in building programs and initiation of school-community controls.

Sports for the Handicapped

The Committee on the Medical Aspects of Sports has made it clear that children with medical or disabling conditions need the opportunity to take part in both intramural and interscholastic competition.[15] Since there is a wide range of sport choices it should be possible to make a sport selection in keeping with the handicapping condition so as not to incur increased risk of serious injury through such sport participation.

In the past, many disabled persons have not been able to obtain the chance to compete with equals. Developmental programs have lacked funding, opportunities, and coaches, and public awareness was low. Today, under various state regulations and Public Law 94–142, programs are being developed, athletic games are being modified, and research and development activity are being directed to the design and production of prosthetic devices and other aids intended to assist mentally and physically handicapped persons. While therapeutic horseback riding goes well in England, in this country wrestling for the deaf, golf for the blind, and archery-basketball-volleyball by wheelchair students are played competitively in regional tournaments. And numbers of emotionally disturbed children have been helped by swimming and diving competition. Lists of suitable athletic activities for all classes of disabled children should be developed in each school system just as other instructional topics are developed and upgraded periodically.

QUESTIONS FOR DISCUSSION

1. From your experience, what are the trends in providing athletic competition for disabled children?
2. Why do athletes seem to belong to more clubs, have wider interests, and be more extroverted and better adjusted socially than nonathletes? Does participation in athletics develop these qualities or do students with these qualities tend to participate in athletics?
3. Should a school sponsor a wide variety of intramural, interscholastic, and

[15]Committee on Medical Aspects of Sports, *Medical Evaluation of the Athlete: Guide*, (Chicago: American Medical Association, 1974 and 1976).

recreational extraclass activities if the community as a whole has a fairly extensive program? Explain your answer.
4. How do you determine which sports and games to include in the intramural program of a given school?
5. It has been said that it is no longer a desirable practice to divide sports into established seasons. What might be the several reasons for this viewpoint?
6. Indicate why it is important that coaches, players, students, and the community understand the school's philosophy of athletics.

SUGGESTED ACTIVITIES

1. Survey the opinions of two or three directors of physical education relative to broadening the girls' intramural and athletic programs. What are the several problems that stand in the way of accomplishing this while meeting Title IX regulations?
2. Having completed question 1, survey the opinions of two or three women who coach girls' programs, relative to the same problem. How do their answers compare with those of the directors? Are they about the same, or do they differ?
3. Read several pieces of literature dealing with interscholastic athletic competition for students of junior high school age. Summarize the conclusions and relate them to the opposing viewpoints.
4. Outline a plan for the organization of a girls' athletic association in a small high school. Is such an association necessary?
5. What can you find out about the operation of the National Association for Girls and Women in Sports (AAHPER)? Contact the Washington office for general information relative to program suggestions, guides, and other interesting printed matter.

SELECTED REFERENCES

BUCHER, CHARLES A., *Administration of School Health and Physical Education Programs* (6th ed.). St. Louis: C.V. Mosby Co., 1977.

CHEFFERS, JOHN, and TOM EVAUL, *Introduction to Physical Education: Concepts of Human Movement*, chap. 9. Englewood Cliffs, N.J.: Prentice-Hall, Inc., 1978.

CLELAND, DONNA, "Preparing Women Coaches and Athletic Administrators," *Journal of Physical Education and Recreation*, 48 (October 1977), 18–20.

CRASE, DARRELL, "Athletics in Trouble," *Journal of Health, Physical Education and Recreation,* 43 (April 1972), 39–41.

CRATTY, BRYANT, *Psychology in Contemporary Sports.* Englewood Cliffs, N.J.: Prentice-Hall, Inc., 1973.

FREEMAN, WILLIAM H., *Physical Education in a Changing Society,* part 4, Boston: Houghton Mifflin Co., 1977.

FROST, REUBEN B., *Physical Education Practices, Principles,* chap. 10. Boston: Addison-Wesley Pub. Co., 1975.

———, and STANLEY J. MARSHALL, *Administration of Physical Education and Athletics.* Dubuque: Wm. C. Brown Co., Publisher, 1977.

FORSYTHE, CHARLES E., and IRVIN A. KELLER, *Administration of High School Athletics* (6th ed.). Englewood Cliffs, N.J.: Prentice-Hall, Inc., 1977.

GALLON, ARTHUR J., *Coaching: Ideas and Ideals.* Boston: Houghton Mifflin Co., 1974.

GERON, NANCY, "Intramurals and Recreation Belong Together," *Journal of Health, Physical Education and Recreation,* 44 (January 1973), 28.

HILLMAN, WILLIAM H., "Intramurals Via the Physical Education Class," *Journal of Health, Physical Education and Recreation,* 43 (April 1972), 63–64.

KELLY, BARBARA J., "Implementing Title IX", *Journal of Physical Education and Recreation,* 48 (February 1977), 27–30.

LOPIANO, DONNA A., "A Fact-Finding Model for Conducting a Title IX Self-Evaluation Study in Athletic Programs," *Journal of Physical Education and Recreation,* 47 (May 1976), 26–30.

LOWE, BENJAMIN, *The Beauty of Sport.* Englewood Cliffs, N.J.: Prentice-Hall, Inc., 1977.

MICHENER, JAMES A., *Sports in America,* New York: Random House, 1976.

OLDS, GLENN A., "In Defense of Sports," *Journal of Health, Physical Education and Recreation,* 32 (January 1961), 18.

MOYER, LOU JEAN, "Women's Athletics—What Is Our Future?" *Journal of Physical Education and Recreation,* 48 (January 1977), 52–53.

PENMAN, KENNETH H., *Planning Physical Education and Athletic Facilities In School.* New York: John Wiley and Sons, 1977.

PESTOLESI, ROBERT A., and WILLIAM A. SINCLAIR, *Creative Administration in Physical Education and Athletics,* chap. 5. Englewood Cliffs, N.J.: Prentice-Hall, Inc., 1977.

POINDEXTER, HALLY B., and CAROLE L. MUSHER, *Coaching Competitive Team Sports for Girls and Women.* Philadelphia: W.B. Saunders Co., 1973.

RESICK, MATTHEW C., BEVERLY L. SEIDEL, and JAMES G. MASON, *Modern Administrative Practices in Physical Education and Athletics,* (2nd ed.), part 3. Boston: Addison-Wesley Pub. Co., 1975.

———, and CARL E. ERICKSON, *Intercollegiate and Interscholastic Athletics for Men and Women.* Boston: Addison-Wesley Pub. Co., 1975.

SHULTZ, FREDERICK D., "Broadening the Athletic Experience," *Journal of Health, Physical Education and Recreation*, 43 (April 1972), 45–47.

ULRICH, CELESTE, "Sports in America," *Journal of Physical Education and Recreation*, 47 (September 1976), 6.

WIND, HERBERT W., *The Realm of Sport*. New York: Simon and Schuster, 1966.

ZEIGLER, EARL F., and MARCIA J. SPAATH, *Administrative Theory and Practice in Physical Education and Athletics*. Englewood Cliffs, N.J.: Prentice-Hall, Inc., 1975.

Evaluating

the Curriculum

chapter twelve

Grant me the strength, time and opportunity always to correct what I have acquired, always extend its domain; for knowledge is immense and the spirit of man can extend indefinitely to enrich itself daily with new requirements. Today he can discover his errors of yesterday and tomorrow he may obtain light on what he thinks himself sure today.

MAIMONIDES

The essential concept of evaluation—of searching for indications that ends have been achieved, and to remain open-minded—is perfectly expressed in the Maimonides quotation. In fact, the essence of the much-overworked word "accountability" begins with the attitude of the individual teacher toward truth-seeking in general.

The Intent of Measurement and Evaluation

Measurement in education is always related to preconceived aims and objectives. It is a process of making comparisons and relating them to one's needs in an effort to find out where one is headed.

To evaluate, says Webster, is "to appraise carefully," and to appraise is "to set a value on." Value is determined by relative "worth, excellence, or importance." The process of evaluating, therefore, should be considered along with measurement. Measurement answers the questions of how much, how many, and how often; it is concerned with quantities and qualities in evidence. Evaluation goes beyond the mechanics of testing and measuring to judgment in the light of aims and objectives.

Evaluation answers the question of whether or not a particular experience has value. It is a continuous process. In its broadest sense, it concerns the advancement of the total program and involves data about not only the excellence of the school plant or pupils but also the way in which the school serves the community.

The current emphasis is not too much on tests themselves, but on their application to problems in physical education. In the end, therefore, measurement devices and evaluation techniques become an administrative means to aid teachers in helping their pupils. They are used in the following ways:

1. to appraise behavior, knowledge, attitudes, and appreciation
2. to classify pupils
3. to determine pupil, teacher, and program status
4. to measure program efficiency
5. to measure progress
6. to analyze students
7. to measure teacher efficiency
8. to measure pupil efficiency
9. to contribute to research
10. to help win the support of the administration and the public for a new or revised program, method, or facility

There are a number of very practical uses for the fruits of measurement.

1. *The director of physical education* can inform superiors and other members of the community regarding the success of the program. Revisions and additions to the existing curriculum can be planned.
2. *The teacher* can determine the extent to which each student's achievement is commensurate with his or her ability. Plans can be devised to help students whose achievement is less than might be expected. Parents can be advised regarding the achievement of their sons and daughters in an effort to secure their cooperation in getting the pupils to put forth a greater effort and in following up deviations in physical fitness, motor skills, body mechanics, handicapping conditions, and so forth. Program changes can be recommended to the administrator.
3. *The students* can analyze their abilities, interests, and limitations and can determine ways in which to realize the greatest value from their physical education. Grades and other indications of accomplishments in physical education can be understood more clearly.

The Program of Evaluation

Today there are important trends in evaluation. There is widespread use of physical fitness tests and study of the factors that contribute to physical fitness. Motor coordination is being appraised through appropriate measures of general motor ability. Specific sport skills for individual pupils are being measured. The quality of after-school participation is being rated in terms of student goals. Total health behavior, academic achievement, self-concept, and personal happiness are being related more and more to physical performance and such specific factors as body mechanics, muscular strength, and endurance. Short written tests pertaining to knowledge, understanding, and general attitudes about physical education are becoming more common. Highly significant is the fact that numerous state and local curriculum guides have set forth achievement standards for sport skills, general motor skills, social behavior, and physical fitness. The users of such guides and courses of study are expected to compare their students with the standards in order to obtain some indication of immediate pupil needs. In the New York State guide, for example, any girl or boy in grades 7 to 12 can be appraised in terms of expected achievement in such major qualities as endurance, agility, speed, strength, and balance. According to these standards, two-thirds of the seventh grade boys and girls should be able to run the 50-yard dash in 8.4 and 9.1 seconds respectively. If these figures appear difficult to reach in a particular school, some thought should probably be given to the nature of the program. Is there enough opportunity to run? How many times per week do boys and girls have physical education? Is the program more instructional or more recreational?

Bloom makes it clear that evaluation practices have contributed little to teaching and learning, and there is a great variety of evidence that can be obtained and put to use beyond the usual paper-and-pencil examinations.[1] He calls for more quality control—so necessary in the manufacturing world. When this is coupled with a model of the outcomes of instruction and a table of specification, it is possible to really know where a student or program is headed. Currently there is some attempt to define behaviors students should attain—the way they think, feel, or act about the subject matter. The creation of *behavioral objectives* or *performance objectives* in precise terms has been helpful for both students and teachers in measuring accomplishments. In late 1977, the Subcommittee on Elementary and Secondary Education of the United States House of Representatives called for competency testing requirements. Although the regulation did not become law, its consideration is indicative of the seriousness that Congress attaches to high-level competencies in all fields of education. David Field writes about the value of breaking down vague objectives into meaningful terms for *all* individual, couple, and group activities taught in the school.[2] He does much to interpret physical education to students and administrators.

[1]Benjamin S. Bloom, J. Thomas Hastings, and George F. Madaus, *Handbook on Formative and Summative Evaluation of Student Learning* (New York: McGraw-Hill, 1971), chap. 1.
[2]David A. Field, "Accountability for the Physical Educator," *Journal of Health, Physical Education and Recreation*, 44 (February 1973), 37–38.

In the Irwin County Schools, Ocilla, Georgia, federal funding permitted the establishment of a *model* physical education program in which specifications for grades 1 through 8 were carefully laid down. Evaluation was an integral part of the program. The AAHPER Cooperative Physical Education Test of knowledge and understanding was given in grades 4 to 8;[3] physical fitness was measured by the AAHPER Youth Fitness Test and the Washington State Elementary School Fitness Test (grades 1 to 3); motor capacity was appraised in grades 1 to 6 with the Minnesota Motor Performance Test; and the SAR Reading and Math Tests and the California Test of Personality were also given. Scores were studied and programs were based on the needs of the children. Comparative scores of reading, math, personality, and fitness were employed to reveal relationships between physical condition and academic achievement. Similar kinds of evaluations have been carried on in Darien, Connecticut. There the usual measurements were supplemented by the findings from class tournaments, community reaction by questionnaire, and the degree of participation by students in community physical activities after graduation.

Forethought is essential to the evaluation program. Planning and organizing of time and resources is necessary to prevent a haphazard approach to the measurement of program efficiency. It is a good practice to measure students' physical fitness three times during a school year: at the start, in the middle, and at the end. Pupils in adapted physical education classes will need to check their progress in physical conditioning more often. Tests of skill and achievement, as well as short written knowledge tests, will generally follow each unit of instruction. Once or twice a year it may be desirable to test the students in a more comprehensive manner, especially at the secondary school level, where it is expected that students will achieve a sound understanding of the nature and values of the physical education experience.

Some schools' curriculum guides indicate testing programs that are just as carefully scheduled and explained as are any other part of the total curriculum. In the program of one high school, copies of the testing program are made available to all students early in the school year so that they know what to expect in the months ahead.

Measuring Progress in the Elementary School

There is nothing unique about elementary school programs that suggests anything out of the ordinary in evaluation practices. However, it does appear to be necessary to remind elementary school teachers of physical

[3]The *AAHPER Cooperative Physical Education Test* was developed by Educational Testing Service, Princeton, New Jersey for AAHPER. The knowledge of skills was combined with a knowledge of the "why." Answers to multiple-choice type questions indicate how well the student understands the various kinds of physical activity, their value, and effects.

FIGURE 12-1. Measuring achievement contributes to curriculum validity. (Courtesy, Milwaukee Public Schools)

education that the results of their efforts need appraising every bit as much at this level as they do at the secondary school level. Because of so many loosely organized and infrequently taught elementary school physical education programs, a strong tendency exists to do little or no evaluation of pupil and program progress. This is especially true in those schools in which the physical education instructor teaches each class as a special visiting teacher once every week or ten days. In these instances, the instructor is likely to feel that the instructional exposure is so inadequate that to measure the effect of the program would be difficult. Nevertheless, the director of the local programs should be interested in knowing how well these children compare with others of similar age and maturity in physical condition, skill development, and social-emotional adjustment. By using tests to make an administrative point, it may be possible to determine that the elementary pupils in question need much more physical education programing than they are currently receiving. Are they gaining the knowledge and skills referred to in Chapter 8? How do they compare with children in other elementary schools in the community?

Children enjoy being challenged, whether through formal tests of strength, speed, skill, and so forth, or through self-testing activities. Experience indicates that they respond well to teachers who post achievement goals. The goals, of course, should be realistic and represent the experience of the teacher coupled with information gained from standardized tests of selected motor skills, sport skills, and physical fitness. Moreover, it can be fun taking a test such as the Johnson Fundamental Skills Test, which involves throwing and catching, kicking, jump-and-reach, and a zigzag run.[4] Percentile norms are available for the primary grades.

A number of years ago, Professor Marjorie Fish of Trenton (New Jersey) State College prepared a list of physical education achievement goals that were immediately useful. They are especially valuable in a large number of schools in which the elementary teacher does not have access to a physical education consultant or special teacher of physical education. Professor Fish set up her goals in simple form so that they could be easily interpreted and measured. They may be used as *minimum achievement goals*.[5]

PHYSICAL EDUCATION ACHIEVEMENT GOALS

GRADE 1

I. Ball Skills: Should be able to
    1. Throw a rubber ball the size of a volleyball a distance of 12 feet, accurately enough for another child to catch it.
    2. Catch a rubber volleyball thrown from a distance of 12 feet.
    3. Hit a fixed target, an Indian Club pin, or another child with a rubber volleyball from a distance of 12 feet.
    4. To kick a ball between two pins which are placed 3 feet apart, from a distance of 16 feet.

II. Running Skills: Should be able to
    1. Play running games without falling down.
    2. Run correctly—on their toes, lightly, feet pointed straight ahead and no swinging of ankles inward or outward. Arms should move easily from the shoulders, head held in normal position.
    3. Dodge another player without falling down.
    4. Increase running speed during the year.

III. Balance and Jumping Skills: Should be able to
    1. Take a squat or deep knee bend position and hold it for 3 seconds.
    2. Walk a 15-foot straight line placing one foot directly in front of the other at each step.
    3. Broad jump, one foot take-off, a distance of 3½ feet.
    4. Jump over an object knee high.
    5. Jump down from a height two feet from the ground and land on the toes with the knees bent, keeping their balance.
    6. Run and jump upward touching a wand 5 feet above ground.
    7. Hop 10 times on one foot progressing forward.

[4]For details see Appendix C in Evelyn L. Schurr, *Movement Experiences for Children,* 2nd ed. (Englewood Cliffs, N.J.: Prentice-Hall, Inc.,) 1975.

[5]Originally set up by Professor Marjorie Fish, Trenton State College. (Used by permission).

IV. Rhythm Skills: Should be able to
1. Walk, run, skip, slide, and gallop in rhythm to music.
2. Developing ability to interpret and respond to the beat, tempo, light and heavy, soft and loud, pitch, and changes in music.
3. Develop ability to interpret the music and to create activities to it.

V. Social Values and Appreciations:
1. Should be growing in ability to take turns, share equipment with others, wait his or her turn, play with others without quarreling, and to understand the necessity for respecting those in authority.
2. Should be able to play in groups happily and to take directions given either by the teacher or a pupil leader.

GRADE 2

I. Ball Skills: Should be able to
1. Throw a rubber ball, the size of a volleyball, a distance of 15 feet accurately enough for another child to catch it.
2. Catch a rubber volleyball thrown from a distance of 15 feet.
3. Hit a fixed or moving target 15 feet away with a rubber volleyball.
4. Kick a stationary ball accurately between two pins set 2½ feet apart, from a distance of 20 feet.
5. Stop or trap a kicked ball (rubber soccer size) passed to him from a distance of 20 feet.

II. Running Skills: Should be able to
1. Play running, chasing, and dodging games without falling.
2. Run correctly on their toes, streamlined.
3. Increase speed and agility in running, throughout the year.

III. Balance, Jumping, Climbing, and Hopping Skills: Should be able to
1. Grow in ability to hold balance in performing simple stunts as standing on one foot, the other foot raised in front, knee bent and hold for 10 seconds; walking a straight line for a distance of 20 feet; holding squat position—back erect—for 5 seconds.
2. Broad jump, one foot take-off—a distance of own height.
3. Jump over an object knee high or higher.
4. Jump down from a higher level and land with knees bent and on the balls of the feet and toes, and keep balance.
5. Jump up and touch an object 6 feet above them.
6. Jump rope forward and backward and on one foot.
7. Hop forward into blocks (30″ × 12″) 10 of them and return without losing balance or putting foot down.
8. Climb twice own height on apparatus—ropes, jungle gym.

IV. Stunts—Self-testing Skills:
1. Should be able to do stunts of balance, agility, strength, flexibility, and speed on second grade level, such as walking 10 feet carrying bean bag on head, foot, or hand with arm outstretched; bean bag and wand stunts.

V. Rhythm Skills:
1. Should be able to walk, run, hop, skip, slide, gallop in rhythm with the music not only alone, but also with a partner.

2. Should be growing in interpreting and responding to changes in music and to put their interpretation into movements.
3. Should be able to express simple ideas in bodily movements.

VI. Social Values and Appreciations:
1. Should be growing in ability to give and follow directions, wait turn, play happily with others, share and respect school equipment.

GRADES 3 AND 4

I. Ball Skills: Should be able to
1. Throw and catch a rubber volleyball a distance of 30 feet.
2. Kick a rubber soccer ball a distance of 40 feet.
3. Kick pass accurately to a player 30 feet away and be able to stop or trap a kick pass from a distance of 30 feet.
4. Dribble a soccer ball without losing control of it a distance of 20 feet and at almost normal running speed.
5. Catch a kicked ball from a distance of 20 feet.
6. Hit an object or a moving target at a distance of 30 feet.
7. Throw a softball a distance of 30 feet accurately enough for a team member to catch it; and be able to catch a softball thrown 30 feet away.
8. Hit 3 out of 10 good pitched balls from a distance of 15 feet.
9. Field a ground ball with a fair degree of accuracy.
10. Pitch a softball 3 out of 10 from a distance of 15 feet.
11. Throw and catch a junior size rubber football 15 feet.

II. Running Skills: Should be able to
1. Run simple relay races involving certain skills: passing object from right hand as runner and receiving it in right hand when about to run.
2. Run lightly on balls of feet.
3. Wait behind starting line until tagged by incoming runner.
4. Run in a straight line or take the shortest distance.

III. Skills in Jumping and Balancing: Should be able to
1. Broad jump the breadth of his or her height.
2. Jump over a wand or stick 3 feet high or leap-frog over another child.
3. Jump rope—turned by self; turned by two children; Double-Dutch; and go in and out; chase the fox; "high water."
4. Do most stunts of grade level.

IV. Rhythm Skills: Should be able to
1. Recognize double and triple meter, musical form A-B-C, and so forth; and to appreciate moods in music and phrases, diminuendo and crescendo, and so forth.
2. Create simple dance forms; move in rhythm with a group; do the simple waltz; change direction of movement at change of phrase.
3. Do simple folk dances, grade level.
4. Express ideas through body movements using a variety of percussive and sound instruments.

V. Social Values and Appreciations:
1. Should be growing in ability to give directions, to be a self-reliant worker.

2. Should be growing in such moral qualities as courage, honor, sportsmanship, cooperation, self-control, and courtesy.

GRADES 5 AND 6

I. Ball Skills: Should be able to
1. Throw and catch a soccer size ball a distance of 35 feet (girls), 50 feet (boys).
2. Throw and catch a football (junior size) 40 feet.
3. Kick pass a soccer ball accurately to another team member 45 feet (girls), 50 feet (boys) away.
4. Kick a moving soccer ball through a soccer goal anywhere within 36 feet of the goal.
5. Dribble a soccer ball a distance of 18 yards at good speed and keep good control of the ball.
6. Keep the eyes on the ball at all times.
7. Trap, block, volley, punt, and drop kick a soccer ball.
8. Pitch a softball over an 18-inch home plate between the knees and the shoulders of the batter from a distance of 45 feet (boys), 30 feet (girls), 2 out of 5 times.
9. Throw and catch a softball from a distance of 85 feet over home-plate 2 out of 5 times (girls), 3 out of 5 times (boys).
10. Bat a pitched ball thrown from a distance of 35 feet over home-plate 2 out of 5 (girls), 3 out of 5 (boys).
11. Catch 2 out of 5 fly balls.
12. Stop grounders 2 out of 5 (girls), 3 out of 5 (boys).
13. Make 5 out of 10 baskets using a volleyball near the basket (ideal spot).

II. Jumping Skills and Stunts:
Boys and girls should know the correct form for approaches, execution, and landing for all jumps and stunts and apparatus work if given. Should be able to:
1. Jump up and reach a distance of 7 inches.
2. Broad jump a distance of 4' 10" (boys), 4' (girls).
3. Boys—high jump 3 feet or more.
4. Girls—do Double-Dutch and Double Irish with jump rope.
5. Execute with skill at least half of the stunts presented in class.

III. Dancing Skills: Should be able to
1. Do the waltz, polka, schottische, and mazurka and understand the music appropriate for each.
2. Do folk, national, tap, and square dances suitable to this age level.
3. Do marching to music, keeping in step and rhythm, following simple command.
4. Do exercises to music—girls modern dance types, and boys stunt types.

IV. Social Values and Appreciations:
1. Should be developing courage, honesty, courtesy, kindness, and so forth.
2. Should be increasing interest in physical welfare of others.
3. Should be growing in leadership ability and in taking responsibility.

Secondary School Evaluation

With one or more specialists assigned to physical education classes almost everywhere today, there should be no excuse for failing to chart the progress of pupils and the ultimate efficiency of a current program. The variety of physical fitness tests is extensive. The number of sports skill tests increase every year. By far, the most practical are those published by the American Alliance for Health, Physical Education and Recreation.[6] A short battery of tests has been devised for each sport and for each sex. Norm tables are included for ages ten through eighteen. The unique characteristic of these tests, which are available on request, is that they were developed as an aid to class instruction and a ready means of noting pupil improvement and how local pupils compare with others on a national basis. They can answer the questions: Just where are skill levels locally? With instruction, how long will it take to raise the skill level?

By employing regular skill knowledge and fitness tests, it should be possible to ascertain the extent to which a current physical education program is adequate. This is the only valid way questions relative to the effectiveness of a particular course of study can be answered. Eventually all questions having to do with program emphasis, time allotted, schedule changes, staff coverage, and teaching stations are answered from the fruits of the measurement effort.

Evaluation in secondary school physical education frequently provides feedback and guidance only for the teacher or administrator. The greatest need, certainly, in terms of future motivation, is for learners—those who need to know themselves—to see more clearly the tasks ahead. In short, what does the measurement activity do for learners' self-reliance? Finke gets at self-evaluation by asking, "Does the evaluation of a student's progress in tennis or golf *increase* his desire and ability to move on to new goals?"[7] How can the appraisal of skill experiences be productive for both student and instructor? One way is through the contract system, which allows students some freedom for directing their learning, although the freedom is still limited by certain instructor-made objectives. Because the level of competence is established ahead of time, the completion of a contract affords a kind of instant measurement. Note the specifics from a section of a high school contract:

BOWLING CONTRACT

Contract 1 (20 points):   Bowl six games at any lane. Keep your score. Copy your game scores on the enclosed sheet in this packet. On a separate piece of paper, state the two basic rules for scoring. List the symbols used in scoring and tell their meaning. Your score sheets will be graded for accuracy.

[6]AAHPER, 1201 16th Street, N.W., Washington, D.C. 20036.
[7]Charles F. W. Finke, "Use Evaluation Positively," *Journal of Health, Physical Education and Recreation*, 43 (November-December 1972), 16–17.

Contract 2 (10 points): Learn the correct way to pick up a ball, how to hold the ball, and be able to demonstrate the hand position that creates a hook ball, a straight ball, and a backup ball. Evaluation will be based on an oral explanation to the instructor.

Assessing the Fitness-Motor Domain

Highly related to success in fundamental movements and the more involved game skills is the level of physical condition as it pertains to general motor performance. Determining this level and relating it to program characteristics may contribute significantly to curriculum analysis and ultimate adjustments.

Available data from national probability samples of public school children compare the results of 1958, 1965, and 1975 on the AAHPER Youth Fitness Test—a study sponsored by the United States Office of Education. Although there were dramatic gains for both boys and girls from 1958 to 1965, in the following ten years the girls scored only slightly better while the boys' performance remained about the same.[8] Both physical fitness and general motor capacity are demonstrated through fun-to-do activities in test examples such as those that follow in Table 12-1.

TABLE 12-1

AAHPER Youth Fitness Test	Pull-ups, sit-ups, shuttlerun, standing broad jump, 50-yard dash, 600-yard run-walk or 1 mile or 9 minute run for ages 10 to 12; and 1½ miles or 12 minute run for ages 13 and over.	Grades 5 to college
New York State Physical Fitness Test	Target throw, modified push-ups, posture test, side-step, 50-yard dash, squat stand, treadmill	Grades 4-12
North Carolina Fitness Test	Sidestepping, sit-ups, standing broad jump, pull-ups, squat thrusts.	Grades 4-12
Washington Physical Fitness Test	Pull-ups, zigzag run, sit and reach, sit-ups, standing broad jump, softball throw, side step, 300-600-yard walk-run.	Grades 6-12
Oregon Motor Fitness Test	Standing broad jump, flexed arm hand and curl-ups (girls), push-ups and sit-ups (boys).	Grades 4-6
Amateur Athletic Union Physical Fitness and Proficiency Test	Sprints, sit-ups, pull-ups, push-ups, standing broad jump, basketball throw, hike for distance, high jump.	Grades 1-12

With the growing popularity of aerobics programs and research linking endurance fitness to physiological well-being, a renewed interest has oc-

[8]Paul Hunsicker and Gary G. Reiff, "Youth Fitness Report," *Journal of Physical Education and Recreation*, 48 (January 1977), 31–32.

curred in physical fitness assessment. From the early work of Bruno Balke in 1963 to the present it has been shown that walk-run tests for distance have been appropriate field tests suitable for elementary age pupils and above. Both 9-minute and 12-minute runs are significantly related with maximum oxygen uptake; and the nine-minute distance run is especially appropriate for elementary school boys and girls.[9]

Handicapped students should have the opportunity to participate in some of the fitness measurement activities and in those tests that are suitable to the handicapping condition. Fait has worked out a set of physical fitness tests for the mentally retarded that are given in the following order: 25-yard dash, bent arm hang, leg lift, static balance test, squat thrust, and 300-yard walk-run.[10] Norm tables are available for boys and girls 9 to 20 years of age.

Observing students for perceptual-motor shortcomings should be accomplished with the assistance of classroom teachers, speech therapists, and special education teachers. When a number of the following conditions are present in an individual, further perceptual-motor measurements should be taken:

confuses right and left sides
fails to transfer weight from one foot to other when throwing
confuses up and down directions
does not show opposition of limbs in throwing, walking, and sitting
is unable to move body parts on command
employs one extremity more often than the other
is unable to clap out a rhythm with both hands or stamp rhythm with feet
cannot keep balance in squat position
cannot hop rhythmically
shows difficulty getting in and out of seat
demonstrates irregular handwriting
runs or walks with awkward gait
spills and drops objects; lacks body awareness
loses place while reading; shows poor ocular control
is unable to walk sideward either direction on balancebeam
has tendency to avoid using left side of body

In Schilling's Body Coordination Test (BCT) it is possible to differentiate between brain-damaged and non-brain-damaged children. The four items in this German test consist of balancing backwards, one-foot hopping over mats,

[9]Andrew S. Jackson and A. Eugene Coleman, "Validation of Distance Run Tests for Elementary School Children," Research Quarterly, 47 (March 1976), 86–93.
[10]Maryhelen Vannier and Hollis F. Fait, Teaching Physical Education in Secondary Schools, 4th ed. (Philadelphia: W.B. Saunders Co., 1975), pp. 564–68.

jumping sideways over an obstacle, and a body-shifting activity. Several studies have shown that BCT measures body coordination and movement control very well.[11]

Measuring Affective Behavior

Although difficult to fully measure, an attempt should be made to sound out the feelings and appreciations that students take with them after a reasonable exposure to physical education. Of course, positive or negative results cannot be attributed entirely to the movement experiences but are the result of the total school program in concert with various peer group and community-home influences. A partially successful curriculum is one in which large numbers of students enjoy their movement activities.

In singling out four currently available instruments for use in measuring affective behavior, McGee stresses their use in physical education:[12]

1. *Martinek-Zaichkowsky Self-Concept Scale*—a non-verbal, culture-free instrument for grades 1 to 8. Non-English speaking groups can take this test because it is in a form of a 25-item pictorial scale. It is sensitive to individual changes in self-concept brought about through physical education skills and contacts.[13]

2. *Wise Student Inventory Toward Athletic Competition*—a means of checking student and parent attitudes at the sixth grade level.[14]

3. *Measures of Self-Concept*—a word choice instrument for grades K–12, designed to show how a student thinks his friends would describe him, i.e., friendly or not friendly, etc.[15]

4. *Attitude Toward School*—a variety of scales that assess ways in which a student views school—the teacher, the instruction, climate, and peers.[16]

[11]Friedhelm Schilling and Ernst J. Kiphard, "The Body Coordination Test," *Journal of Physical Education and Recreation*, 47 (April 1976), 37.

[12]Rosemary McGee, "Measuring Affective Behavior in Physical Education," *Journal of Physical Education and Recreation*, 48 (November/December, 1977), 29–30.

[13]Martinek-Zaichkowsky Self-Concept Scale (1977), Psychologists and Educators Inc., Suite 212, West State Street, Jacksonville, Illinois 62650.

[14]Mary K. Wise, "A Comparison of Attitudes of Children and Their Parents Toward Athletic Competition at the Elementary School Level (Doctoral Dissertation, University of Nebraska, 1976).

[15]*Measurement of Self-Concept—Grades K-12*, revised edition, 1972, Instructional Objectives Exchange, Box 24095, Los Angeles, California 90024.

[16]*Attitude Towards School—Grades K-12*, revised 1972, Instructional Objectives Exchange, Box 24095, Los Angeles, California 90024.

FIGURE 12-2. A visual evaluation can be objective.

Appraising the Total Curriculum

The purpose of this book has been to take a look at the total physical education curriculum. Although its parts have been examined, the objective all along has been to relate them to the whole program and to effect a proper balance between grade level progression, developmental and adapted class instruction, intramurals, interscholastics, and school recreational activities. No one area has been singled out as all-important. They are *all* important.

Alert school administrators and directors of physical education frequently want to know how well their programs are working and how they compare with others in neighboring communities or on a national level. Such a comparison may be accomplished in part by the employment of an already developed administrative measure. Such appraisal instruments are designed to provide the administrator with a somewhat broad view of the physical education program, and they permit the local community to evaluate itself. Self-examination is almost always a good practice, for it encourages soul-searching and an honest attitude toward what the program *should* be. When an administrator and staff appraise their total curriculum, they have, in effect,

384

opened their minds and humbled themselves just enough to be able to see the changes needed. Therefore, the simple act of deciding to appraise a program is in itself significant. It is a first step along the road to program modifications in a changing society.

· The process of *quality control* in any educational program is important. Quality control is a way of telling whether the program is executed well and whether it remains as effective over time as it was when first implemented. Since new programs frequently deteriorate, one must measure the deterioration by comparing base-line data with current achievement results. Scores relative to fitness, sport skills, knowledge, and attitudes toward the program can be compared with scores obtained after the implementation stage. Signs of program deterioration frequently relate to a weak implementation practice because of such variables as poor teacher morale, teacher indifference, inadequacy of teaching stations, and school learning climate in general. Usually, if a curriculum is properly planned, exposed to a preliminary tryout, field tested, and implemented by the planners themselves, quality control and its questionnaires and checklists will probably not be needed to discover the cause of the deterioration.

Administrative Measures

There are a number of self-appraisal instruments designed for the physical education program. Several are standardized and have had wide use over a period of years. Several states have taken the lead in developing instruments for this kind of appraisal. Texas, Indiana, Ohio, New York, Wisconsin, California, and Florida are examples.

The Indiana Physical Education Score Card for Elementary and Secondary Schools (revised) was developed to improve the quality of physical education programs.[17] It is primarily a self-evaluation instrument that encourages follow-up studies. The score is divided into four areas, which are weighted in the following manner (Table 12-2).

TABLE 12-2

Area	Percent of Total Value
1. Class management and instruction	40
2. Program activities	30
3. Facilities and equipment	20
4. Administration	10

[17]Copies may be obtained from the Indiana State Department of Public Instruction, 1330 West Michigan Street, Indianapolis, Indiana.

Because of differences in programs for boys and girls at the different levels, the score card is divided into three parts: elementary grades 1, 2, and 3; elementary grades 4, 5, and 6; and secondary grades 7–12. Each group is scored in each area after several questions have been answered. For individuals concerned with curriculum instruction, areas one and two are the most helpful. Table 12-3 presents an example of two pages from this forty-eight page score card:

TABLE 12-3

ELEMENTARY—GRADES 1, 2, 3

Program Activities—Boys and Girls

A. Instructional Program

1. Arranged so that time for the year devoted to   (Average)
   Physical Education is allocated as follows:
   (Refers to time devoted to instruction)
   Activity

Games, races, and relays	50%
Rhythmics	20%
Self-testing (stunts, tumbling, apparatus)	20%
Mimetics and story plays	10%

Approximately as above	9	_____
Time allotted in all areas, but quite different from above	6	
Heavily weighted in one area	3	

2. Provides activities in games, rhythmics, mimetics and story plays, and self-testing including stunts and tumbling

All areas	12	_____
3 areas	9	
2 areas	6	
1 area	3	

3. Each grade level shows progression

Marked	9	_____
Some	6	
Very little	3	

4. Activities prepare children for recreation outside of school

Systematically planned	6	_____
Incidentally planned	4	
Left to chance	2	

5. Activities suitable to interest and ability of children

Marked	9	_____
Some	6	

TABLE 12-3. *Continued.*

6. Activities provide for:
   Maximum active participation   9   _____
   Active participation for most of class   6
   Active participation for few   3

7. Self-testing, including stunts and tumbling, provides that running, jumping, throwing, catching,
   climbing, hanging, dodging are basic skills in
   tumbling and stunts
   All activities   15   _____
   5 activities   10
   4 activities   5

Program Activities—Boys and Girls

8. Mimetics and story plays are planned to include
   vigorous, big muscle activity for:
   All parts of body   15   _____
   Most parts of body   10
   Some parts of body   5

9. The dance program includes:
   a. Creative activities   _____
   b. Fundamental rhythmics
   c. Singing games
   d. Folk dances
   e. Nursery rhymes
   All items   15
   Items a, b, and one other   10
   Any two   5

		Total Actual	_____
Actual		__X 100 =	_____
Maximum	99		_____

The Indiana Score Card is an excellent choice for use in appraising the full K–12 program, and has had wide use.

The Florida State Department of Education, after extensive study, developed a checklist entitled *An Evaluation in Physical Education* (revised), to be used primarily for self-evaluation at the local community level.[18] It is a complete booklet of standardized items with which the supervisor or director in the city or town can compare his total program at all levels.

The LaPorte Health and Physical Education Score Card (I,II) has been in use longer than any other similar instrument.[19] It is intended to measure all aspects of the health, safety, recreation, and physical education programs.

---

[18]May be obtained from the Department of Physical Education, State Department of Education, Tallahassee, Florida.

[19]William R. LaPorte, *Health and Physical Education Score Card*, I, II (Los Angeles: Parker and Co., 1951).

The card is set up so that it centers attention upon the characteristics of a good program. There are ten program elements, which can be rated from 1–30 points; a perfect score is 300 points. If 200 points are scored, the program is considered fair to good. If only 100 points are scored, the program is considered poor. One of the largest surveys employing the score card for secondary schools was carried out on 135 North Carolina high schools as part of a larger study. Scores ranged from 32 to 201, with a mean of 91.38 and a median of 76. As in previous New York and Ohio studies, school size was significantly related to favorable scores.

The Evaluative Criteria, National Study of Secondary School Evaluation, which was developed in 1960 and updated in 1970 by the American Council on Education, is available as *Physical Education for Boys* (D-14) and *Physical Education for Girls* (D-15).[20] These criteria, in checklist form, are concerned with the organization of the program, the nature of the offerings, the physical facilities, and the direction of learning. In the last category some excellent questions are raised relative to instructional staff, instructional activities, instructional materials, and methods of evaluation. This instrument is probably the most widely used in the field today. Because programs for boys and girls are separated, it needs revising.

In Wisconsin, *Standards for Physical Education Grades One through Twelve* (revised) was prepared, in booklet form (64 pages), so that a given community program of physical education could be evaluated.[21] Part One is qualitative and foundational in nature. It questions program values and philosophy. Part Two is quantitative and places emphasis on the elements of physical education that yield optional development during the various stages of maturation. Outcome standards for all grade levels follow. Then follows a section on standards for the selection of activities for grades 1–3, 4–6, 7–9, and 10–12. This section is thorough and especially well-prepared. In fact, the whole standards manual is immediately useful. Moreover, each section has an introductory paragraph or two, indicating briefly how it is to be used. As suggested, if at least three-fourths of the answers are not in agreement with the standards as stated, perhaps some examination of the separate parts of the score card should be examined closely. Before the standards were distributed they were carefully tested out as pilot studies in a dozen Wisconsin communities.

The School-Community Fitness Inventory (revised) was prepared by the American Association for Health, Physical Education and Recreation as a general survey instrument.[22] Part II suggests standards for physical edu-

---

[20]May be obtained from NSSSE, American Council on Education, 1785 Massachusetts Avenue, N.W., Washington, D.C.

[21]Copies may be obtained from the State Superintendent of Education, State Department of Public Instruction, Madison, Wisconsin.

[22]Copies may be obtained from AAHPER, Publication Division, 1201 16th Street, N.W., Washington, D.C. 20036.

cation—instructional program, intramural program, interscholastic athletic program, leadership, facilities and equipment, and the participant.

Bucher has developed the complete and lengthy *Checklist and Rating Scale for the Evaluation of the Physical Education Program* (1977), which combines the evaluation standards required by several state departments of education and those recommended by leading authorities in the field.[23] The scale is admirably suited for a total school program appraisal. Not all of the scale must be used for a particular school evaluation. There are enough items in each of the following sections to enable a school to appraise a part of its program:

1. General Administrative Considerations: Philosophy, objectives, curriculum, general.
2. Considerations in the administration of physical education programs: Excuses, attendance, required program, required classes per week, length of each class, time provisions for showers and dressing, class grouping, determining class size, pupil-teacher ratio in each class, total program financed, extramural program, public relations, athletic standards, supervision of intramural and extramural activities, teacher schedules, coeducational instruction and supervision, proper equipment.
3. Components of the Physical Education Program: Program design, specific activities offered, aquatics, intramural program, interscholastic activities, recreational program, combative activities.
4. Staff: Status and tenure, background preparation.
5. Facilities and Equipment: General standards, indoor facilities, indoor equipment, training room, faculty offices, locker, shower, drying rooms, outdoor facilities.
6. Measurement and Evaluation Techniques: Student status and progress, staff evaluation.

A rather brief but well-formulated set of questions was developed by the California State Department of Education (*Criteria for Evaluating the Physical Education Program*).[24] Each question is answered in terms of quality of practice—*yes, no, good, fair,* and *poor.* The first six questions are as in Table 12-4.

The Texas Education Agency has worked with *Standards for Secondary Schools* for a number of years.[25] Important in the state evaluation is the degree to which the standards are met. In Missouri, the State Department of Education has a similar set of standards used extensively in the state since late 1969.[26] The *Missouri Physical Education Program Review Scorecard for*

[23]Charles A. Bucher, *Administration of School Health and College Health and Physical Education Programs,* 6th ed. (St. Louis: C. V. Mosby Co., 1977).

[24]*Education Program, Senior or Four-Year High School* (Sacramento, Calif.: California State Department of Education, revised).

[25]Texas Education Agency, *Standards for Secondary Schools as Recommended In Texas Education Agency,* Bulletins 615, 617, and 625. Dallas, Texas.

[26]Missouri State Department of Education, *Missouri Physical Education Program Review Scoreboard for Secondary Schools,* Jefferson City, Missouri.

TABLE 12-4. Criteria for Evaluating the Physical Education Program

Questions	Grades 7, 8, and 9					Changes Needed and Action Necessary
			Quality of Practice			
	Yes	No	Good	Fair	Poor	
1. Is there a workable plan to acquaint members of the community with the physical education program?						
2. Are channels provided for utilizing laymen's suggestions for improving the program?						
3. Does the physical education program have community approval?						
4. Is there a written up-to-date course of study?						
5. Is the course of study available upon request?						
6. Are there written school policies that govern the operation of the physical education program?						

Secondary Schools affords a thorough appraisal of instruction, administration, space and facilities, and supplies and equipment. Even more involved, and highly recommended, are the two instruments developed for New York State schools: *A Guide for the Review of Elementary School Physical Education* and *A Guide for the Review of Secondary School Physical Education.*[27] These have been used since 1968 to evaluate program objectives, program organization, curriculum offerings, quality of instruction, facilities, equipment, and local evaluation practices.

Because the school athletic program has become such a significant part of the physical education curriculum, it is necessary to submit it to a thorough examination from time to time. In addition to administrators and coaches, the members of the local school board will want to appraise athletic programs in terms of the excellent standards set up years ago by the Educational Policies Commission.[28] Their "Checklist On School Athletics," which follows, contains questions that may be answered with a Yes (Y), No (N), or Unknown or Uncertain (U). Each question is also answered with a checkmark under Agree (A), Disagree (D), or Uncertain (U). The degree to which a school administrator answers a question with a Yes (Y) indicates whether practices are in keeping with the policies recommended by the Commission. The degree to which questions are answered with Agree (A) measures the extent to which the administrator's opinion coincides with that of the Commission. There might be some disagreement today about questions 57 and 79.

Study the checklist carefully. Note that intramurals are evaluated, and that elementary and junior high school programs are considered. There are also eleven pertinent questions relating specifically to athletics for girls.

CHECKLIST ON SCHOOL ATHLETICS

PURPOSES OF SCHOOL ATHLETICS

1. Does your school have clearly defined goals for its athletic program?
   Y............... N............... U............... A............... D............... U...............
2. Do other teachers, as well as coaches and teachers of physical education, have a part in formulating the purposes of athletics in your school?
   Y............... N............... U............... A............... D............... U...............
3. Do lay citizens have opportunity to express themselves with respect to the purposes of athletics in your school?
   Y............... N............... U............... A............... D............... U...............
4. Are athletics recognized by your school as an integral part of complete education?
   Y............... N............... U............... A............... D............... U...............
5. Are athletic activities in harmony with the objectives of the total educational program?
   Y............... N............... U............... A............... D............... U...............

[27]The University of the State of New York, *Physical Education Program: Elementary School* and *Physical Education Program: Secondary School*, the State Education Department, Albany, N.Y.

[28]The Educational Policies Commission, *School Athletics: Problems and Policies*, Washington: National Education Association, 1953.

6. Does your school's athletic program encourage participation in satisfying play by *all* pupils?

     Y.............. N............... U................ A................ D................ U...............

7. Does your school in its athletic program seek to contribute to the development of wholesome personalities?

     Y.............. N............... U................ A................ D................ U...............

8. Does your school conduct athletics in ways intended to help participants develop health and physical fitness?

     Y.............. N............... U................ A................ D................ U...............

9. Does your school seek to conduct athletics in such a way that participants develop enduring play habits, skills, and attitudes?

     Y.............. N............... U................ A................ D................ U...............

10. Does your school encourage athletic activities which aid development of desirable social growth and adjustment?

     Y.............. N............... U................ A................ D................ U...............

11. Does your school conduct athletics in such a way as to avoid excessive emotional strains and tensions on the part of both players and spectators?

     Y.............. N............... U................ A................ D................ U...............

12. Does your school take steps to prevent athletic practices which might be detrimental to the welfare of pupils as individuals?

     Y.............. N............... U................ A................ D................ U...............

HEALTH AND WELFARE OF ATHLETIC PARTICIPANTS

13. In determining policies and procedures for athletics in your school is the health and welfare of participants considered paramount?

     Y.............. N............... U................ A................ D................ U...............

14. Does the school provide adequate protective equipment and other health safeguards for all participants in athletic contests?

     Y.............. N............... U................ A................ D................ U...............

15. Are all games and practice sessions conducted in facilities that are hygienic, clean, and safe?

     Y.............. N............... U................ A................ D................ U...............

16. Is adequate training and conditioning required for all types of athletic competition?

     Y.............. N............... U................ A................ D................ U...............

17. Has the approval of a physician been secured for the practices of your school's interscholastic athletic program which involve conditioning, training, and health?

     Y.............. N............... U................ A................ D................ U...............

18. Is a thorough health examination required of all participants in both intramural and interscholastic sports before they take part in vigorous athletic competition?

     Y.............. N............... U................ A................ D................ U...............

19. Is a postseason health examination required of athletes?

     Y.............. N............... U................ A................ D................ U...............

20. Is emergency medical service available during all practice periods, intramural games, and interscholastic contests held under school auspices?

     Y.............. N............... U................ A................ D................ U...............

21. Are athletes who have been injured or ill readmitted to participation only with the written approval of a physician?

    Y.............. N.............. U.............. A.............. D.............. U..............

22. Does your school have a written and well-publicized policy regarding the legal and financial responsibilities for injuries incurred in athletics?

    Y.............. N.............. U.............. A.............. D.............. U..............

23. Even when not legally responsible, does your school have a plan for making financial provisions for the care of injuries incurred in school athletics?

    Y.............. N.............. U.............. A.............. D.............. U..............

24. Does the school seek to prevent injury to the personality development of star athletes from overattention and ego-inflation?

    Y.............. N.............. U.............. A.............. D.............. U..............

ORGANIZATION AND ADMINISTRATION OF SCHOOL ATHLETICS

25. Are all athletic activities in your school recognized as the responsibility of the school and under its control?

    Y.............. N.............. U.............. A.............. D.............. U..............

26. Are all athletics in your school administered as part of the school's total program of physical education?

    Y.............. N.............. U.............. A.............. D.............. U..............

27. Is your school (if a high school) a member of your state high school athletic association or similar organization?

    Y.............. N.............. U.............. A.............. D.............. U..............

28. Does your school accept the aid of your state's department of education (or public instruction) in establishing and maintaining high standards in the conduct of school athletics?

    Y.............. N.............. U.............. A.............. D.............. U..............

FACILITIES FOR SCHOOL ATHLETICS

29. Does your board of education provide adequate facilities in athletics for *all* students?

    Y.............. N.............. U.............. A.............. D.............. U..............

30. Are physical education facilities in your school available to all phases of the program, including required activity classes and intramurals?

    Y.............. N.............. U.............. A.............. D.............. U..............

31. Do girls share equally with boys in the use of your school's athletic facilities?

    Y.............. N.............. U.............. A.............. D.............. U..............

32. Does your school provide a standard field, court, or play space for each team game and individual sport most popular in your section of the country?

    Y.............. N.............. U.............. A.............. D.............. U..............

PERSONNEL FOR THE ATHLETIC PROGRAM

33. Are all who coach athletic teams in your school competently trained and certified as teachers?

    Y.............. N.............. U.............. A.............. D.............. U..............

34. Do the athletic coaches have professional training in physical education equivalent to a minor or more?

   Y.............. N.............. U.............. A.............. D.............. U..............

35. Do the athletic coaches consistently set good examples in the matter of sportsmanship and personal contact?

   Y.............. N.............. U.............. A.............. D.............. U..............

36. Do athletic coaches use their influence with students to help them with personal problems?

   Y.............. N.............. U.............. A.............. D.............. U..............

37. Are those members of the school staff whose chief work is coaching athletics generally regarded by other faculty members as fellow teachers of comparable professional status?

   Y.............. N.............. U.............. A.............. D.............. U..............

38. Does the school provide sufficient personnel for the proper instruction and supervision of all participants in the required activity classes, in corecreation, in intramural sports, and in interscholastic athletics?

   Y.............. N.............. U.............. A.............. D.............. U..............

39. Do school authorities seek to maintain at all times a balance in the amount of staff time and instruction given to all phases of physical education, including required activity classes, corecreation, intramural sports, and interscholastic athletics?

   Y.............. N.............. U.............. A.............. D.............. U..............

INTRAMURAL PROGRAMS

40. Does every student in your school system have opportunity for participating in a variety of intramural sports?

   Y.............. N.............. U.............. A.............. D.............. U..............

41. Is the intramural sports program conducted as an integral part of the total program of physical education and not as a "feeder" system for interscholastic athletics?

   Y.............. N.............. U.............. A.............. D.............. U..............

42. Does the intramural sports program serve as a laboratory where students can test things they are taught in physical education classes?

   Y.............. N.............. U.............. A.............. D.............. U..............

43. Do most of the students in your school find the intramural program sufficiently interesting, diverse, and convenient that they voluntarily participate in it?

   Y.............. N.............. U.............. A.............. D.............. U..............

44. Does the school provide opportunities for corecreation (that is, for boys and girls to play together) through intramural sports?

   Y.............. N.............. U.............. A.............. D.............. U..............

45. Does the intramural athletic program have good equipment rather than handed-down equipment, worn-out balls, unmarked fields, and poorly organized game situations?

   Y.............. N.............. U.............. A.............. D.............. U..............

ELEMENTARY SCHOOL POLICIES AND PROGRAMS

46. Does your elementary school program recognize that children need to engage in vigorous muscular activities as a part of the growing process?

   Y.............. N.............. U.............. A.............. D.............. U..............

47. Do the practices of your school reflect the policy that interscholastic athletics are not desirable in elementary schools?

    Y............... N............... U............... A............... D............... U...............

48. Are sports adapted to the needs of children of elementary school age by modification of such things as rules, size of courts and fields, and the size or weight of equipment?

    Y............... N............... U............... A............... D............... U...............

49. Are athletic activities in your elementary school planned cooperatively by teachers, pupils, and parents?

    Y............... N............... U............... A............... D............... U...............

50. Are children of elementary school age given opportunities to develop responsibility through the athletic program by participating in the planning, by organizing groups, by holding office, and by helping with equipment?

    Y............... N............... U............... A............... D............... U...............

51. Do the school authorities discourage and seek to prevent outside interests from forcing undesirable patterns of athletic competition upon children?

    Y............... N............... U............... A............... D............... U...............

JUNIOR HIGH SCHOOL POLICIES AND PROGRAMS

52. Is the athletic program for junior high school pupils suited to the needs of children who are undergoing rapid changes in physical growth?

    Y............... N............... U............... A............... D............... U...............

53. Is the athletic program of your junior high school planned cooperatively by teachers, pupils, and parents?

    Y............... N............... U............... A............... D............... U...............

54. Does your junior high school provide a broad athletic program for every boy and girl in the school?

    Y............... N............... U............... A............... D............... U...............

55. Does the athletic program in junior high school consist primarily of sports organized and conducted on an intramural basis?

    Y............... N............... U............... A............... D............... U...............

56. Are junior high school pupils given an opportunity to develop responsibility through the athletic program by participating in the planning, by organizing groups, by holding office, and by helping with equipment?

    Y............... N............... U............... A............... D............... U...............

57. Is tackle football prohibited as an athletic activity in your junior high school?

    Y............... N............... U............... A............... D............... U...............

58. Does your junior high school refrain from participation in varsity-type interscholastics?

    Y............... N............... U............... A............... D............... U...............

59. Are the leaders of athletic activities in your junior high school competently trained teachers?

    Y............... N............... U............... A............... D............... U...............

INTERSCHOLASTIC ATHLETICS FOR BOYS IN SENIOR HIGH SCHOOL

60. Are interscholastic athletics conducted primarily to serve the needs of students with superior athletic skills?

    Y............... N............... U............... A............... D............... U...............

61. Are games and practice periods for interscholastic athletics worked into the school schedule with a minimum of interference with the academic program?

Y............. N............. U............. A............. D............. U.............

62. Are interscholastic games played only with schools that maintain acceptable principles and policies in their conduct of interscholastic athletics?

Y............. N............. U............. A............. D............. U.............

63. Are interscholastic games played only on school or public property?

Y............. N............. U............. A............. D............. U.............

64. Does the school observe the rules of its state high school athletic association?

Y............. N............. U............. A............. D............. U.............

65. Does the school refuse to participate in all postseason tournaments and post-season championship games?

Y............. N............. U............. A............. D............. U.............

66. Is the board of education adequately informed regarding the interscholastic athletic program?

Y............. N............. U............. A............. D............. U.............

67. Is the board of education adequately informed regarding the rules and regulations of the state high school athletic association?

Y............. N............. U............. A............. D............. U.............

68. Are athletes engaged in interscholastic sports held to the same standards of scholarship as other students?

Y............. N............. U............. A............. D............. U.............

69. Are boys who participate in interscholastic athletics required to attend regular classes in physical education (except during the actual period of their interscholastic participation)?

Y............. N............. U............. A............. D............. U.............

70. Does the school try to prevent solicitation of its athletes by colleges and universities through tryouts and competitive bidding?

Y............. N............. U............. A............. D............. U.............

71. Does the school make an effort to develop high standards of good sportsmanship on the part of all students?

Y............. N............. U............. A............. D............. U.............

ATHLETICS FOR GIRLS

72. Does the school athletic program for girls provide opportunities for all girls to participate according to their needs, abilities, and interests?

Y............. N............. U............. A............. D............. U.............

73. Are facilities for girls' athletics provided in accordance with the requirements of the girls' program and not on the basis of causing minimum inconvenience to the boys' program?

Y............. N............. U............. A............. D............. U.............

74. Is the school athletic program for girls under the direction of a competent woman leader who is professionally trained in health and physical education?

Y............. N............. U............. A............. D............. U.............

75. Does the school include in its girls' athletic program such dual, individual, and recreational sports and games as archery, badminton, bowling, croquet, horse-

shoes, golf, riding, shuffleboard, skiing, swimming, table tennis, and tennis?

Y............... N............... U............... A............... D............... U...............

76. Does the school include in its girls' athletic program such team sports as basketball, field hockey, softball, soccer, speedball, and volleyball?

Y............... N............... U............... A............... D............... U...............

77. Does every girl in the school have an opportunity to compete in team games?

Y............... N............... U............... A............... D............... U...............

78. Is participation of girls in athletics based on an appraisal of the health status of each participant which takes into account quality and extent of participation, type of activity, individual differences, and general organic condition?

Y............... N............... U............... A............... D............... U...............

79. Are girls prevented from participation, under school auspices, in sports that involve rough and tumble body contact?

Y............... N............... U............... A............... D............... U...............

80. Are girls provided opportunities for athletic competition with girls of other schools through such means as play days and sports days?

Y............... N............... U............... A............... D............... U...............

81. Are all school athletic contests for girls conducted in accordance with girls' rules?

Y............... N............... U............... A............... D............... U...............

82. Is the school's athletic program for girls conducted in conformity with the policies and recommendations contained in *Standards in Sports for Girls and Women*?

Y............... N............... U............... A............... D............... U...............

FINANCING ATHLETIC PROGRAMS

83. Does the board of education control the financing of the athletic program?

Y............... N............... U............... A............... D............... U...............

84. Is the welfare of participants considered more important than financial gain in determining the athletic policies and practices of your school?

Y............... N............... U............... A............... D............... U...............

85. Is the size of the budget for athletics in sound proportion to the size of the budget for the rest of the school program?

Y............... N............... U............... A............... D............... U...............

86. Is balance maintained in the financial support of all phases of the physical education program, including required activity classes, corecreation, intramural sports, and interscholastic athletics?

Y............... N............... U............... A............... D............... U...............

87. Are the salaries of other teachers equitable in comparison with the salaries of coaches?

Y............... N............... U............... A............... D............... U...............

88. Are all athletic moneys, including gate receipts, considered as school funds with records accurately kept and audited?

Y............... N............... U............... A............... D............... U...............

89. Is the intramural sports program of your school financed entirely by appropriations from tax funds?

Y............... N............... U............... A............... D............... U...............

90. Is your school district moving toward complete financing of the athletic program from tax funds?

  Y................ N................ U................ A................ D................ U................

COMMUNITY RELATIONS

91. Is the school actively concerned with providing adequate community athletic facilities for children and youth?

  Y................ N................ U................ A................ D................ U................

92. Does the school staff study your community to determine how to use, to improve, and to increase available space for wholesome play for the students enrolled in your school?

  Y................ N................ U................ A................ D................ U................

93. Is the school actively interested in providing community athletic programs for children and youth during vacation periods?

  Y................ N................ U................ A................ D................ U................

94. Do community organizations look to the school for expert counsel and advice regarding athletic programs?

  Y................ N................ U................ A................ D................ U................

95. Does the school assume responsibility for informing the community regarding the standards of good sportsmanship that should be observed at all athletic contests?

  Y................ N................ U................ A................ D................ U................

96. Is the conduct of spectators at interscholastic games such as to reflect favorably on the school?

  Y................ N................ U................ A................ D................ U................

97. Does the board of education enjoy as much freedom from outside pressures in the selection of a coach as it does in the selection of other teachers?

  Y................ N................ U................ A................ D................ U................

98. Does the community support the coach of a boys' varsity team that has a losing season?

  Y................ N................ U................ A................ D................ U................

99. Do local newspapers, radio stations, and television stations support clean athletics and have a high regard for standards of good sportsmanship?

  Y................ N................ U................ A................ D................ U................

100. Are the schools comparatively free from undesirable activities on the part of outside organizations primarily concerned with winning teams in interscholastic games?

  Y................ N................ U................ A................ D................ U................

QUESTIONS FOR DISCUSSION

1. Differentiate between measurement as a tool and evaluation as a process of determining direction.
2. Much has been written by philosophers of physical education relative to the place of measurement in the program. What seems to be the prevailing viewpoint today?

3. How do you feel about setting up achievement goals for boys and girls of all ages, grades K–12? Are such goals readily acceptable by students as worthy of in-class and out-of-class activity?
4. At what point in the evaluation process do measurement activities become "too" time-consuming? Explain your viewpoint and illustrate it with an example or two.
5. Explain how you might use the results of measurement in a secondary school to revise a given curriculum.
6. Is it possible through program evaluation to improve the effectiveness of teachers? Explain your answer and give an illustration.

SUGGESTED ACTIVITIES

1. Inquire about current quality control practices in some industry. How do these compare with those employed in schools?
2. Formulate a list of suitable sports skill tests that could be used in physical education classes at the junior high school level. What will you use as your criteria for test selection? Do these appear to eliminate many existing tests? Explain.
3. Examine several curriculum guides from the states and larger communities. Do you find that measurement and evaluation are considered part of the total program? How do your findings compare with those of your classmates?
4. Obtain a copy of one of the program evaluation instruments referred to in this chapter. Look it over carefully. In order to get the "feel" of the instrument, try it out on a school. This may be accomplished in several ways, one of which is to interview personally the director of the physical education program for the community.
5. Develop a short statement relative to the significant relationship between educational aims and objectives and evaluation practices. Before doing this, read what several authors have had to say on this topic.
6. Select for yourself an imaginary school system in a city of 50,000 people. Assume that you are going to revise the curriculum, partly on the basis of measurement findings. What procedures would you follow? Lay out a plan for relating evaluation results to curriculum revision.

SELECTED REFERENCES

ANDERSON, S. B., and others, *Encyclopedia of Educational Evaluation* (1973).
American Association for Health, Physical Education and Recreation, *Knowledge and Understanding in Physical Education*. Washington, D.C.: AAHPER, 1969.

BARROWS, HAROLD M., *Man and His Movement: Principles of His Physical Education.* (2nd ed.), chap. 18. Philadelphia: Lea & Febiger, 1977.

BARROWS, HAROLD M., and ROSEMARY MCGEE, *Measurement in Physical Education* (2nd ed.), Philadelphia: Lea & Febiger, 1972.

BAUMGARTNER, TED A., and ANDREW S. JACKSON, *Measurement for Evaluation in Physical Education.* Boston: Houghton Mifflin Co., 1975.

CHEFFERS, JOHN, and TOM EVAUL, *Introduction to Physical Education: Concepts of Human Movement,* part 4. Englewood Cliffs, N.J.: Prentice-Hall, Inc., 1978.

CLARKE, HARRISON H., *The Application of Measurement to Health and Physical Education,* (5th ed.). Englewood Cliffs, N.J.: Prentice-Hall Inc., 1976.

COLVIN, WILLIAM W., and ELMO S. ROUNDY, "An Instrument for the Student Evaluation of Teaching Effectiveness in Physical Education Activity Courses," *Research Quarterly,* 47 (May 1976), 296–99.

DAVIS, O.L., JR., ed., *Perspectives on Curriculum Development.* Washington: Association for Supervision and Curriculum Development, 1976.

FRANGIONE, FRANK J., "Integrating the 'Why' in Measurement and Evaluation," *Journal of Physical Education and Recreation,* 48 (March 1977), 56.

FRANKS, B. DON, and HELGA DEUTSCH, *Evaluating Performance in Physical Education.* New York: Academic Press, Inc., 1978.

GRUIJTER, D.N.M., ed., *Advances in Educational and Psychological Measurement.* New York: John Wiley and Sons, 1977.

HUNSICKER, PAUL, and GUY G. REIFF, *Youth Fitness Manual,* revised, Washington: American Alliance for Health, Physical Education and Recreation, 1976.

LEWY, ARIEH, *Handbook of Curriculum Evaluation.* New York: Longman, Inc., 1977.

MATTHEWS, DONALD K., *Measurement in Physical Education,* (5th ed.). Philadelphia: W.B. Saunders Co., 1978.

SHEEHAN, THOMAS J., *An Introduction to the Evaluation of Measurement Data in Physical Education.* Reading, Mass.: Addison-Wesley Co., 1971.

SPRAY, JUDITH A., "Interpreting Class Performance Using AAHPER Test Norms," *Journal of Physical Education and Recreation,* 48 (September 1976), 56–57.

WILLGOOSE, CARL E., *Evaluation in Health Education and Physical Education.* New York: McGraw-Hill, 1961.

Index